63-819996   (2-16-69)

FRANCE IN THE
EIGHTEENTH CENTURY

FRANCE IN THE EIGHTEENTH CENTURY

Its Institutions, Customs and Costumes

PAUL LACROIX

Illustrated with over 300 wood engravings

FREDERICK UNGAR PUBLISHING CO.
NEW YORK

Republished 1963

First published in 1876 under the title
THE EIGHTEENTH CENTURY:
Its Institutions, Customs, and Costumes. France 1700-1789

Printed in the United States of America

Library of Congress Catalog Card No. 63-21996

CONTENTS.

CHAPTER I.

THE KING AND THE COURT.

CHAPTER II.

THE NOBILITY.

CHAPTER III.

THE BOURGEOISIE.

CHAPTER IV.

THE PEOPLE.

CHAPTER V.

THE ARMY AND NAVY.

CHAPTER VI.

THE CLERGY.

CHAPTER VII.

THE PARLIAMENTS.

CHAPTER VIII.

FINANCE.

CHAPTER IX.

COMMERCE.

CHAPTER X.

EDUCATION.

CHAPTER XI.

CHARITY.

CHAPTER XVIII.

TRAVEL.

CHAPTER XIX.

DRESS AND FASHIONS.

LIST OF ILLUSTRATIONS.

PAGE ENGRAVINGS.

ENGRAVINGS IN THE TEXT.

FRANCE
XVIIITH
CENTURY.

CARTOUCHE-FRONTISPIECE; AFTER MEISSONNIER.

THE EIGHTEENTH CENTURY.

CHAPTER I.

THE KING AND THE COURT.

Historical Introduction.—End of the Reign of Louis XIV.—The Regency.—Louis XV.—Louis XVI.
and Marie Antoinette.—The Court and its Charges.

THE last years of the reign of Louis XIV. threw some little
éclat upon the early part of the eighteenth century ; but the aged
monarch who, notwithstanding the defeats of his armies and the
disasters of his navy, the loss of a portion of his conquests, the
dilapidation of his finances, and the suffering of his subjects, still
sustained the prestige of his past glories and his great place amongst
the sovereigns of Europe, must have foreseen in his last hours that
the monarchy which he had raised to such a pitch of grandeur and
prosperity was likely to follow him to its grave.

Louis XIV., whose unbounded ambition had been so well
served by men and by events, was not, moreover, ignorant of the
duties which his position entailed upon him, and he endeavoured to
fulfil them to the best of his ability. To use his own words : " The
kingly calling is a great, a noble and a flattering one, when one is
worthy to fulfil all the engagements which it entails ; but it brings
with it many annoyances, much fatigue and anxiety. When a king
has the good of the State in view, he is labouring in his own cause,
for the welfare of the one is the glory of the other ; when the State
is contented, great and powerful, he who makes it so is glorified, and
must therefore derive greater satisfaction than his subjects. When a
mistake has been committed, it must be repaired as soon as possible ;

no consideration, not even that of mercy, should stand in the way." These noble maxims which Louis XIV. had framed for his own use, show that he was not blind to his faults and errors, inasmuch as he was always providing to repair them. If he was not always and altogether a good king, it may be said that he desired and endeavoured to become one. As Voltaire says : "a really good king is the noblest gift of heaven."

The character and aspect of the French Court underwent a complete change towards the close of this reign, which opened so brilliantly and terminated in the most sombre monotony. The influence of Madame de Maintenon was the sole cause of this change, which, beginning in 1681, became more marked as the King fell more and more under the domination of the crafty and ambitious woman whom he had married in secret, without ever having the courage to declare that the widow Scarron was his wife. The Marquise de Maintenon, who had been beautiful and who was well-educated, clever and amusing, soon acquired a complete supremacy, while appearing to take no part in public affairs. She established over the King an influence which she had exercised upon his affections, and obtained his confidence so completely that his imperious will was mastered by a real queen who masked her power under the veil of extreme timidity. Madame de Maintenon's piety was sincere, though exclusive, and by means of it she exercised the greatest authority over the King, whom she had brought to be very particular about religious observances, for himself and for others, but at the same time morose and melancholy.

The example of the King effected a transformation in the Court ; no more fêtes or theatrical spectacles were given, and there was little beyond evening receptions where the guests strolled through the galleries or collected round the tables at which ombre, hookey and other games of cards were being played. The King played with the princes and princesses and with a few of the persons of the household. Madame de Maintenon never appeared at these *apartments* as they were called, though her invisible personality was always present, so to

THE GRAND TRIANON; AFTER RIGAUD.

speak, in the conversations of the courtiers. There were a few concerts of instrumental music ; and upon certain exceptional occasions,
such as victories, treaties of peace, baptisms or marriages in the royal
family, singers either from the theatre or the churches took part in
them. The last ballet danced before the King was *The Triumph of
Love* in 1681 ; the last representation of the Royal Academy of
Music at which the King and the Court were present was in 1685.
As to the performances of the ordinary Court comedians, they were
altogether suppressed, and Louis XIV. only honoured with his
presence the theatre of the royal school at Saint Cyr, where the young
ladies of the establishment sometimes played before him and
Madame de Maintenon the two tragedies of *Esther* and *Athalie*
which, written by Racine expressly for these performances, partook
more of a religious than a secular character.

Madame de Maintenon hardly ever left her apartments, where she
lived in retirement with two or three ladies, pious like herself. The
King came to see her several times a day ; after dinner, before and
after supper. He remained until past midnight, transacting business
with his ministers and regulating State affairs, Madame de Maintenon
listening to and directing everything, while she seemed to be wholly
intent upon her books or her needle work, only speaking when the
King asked her a question, and couching her replies in the most
reserved terms. Louis XIV. sometimes accompanied her in her
drives, especially to Marly, where she went frequently. "Shut up in
a close chair," says Duclos, "to avoid the least breath of air, the
King walked by her side, taking off his hat each time that he stooped
to speak to her" (Figs. 1 and 2). There was no doubt as to her being
a queen, and all the more exacting and powerful because she affected
not to claim any sort of supremacy. She never failed to attend the
chapel of the palace whenever the King went either alone or with his
household, and she always occupied a sort of private gallery, behind
the closed curtains of which nothing was visible but the shadow of the
black silk coif in which her yellow and livid face was always buried.

This Court, majestic rather than brilliant, seemed to have lost all

recollection of what it had been twenty or forty years before, when
Louis XIV. at the apogee of his glory, following the inspirations of
his youth and gallantry, thought only of pleasure, fêtes and displays
of magnificence, to celebrate the ephemeral reign of the Duchesse de
la Vallière, the Marquise de Montespan, and Mlle. de Fontange.

An idea of the severe etiquette which presided at all the details in
the private life of Louis XIV. may best be conveyed by borrowing
from the Memoirs of the Duc de Saint-Simon a short account of what
took place at his rising and at his retiring for the night.   At 8 a.m.
the first valet de chambre on duty, who had slept in the King's
chamber, went to wake him.   The first physician and the first

Fig. 1.— Royal Promenade in the Park at Versailles.   (Fac-simile, from Rigaud.)

surgeon then entered the room and consulted as to the state of his
health.   At a quarter past eight, the grand chamberlain, or in his
absence the first gentleman of the chamber, was called, as also were
the *grandes entrées*, that is to say the persons who occupied the
highest posts at the Court and in the royal household.   The first
gentleman or the grand chamberlain opened the curtains and presented to the King, still in bed, the holy water and a book of prayer ;
and then all the persons present withdrew into the next room.   The
King, having been aided in rising by his valet, and having hastily
made his ablutions, recalled the grand chamberlain or first gentleman, who handed him his dressing-gown.   The door was then opened
and admittance given to those who had been waiting outside, that
is, to use Saint-Simon's words, " to the second entrées and the
patented tradesmen, then to persons of distinction and notoriety."

The King "did nearly everything for himself with rapidity and grace;" he put on his stockings, combed, washed and dressed himself without any toilet-table in front of him ; nothing but a looking-glass. As soon as he was dresssed, he said his prayers by his bedside, the ecclesiastics who were present, including the cardinals, knelt down, the laymen remained standing, and the captain of the guard, his drawn sword in his hand, leant against the

Fig. 2.—Sedan-chairs for the Park. (Fac-simile, from Rigaud.)

balustrade of the bed. His prayers said, the King passed into his cabinet, where those whose functions gave them the right of entry were awaiting him. There he gave the orders for the day. That done, all the persons in attendance withdrew, and the King, remaining alone with his children, their governors, and a few privileged courtiers, received the intendants of his palaces, his gardens, and "other pleasures." There were, sometimes, *secret* audiences, so called to distinguish them from those granted at the bedside, which were called *private* audiences. During these audiences and conversations, the Court waited in the gallery, and if the King attended mass followed him to the chapel. When the King went from the chapel to the council chamber, persons belonging to the Court had the right of speaking to him without first notifying their intention to the captain of the guard.

The orders having been given, down to the most minute details, for the day, every step which the King took was accompanied by some ceremonial, especially when Louis XIV. desired to exhibit the prestige of royalty, as, for instance, at the reception of ambassadors or foreign ministers. At the chase or the promenade, the King, though still surrounded by the same amount of state, would relax to a certain extent the severity of the etiquette, signifying to the persons present that they were not to remain uncovered.

Dinner and supper were also hedged about by the same amount of ceremonial. After supper, the King returned to his chamber, surrounded by all the Court; he remained standing for a few minutes, with his back to the balustrade of the bed, then, after bowing to the ladies, withdrew to his cabinet, where the royal family had, as a rule, assembled. He remained an hour with them, only leaving them a moment to go and feed his dogs; returning to wish them good night, he again passed into his chamber, where the persons with the grand and second entrées and the purveyors of the Court were awaiting him. He talked to them while undressing, and as soon as he was in bed they all withdrew, except the first valet on duty. The ceremonial of the *grand coucher* terminated at the moment when the King, returning to his chamber, said his prayers at the bedside and dismissed the attendants by an inclination of the head which signified : " Good night to you, gentlemen."

There was no *grand coucher* during the last twelve years of his reign, but the *petit coucher*, at which the grand and second entrées assisted, continued to the last in the usual form. These severe rules were somewhat relaxed at the Grand Trianon, one of the King's favourite creations; when he paid a visit to it, everyone was allowed to pay his court to the King, and the ladies had the honour of eating at the same table.

Moreover, the Court ceremonies which Louis XIV. had himself regulated down to their least details subsisted in all their rigour under Louis XV., and were only modified at the accession of Louis XVI.

If the life of the courtiers became more and more dull and

RECEPTION OF AN AMBASSADOR AT VERSAILLES; AFTER PARROCEL.

monotonous during the old age of Louis XIV., there is reason to believe that the King himself did not fare much better. His eternal solitude with Mme. de Maintenon began to weigh upon him, when death, a death sudden and terrible, entered his family, accompanied by all the horrors of the unforeseen and the mysterious. Yet the loss of his only son, the grand dauphin (1711), had not left him without a direct heir. His grandson, the Duc de Bourgogne, had two sons of tender years, while of the grand dauphin's two other sons, one was Philip V. of Spain, and the other, the Duc de Berry, was childless. But a sudden and mysterious illness, lasting only a few hours, carried off the Duchesse de Bourgogne and her husband together with their eldest son in the course of a few days (1712). Their second son, the Duc d'Anjou, afterwards Louis XV., was attacked with the same malady, and only cured by a desperate remedy which his governess administered to him unknown to the physicians. Rumours of poisoning, since accepted as true by many historians, circulated freely at the time.

The Court became a very sepulchre : "everything is dead here, life has fled from us," wrote Mme. de Caylus : "There is a complete void, no gaiety or pleasure," wrote Mme. de Maintenon to her intimate friend Mme. des Ursins. Another letter to Mme. de Maisonfort, complaining of being "old and melancholy and secluded from the world," expresses still more strongly the dejection which prevailed. "If I could but let you see the melancholy which besieges the great, and the difficulty they experience in killing time ! Can you not see that I am bored to death, though raised to a position of inconceivable eminence ?" If the King had confided his impressions to any one, they would not assuredly have been less dismal. Mme. de Maintenon had succeeded in obtaining from him, in favour of the Duc du Maine, one of the legitimized princes, a will removing the Duc d'Orléans from the regency. Louis XIV. on his death-bed regretted this step, and in an undertone expressed his hope that the will would be set aside. He died like a King and a Christian. Holding the Dauphin in his arms, he said to him : " You are about to reign over a great kingdom, endeavour to keep at peace with your neighbours. I have been too fond of war, do not imitate me in this, nor in my excessive expenditure. Take advice on every point; endeavour to obtain the best, and always follow it. Relieve your subjects whenever you can, and do what I have not unfortunately been able to accomplish." The great King's eyes were not yet closed before he was deserted by all save two or three under servants. The Court was divided into several groups, one party siding with the Duc du Maine, and another with the Duc d'Orléans. Mme. de Maintenon, ere her royal spouse had drawn his last breath, retired to Saint-Cyr. The Court was, just then, part at the Château de Sceaux and part at the Palais Royal in Paris. There were only a few courtiers with the young King at the Louvre.

The French people had always loved its sovereigns. This national tradition seemed to be broken at the death of Louis XIV., who had been Louis le Grand. The Duc de Richelieu, writing some time after that event, said : " I cannot look back without a feeling of horror upon the indecent behaviour of the people of Paris upon the day of his burial. The death of the most odious tyrant could not have excited greater pleasure. His death was looked upon as a divine favour. A few years of disgrace had destroyed all recollections of the past, his former glory was utterly forgotten; the people cursed his memory and insulted the coffin of a King who had conferred immortal honour upon France, and whose remains were scarcely safe in the tomb of his forefathers."

The breath of revolution, which had stimulated the League and the Fronde, threatened to overthrow the monarchy of Louis XIV. before his body was laid in the basilica of St. Denis. The Duc d'Orléans, fortunately for France, had never designed to lend himself to any great changes in the political order of things; he, no doubt, was anxious to govern the kingdom during the minority of the young monarch, but he did not wish to become King himself by an act of unblushing usurpation. The will of Louis XIV., removing him as far as possible from the regency to put the Duc du Maine in his place, was to be opened in the parliament.   Philip of Orleans, having at his back the grandees, the Court, and the people who pronounced strongly in his favour, had but one ambition, that of administering the State well.   In the sitting of parliament when the late King's

Fig. 3.—The Rocking-cradle of the Duc d'Anjou (afterwards Louis XV.)

will was opened, he said : "I consent to my hands being tied for evil, but, as for what is good, I will not be fettered."   The nation already welcomed him as a liberator, and three days before the funeral of Louis XIV., when Louis, only five years of age, accompanied by his governess Mme. de Ventadour, went to hold a bed of justice at the

Tuileries, that same people which, three years before, was ready to stone the Duc d'Orléans to death, because they suspected him of having poisoned the princes, now gave him a great ovation and escorted him back in triumph to the Palais Royal.

The Duc d'Orléans, who, till his death in 1723, was the absolute and irresponsible head of the Council of Regency, did not like either courtiers or flatterers. The latter did not spare him in their calumnies, and they have done their best to have him pilloried in history as a monster. It was the Court, more especially the old Court, which supplied the venom for the *Philippiques* of Grange-Chancel. The following true and accurate picture of what he was gives the lie to the hideous caricatures of the *Philippiques*. " The Duc d'Orléans had a pleasant open face, he was of about the middle height, and there was a great amount of ease and grace in all his movements. Endowed with rare penetration and sagacity, he expressed himself fluently and accurately. His repartees were prompt, just and amusing. His first resolves were generally the best ; reflection rendered him undecided. A rapid course of reading, aided by a retentive memory, stood him in the stead of continuous study ; he seemed to guess at rather than to think out a subject ; he had something more than a superficial knowledge of painting, music, chemistry, and mechanics. With great courage, and as modest about himself as he was severe upon others whose bravery was doubtful, he would have been a general had the late king allowed it, but he was always kept in subjection at Court and under tutorage in the army. A dignified familiarity placed him on a level with all those who came near him ; he felt that a personal superiority dispensed him from insisting upon his rank. He was not of a resentful disposition, and drew an advantageous comparison between himself and Henri IV. in this respect. His indifference on this head arose from his contempt for mankind." The philosopher Duclos, who was a contemporary of the Regent, and who judged him thus after contemporary evidence, reproached him only with having sometimes been fond of making a boast of his vice and immorality.

It was soon seen that the Duc d'Orléans would have nothing to do with the old Court, which was nicknamed the *antiquaille;* he had closed the gates of the Palais Royal in their face, and remained at liberty with his friends and the companions of his pleasures—the *roués* as they were called. His suppers, which were given every evening, lasted the whole night, and the Duke had become so accustomed to them that he could not live in any other way, in despite of the fatigue and excesses which they entailed. Yet he was naturally sober, and was ashamed of getting intoxicated like his guests. He said that " on these occasions he formed his judgment as to the worth of the persons about him, and, as every one was at liberty to say what he chose, he got at public opinion ; but he kept his own secret, not letting his companions know what advantage he derived from these excesses."

It will be readily understood that such habits must have been very distasteful to the Versailles Court, such as Louis XIV. had moulded it during his long reign, and which still preserved the impress of this slavish etiquette, with its aristocratic pride, its arrogant preten-sions, its inexhaustible fund of intrigue. It followed, therefore, that such a Court, stiff and prim, prude and obstinate, must either abandon its authority for ever, or wait till the young King was at all events old enough to have courtiers about him. But the King, who seemed already qualified to hold a bed of justice, had at present only servants who were under the eye of his governess, the Duchesse de Ventadour ; and even when he was placed under the tutelage of Marshal de Villeroy, whom the will of Louis XIV. had appointed his governor, the time was still distant when the Court could hope to group itself around the King and resume the habits of Court life. Louis XV., hedged in by excessive and often ridiculous precautions, which injured only the Regent, was guarded like a prisoner at Vincennes, the Tuileries (see Fig. 4), and the Louvre, and his governor was always pretending to fear for his young charge a thousand imaginary dangers. The Court was absolutely banished from the palace, being only convoked on state occasions or for official

ceremonies. This was a sort of exile which it found very insup-
portable; its members never put in an appearance at the Palais
Royal, and rarely at the Château de Sceaux, the residence of the
Duc du Maine. The courtiers shut themselves up in their hotels at
Paris and Versailles, or withdrew to their country houses, nursing
their grievances and their hopes.

The preachers in the reign of Louis XIV., Bossuet, Bourdaloue,
and Massillon, had often had occasion to say some hard things to
the courtiers, and to represent the Court in anything but a flattering
light. Yet their boldness had not excited any feelings of anger,
though there was much exaggeration in the vague and incoherent
pictures which they drew like riddles for the persons concerned to
guess. Massillon, in a sermon which seemed to spare no one but
the King, said: " The blood touches the blood, the father shames the
child, the brother lays snares for the brother, the husband seeks to
abandon his wife. The only tie which binds men together is that of
interest, passion, ill-feeling, and caprice ; crime is respected by the
great; virtue is only to be found amongst the simple, and piety
amongst the poor." It was the Court, and the Court alone, that the
preacher ventured to arraign before the bar of public opinion, in the
presence of the aged King, who had not the generosity to take up the
defence of his courtiers, though he knew them to be better and less
criminal than the preacher made them out, so as to have a pretext
for flattering the people at the expense of the great.

It will readily be believed that the Court was better studied and
judged more justly by moralists and philosophers than by the most
eloquent pulpit orators. Dufresny, a comic author, wrote, in 1705, a
charming sketch, in which the characteristics of the Court are very
cleverly delineated. In his " Serious and Comic Amusements " he
says: "The Court is a very amusing country. One breathes a very
good air in it; the avenues are inviting, the approach to them agreeable, and they all lead to one point. The courtiers' fortune seems to
await us, at the end of a wide road open to all the world ; it would
appear as if one had only to set foot there to reach one's destination ;

yet one only attains the goal by covered bye-ways, which are so
arranged that the straightest road is not always the shortest. I
don't know whether the ground of the Court is very solid; I have
seen new arrivals walk upon it with confidence, and old campaigners

Fig. 4.—Louis XV., as a child, being wheeled about the Tuileries Gardens. (Communicated by M. Bonnardot.)

who could only advance with fear and trembling; it is a high and a
low land, where every one endeavours to reach the highest part.
But to attain this part, there is only one path, and that so narrow
that an ambitious person can only advance along it by elbowing
others out of his way.

"Travelling through the Court country, I have remarked that the denizens are of idle habits. I only speak of the people, for the grandees and those who aspire to become such have their work cut out for them. The courtier's task is a harder one than it seems. In regard to the subordinates, they have only to crawl and supplicate : that is all their work, and their only merit consists in their long term of service. I except a certain number of officers, who, without any complacent servility, limit their ambition to doing their master's work to the best ability, and who live peaceably in that moderate state of life where true merit is mostly to be found. In this moderate state, which I place between the people and the great nobles, one may be polite without being double-faced, and open without being ill-mannered ; one may be free from the baseness of the people and the haughtiness of the great ; in a word, one may be what is called a man of honour."

To this subtle and ingenious picture must be added the portrait of the courtier, traced by the master hand of Montesquieu, who had himself too much taste and politeness not to admit that these two qualities were natural to the Court. He says : " In a monarchy politeness is naturalized at Court. At the Court one finds, in all things, a delicacy of taste which arises from a continual use of the superfluities of a large fortune, from the variety, and especially from the lassitudes of pleasure, from the multiplicity and the very confusion of fancies which, when they are agreeable, are always well received there." But, while appreciating what was distinguished and charming at the Court, he was severe and impartial in his judgment of the courtiers. "Ambition with sloth, baseness with pride, the desire to get rich without labour, an aversion to hearing the truth, flattery, treason, perfidy, the neglect of solemn engagements and civic duties, the fear of the virtue of the sovereign, the hopes based on his weaknesses, and, above all, the perpetual ridicule cast upon virtue, enter, I think, into the composition of most courtiers, in all times and at all places."

The French Court consisted of an immense agglomeration of

persons of all ages, all ranks, and all conditions, knitted the one to the other by the fact that they "belonged to the Court;" as is well expressed by Dufresny when he points out the different degrees which separated the people and the grandees of Court-land. Nor is this all. After the masters came the servants and the subordinates, who also had the honour of belonging to the Court, and were very proud of it. A host of noble or commoners' families had belonged to the Court for five or six hundred years, occupying the same post from father to son—posts, some of which were salaried and entailed actual duties, while others were honorary, and, in certain instances, implied the possession of a title of nobility. Everyone attached to the Court had his duties carefully marked out, his privileges minutely defined, and his rights regularly recorded. Everyone who was of the Court or in the Court, down to the men who pushed the King's sedan-chair, were jealous about their titles and special duties.

Piganiol de la Force, before enumerating the officers who composed the household of Louis XV., points out that it was "the image and miniature of the kingdom, being composed of the clergy, the nobility, and the third estate." He might well have added that even the people had its representatives.

The grand almoner of France, at the King's table, where he said the grace before and after meat, and at the chapel, where he gave the communion and other sacraments, was replaced in the event of forced absence by the first almoner, who was often himself replaced by one of the eight almoners in residence. The King's chapel had, in addition, eight chaplains taking the duty by turns, eight clerks, a sacristan, and a chapel-master having the musical department and the choristers under his control.

The grand master of the household, whose functions consisted mainly in regulating the expenses of the table, had jurisdiction over the seven offices belonging to this department, and it was before him that the officers of it, from the almoners to the equerries, took the oath of fidelity to the King. He presided at the King's bureau, which held its sittings twice a week, and at which were present the first maître d'hôtel and his assistants on duty, the masters of the counting-house, the controller-general of the table, the controllers of the different departments, and several book-keepers.   Each member of the King's bureau had a special duty at the Court.   The first maître d'hôtel had under his personal superintendence the seven offices, viz. : the goblet, the kitchen, the pantry, the wine-cellar, the common kitchen, the fruitery, and the pinfold.

Fig. 5.—The Grand Pantler.
(Duc de Cossé-Brissac, 1782.)

Fig. 6.—The Grand Cup-bearer.
(André de Gironde, 1731.)

He did the honours of the grand-master's table, and if the King expressed a wish for some bouillon when he woke in the morning, it was the first maître d'hôtel who brought it into the presence.   In his absence the duty devolved upon one of the ordinary maîtres d'hôtel. These latter, to the number of 12, carried the King's meat, bearing silver-gilt wands, and presented to his Majesty the moistened napkin which he used for his hands before meals.   The functions of the three masters of the counting-house consisted in paying all the charges of the table and the wages of the servants belonging to the great and small livery.   As to the controller-general of the household, he kept an account of the table expenses, and had charge of all the plate—gold, silver, and silver-gilt.   The grand chamberlain, who occupied such a high position in the old Court, was no longer entrusted with any duties but the interior service of the King's chamber.   His place was, as a rule, taken by one of the four first gentlemen of the chamber, who had the direction of the numerous *personnel* attached to the King's chamber. Next to them were the four first valets, who served by turns and exercised several honourable functions : they slept at the foot of the King's bed, and kept the keys of the coffers.

Fig. 7.—The Duc deGesvres, First Gentleman of the Chamber, in State Dress ; after Vanloo the younger (1735).

In enumerating the officers of the chamber, it will be sufficient to mention sixteen ushers, thirty-two valets of the chamber, twelve mantle bearers, two arquebuse bearers, eight barbers, a surgeon-dentist, eight upholsterers, three watchmakers, six grooms of the chamber, two chairmen, etc. No post in connection with the King's household was looked upon as undignified or degrading. Amongst

the other officers of the King's chamber, under the generic title of
"valets of the chamber without a fixed rank," were included the
painters, the sculptors, the glaziers, etc., the kennelmen, and the men
who had charge of the hawks employed in a sport which was rapidly
falling out of fashion. The twenty-six gentlemen of the chamber
served in rotation, and their functions were essentially honorary.
They belonged, as may be supposed, to the old nobility, and they
had to prove the purity of their extraction. The grand-master of

Fig. 8.—Grand-Chamberlain
(Prince de Turenne, 1747).

Fig. 9.—Captain of the Gate
(Vicomte de Vergennes, 1783).

the wardrobe, who was one of the highest persons in the kingdom,
had under his superintendence the wearing apparel, the linen and
the hose. When the King dressed, the grand-master assisted him to
put on his under waistcoat, his blue sash and his justaucorps; when
the King undressed, he handed him his nightdress, nightcap, and
handkerchief : but as a rule his duties devolved upon one of the
two masters of the wardrobe, who were always present in the
chamber to give the King his handkerchief, gloves, cane, and hat, or
to assist him in emptying his pockets when he came in to change
his dress, for the King's pockets were always full of letters,
memorials, and petitions. The officers of the wardrobe comprised
four first valets, sixteen valets, one trunkbearer, four grooms in
ordinary, three tailors, one linen-starcher, and two laundresses. The
officers of the King's cabinet were quite distinct from the officers of
the chamber. They were not compelled to prove their nobility,

but they became noble from the moment of their appointment. They consisted of the four secretaries of the cabinet, who had the rank of councillors in ordinary of the King, the four readers in ordinary, and the interpreters ; there were also, but of a somewhat lower rank, the two ushers of the cabinet, who ranked as equerries, and the cabinet couriers. The court charges were ranked according to their seniority, even when they had fallen into disuse and had become mere sinecures. Thus, there was a captain-general of the

Fig. 10.—Grand-Falconer (Comte de Vaudreuil, 1780).

falconries of the King's cabinet, who was not under the control of the grand-falconer, and whose duties merely consisted in taking the King's commands for all the hawking parties, and in receiving the birds which were sent to the King as presents from all parts of the world. Another department, which had become annexed to the cabinet, was that of the royal palaces and buildings, and it comprised important functions, filled by a large number of persons. The inspection and management of the royal buildings, gardens, and manufactures, had always been entrusted to great noblemen, and afterwards to eminent artists, such as Mansard, or to princes, like the Duc de Antin, who were entitled "superintendents of the royal buildings." This superintendent had under him a first architect, several architects in ordinary, three surveyors and controllers of buildings, two treasurers, an inspector of the waterworks, a surveyor of plans and inscriptions, a first clerk of the archives, and several other officers of different grades, each having his title, function, and pay. For instance, in the service of the royal palaces, we find for the Versailles canal a regular fleet with a captain, first officer, mariners, gondoliers, and calkers; amongst the staff employed in the gardens was a cleaner of the statues and a mole-catcher.

It must not be supposed that all these subordinate posts, many of which were mere sinecures, were gratuitous, or that the salaries were small; the great charges and the second charges were very valuable, for the caution money, or the price of the charge guaranteed by the King, was 500,000 livres for the first gentlemen of the chamber, and 400,000 for the first maître d'hotel of the King. These charges procured a large revenue to their holders. The subordinate posts were relatively as profitable; many of them conferred the right of free domicile, board, and clothing (or livery). Thus, the captain of the King's greyhounds received 2500 livres a year, exclusive of perquisites; the keeper of the fancy dogs had a salary of 1500 livres and 200 livres for livery. The four apothecaries of the King, serving in rotation, received a salary of 1000 livres and 600 livres indemnity for their horse; their four assistants, whom Molière held up to such ridicule in his comedies, had only 200 livres each, but various perquisites brought their pay up to 400 livres, exclusive of the right of having a shop in Paris. The ordinary servants, as well as those who occupied the higher functions, had bouche à cour; that is to say, they were lodged and boarded at the King's expense. The very sweeper, with wages of only 350 livres, was well off, for he only had to work two or three hours a day, and the relative value of money has increased very much during the last hundred years. Thus the functions which appeared to be the most humble were much sought after, and looked upon as honourable by persons of gentle or even noble birth, and in 1735 one of the two chairmen of the King was the Sieur Jacques Calabre de Perrault, who received wages of 600 livres paid out of the privy purse, and an indemnification of 200 livres out of the royal treasury.

All those who held a post at Court were very punctilious as to fulfilling the functions attaching to it, however embarrassing and peculiar these functions might be. In this respect, every one made a point of serving the King, without letting it be seen that his duties appeared onerous or distasteful. But, upon the other hand, no one was disposed to exceed the limits of his duty, nor to encroach upon the higher or less important functions of his neighbour. Hence arose an unbending and pitiless etiquette which knew no law

Fig. 11.—The Grand-Marshal of the Palace (Chamillart, Marquis de la Suze, 1774).

but that of precedent. The King, the Princes and Princesses of the royal house would have felt its inconvenience, had they not been accustomed to it from childhood. "These servile regulations," as Madame de Campan very sensibly remarks, "were raised to the dignity of a code; they enabled a Richelieu, a La Rochefoucauld, a Duras, to make their domestic functions subservient to their fortune; and, to indulge their vanity, they discovered an affection for usages which converted into prerogatives the right of handing a glass of water, of putting on a shirt, and removing a basin. Princes who had been accustomed to be treated as if they were demi-gods naturally got to believe that they were of a nature apart, of an essence purer than their fellow men."

This multiplicity of charges and offices necessitated an enormous expenditure, and it is not surprising that the King's ordinary resources were insufficient to meet it, when we remember that his military was even more costly than his civil household. No exact calculation has ever been made of the general expenditure of the King's household. The most economical ministers, such as Colbert, his nephew, the controller-general Desmarets, never succeeded in making both ends meet. The receipts amounted to forty-nine million livres in 1709, and in the early part of 1715 the financial requirements of the treasury were so pressing that it was necessary to negotiate bills for thirty-two millions in order to obtain a fourth of

Fig. 12.—Grand-Veneur (Huntsman)
Duc de Penthièvre, 1737).

Fig. 13.—Grand-Louvetier, or Master of the Wolf-
hounds (Comte d'Haussonville, 1780).

that sum in specie. Louis XIV., a few months after this ruinous loan, left debts amounting to nearly three milliards of livres. Yet no diminutions were ever made in the charges of the Court ; not a single kennelman was dismissed, there was not one turnspit the less in the kitchen, nor one upholsterer's man the less in the King's chamber.

When Louis XV. was but five years of age, his civil household was as complete and well organized as that of his predecessor had been, and awaited his majority to serve him with the usual amount of ceremony. The Duchesse de Ventadour, the governess of the young King, under the superintendence of the Duc de Bourbon, was absorbed in the important functions which Louis XIV. had confided to her. Moufle d'Angerville, one of the most impartial historians of that reign, says : " She was of a mild and yet resolute disposition ; she was passionately fond of her royal pupil, and her attention to him resembled rather that of a tender mother than of an ambitious stranger. Her vigilance was redoubled by the events of the day ; she knew what terrible suspicions were afloat, and she had scarcely a moment's peace during the eighteen months that she was in the King's service." The young King was afterwards entrusted to the care of his governor, the Duc de Villeroy, who watched over him with equal solicitude, though he was the first to spoil his native good qualities by undue flattery. He it was who was always taking the young King to the different windows of the Tuileries and who, showing him the

Fig. 14.—The Grand-Master of France (Prince de Condé, 1740).

crowd which assembled in the Place du Carrousel to cheer him, used to say : " Look, Sire, at these crowds of people ! they all belong to you, you are their master ! " These unwise precepts naturally developed and increased the innate egotism of the young Prince who received no moral education, in spite of the lessons of his tutor Cardinal de Fleury. Louis XV. was of a delicate constitution ; he had been very ill when three years of age, and it was thought imprudent to fatigue him by a course of prolonged study for which he himself had a great distaste.

Upon the other hand, he was very fond of physical exercise, and took to it with such impetuousness that his governor was often obliged to interfere. As soon as he was old enough, he had a fencing-master, a singing-master, a dancing-master, and even a vaulting-master. The latter, Louis Scially, received only two hundred livres, but the fencing-master. Henri Rousseau, who was a man of great skill, and whose lessons were very eagerly looked forward to by the young Prince, received 2000 livres.   This was not nearly so much as the dancing-master got, for he received a salary of 2000 livres, 2000 livres as a gratification, and 3600 livres by way of indemnity.   The King was very fond of dancing, and soon became the best dancer at the Court.

He readily learnt anything that tended to increase the grace of his manners and the charm of his person, and he would have been one of the most attractive of lads but for the melancholy and preoccupied look which never left him.   His natural quickness was never culti-vated, nor was any effort made to overcome his slothfulness of mind and his indolent memory.   "Mind the King's health," the doctors were always saying, and all the household took up the parrot cry. These suspicions were directed against the Duc d'Orleans who did not deign to take any notice of them.   Still there was much real anxiety felt as to the King's health ; notably in 1721, when he had a very bad throat complaint.   Immediately it was said that he had been poisoned, and of course it was the regent who had committed the crime.   " The Duc d'Orleans," says Saint Simon, " behaved in such a simple and proper manner during the King's illness, that he raised himself a great deal in the estimation of the public ; his uneasi-ness was natural, but not overdone . . . . He took care never to say that he thought the King either better or worse than he really was, so that it might not be said that his fears were too true, or his hopes of evil omen."   The truth is, that he never had any wish to occupy the throne.   The King got well, and it was easy to see that the French still felt the same affection and respect for their Sovereigns.   " It would be impossible to describe," wrote Duclos, "the transports of joy succeeding to a general feeling of consternation which the King's convalescence excited.   There was no need to stimulate their loyalty. People were dancing and feasting in the streets.   The tradespeople took their meals at their doors and invited the passers-by to come and partake of them ; all Paris seemed to give a family feast every day.   This went on for two months ; the foreigners shared our joy, and the Emperor openly declared that Louis XV. was the Child of Europe."

The Duc d'Orleans was not the person least pleased at his recovery, for he was very fond of the young King, who, in spite of

Fig. 15.—Minuet danced at the State Ball given by the King, February 24th, 1745, in the covered Riding-school of the Grand Stables at Versailles, after Cochin.

the efforts made to excite his distrust, reciprocated the affection. Thus Louis XV., when at the age of thirteen he held a bed of justice at which he proclaimed his majority, asked the Duc to continue his attentions and advice, and still to give him the benefit of his experience. He regretted him, as if he had been his father, when he died suddenly on the 21st of December, 1723. Louis had been crowned in the previous year. One of his ministers, the Marquis d'Argenson, says: "The King's face was charming. On the morning of his coronation at Rheims, with his long robe and silver cap, in the dress of a neophyte or a king-candidate, he was marvellously like Cupid .... I have never seen so touching a face, the tears came into one's eyes as one thought how this poor little Prince, the sole offshoot of a once numerous family, had escaped so many dangers."

The reign of Louis XV. had now began, and the place of the Duc d'Orleans was taken by the Duc de Bourbon, the prime minister, and afterwards by the Cardinal de Fleury, for the King would not be burdened with the affairs of state, and left them to his ministers who were governed by Court influences.

The King, as a young man, did not care either for fêtes or state entertainments or ceremonies. He was silent, reserved, and absent-minded ; he avoided anything like noise or crowds, though, to quote the Duc de Richelieu, he combined politeness and attention to details with the stately manners of royal personages. Marshal de Villeroy, who was looked upon as a pattern of the accomplished courtier, had made him very particular about points of etiquette, and his tutor, Cardinal de Fleury, teaching him to pay strict attention to his religious duties, had no difficulty in developing a piety the only defect of which was its narrowness. Louis XV. in his early years devoted all his spare time to the chase ; he never read, wrote but little, and worked a good deal at embroidery. His personal appearance became more and more attractive, and the Duc de Richelieu wrote ; "his physical beauty was so great at the age of seventeen that he was reputed to be the most handsome youth in the kingdom. Nature had not forgotten a single point of importance or of detail." He avoided female society, and would not even look a lady in the face. "The King does not at present deign to bestow his bright looks upon any sort of object," wrote Marshal de Villars in his journal. His cousin, the Infanta of Spain, who had been brought up near to him, with a view to making her Queen of France, was sent back to Madrid. Thus the courtiers were concerned to see that

there was no present prospect of a direct heir to the crown. The
prime minister, the Duc de Bourbon, set himself to bring about the
marriage of the young King, and the latter accepted, without en-

Fig. 16.—Louis XV. as a youth, after Vanloo.

thusiasm, but without repugnance, the wife whom his ministers had
selected for him. This was Marie Leczinska, a daughter of
Stanislaus, the dethroned and fugitive King of Poland. France,
always attached to its Kings, approved of this marriage which

promised to be a happy one (Sept. 5th, 1725). Marie Leczinska could not be called beautiful; there was nothing striking about her features, but she had a soft and pleasing expression, and a good and aristocratic figure. Her youth and gracefulness made up for other deficiencies. Intellectually, her mind was not very brilliant or highly cultivated, but she was of an excellent disposition and her kindness of heart was her chief charm. Louis XV. thought her agreeable, interesting and almost pretty, for, to the corrupt persons who pointed out to him the beauty of one of his subjects, he replied: "She is not so good-looking as the Queen!" But the relations between the royal couple were by no means hearty, very ceremonious, and cold. This coldness was mainly due to the excessive mistrust of the Queen. The King, however, lived upon good terms with her, and she bore him two sons and eight daughters. Until 1732, his conduct as a husband was almost irreproachable. It was in the society of the Comtesse de Toulouse at the Château de Rambouillet that the King became initiated into the habits of high life, those habits of suavity and politeness which add an increased lustre to the prestige of the crown. One of the most judicious historians of the eighteenth century, M. de Lacretelle, writing of the Court at this epoch, says: "The Court, a country in which the course of events is never more stirring, nor the intrigues more complicated than during the minority of the Sovereign, was governed as might be a quiet and well-to-do family . . . . License was tacitly suppressed, and vice was no longer a fashion."

The Court regained, in the course of time, the éclat and animation which it had lost during the old age of Louis XIV. and the minority of his grandson. Amongst other entertainments we may mention the splendid fêtes given at Versailles to celebrate the first marriage of the Dauphin, eldest son of Louis XV., with Marie-Thérèse Bourbon, Infanta of Spain, in 1745, which was the year of the battle of Fontenoy, that is to say, the most brilliant period of his reign. The recollection of these fêtes has been preserved to us by the engravings of Charles Nicholas Cochin the younger. These entertainments were organized by the Duc de Richelieu, then first gentleman of the chamber; and the most remarkable, in addition to a grand masked ball in the Galerie des Glaces (for which see chromo-lithograph 3), were a representation in the riding-school at Versailles of Voltaire's comedy-ballet, "La Princesse de Navarre," which was

Fig. 17.—Marie Leczinska, Queen of France ; after Nattier.

set to music by Rameau (February 23rd, 1745 ; see p. 30), and a state ball given at the same place on the following day (see figs. 15 and 18.)

A complete change took place when the King, ceasing to have any other feelings for the Queen than those of respect, was led away by bad advice into the temptations to which Sovereigns are especially prone. He had hitherto reigned through his ministers, now he began to reign through his favourites, and the bad example which he set his Court were only too soon followed. His subjects had surnamed him *the Well-beloved* when they feared they were about to lose him, but in the course of his long reign he seemed anxious to ensure that he would not be regretted. He proclaimed his selfishness when he said one day, " After us the deluge ! "   Never did a French monarch make so sad a use of the good qualities which even his enemies admitted that he possessed.   Pidaunsat de Mairobert, who speaks of him as "the mildest of men, the most affable of masters, the most honest man in the kingdom," thus

Fig. 18.—Card of Invitation or the Court Ball ; after Cochin.

explains in *L'Espion Anglais* how it came to pass that his acts were never in harmony with his ideas and feelings : " He is fond of honest people, and when he comes across them he pays no heed to them ; he would like to be told the truth, and he repels the only bodies (parliamentary bodies) which could convey it to him : he is just, and he knows that every kind of injustice is done under cover of his name.   He is benevolent, and he will not take any trouble ; those who want to approach him must first see his ministers, what- ever favour they may happen to want.   He is very orderly in regard to his own affairs ; he is careful and even economical, and he wastes the money of the State in superfluous expenses and undeserved largesses ; he knows that he is being robbed right and

REPRESENTATION OF "LA PRINCESSE DE NAVARRE," AT VERSAILLES; AFTER COCHIN.

left, and he does nothing to stop it. The key to this enigma is that he is easy-going." His disorderly conduct, which had not even the excuse of youth, was perhaps solely due to his wanting something to divert his mind. " He is in the habit," said *L'Espion Anglais*, " of taking a great deal of exercise; whenever he is detained indoors for a few days his bile gets the better of him. He suffers from a still worse complaint, and that is the feeling of ennui, to shake off which he must be always moving about, and which leads him from one palace to another until he has completed the whole series." When the King was not going to the chase, the courtiers always used to say, " The King is not going to do anything to-day."

After the military and naval disasters of this reign, after the scarcity and sufferings of the nation, after the bickerings of the clergy and the parliament, after the scandals of the domination of Madame de Pompadour, and the shameless favour accorded to Madame du Barry, the attachment of the people for *Louis the Well-Beloved* was changed into hatred and contempt. This was made only too plain during his last illness when his death-bed was abandoned even by the most devoted of his servants. The grand-almoner, before administering to him the sacraments, had drawn up the following retractation : " Although the King owes an account of his conduct to God alone, he regrets having been the cause of scandal to his subjects, and declares that in future he will think only of the maintenance of religion and the happiness of his people." His eyes were no sooner closed (May 10th, 1774) than his body, black with corruption, was hastily conducted in a hunting-carriage to St. Denis, with an escort of forty body-guards and a few pages bearing torches. The populace, cursing his memory, dancing, singing, shouting, and drinking, were the only spectators of this shabby funeral procession.

The Dauphin, his eldest son, had died in 1765, at the age of thirty-six. Left a widower a year after his marriage with Marie Thérèse of Spain, he had afterwards espoused the Princess Marie Joséphine of Saxony, by whom he had, amongst other children,

Louis XVI., Louis XVIII., and Charles X. The death of this Prince was much to be regretted, if the testimony of Louis XV. may be taken, for that Sovereign, speaking before Madame du Hausset, said : " My son is of an indolent disposition, and his temper, like that of most people with Polish blood in their veins, is quick and variable; he has no taste ; he cares nothing for the chase, women, or good living. Perhaps he thinks that if he were in my position he would be happy. At first he would change everything, appear to make a fresh start in every particular, and would soon be tired of the position of King as he is now of his own. He is made to live like a philosopher with men of intellect ; he likes to do good, he is really virtuous and intelligent." The people never had an opportunity of knowing or appreciating him, but they had conceived a great liking for the new Dauphin who was to succeed his grandfather ; since the marriage of that young Prince with the daughter of Maria Theresa Empress of Austria (1770). When his bride passed through Paris on her way to Versailles, all the inhabitants came out to greet her, and cheered her almost to delirium. These were the same people who, four years later, threw mud at the coffin of Louis XV. Marie-Antoinette feigned to believe that the enthusiasm which she excited was meant for the King, and she said: " The French do not see enough of their King; they cannot pay me a higher compliment than in letting me see they love him whom I already look upon as a second father." This display of the popular sympathy was intended for her, but her husband profited by it. The public satisfaction was still more marked upon his accession, and his reign was ushered in by universal rejoicing.

Weber, the Queen's foster-brother, has drawn the following life-like portrait of her : " Nature herself, as Madame de Polignac has pointed out, intended Marie-Antoinette to occupy a throne. A majestic figure, features of aristocratic beauty, and a way of carrying the head difficult to describe, inspired respect. Her features, though not regular, were, what is still better, very harmonious ; the whiteness of her skin set them off and gave a dazzling radiance to her face. A most seductive manner heightened all these charms, and in this first flower of her youth, the elegance and sprightliness of her movements, the frank and innocent outflow of a genial disposition and a natural wit, could not but please the Frenchmen of that day. She charmed her husband the King, and his family, the city, the grandees and the people ; in fact persons of all ranks and all ages."

Fig. 19.—Louis XVI., Marie-Antoinette, and the Dauphin ; after Saint-Aubin.

Now for the portrait of Louis XVI. We cannot do better than quote Madame de Campan, who wrote from memory long after his execution : "Louis XVI. had rather aristocratic features, tinged with melancholy ; his gait was heavy and by no means majestic ; his hair, however well the hairdresser had arranged it, would, so careless was he in these matters, soon fall into disorder. His voice, though not harsh, was by no means pleasant. His tutor, the Abbé de Radonvilliers, a gentle and kind-hearted bookworm, had impregnated him with the love of study. The King had kept up his course of instruction ; he was well acquainted with English, he was a good geographer, and he was very fond of drawing maps ; he was well versed in history, though perhaps he had not sufficiently seized its teaching. . . . . This Prince united to so much knowledge all the qualities of a good husband, a kind father, and an indulgent master. . . . Unfortunately, he was too fond of mechanical studies ; he was so fond of masonry and locksmith's work that he used to have a locksmith at the palace to work with him at the latter's trade. . . . Austere as regarded himself alone, he carried out all the ordinances of the church, fasting throughout the whole of Lent. . . . Of a pious disposition, he was none the less disposed to be tolerant, modest, and simple. Turgot, Malesherbes, and Necker had thought that a prince such as he was would sacrifice the royal prerogatives to the real greatness of his people."

The profound feeling which had so long attached the French people to their kings still subsisted when Louis XVI. was on the throne, and was never displayed more strikingly than upon the birth of the Dauphin. Marie-Antoinette was no longer so much admired, and the people were beginning to look upon her with suspicious dislike. All the faults and troubles of the government were attributed to her ; her influence in politics was dreaded, and, in secret, she was accused of being ready to sacrifice France to her pride, her whims, and her intrigues. An unscrupulous party, of which the Duc d'Orleans was, in secret, the leader, did all in their power to discredit the royalty and dishonour the King, by inventing the blackest and the foullest calumnies against the Queen. These calumnies were originated at the Court, and grew with incredible rapidity, being propagated amongst the populace in the shape of scandalous pamphlets, songs, and caricatures.

Marie-Antoinette was very fond of pleasure, and she loved it with all the passion of a candid and innocent mind. To use the expression of an impartial historian, "the King, in the midst of his Court, was like an indulgent father who good-humouredly tolerates the amusements of his children." Hence arose the continual fêtes, of which the Queen was the life and soul, at Versailles, Marly, Trianon,

MARIE-ANTOINETTE AND HER CHILDREN.

Louis-Joseph-Xavier-François, born in 1781, died in 1789.
Louis-Charles de France, born in 1785 ; afterwards Louis XVII.
Marie-Thérèse-Charlotte de France, born 1778 ; afterwards Duchesse d'Angoulême.

Painted by Madame Vigée-Lebrun (Versailles Museum).

and St. Cloud. He never raised any objection to her fancies, and all she thought of was how to amuse herself by providing diversions for her household and friends. He allowed her to indulge in unlimited expenditure for her amusements as well as for her charity. Play, dress, carriages and horses, visits to Marly, rustic fêtes at Trianon, swallowed up enormous sums. But the Prince de Ligne, who was one of her intimates, endeavours to justify her on this point, and his memoir of the Court, says : " The reproaches as to the Queen's luxury were unfounded. She paid so little attention to her dress, that for many years she allowed herself to be attended by a hairdresser who had been in her service since she was first married, rather than wound his feelings by a dismissal. It is true that after he had arranged her hair she often ran her hands through it so as to make it harmonize with her features. As to her love of play, I have never seen her lose more than 2000 louis, and that was at those games of etiquette at which she was unwilling to win from those who were obliged to join in the game. In fact, I remember that, after having received on the first of the month the 500 louis which formed her pin-money, she was in the course of a few hours penniless. I remember on one occasion having collected some 25 louis from the various servants in attendance for the purpose of giving them to some unfortunate woman whom the Queen wished to relieve. The accusations of improper conduct levelled against her arose from the fact that she displayed a perhaps overstrained feeling of friendship for two or three persons, and from a general desire to be pleasant to everybody."

The calumniators, in fact, who were her implacable and secret foes, transformed a few inconsiderate actions into gross misbehaviour. The disgraceful Necklace Trial, in which her name and her honour were pilloried, was but the sequel of the underground machinations which were resorted to for the purpose of ruining her reputation. But the confidence of Louis XVI. in her virtue and honour was not in the least shaken by these reiterated attacks, which were repeated in every form, so as to make it appear that Marie-Antoinette was a shameless woman, devoid of morality and self-respect, a dangerous councillor for her husband, and a feather-brained squanderer of the public revenues. She was even accused of sacrificing the interests of France to those of Austria, of emptying the treasury into the lap of her brother, the Emperor Joseph II., and of covering the King with ridicule and disgrace by urging upon him a policy fatal to the interests of his crown and country. It was said that Louis XVI. was blinded by his affection for her. It is true that on certain occasions he proved that he was unable to deny her anything, for on one evening she went to the Bal de l'Opera with one of her brothers-in-law and a lady-in-waiting, and, thinking that she would not be recognised beneath her mask, entered into the enjoyment of the evening without any restraint. This, being known, gave rise to much gossip. She then asked the King to accompany her, and he consented to do so. Madame de Campan says that he did not enjoy the spectacle much, and only spoke to two or three persons who recognised him. " The only amusing feature in it was, he thought, the harlequins and the clowns."

Lacretelle says : " The Court no longer affected that aridity of feeling which often arises from the very excess of politeness, and which had become a fashion rather than a law under a selfish and libertine monarch such as Louis XV. ; the Court seemed to conform to the tastes and habits of the Queen. One breathed, so to speak, the air of pleasure at Versailles, and especially at Trianon and St. Cloud, where Marie-Antoinette seemed to be the Queen of the Graces. Everyone tried to appear young, because she was. The manners of the Court were no longer guided by the example of the King, but at all events there was no longer the ostentation of misconduct as during the Regency. Virtue was no longer a butt for ridicule ; there was a good deal of what was wrong, but it was covered with a veil of decency, or people endeavoured to excuse it on the score of profound feeling." Sentiment became the rule of morality, which was relaxed without giving cause to any crying scandal, though this sentimental feeling, nearly always false, exaggerated and unbridled, was

used as an excuse for every sort of imprudence and misbehaviour.
It was put forward without restraint in the books, the plays, the conversation, and all the episodes of social life ; and it must be admitted
that this repulsive sentimentality was imported from Germany with
Marie-Antoinette.

Fig. 20.—The Queen's Lady of the Palace ; after Moreau the younger.

"The Revolution," says Madame de Genlis in her "Memoirs," "had
long been preparing, and it was inevitable ; respect for the monarchy
had altogether died out, and it was considered good taste to make
sport of the Court in every particular. . . . A minister in disgrace
was sure to enjoy the public favour, and if he was sent into exile,
everybody made a point of going to see him, not out of real mag-
nanimity, but so as to follow the fashion of depreciating and blaming

everything done by the Court." Mercier says almost the same, only
in more grandiloquent and defiant terms : " The prevailing opinions
are no longer received from the *Court;* it is from the *city* that originates the approval or disapproval which eventually extends to the
rest of the kingdom." Marie-Antoinette, alas! was in part to blame
for this revolution of ideas and manners—the forerunner of one more
profound and more thorough, more shocking and more terrible, one
of which she was herself the first victim, and the monarchy of Louis
XIV. the second.

Fig. 21.—A Counter used by Marie-Antoinette.

CHAPTER II.

THE NOBILITY.

The Nobility.—The Genealogists.—The Nobility of the Court and the Provincial Nobility.—The Orders of Chivalry.—Foundation of the Military School for the Nobility.—The States-General and the Abolition of Titles of Nobility.

SINCE the learned Charles d'Hozier, genealogist to the King, had been ordered to draw up the general list of the nobility of the kingdom (1683), the commissioners appointed to seek out the counterfeit nobles and the persons who had usurped titles to which they had no right, had been constantly at work, fulfilling their duties with more or less impartiality and success. The object of these researches was not so much to obtain the punishment of delinquents as to make them pay fines and fiscal duties. These heraldic and genealogical enquiries did, as a matter of fact, bring large sums into the coffers of the King. The nobles were exempt from paying the *taille* and most other imposts, but the spurious nobles, and those who had been ennobled within a recent period, paid without murmur and often more than mere commoners. From 1700 to the death of Louis XIV. a great many orders in council were issued, enjoining that the prosecution of those who had usurped titles should go on, and the commissioners even called upon persons of high position to prove their right to the title they bore. Thus, in 1704, the lieutenant of the provostship of the exchequer and of the marshalsea of France, was summoned before the commissioners to show cause why he styled himself by the title of esquire to which he had no right. The fine for assuming a false title was 2000 livres, and the delinquent had also to pay 300 livres for each of the titles he had unlawfully used in any public deeds ;

noble, chevalier, esquire, messire, baron, etc. Yet the usurpers of noble titles were incorrigible and constantly fell into the same snare. Sometimes, the commissioner was authorized to make a special agreement with a town or province, and, in consideration of a certain fixed sum or a voluntary annual contribution, he agreed to abstain for a given period from holding any enquiry or instituting any prosecution against the usurpers of noble titles or the recently ennobled who agreed amongst themselves to provide this sum, each contributing in proportion to his interests.

The office of judge-of-arms in France was suppressed by edict in November, 1696, and d'Hozier, who held this post, was succeeded by Clairambault, whose functions were those of archivist of the nobility. But an order in council (March 9th ,1706) restored d'Hozier to his former post, maintaining in the city of Paris a grand mastership of the nobility and a general armorial or public dêpot of the arms and scutcheons of the kingdom. As a consequence, no one had a right to use crested arms unless they had been controlled by the judge-at-arms and registered in the general book of heraldry. This created great consternation amongst those who owed their titles of nobility to the offices which they had purchased in the finance department, for all coats of arms were inspected by d'Hozier, and many of them were condemned. Complaints arose from all quarters and reached the ears of the King, who enjoined d'Hozier not to be so particular. The provost, the echevins and the other representatives of the city of Paris, were amongst the first to take umbrage at the severity of the grand mastership of the nobility. A royal edict was required to confirm the provost in his title of chevalier, and to retain for the echevins and other representatives the quality of hereditary noble, while they continued to carry on wholesale trade, and so long as they did not sell by retail or keep an open shop.

The creation of nobles and the sale of patents of nobility for the benefit of the King had not, however, been suspended, notwithstanding the measures being taken against those who usurped titles. In 1702, the King had ennobled 200 persons, "selected from amongst those who had most distinguished themselves in his service, by their merit, virtues and good qualities, upon the condition that they lived nobly, without derogation to the said quality, and

Fig. 22.—D'Hozier (Charles-René), genealogist of the King's household, controller of the arms and heraldry of France ; after Hyacinthe Rigaud.

paid to His Majesty the sums which may be named by the decrees of council." Each person ennobled had to pay 3000 livres, in addition to the costs. In 1706, the ennoblement of 500 persons produced a large sum, for the price had been raised to 6000 livres, the total representing at least £800,000 sterling at the present value of money. The concessions and the nobiliary fines amounted to at least £4,000,000 sterling during the last fifteen years of Louis XIV.'s reign.

The number of real nobles in France at this period did not exceed 600,000, inclusive of women and children; and the total had a tendency to diminish rather than increase. About 1750, there were not more than ten noble houses to each square league of land; thus 18,000 square leagues would give 180,000 houses, each composed of three persons on the average. But the condition and the fortune of these nobles varied enormously. The French nobility was, by general consent, divided into two distinct sections; the Court and the provincial nobility.

"The different provinces of the kingdom," says Barbier in his "Journal Historique," (January, 1751), "are filled with an infinity of poor noblemen, overburdened with children, whose fathers and mothers are unable to give them a proper education much less to send them to Court. Their children pass their youth amongst the peasants, ignorant and unpolished, often help to farm their land, and only differ from the peasants themselves in that they wear a sword and call themselves gentlemen."

Abbé Coyer, in his "Noblesse Commerçante," (1756), draws a striking picture of the sad state of the provincial nobility: "This obscure nobility, who see their ancestral castles daily crumbling into ruins without being able to repair them, not the Court nobility always present at the Court ceremonials and so made familiar with the graces of life, but this nobility chained down by want, upon which the sun only rises to expose their poverty, and which have no wings to carry them off to the land of good things . . . . . Cast your eye over those baronial acres which cannot sustain their barons. Look at these homesteads without cattle, these fields either badly cultivated or left waste altogether, these scanty crops which some creditor, judgment in hand, is waiting to seize, this castle which is threatening to fall about its owner's ears, this family which has neither education or clothes, the father and the mother who are only agreed as to their destitution. What good are these marks of honour which poverty degrades ; these worm-eaten coats of arms ; this prominent seat in the village-church, which ought to have in front of it a charity-box for the benefit of its tenant ; these prayers in which the name mentioned by the priest might well be recommended to the charity of the congregation ; this right of chase which is only a pleasure to people who are in easy circumstances and which becomes a burden to those who are not ; this right of justice which is degraded and badly dispensed when the person exercising it is down in the world ? "

Beside this poor and obscure nobility, there shone and, so to speak, reigned, the higher nobility which also had their castles, but castles which, whether of ancient or modern date, were kept in complete repair in the centre of their vast feudal domains. The territorial fortune of these great nobles was sometimes much compromised by excessive expenditure, and especially by voracious stewards. The Duc de St. Simon, in his " Memoirs," admits that he had never interfered in the management of his property, or in his domestic expenditure, because he felt himself incapable of seeing after it. But one wealthy marriage set this terrestrial fortune right again. The great nobles did not as a rule live upon their property ; they only came occasionally for the chase or to save money. They generally resided in Paris, where they possessed splendid residences, many of which, such as the Hôtels de Aumont, de Beauvilliers, de Biron, de Montmorency, de Luynes, de la Force, de Noailles, de Praslin, de Soubise, etc., were named after their proprietors. The owners of these hotels which were magnificently decorated and furnished, with spacious courtyards in front and at the rear, were large enough for the reception of a whole household, and for giving entertainments of every kind. The people derived pleasure from the passage through the streets of their carriages with its accompaniment of lackeys and running footmen, brilliant in gold lace and epaulettes, with their long gilt-headed canes.

This wealthy Court nobility, which inhabited Paris and Versailles, monopolized, and divided between themselves all the favours of the

Sovereign, the pensions, the lucrative appointments, the grades in the army, the ecclesiastical benefices and the honours of the Court. Abbé Coyer, who has drawn so epigrammatic a picture of the manners of the time, says : " A gentleman is quite persuaded that the King can only be served by arms ; he wishes his eldest son to play the leading part, and, while he is still sucking his coral, he shows him a sword. The child grows into manhood, and his first survey of his military calling shows him distractions of every kind, dogs,

Fig. 23.—Chariot with running ootmen (fac-simile after Rigaud).

horses, brilliant uniforms, play, the table, etc. ; he throws himself headlong into the service of the King."

Barbier completes this picture in his " Journal Historique," which never presented a favourable view of the nobility. He says : " Those who are most in favour obtain the command of a regiment at eighteen or twenty without any practical knowledge of military matters. They pass their youth in luxury and dissipation ; they have plenty of intelligence and politeness, but no acquaintance with the necessary sciences ; plenty of courage to fight, but no ability to command ; and this is why we have so few good generals or even good officers." Yet these effeminate libertines acted very bravely in the field. "Our young men apparently so enervated and feeble, so worn-out by luxury and pleasure," said the Comte d'Argenson who had seen them at the battle of Fontenoy, "are all the more praiseworthy for exposing themselves of their own free will to the hardship of war, whereas our fathers, semi-barbarous and of strong constitutions, were merely acting in obedience to their savage impulses."

The French army and navy required but 30,000 officers, and more than three times that number of nobles applied for employment in these services. The government took no thought of what must become of so many young men without a calling and without the means of existence, who were only willing to serve as officers, and who solicited in vain the honour of being exposed to death or wounds beneath the national flag.

Most of the nobles vegetated miserably in their provinces. The eldest of the family was generally in the service, with the rank of officer ; but his brothers and sisters had great difficulty in keeping body and soul together upon the soil of their ancestors, for it was considered derogatory for them to embark upon business of any kind. Thus the father was obliged to make his second son a priest or a monk, and his portionless daughters, whom no one would marry, nuns. The ecclesiastical state was not, for the nobles at least, incompatible with nobility. There were also a large number of benefices, abbeys, priories, canonries, and prebends which were the apanage of the young nobility and especially of the Court nobility. They were rarely given as a reward of merit ; the appointments nearly always went by favour. A nobleman in good repute at Court had little difficulty in getting one or even two or three of his sons inscribed upon "the list of appointments ;" in obtaining a place of canoness for his daughter and a grant of church tithes for other relatives. Still, as the young noblemen who were in need of appointments outnumbered by ten to one the posts to be filled, it was thought advisable to dub them *chevaliers* or *abbés*, though, as a rule, they had nothing military or ecclesiastical about them, save these titles which they assumed for the purpose of pushing their fortune.

The nobility of the provinces, however, remained proud amidst its poverty, and never humiliated itself to the enriched parvenus. The Court nobility, on the contrary, was not so proof against temptation, and had little scruple in flattering those who enjoyed the favour of the King and his ministers. Thus, when Cardinal de Fleury made Barjac, who had formerly been his lackey, the dispenser of the graces and favours of power, the greatest gentlemen in France so far forgot themselves as to become his courtiers and guests. The nobility, however, thought that no function, however humble, was derogatory when it was one imposed by their service of the King. Thus, as Abbé Coyer remarked : " In order to be *something*, a great part of the nobility is plunged in nothingness."

The regent Philip of Orleans had never felt any great esteem or liking for the nobility ; however he gave his approval to the renewed prosecution of the spurious nobles, because the fines increased the royal revenue without exciting any discontent. In consequence, the research was rigorously carried on from 1716-18, as also was the collection of the freehold tax upon all commoners possessing property that had belonged to nobles, notwithstanding the privileges and exemptions which their ennoblement carried with it. The number of persons ennobled did not increase until after the death of the Duc d'Orleans, who, on two special occasions, manifested his want of sympathy with the old nobility. The Breton gentlemen, implicated in the conspiracy of Cellamare and the accomplices of the Duc du Maine, had been sentenced to different modes of capital punishment which involved degradation ; and the efforts of the whole French nobility were powerless to procure their respite. Upon March 27th, 1720, four of them were beheaded at Nantes, sixteen others were hung in effigy. At Paris, on the previous day, the young Comte de Horn had been broken on the wheel in the Place de Grève for having murdered a wealthy stockjobber of the Rue Quincampoix, whom he had endeavoured to rob. " It is reported that the murderer, acquiescing in the justice of his sentence, said : " I deserve the wheel, but I hope that, out of consideration for my family, the punishment will be changed into decapitation." It was even said that the regent

THE HOTEL DE ROHAN SOUBISE; AFTER RIGAUD.

would have assented to this but for the remonstrances of Dubois and Law who, according to Duclos, declared "that the people would be very displeased and humiliated at any distinction being accorded for so foul a crime." The old nobility were very angry that their ancient privileges had not been taken into consideration.

At the expiration of the regency, the nobility regained its former supremacy after having been attacked and almost worsted by the parvenus of finance and politics. Louis XV., governed by the advice of Marshal de Villeroy, placed himself at the head of his old nobility and entrusted to them the destinies of the kingdom. He put in practice the feudal system of the learned Comte de Boulainvilliers, who looked upon the nobles as the feudal servants of the King. President Montesquieu, notwithstanding his connection with the sect of philosophers who had set themselves up as the irreconcilable enemies of an hereditary nobility, remembered that he was noble by profession and, in his "Esprit des Lois," he says : "The nobility enters, to a certain extent, into the very essence of the monarchy." Voltaire, who was also in a degree noble, as being the son of a notary to the King, indirectly supported Montesquieu's statement, and admitted that a nobility was necessary in a monarchical State, while he blamed the abuses which had grown around that institution in its decadence. He says : "In every moderate monarchy where property is safe, there will be families which, having saved money and rendered services to their country for several generations, will obtain an hereditary recompense : but there is a great difference between this and the nobility with its exactions, its prerogatives, its noble chapters, its tabourets, its ribands, its genealogists' certificate and all the noxious and ridiculous inventions which are certainly not essential parts of a monarchy."

Royalty and the government did, however, make certain concessions to the philosophical ideas which had penetrated even to the nobles themselves. Thus it had long been urged that the nobles should be allowed to embark in trade without being exposed to the loss of their privileges. Yet many intelligent persons, generally free from prejudice, continued to look upon commerce as incompatible with nobility, in spite of the example set by England and most other nations. Montesquieu himself maintained this view, without however asserting that trade was derogatory. He said that it would destroy the nobility without doing any good to commerce. However, the Council of State, by a decree dated April 27th, 1727, renewed that of December, 1701, which had become a dead letter, making a formal distinction between the merchant and the tradesman, and declaring that wholesale business did not entail loss of dignity. So it was that commerce, more especially maritime and colonial commerce, opened to the nobility an honourable career; but prejudice and even the jurisprudence of their order, prevented them from going into ordinary trade. The Abbé Coyer, appealing on behalf of the economists of the day to the nobility, wrote, in 1756 : " Become the sustainers of the soil, the supporters of the population, the force of our navy, the soul of our colonies, the nerve of the State, the promoters of the public fortune ! "

Just as it seemed as if the former exigencies of the nobility were about to be released, etiquette, which had never been more severe at Court, became established on a fixed and durable basis, by a minute regulation of the rights and privileges of the nobles. It was in the reign of Louis XV. that orders in council definitely regulated the conditions for being admitted to the post of page of the chamber, page of the great or small stable—posts which were much sought after by youths belonging to the highest families, as, in addition to serving the King, they were enabled to perfect themselves in fencing, dancing, and equitation, which formed so important a part in aristocratic education, and served as a preparation at once for their military career and their subsequent duties at Court. These conditions were not pecuniary; the candidate had to produce, verified by the judge-at-arms, the proof of his noble origin.

To form an idea of the number of documents required to prove the nobility, it will be sufficient to mention that, to be one of the pages of the Grande Ecurie, it was necessary to have belonged to the military nobility since 1550, and that the gentleman who was a candidate for the Petite Ecurie, had to prove his descent in four generations, that is from 1560, without any subsequent ennobling having taken place.

Fig. 24.—The Riding-lesson; after Parrocel (communicated by M. Bonnardot).

Every sub-lieutenant in the body-guard had proved that he was of a family noble for three and a half centuries.

It was even more difficult to attain the honours of the Court, to assist at the "Jeu du roi" (see Chromolithograph 4), to ride in the royal carriage. Every man or woman, before being presented to the

King, had to produce, before the genealogists of the royal orders, three titles establishing his descent from the beginning of the fifteenth century.

Fig. 25.—*Parade de prime* after a *coup de seconde.*

Admission into the noble chapters, both of men and women, was also subject to rigorous verifications of nobility. Nobles by birth

Fig. 26.—Disarmament after a *coup de tierce* or *de quarte.*

were alone admissible, and persons recently ennobled were invariably rejected, except upon the special authority and at the good pleasure of the King.

The nobility also opened the way to the orders of chivalry, more especially to the three highest, properly called *the King's orders;* that is to say, the order of the Holy Ghost, founded by Henri III.,

Fig. 27.—Position after having disarmed upon the *coup de tierce.*

of which the King was the immediate head, and which did not number more than a hundred members. Of the two other orders, one, that

Fig. 28.—Position after having disarmed upon the *coup de tierce* or the *coup de seconde* warded off *de prime.*
(Taken from Angelo's work on fencing, published in 1760.)

of St. Louis, founded by Louis XIV., was purely military; the other, that of St. Michel, dating from Louis XI., was not in-accessible to the ennobled bourgeoisie, and particularly to the members of the long robe. Nine degrees of nobility were required for admission into the order of St. Lazarus of Jerusalem, which was of very ancient foundation, and which had been incorporated with that of our Lady of Carmel, and which was sanctioned by Louis XIV. in 1664, and by Louis XV. in 1722.

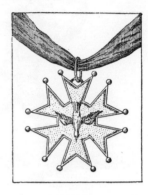

Fig. 29.—Collar of the Order of the Holy Ghost, founded by Henri III.

Fig. 30.—Collar of the Ultramontane Order of the Holy Ghost, established by the Popes and confirmed by various ordinances of the Kings of France.

The genealogists of the King's orders and the judges-at-arms were not, it was whispered, altogether incorruptible, however honest d'Hozier and Clairambault may have been. But the commissioners-general, who were deputed to inquire into the validity of titles, as well as their subordinates, lent themselves to frauds and illicit compromises with certain personages who were unable to justify the titles they had assumed. The fabrication of false titles of nobility was an art which had been carried to a high pitch of perfection at this period ; and it was practised almost with impunity beneath the severe eyes of the most respectable genealogists. The Marquise du Prat, in the " Memoirs " recently published by one of her descendants, says that she should like to have seen "many of the procureur-generals of certain parliaments burnt, and ten of their notaries sent to the galleys, for having falsified, either out of good-nature or self-interest, acts which ennobled persons who were anything but noble, and for having invented cradles for families which had only hovels and cribs."

Louis XV., who felt his throne menaced by the audacious attacks of the parliamentary authority, naturally looked for support to the old nobility, the decadence and gradual extinction of which he

Figs. 31 and 32.—Grand Cross and Collar of the Royal and Military Order of St. Lazarus of Jerusalem and of our Lady of Carmel.

witnessed with regret. It was not enough to reform and revivify this nobility, by grafting new branches on to ancient trunks which had nothing left but their roots, or by renewing with patents of

Fig. 33.—Order of the Ampulla, said to have been founded by Clovis; very rare.

Fig. 34.—Order of the Counts of Lyons, instituted by Louis XV. in 1745.

maintenance and filiation noble families which were on the point of extinction. The King and his ministers had recourse to the young nobles who were destined to serve in the army, and who had not the means of acquiring a military education previous to becoming officers. This was the origin of the Royal Military School, created in 1751, in which lads of noble parentage, who had no private fortune, were received at the age of eight, and carefully educated until they were old enough to become sub-lieutenants. At the same time, Louis XV. conceived the idea of counterpoising, so to speak, the nobility acquired by court functions and civil duties by a military nobility won by the sword on the field of battle. The edict of November, 1750, therefore granted the privileges of hereditary nobility to all the general officers on active service who were not noble at the time, and to any other officer without a title who had obtained, without giving proof of nobility, a rank inferior to that of marshal of the camp, but only after thirty years of uninterrupted service, during which period he was to be exempt from the *taille* and the poll-tax.

The object of these creations was, of course, to form a new military nobility, to counterbalance that of the long robe and other civil professions, for some immediate measures were required to stem the decadence and the diminution of the old territorial nobility. "If we passed in review our poverty-stricken nobility," wrote Abbé Coyer in 1756, "what should we see? An eldest son goes into the army, if he can. Will he eventually marry? It is impossible to say. The younger sons wed the Cross of Malta, a cassock, or a cowl. Sometimes, without embracing any profession, they lead a life of celibacy, which is as undesirable as it is profitless; and the daughters, instead of bearing children, shut themselves up in a cloister. The nobles, who were not particular about marrying beneath them, did not look for a title in their wife's dowry, all they thought of was the amount of the dowry, for they did not consider themselves demeaned by marrying a commoner's daughter; and this they called 'manuring their land.' These marriages were, it need hardly be said, rarely prompted by other than mercenary motives. Moreover, the habits of the great noblemen and the landed gentry disinclined them to the domesticated life which was, as a rule, led by the upper class amongst the bourgeoisie. With the nobility, there was an almost complete separation of man and wife, each living a life apart, and only appearing together on state occasions, or at some special ceremony. This disdainful neglect of family duties and family life contributed in no small degree to the decadence of the nobility. Nor was their mode of life calculated to gain them the respect of their inferiors ; they lowered themselves by the unfavourable opinion which their ruinous luxury, their pride, their arrogance, and their despotism could not fail to excite. This very luxury, so characteristic of the great nobleman, was often a proof

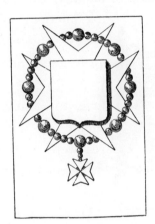 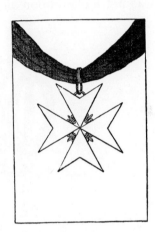

Figs. 35 and 36.—Grand Cross and Collar of the Order of St. John of Jerusalem (the Knights of Malta).

that he was in debt ; but, as Abbé Coyer remarks in his " Bagatelles Morales," " It is very vulgar to mind being in debt ; debts are a proof and confirmation of a man's greatness. It may be assumed that a nobleman who owes two millions is twice as great a nobleman as he who owes only a million."

The last act of Louis XV. in reference to the nobility was looked upon as a grave encroachment upon their rights, though it was only a fiscal measure intended to fill the King's coffers. A royal ordinance of July 29th, 1760, addressed to the tribunal of the Marshals of France, imposed a tax of thirty livres upon all those who had a coat of arms, from the princes of the blood downwards ; another tax of 220 livres was imposed upon those who had not had their right attested since 1700, and a further tax of 250 livres was to be levied on those who, not having any arms, wished to adopt some. But the Paris Parliament refused to register this decree, and prohibited its being carried into effect. The King did not venture to persist in a scheme which would have brought him in more than a million sterling, but which would have alienated the sympathies of the nobles, by its pressure upon the provincial nobility, and by multiplying enormously the number of heraldic devices at a time when the habit of having arms upon carriages, silver-plate, and seals was not looked upon as an assumption of nobility.

Fig. 37.—Grand Equerry (Prince de Lorraine, 1718).

Louis XVI., when he came to the throne, did not attempt to reconstitute the nobility by promulgating a new code, but he endeavoured to preserve, as far as possible, the relics of the ancient nobility, territorial as well as military. Hence arose a still stricter rule as to the proofs of nobility, which had to be produced before being nominated to one of the orders, admitted to a seat in the royal carriages, to the Grande-Ecurie, or to a grade in the army. There was still a mania for being deemed noble, especially at Court and in the aristocracy of finance. As for the real situation of the nobility it was very precarious. The Marquis de Bouillé says, in his " Memoirs : " " The nobility had undergone great changes ; it had lost, not only its former splendour, but its very existence, and it was fast going to decomposition. In France there were about 80,000 noble families : out of this number, a thousand or so dated back to the earliest ages of the monarchy, and of them not more than two or three hundred had escaped ruin. A few great names were still to be found at Court, recalling the memory of the famous personages who had made them illustrious, but too often degraded by the vices of their heirs. In the provinces there were still a few families of high standing who had preserved their patrimony, notwithstanding the restrictions placed on the substitutions which had formerly been the rule amongst the nobility, or rather because they had been able to repair the inroads upon their ancestral fortunes by

Fig. 38.—A Royal Chariot (fac-simile, after Rigaud).

wealthy marriages. The remainder of this ancient nobility languished in poverty, like those ancient oaks, mutilated by time, which have nothing but their naked trunks."

Several public scandals, such as the bankruptcy of the Prince de Guémené in 1782, and many shameless deeds of violence which had remained unpunished, served to complete the disgrace which had fallen on the great historic families, and this it was which caused Mercier, in his "Tableau de Paris," to say : "These names deserved personal consideration, but it was equally difficult to bear them and to propagate their lustre."

Louis XVI., though he adhered to the philosophical maxims of equality before the law and before society, attempted to restore in some degree the prestige of the nobility by birth, by decreeing that all those who were candidates for the grade of sub-lieutenant in the infantry or cavalry should produce the same proofs of nobility as those who sought for admission into the Royal Military School (May 22nd, 1781). Afterwards he decreed that nobles only should be eligible for admission into the colleges of the royal navy (January, 1786).

Under the influence of the return to these ancient privileges, the preponderance of the judges-at-arms once more asserted itself. Yet Henri Chérin, councillor to the court of excise and genealogist of the royal orders, did not hesitate to state, in the preface of his "Chronological summary of edicts, etc., concerning the nobility," (1788) that "in this countless multitude which makes up the order of privileged persons, scarcely a twentieth part has any real right to be classed amongst the nobility of ancient race."

These attempts were condemned to failure, and could but delay, without arresting, the march of those new ideas which the treatises of the philosophers had promulgated throughout the kingdom. Thus the decree of Louis XVI., conferring upon the nobles alone all the grades in the army, only served to excite discontent and ill-feeling. "The injustice and absurdity of this law," says Madame de Campan, "was no doubt one of the secondary causes of the Revolution ; only those who belonged to that honourable class called the third estate, can conceive the vexation or rather the anger which it created. . . . Another decision of the Court, which could not be proclaimed by edict, was that for the future all ecclesiastical property, from the humblest priory to the richest abbeys, should be the apanage of the nobility."

The effect of these exorbitant favours, conferred upon the nobility by birth, upon the eve of a social revolution, was to raise their pretensions and to intensify the opposition of the third estate. Yet there was just then a sort of recrudescence in the *noblomania.* People talked of nothing but heraldry and genealogy ; coats of arms were exhibited upon every possible object. Of counts, barons, and chevaliers, there was no end, in spite of the protestations of the royal

OPENING OF THE STATES-GENERAL IN 1789.

genealogist, who did not venture upon prosecuting their bearers. "These nobles," says Mercier, "are the greatest enemies of our national morality: they will not pay in any other coin than genealogy. To the secret league of those who are the enemies of merit of any kind whatever, are due certain underhand arrangements for excluding, wherever it is possible to do so, those endowed with personal talents." Mercier could not well designate more pointedly than this, the edicts in favour of the old nobility.

The crowning manifestation of this nobility, was an act of government, upon the nomination of the members of the assembly of Notables (1784), and still more so at the formation of the States-General of 1789. But these States-General, in which the third-estate had as many representatives as the clergy and nobility combined, was destined to witness the disappearance of the nobility, with all their rights and privileges, upon that night sitting of August 4th, when the nobles seemed themselves anxious to justify the fatal prediction of Mercier: "Now that the nobility has no more true courage or real ability than the enlightened and patriotic part of the nation, equality is imperceptibly but surely forcing its way to the front. The services rendered to the throne, to the nation, and to art, must no longer be distinguished by syllables of more or less length; man, more than ever before, is noble according to his works."

Fig. 39.—A Lady of Quality (fac-simile after Rigaud).

CHAPTER III.

THE BOURGEOISIE.

The Role of the Bourgeoisie.—Declension of its Primitive Characteristics.—The Upper, the Middle, and the Lower Bourgeoisie.—Their Habits.—The Provincial Bourgeoisie.—The Bourgeoisie upon the Eve of the Revolution.—The Third Estate.

OUR bourgeoisie had been losing its original characteristics and its ancient prerogatives during the reign of Louis XIV., who never forgot the Fronde, and who looked upon their political aspiration as seditious inroads upon his absolute authority. Thus, the old leaven of their opposition was only to be found in the parliaments, which were the image and expression of the aristocracy of commerce. Strictly speaking, the bourgeoisie as a body—a body at once powerful and jealous of its privileges—had ceased to exist at the beginning of the eighteenth century, or did not, at all events, exercise any direct influence or play any active part in state affairs. There was still a provost and a body of echevins (aldermen) for the administration of Paris; the other cities of the kingdom also possessed their elected municipalities, but nowhere did the bourgeois, as such, enjoy any share in the government of the country. When he happened to shake off his passive indifference, he only ventured upon a few criticisms, more or less measured, or some popular rhymes and epigrams.

Montesquieu did not even deign to mention the bourgeoisie by name when he enveloped it, so to speak, in the long robe, for, in his "Lettres Persanes," we read : " There are three estates in France ; the Church, the Sword, and the Gown. Each one of the three has a sovereign contempt for the other two, and thus, an individual who ought merely to be despised because he is a fool, is often treated with contempt simply because he is a Gownsman." At this period there were few members of the select bourgeoisie, either in Paris or the provinces, who stooped to claim, for themselves and their families, that semi-nobility which the French Kings, from Jean I. to Henri II.,

Fig. 40.—The Bourgeois, his Wife and Child; after Dupin's costumes Français.

had conferred upon the notables of their chief cities. They still termed themselves *bourgeois de Paris* upon their funeral invitations and their epitaphs when they died in some business profession, but, during their lifetime, they would have thought it derogatory to call themselves *bourgeois.*

This name had become almost a term of reproach, at least, when used in a certain sense. The decadence of the title dated, perhaps, from Molière's comedy, "Le Bourgeois Gentilhomme." La

Fontaine, in one of his fables, contributed to depreciate it by the following verses, which were very applicable to the chief defect of the wealthy bourgeoisie :

> " Se croire un personnage est fort commun en France ;
> On y fait l'homme d'importance,
> Et l'on n'est souvent qu'un *bourgeois*.
> C'est proprement le mal françois."

This proverb had served to affix to the name of *bourgeois*, once so respected and so respectable, a meaning which was anything but flattering and the impress of ridicule. Comedy had turned it into contempt, by holding up to derision what ought, on the contrary, to have raised it in esteem. To pay one's debts, or rather not to incur any, was to live like a *bourgeois;* to contract a marriage of affection was *bourgeois* and *ultra-bourgeois*, as Léandre says in the comedy of " The Philosophe Marie," wherein Destouches copies La Fontaine's well-known line :

> " Laissons les bons bourgeois se plaire en leur ménage."

And it was upon the stage, during the last fifteen years of the reign of Louis XIV., that we find the most life-like picture of the bourgeoisie of the long robe. Dancourt depicted these failings in several comedies of great wit and very true to nature, notably in his " Bourgeoises à la mode " and his " Bourgeoises de qualité." Women, in particular, the widows of notaries, registrars, commissaries, etc., profess the greatest possible indifference for their late husbands, waste their substance at the gaming-table, borrow money at an exorbitant rate of interest, indulge in the most reckless expenditure, and whose chief ambition is to obtain a titled son-in-law, or to get married themselves to some ruined nobleman. Thus, we are told that the wife of notary Simon " is one of the most extravagant women in the world; all she wants is more money. She is a woman of very good sense, who is fond of amusement, play, and society. She has been persuaded to let play take place at her own house." When the husband, who is not himself less to blame in other respects, remonstrates with his spouse, she retorts upon him, " I shall only want music three times a week ; on the other three evenings there will only be a little lansquenet and ombre, followed by a large supper. Thus, there will only be one day, which will be devoted to conversation ; we shall read clever books, discuss the news, and, in fact, employ ourselves the whole day upon ' things of the mind.' " Master Simon, "who is a bourgeois from the crown of his head to the sole of his feet," could find nothing to say, for he and his wife were not on

Fig. 41.—Gaming ; from the *Occupations des Dames*, by Chodovieski.
(Communicated by M. Eug. Sauzay.)

worse terms than the majority of their class. A soubrette, serving in such a family, when asked how her master and mistress lived, would immediately reply : " Like man and wife. They are always at loggerheads, frequently come to high words, rarely make it up, are always sulking with each other, and each complains, perhaps with justice, that the other is in the wrong."

Madame Blandureau, wife of a procureur of the Châtelet, gives the following reasons why she cannot abstain from play : " What else is there to be done, especially in the country ? " Her husband does not think it proper that a woman of *position, une femme en charge,* should pass her days and nights in this way; "It is ridiculous to invite eight or ten women, the one more ridiculous than the other, and with whom you are not intimate, to come and sup at your expense." Madame Blandureau was not worse than her cousin, the registrar's widow, who, left a large fortune by her deceased husband, immediately set about finding a second amongst the nobility. "I want a title," she wrote to one of her friends, "that is all I care about." The *bourgeoise* who married a noble might expect to enjoy a fair amount of consideration, especially if she bore children to her husband, for these children would be noble, notwithstanding the plebeian origin of their mother. But, upon the other hand, the bourgeois who married a young lady of noble birth met with nothing but contempt and slights. In Allainval's amusing comedy, "L'Ecole des Bourgeois," which was represented in 1728, M. Mathieu is thus made to describe his married disappointments: "Being a rich banker, I was induced, by my ridiculous aspirations after nobility, to marry a young lady whose only fortune was her pedigree. To what ridicule and vexation did she not expose me during her lifetime! She and all her family fed upon my purse, and then she thought that I had not paid enough for her. I was only her nominal husband; she looked upon me as beneath her. In fact, I was the Georges Dandin of the comedy."

What most marked the difference between aristocratic alliances and the marriages of the bourgeois was the harmony which generally prevailed in the latter class between husband and wife, who saw nothing to be ashamed of in living together, whereas in the nobility husband and wife affected to live apart, at least in public. The bourgeois households caused no scandal, and had the outward appearance of happiness, even when the man and wife were not very attached to each other. Montesquieu, in the "Lettres Persanes," gives the following picture of one of these bourgeois homes:

"We can boast of many marriages which turn out happily, and of many very virtuous women. The people to whom we refer live in unbroken harmony, they are liked and respected by everybody.

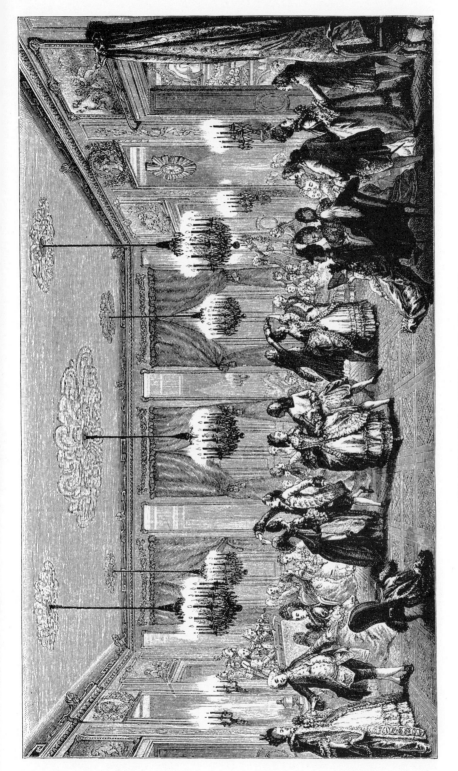

THE FANCY BALL; AFTER A. DE ST. AUBIN.

The only drawback is that their innate kindness of heart prevents them from being very particular as to whom they receive, and thus they are often surrounded by questionable company. Not that I blame them, for one must live with people as one finds them.

Fig. 42.—A Newly-Married Couple ; after Schénau.

Those who are looked upon as good company are, in many cases, persons whose vices are more refined, and who perhaps, as with poisons, are all the more dangerous on that account."

Dufresny, Montesquieu's predecessor, speaking of the *bourgeois circles,* the bourgeois society which was looked down upon so contemptuously by the nobility, says, " The bourgeois circle is a familiar assembly, a sort of free council, in which disputes between individuals are decided without the evidence of the parties. These decisions are governed by caprice, and there are as many different opinions as there are persons present; the same judge is severe one day, indulgent the next; sometimes grave, sometimes playful. The transition from grave to gay, from matters of importance to trifles, is instantaneous, and occasionally a sudden remark about a woman's head-dress defers the decision as to some point of morality which was being discussed at the time. Twenty different conclusions are formed at once; the men give their opinions when they can, and the women when they like, having two votes to one. The liberty which reigns in the *bourgeois circle* gives an insight into the character of those who belong to it, for every one speaks according to his views, inclinations, and genius." Dufresny delineates very wittily the different characters which composed the *bourgeois circle:* the young feather-pate and the man of advanced years, the sluggard, Lucretia and Lais, the self-made man, the blue-stocking and the poet, the heir in mourning for his legatee, the young magistrate, the female gambler, the good-looking man and the ladies' favourite, the man of money and the valet, the eccentric, and, lastly, the man whose voice is always being heard, and who is, in fact, a stray noble who has found his way into this assembly of bourgeois and their wives.

The bourgeoisie, like the nobility, was moreover composed of different classes quite distinct from each other, which did not seem to belong to the same order, for the economists and philosophers had not yet grouped the various members of this social body under the generic name of the *third estate,* and so made it a political power. It was not until the middle of the reign of Louis XV. that they invented the title of *bourgeois* which was contrasted, in the "Encyclopædia of Diderot and d'Alembert," with the shafts of ridicule shot from the stage at the extravagances of the *bourgeoisie:* "The *bourgeois* is a person who ordinarily resides in a town; the *citizen* is a bourgeois, taken in regard to the society of which he is a member." Subsequent to this categorical definition of the *bourgeois*, the word was hardly ever used except by the people, as applied to wealthy persons, and the term *citizen* served, so to speak, to ennoble the bourgeoisie. Voltaire, who was a bourgeois by birth, his father having been a Paris notary, seems to avoid mentioning the word *bourgeois* in his writings, but he does not appear much inclined to

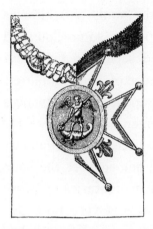

Fig. 43.—The Order of St. Michel, one of the king's orders, open to artists and to bourgeois who had been ennobled.

transform them into *citizens*, for, when he does happen to allude to them, he gives them the somewhat disdainful appellation of *Parisians* and *financiers*. Addressing a typical personage who cannot be other than a bourgeois, he says: "And you, pleasure-loving Parisian, who have never travelled further than Dieppe, where you went to eat fresh fish, who know nothing beyond your well-kept town house, your country villa, and your box at the Opera, which all Europe is weak enough to frequent; who can speak your own language pretty fairly, because you know no other, you think all this very pleasant, and you enjoy your champagne from Rheims, your funds the interest of which is paid every half year, and you say you love your country!" Voltaire, who set up for being a patriot and a good citizen, always had something of the bourgeois about him, flattering and paying court to the great, bantering and finding fault with the nobles, fond of luxury and good cheer, lending his money at a high rate of interest, and caring little about the people though he did tickle their vanity.

The *bourgeoisie* comprised several classes which, though they were its typical representatives, were by no means anxious to claim their place in it; viz., the ennobled families, the members of the parliaments and the supreme courts, and the financiers. They seemed inclined to leave to the tradesmen and those who had small independent fortunes the rank and title of *bourgeois* which had formerly been looked upon as so precious and so honourable. They had of their own accord separated themselves from the bourgeoisie, though they had no chance of being admitted into intimacy with the nobles who inexorably repelled their advances on the score of birth. The letters of ennoblement, which were frequently issued and the granting of which was a necessary preliminary to a nomination in the order of St. Michel, did not convert the bourgeois into a noble, until confirmed by three or four centuries of possession, and, except in a case of this kind, which was very rare, the person ennobled continued to be a bourgeois, even while styled chevalier, esquire, baron, or count, after having acquired by payment the right to bear these titles. Still, the bourgeoisie was composed of three special categories which usage alone had made hierarchical : the upper bourgeoisie, which comprised the persons ennobled by letters patent or by the nature of their functions, the long robe, and finance ; the middle-class bourgeoisie consisting of those who were bourgeois by birth, together with the holders of subordinate posts in the magistracy and municipality, as well as all the wealthy tradesmen, and the inferior bourgeoisie, which was very numerous, abounding in the provincial towns as well as in Paris, and including in its ranks all the laborious and industrial part of the population, as also those who lived unobtrusively upon a modest competence.

The upper bourgeoisie was not very different from the upper ranks of the nobility, for, like it, its members lived in great style and were very wealthy; they were even more wealthy, especially as they took better care of their fortune, and did not permit themselves the expensive luxury of a steward. They spent their money honourably, without having recourse to loans, and regulated their

Fig. 44.—The Industrious Mother ; after Chardin (in the Louvre).

expenditure according to their income. Their households were very well ordered both in Paris and at their country residences. They possessed sumptuous hotels, splendid castles, broad acres, handsome equipages, numerous servants, a good table, pleasant receptions, and everything that makes life agreeable. The chief dignitaries of the parliaments were thought more of than the great noblemen ; the

leading financiers were more courted than princes.   Samuel Bernard
gave a dowry of 800,000 francs to his daughters and grand-daughters,
and the Presidents Molé and Lamoignon sought the honour of
becoming his sons-in-law.

It is impossible to speak too highly of the upper bourgeoisie in
their private as well as in their public life.   Their morals were
pure even to austerity, they exhibited a great deal of home affection,
and father and mother set an example to their children, who
were brought up under their eyes in those simple and laborious habits
so well depicted by Chardin, the delineator of bourgeois life.   So
was it with the middle-class bourgeoisie, which had not been much
affected by the corrupting influences which the upper classes were
accused of propagating during the eighteenth century.   They led an
honourable existence, enjoying the society of a select circle of
acquaintances who belonged to the same social scale, without seeking
or envying the tumultuous pleasures of the great ; the mother and
her daughters attended to household duties (see Figs. 44 and 47,
p. 69, and p. 75), and the father found his daily amusement in a game
of trictrac or piquet (see Fig. 46, p. 73).   The inferior bourgeoisie, far
removed from the sphere of aristocratic society, passed their time
at home, and displayed, perhaps unconsciously, a bright example of
domestic virtues.

But the populace and the small tradespeople displayed towards
the bourgeoisie in general a spirit of distrust and antipathy, which
was made manifest by unjust and malignant prejudices.   They had
no idea of acting in hostility to the nobles, who were too far removed
from them to excite any other feeling than one of indifference ; but
there was always a latent antagonism between them and the
bourgeois, with whom they were continually brought into contact,
living as they did almost in their midst, and having seen them grow
rich, always with their aid, and sometimes at their expense.   Hence
arose those feelings of hatred and envy which lasted until the
revolution, by which time the bourgeoisie had ceased to have more
than a nominal existence.   In the eyes of the people, anyone who

had a fixed fortune, and who led an easy and independent life, was a
bourgeois.

The young bourgeois aristocracy was, it must be said, as fond of
luxury and as dissipated as the young nobles : money established a

Fig. 45.—The *Petite Toilette ;* after Moreau.

sort of connection between them. The young councillors of parliament and the youthful masters of requests outrivalled each other in
gallantry, as everything which denoted habits of luxury, such as
equipages, wearing apparel and jewellery, and high living, furniture,
and objects of vertu, was generally termed. Abbé Coyer, in his
Année Merveilleuse, says : "I had occasion to see a judge of five-and-

twenty. He was in the act of dressing (Fig. 45). I stopped to witness the whole performance, which lasted longer than my business; he might have been going to visit a duchess for the purpose of outrivalling her in perfumes. So we must not be surprised in future when we see individuals of the male sex, with ornaments in their ears, doing embroidery work, giving audience in bed at noon, interrupting a serious discussion to amuse their dog, talking to themselves before the glass, playing with their lace, going into paroxysms of rage over the breakage of a table ornament, fainting because their parrot is ill, and, in a word, usurping all the frivolous airs of the other sex." Was it such puerile occupations as these which Marshal de Richelieu was thinking of when he declared that it was rare to find a bourgeois capable of grand conceptions?

So, too, the Marquis d'Argenson, in his *Memoirs*, speaks very contemptuously of the paltry behaviour of certain ladies of the bourgeoisie class : " There can be nothing more ridiculous than to see the lady of the house fussing about and giving her keys for the servants to go and fetch the very objects that she keeps under her own control, and which she only produces on great occasions ; pressing her guests to taste the dishes which she thinks the best, as if they were not in a position to dine as well every day. These manners are so bourgeois, so provincial, so countrified that they are not now to be seen in the best *bourgeois* families of the capital, the provinces, and the country. In a house everything ought to seem so well regulated that the master or mistress of the house have only a sign to make for their guests to be well waited on. But if in the course of the day the mistress does not appear to be pre-occupied with these details, she must devote some portion of her time, when she is alone with her servants, to giving her orders, and seeing after the expenditure. She ought to know what each object costs and what becomes of it. In establishments, the masters of which are too great to look after such matters, the work must be done by a trustworthy house-steward." The Marquis d'Argenson goes on to instance a bourgeois household in which the husband supplied the place of

steward. He says : " I know a certain establishment, the master of
which is very-well-to-do, where the usual order of things is reversed.
It is the wife, as a rule, who sees to the daily expenditure, but in
this case the husband takes her place ; she prides herself upon being

Fig. 46.—The Game of Trictrac ; after Eisen.

a woman of great intellect." So the duty of paying the bills devolved
upon him, and he fulfilled his task with a very good grace. This
husband, who only opens his mouth to ask his guests what they
will eat or drink, who seems to be entirely at madame's orders,
passes all the morning in settling accounts, ordering the dinner, and

preparing the menu ; he is very strict with the servants, reprimanding them when they have neglected their duties, and prescribing to them how to avoid such faults for the future. His servants are afraid of him ; he even ventures to remonstrate with his wife occasionally when, by some neglect of hers, the expenditure has been too heavy or the fare indifferent." The household which the Marquis d'Argenson was caricaturing as being *too bourgeois* was that of Mme. Geoffrin, at which the leaders of society were proud of being invited to dinner or supper, to meet the most celebrated literary men of the day.

The best class of the bourgeoisie endeavoured, however, to show that they were not inferior to the nobility in point of politeness and good breeding; they even affected to believe that they were superior. Montesquieu puts into the mouth of one of his imaginary persons in the " Lettres Persanes," the story of a friend who, having promised to show him the best *salons* in Paris, takes him " to the house of a great nobleman who receives his guests better than almost any one in the kingdom. ' What does that mean, if you please ? Is he more polite or more affable than others ?' ' No, that is not it !' ' Oh ! I understand ; he makes all his guests feel that he is their superior. . . . I saw a little man so proud, he took a pinch of snuff with such a haughty air, he blew his nose so loudly, he spit with so much indifference, he caressed his dogs in a way which was so offensive to human beings, that I could not help admiring him. Ah, I said to myself, if when I was at the court of Persia I represented in this way, I should represent a ninny.' " Charles de Secondat, Baron de Montesquieu, was merely a wealthy bourgeois who possessed a baronial estate, and who, as President of the Bordeaux parliament, was on an equal footing with the nobles of his province.

Montesquieu might have drawn an attractive sketch of the bourgeois home-life in the provinces ; but he contents himself with hinting that the nobles of Paris were not held in higher esteem than those bourgeois who deserved respect. In Paris, liberty and equality prevail. Birth, virtue, and even warlike renown, however brilliant, are insufficient to distinguish an individual from the crowd in which he is lost. Jealousy of rank is unknown there. It is said that the greatest person in Paris is the man who has the best horses in his stable. In the provinces, more especially in the small towns, the inferior bourgeoisie had preserved their primitive habits. Marmontel,

Fig. 47.—The Servant ; after Chardin.

in his " Instructions of a father to his children," gives a touching description of the paternal house at Bort, a small town in the Limousin province : " My father, somewhat strict but essentially kind-hearted withal, loved his wife most devotedly, and with good reason. My dear mother was the best and the most pleasing of women. . . . My father venerated her as much as he loved her. His only reproach to her was that she was too fond of me, but this was excusable, for I was the only one of her children that, owing to delicate health, she had been able to bring up herself. My grand-mother was also very fond of me, and I fancy that I can see her, with her subdued gaiety and charm of manner. My mother was an excel-lent manager and presided over the household, setting us an example of filial piety ; for she too had her mother in addition to my paternal grandmother, to whom she was very attentive. There were also in the house, three sisters of my paternal grandmother, and my mother's sister. . . . My father was alone amongst all these women and a host of children ; his means were not very large, but still there was enough for all. Order, economy, a modest business, and, chief of all, frugality enabled us to live comfortably." The Parisian bourgeoisie had maintained the same orderly habits, for even during the Regency it was not led away by the deplorable example which the court set. The " Chronique Scandaleuse," which the *Duc de Richelieu* is said to have written in 1721, says : " The ladies of title soon imitated the court and the princesses. The bourgeoisie alone appeared to have kept command over itself. Modest in its habits, it did not make itself conspicuous like the persons of quality who, owing to their rank, displayed greater boldness and effrontery." Duclos, in his " Secret Memoirs of the Regency," also contrasts the simplicity of the bourgeoisie with the follies and debauchery of the time : " The middle class of citizens, more attached to the state and to morality, saw the fruits of their economy lost, their patrimony wasted, their property threatened, and, with all this, they saw vice which made no effort at concealment, decency despised, and scandal accorded the place of honour. They absolutely came to regret the hypocrisy of the ancient court." And, in praising the citizens of the middle class, it was to the bourgeoisie that he referred.

The bourgeoisie did not imitate the bad habits of the court and the nobility, but it copied their fashions with an exaggeration, perhaps, of bad taste. The court and the nobility complained about this and clamoured for sumptuary laws, which were promulgated for the last time on March 29th, 1700. This decree was partially revoked on February 28th, 1702, when the wives and daughters of

notaries, procureurs, registrars, and merchants, were allowed to wear
jewellery to the value of 2000 livres. For the future, there was no
sumptuary tax upon dress, notwithstanding "the impertinence of
petty *bourgeoises* who dared to imitate the noble inventions of
veritable ladies" (from Chevalier de Nizart's satire on hoops,
panniers, etc., published in 1712). The final effort of this fiscal
war, which was declared, not against luxury of dress, but
against the bourgeoisie, was a prohibition for them to wear
diamonds, pearls, or other precious stones, and to use gold or
silver plate (1720).

Henceforward their habits of luxury were to be combated, not
with sumptuary laws, but with the arms of the philosopher and the
economist. Montesquieu in his "Lettres Persanes," writes : "For
one man to live at ease, a hundred others must always be working
hard. A lady takes it into her head to appear at a ball in a certain
dress ; from that instant fifty work people will have no sleep, scarcely
even the time for refreshment, until the order is executed ; she
commands, and is obeyed more promptly than our monarch, and this
because self-interest is the greatest monarch in the land." Sixty
years later, Mercier, who had declared himself the enemy of the
bourgeoisie, out of his unreasoning enthusiasm for the citizens,
repeated this saying of Montesquieu, adding to it still greater bitterness and injustice : "An empty-headed bourgeois with an income of
50,000 francs may consider himself the centre of three hundred
thousand men, who slave and toil for him night and day. . . . By
means of all the arts linked one to the other, the position of this
private individual becomes almost equal to that of a king, for he
commands all the ease and pleasure which a sovereign can enjoy."
Mercier, like most philosophers, was not fond of the bourgeoisie,
especially on the eve of a revolution which would raise up a new
race of citizens. He might have remembered that the two greatest
ministers of Louis XVI. were but two *bourgeois ;* one a native of
Geneva, the other of Paris. As to the lower bourgeoisie which,
according to Mercier, "is closely allied to what is known as the

common people," he covers it with ridicule for having remained true
to the faith of its fathers.

The Marquis de Bouillé, in his "Memoirs," takes a juster view
of the position occupied by the bourgeoisie at the time when the
third-estate was about to reappear in the political assemblies : "All
the little provincial towns were peopled with small bourgeois, who
were richer and more industrious than the nobles, and who had
found means, either by themselves or their ancestors, to grow rich
upon the farms which they rented of the great nobility, or even in
their service . . . they had received, as a rule, an education which
was more necessary to them than it was to persons of gentle birth.
Thus, in Paris and the large cities, the bourgeoisie was superior in
point of money, ability, and personal merit. So, too, in the
provinces ; yet, in spite of this superiority the bourgeois were
excluded, by the rules of the service, from employment in the army,
and, to a certain extent, from the higher clergy. . . . They could not,
moreover, gain admittance to the higher magistracy, and most of
the supreme courts were only open to noblemen." This sufficed
to create a permanent and fatal antagonism between the nobility
and the bourgeoisie.

The latter ceased, as in former days, to exact from its members
descent from ancestors who had belonged to the magistracy, commerce, or finance ; it opened its ranks to all those who boasted of
being self-made. Many barristers, procureurs, physicians, journalists,
etc., were the sons or grandsons of stewards, valets, and domestic
servants of the old nobility. They took care not to proclaim this,
pretending to be very indifferent as to their origin. They were well
aware that their certificate of birth would give a signal contradiction
to their vain boasting.

This insatiable vanity was only too much stimulated by the
famous pamphlet of Abbé Sièyes : *What is the Third Estate ?* His
answer was : "Everything, but it is oppressed and hampered in every
direction. What would it be, but for a privileged order? Everything, but it would also be free and prosperous." The third-estate

reappeared stronger and more audacious than ever it had been before ; the bourgeoisie again became a political body, but it pronounced its own deposition, when it lost its ancient title, abdicated its social predominance, and became confounded in the popular element which soon absorbed it and dragged it down into the abyss of revolution.

Fig. 48. – Small Movable Diamond Cross, to be worn round the neck.

CHAPTER IV.

THE PEOPLE.

MASSILLON, preaching before Louis XIV. at Versailles in 1701, had the courage to pronounce the following words, the sense of which was purposely misinterpreted by the philosophers of the eighteenth century : " The great would be useless upon the earth if there were neither poor nor unfortunates ; they only owe their lofty position to the public necessity, and, instead of the people having been made for them, they are only what they are for the good of the people. What could we think of Providence if the whole multitude of men was only placed upon the earth to serve a select few of its most favoured inhabitants ! Their real greatness consists in the usage they make of it to relieve suffering." Louis XIV. often talked about this sermon, but he did nothing to relieve the miseries of the poor, which grew greater and greater. A few years after Massillon had reminded the King and his nobles of their duties towards the poor, Vauban, in his " Dixme Royale," wrote : " I have noticed that in these recent times nearly a tenth of the people is reduced to beggary ; that of the other nine-tenths, the majority are more in a condition to receive than to give charity." Vauban did not hesitate to plead before the King and his ministers the cause of " this part of the population, so useful and so despised, which has suffered so deeply, and suffers still." In the following terms this generous champion of the people's cause sets forth their neglected claims : " It is the lower class of the people which, by their labour and industry, and by their contributions to the royal treasury, enrich the sovereign, and his kingdom. From this part of the people are recruited the soldiers and sailors, and many officers, all the merchants and the subordinate law-officers. They exercise all the most important trades ; they carry on the commerce and manufactures of the kingdom ; they supply the labourers and farmers of the soil ; they rear the cattle, sow and reap the corn, trim the vines and make the wine, and, in a word, do all the most important work both in town and country." Vauban went on to draw a sad picture of the state of the country and its inhabitants ; borne down by taxation, most of these poor people had to live on oatmeal and barley bread, and had only a few rags to wear, many houses were in ruins and the land left fallow.

By this time, it is true, the people had lost their best and most natural supporters ; the magistrates, merchants, financiers, men of letters, and artists had separated from the people more or less openly, so as to gain admittance into the bourgeoisie and nobility. "The people," says Abbé Coyer, "were formerly the most useful, the most virtuous, and, consequently, the most respectable part of the nation. They were composed of husbandmen, artizans, merchants, financiers, men of letters, and lawyers. The men of the law came to think that there was as much glory in administering justice to men as in slaughtering them. So they ennobled themselves without the assistance of the sword. The men of letters, following Horace's example, looked upon the people as profane, and turned their backs upon them. The financiers soared so high that they found it difficult to keep on so low a level as the great. There is no possibility of confounding the merchants and the people, since the former have become ashamed of their calling, and affect to have abandoned it before they really have. Thus the people merely consist of the husbandmen, the domestic servants, and the artizans. . . . The people, even thus reduced, are, nevertheless, the most numerous and most indispensable part of the nation."

The population had decreased by nearly a million since the

revocation of the edict of Nantes, and its wretched condition had prevented any increase during the last years of Louis XIV. " If France contained as many inhabitants as she could support," wrote Vauban in 1709, "she would possess, at the rate of 700 to a square league, 21 millions ; " but the census recently taken in several provinces showed that there were not more than 627 inhabitants to a square league. The calculation, therefore, was that at that period the population of France was 19,094,144, out of which number 300,000 belonged to the nobility, and 1,800,000 to the bourgeoisie. Yet the people, who, as the philosophers were never tired of repeating, were everything, counted for nothing, and their only share in state affairs was to pay the taxes, for the privileged classes were exempt from most of the public imposts. It was not till the year 1713 that the population began to increase afresh, progressing slowly but gradually until, at the death of Louis XVI., it numbered 20,000,000.

The people, like the bourgeoisie and the nobility, were divided into several classes or categories, quite distinct from each other, viz., the people of Paris, the people of the provincial towns, the country people. It might also be said to consist of three kinds of individuals ; the artizans, the domestic servants, and the tillers of the soil, the latter forming two-thirds of the whole population, and being the halest and most honest as they were the poorest part. Thus the people had different habits, different requirements, and clashing sentiments. There was no affinity between the artizan and the husbandman, and they both looked down upon the domestic servant. The latter, though sprung from the people, which looked upon him as a degraded being who had passed over to the enemy, seemed to repudiate his origin ; he had no imposts to pay, neither the taille nor the poll-tax ; he did not contribute in the least degree to the public weal ; he did not often marry, and had few children, so as to be as unlike the artizans and cultivators as he possibly could.

The people of Paris were, in truth, a people apart ; more intelligent, more impetuous, and more capricious than the rest of the population, but, upon the other hand, comprising many elements of mischief. The dangerous characters, beggars, vagabonds, thieves, swindlers of every description, formed, perhaps, a sixth of the people, who were witnesses of their misdeeds without imitating them. Duclos, in a treatise on the habits of the people, said that their distinctive merit lay in the fact, that "they were the only people whose morality can become depraved without loss of courage or

Popular Types.
Fig. 49.—Père Tranquille and his Wallet ; after Boucher.

hardening of heart ; they ally heroic qualities with pleasure, luxury, and effeminacy ; their virtues are not very steadfast, but their vices are not very deeply rooted. The licentiousness of habits and of thought does not prevent a Frenchman from being frank and good-natured ; his *amour-propre* contributes to make him agreeable, for the more pleasure his conversation appears to give, the more anxious is he to please. The frivolity which interferes with the development of his talents and virtues, preserves him at the same time from the worst sorts of premeditated crime. He is never perfidious, and soon tires of intrigue. The Frenchman is the urchin of Europe." Duclos, in this portrait of the Frenchman, had the people of Paris as his model.

Poullain de Sainte-Foix, the witty author of *Historical Essays on Paris*, drew quite a different picture of this people, which, as a noble, he perhaps looked upon with less favourable eyes, for he says : " The people of Paris consist of a number of men brought together by their equal obscurity of condition ; they dispute, fight, shake hands, do one another a good or a bad turn all at once, they make friends and quarrel anew in a trice. The married people are always talking as if they were going to fight, and this habituates them to a rudeness of manner which does not attract much notice even when it is serious. A woman does not mind much what is said in her presence, while her husband is not surprised if he gets a sharp retort ; his ears tingle too often for that. It is only when they come to fisticuffs that the quarrel is serious. Those who aspire to be religious are only so in respect to outward forms ; true piety is above their heart and understanding."

There was little to recall the former turbulence of the people of Paris, who were so ready to create an uproar in the middle ages, but who seemed to have exhausted their energy during the Fronde. Disturbances in the street were almost unknown under Louis XIV., who did not like the Parisians, and would have made this fact felt at the first opportunity. The only instance of popular effervescence was towards the close of his reign, when Philip of Orleans, whom public opinion designated as having poisoned the Duchesse and the Duc de Bourgogne, was seen riding in a mourning-coach in the streets. He was hooted by the crowd, which threw mud and stones at him, and attempted to break into his residence at the Palais Royal. But this was, in reality, a mark of affection for the king and his family, un- concealed as was the antipathy of Louis XIV. for the Parisians. The affection of the latter for their sovereign was manifested on more than one occasion during the reigns of Louis XV. and his grandson

Duclos tells us that, on the recovery of the former in 1721, " it would be impossible to describe the transports of joy which his convalescence elicited." So, too, in 1744, after his recovery from the illness with which he was struck down at Metz. The author of *The Memoirs of the Duc de Richelieu* says : " When the king was well enough to return to Paris the enthusiasm broke out afresh, and the triumphal

Fig. 50.—A Street Row ; after L. Binet.

entries of victorious emperors into the world's capital could not compare with the delirious joy of the people at the return of their king . . . . all the splendour possible was displayed to delight an enchanted populace, which shed tears of happiness. The money distributed broadcast was not picked up. The sight of a handsome and victorious king, the liberator of France, was thought more of than mere money by the Parisians."

The disturbances which occurred in Paris during the reign of Louis XV. were not directed against the authority of the king; many of them, and those the most serious, arose from quite insignificant causes. In these disturbances, there was a great display of turbulence, but the people quieted down as rapidly as they had flared up. In 1721, the crowd menacing Law with death, on account of the scarcity of money and the dearness of food, assembled round the Palais Royal and threatened to set it on fire. The regent was there, almost unprotected, but he did not lose his presence of mind, and said: "The people are quite right to manifest their indignation; it is astonishing they have put up with it so long." Law, whose carriage was broken into pieces, had the courage to face the people, and to tell those who insulted them that they were a pack of canaille! Upon another occasion, the people took the part of a lackey who had been sentenced to the pillory and the galleys (Nov. 15th, 1721); they broke the pillory, set the lackey free, and did not disperse until several persons had been killed and wounded. A disturbance, caused by a rise in the price of bread (July 14th, 1725), resulted in several of the ringleaders being shot down, and two of them were afterwards hung in the Rue St Antoine.

There was a still more formidable riot in 1750, when the rumour was spread that children were being seized for transportation to the colonies. The people vented their fury upon the police, whom they accused of conniving at these abductions. Not only did they tear several archers of the guard to pieces, but they laid siege to the commissaries in their houses, and tried to sack the residence of Berrier, the Lieutenant of Police, order only being restored upon the appearance of the French guard. There was still a great difference between such disturbances as these and political sedition, with all its horrors and excesses.

It may be easily imagined how Voltaire, being an eye-witness of these disturbances, which were but the forerunners of others still more terrible, should have expressed little sympathy for the people with whom they originated; philosopher though he was, he was hostile to

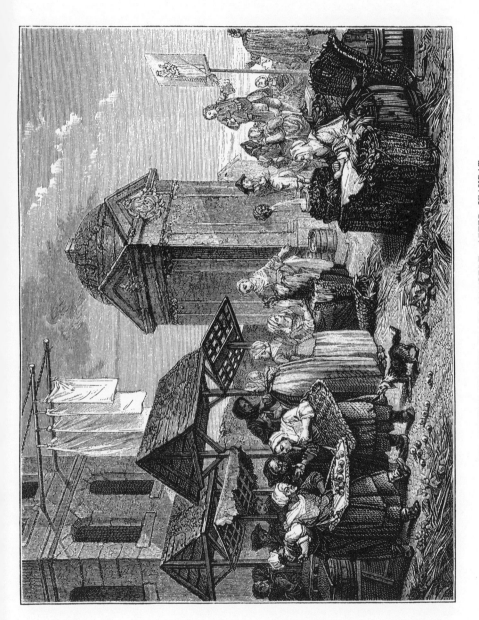

THE MARKET IN THE PLACE MAUBERT; AFTER JEAURAT.

popular instruction. Writing to Damilaville in 1766, he says : "I think we are not agreed as to the meaning of the word *people*, whom you think worthy of receiving education. I mean by *people* the populace which has only manual labour for their support. I question whether this order of citizens can ever have the time or the capacity for instruction ; they would die of hunger before they were educated.

" Thus it seems to me essential that there should be some ignorant clowns . . . . When the people take to reasoning, there will be an end to every thing." Voltaire was not, like his friends and followers, a flatterer of the people, who, throughout the eighteenth century, were always being truckled to and hoodwinked by the philosophers, when they endeavoured to stir them up against their masters and tyrants. " All is not lost," Voltaire wrote, " so long as the people are in a con-dition to see that they have a mind. But the worst may be looked for when they are treated like a herd of oxen, for sooner or later they will goad you with their horns." Abbé Coyer had already made a similar remark, only tempered by greater consideration for the people ; for, in his famous *Dissertation upon the Character of the People*, he says : " We refuse them reason, yet we have laws to punish them : tortures, gibbets, and the rack are ready prepared for them ; yet a bull that has killed its herdsman is not put to death. I will go further ; measuring reason in proportion to punishment, the people must be more reasonable than the classes above them. A poor wretch, whose children have nothing to eat, engages in some contraband trade ; he is found out and punished. A gentleman riding in his postchaise, is caught doing the same thing ; he kills the custom-house officer and gets off scot-free. Grégoire, having drunk too much wine, breaks his mug over the head of one of his boon-companions ; the rope settles his account. Two honourable gentlemen agree to fight a duel : one of them is left upon the field, and the other continues to advance in the service." Abbé Coyer terminates his dissertation by this satirical and insidious conclusion : " The people consist of men, but they are, fortunately for the classes above, unaware of the fact."

The physiognomy and character of the people of Paris underwent

little change from the reign of Louis XIV. to that of Louis XVI.,
when, in response to the flatteries and appeals of the philosophers,
they began to complain loudly of the nobility and bourgeoisie.
Thus, there was little new to be said about this class of the population, which remained much as La Bruyère had described it at the end
of the seventeenth century.   An Avignon barrister, Charles Cotolendi, who had come to Paris to enjoy literary society, conceived the
idea of writing a letter from an imaginary inhabitant of Sicily, so as
to be able to speak his mind about the Parisians.   A few sentences
in it relate to the people.   He says : " It is no exaggeration to call

Fig. 51.—A Tavern Breakfast.

Paris one large hotel ; on all sides I find inns and innkeepers, taverns
and their hosts, kitchen-fires always alight, because there is always
some one to be served. . . . The tables are always well provided ;
the Parisians never eat alone, they like to sip rather than drink,
but then they sip often, and always ask their guests to do the same.
The people never indulge, except on festivals and holidays, working
hard at other times.   There is not a population in the world more
industrious or so badly off, because they spend all their money on
their stomach and their back.   With all this, they are never
contented."

Cotolendi does not omit to notice their preference for second-
hand clothes : " When a garment has lived a longer life than that of

a flower, it is out of date ; hence we have a host of people who make their living by buying and selling discarded garments. They are very finely arrayed in clothes which have been worn by other people; and it is a rather useful custom in a very populous city, where those

Fig. 52.—The Toilette ; after Carle Vernet.

who dislike wearing the same things often can get rid of them at little loss, while others who have not much money can obtain clothing at a very slight expense." Cotolendi admits that at this period (1700) the people were polite, or at least endeavoured to be so. " Civility is thought more of in France than in China ; it is exhibited in a very agreeable fashion by persons of quality, the bourgeois import a certain amount of affectation into it, and the people, though civil, are rather rough withal ; each class has its own way of being polite."

Cotolendi mentions the increase of luxury amongst the people, who endeavoured, by imitating the bourgeoisie, to pass themselves off as such. He says : " An excess of luxury has obliterated the difference between master and man, between the dregs of the people and persons of high rank. Everybody wears a sword ; men do not wear a beard, or their own hair, and they endeavour to preserve their youthful appearance by a profuse appliance of cosmetics."

It was in fact true that the use of wigs was still prevalent, that is to say, that, till the end of Louis the Fifteenth's reign, not only the young men belonging to the lesser bourgeoisie, the merchants' sons, and the procureurs' clerks (see Fig. 52), but even the people, especially the artizans, wore small round wigs with short hair, very much pomaded and slightly powdered ; the sword was invariably worn, especially when they went out walking or to the theatre. The Marquis de Mirabeau, in his "Ami des Hommes," (1756), says : " Every Sunday I receive a visit from some one dressed in black silk and with a well-powdered wig, and as I am about to cover him with compliments, he announces himself as my blacksmith's or my saddler's foreman."

Restif de la Bretonne, in some memoirs published under the title of " Monsieur Nicolas," states that, after having done his work at the printing office (1770), he put on a closely fitting rateen coat, with black drugget breeches and white cotton hose, put under his arm a cocked hat, buckled to his side a small steel-hilted sword, and, with his hair perfumed and curled, walking tiptoe, so as not to soil his patent leather shoes with brass buckles, strolled through the dirty streets, where he was taken for a chevalier or a marquis. The same writer also says that the humblest grisette or needlewoman wore elegant but inexpensive dresses when she took a holiday, and was especially particular about *making her feet small*, wearing narrow shoes of bright-coloured leather, with high heels and bows of ribbon. " Fashion is the veritable demon which torments this country."

He remarks, however, that the people did not neglect their religious duties. " During Lent, the people go to hear the sermon, to which they listen very devoutly, and in the afternoon they are as assiduous in their attendance at the play. . . . There is a crowd at the theatre, where there is more scope for laughter ; this is why the Italian comedians derive a greater profit than their French con-frères out of the popular simplicity. . . . The people are pious in their attendance at church ; the tradespeople go to pray God for the prosperity of their business." Cotolendi also dwells upon the laborious qualities of the Parisians, for he says that " everyone is so rooted to his work that the devil can only put forth his temptations on Sundays and festivals." This energy in work, this arduous appli-cation to trade and manufacture, did not, unfortunately, suffice to frustrate the inevitable results of want of work, illness, and dissipation. " Rich as the city is," says Cotolendi, " he who is penniless, has nothing, that is to say, fire and water are forbidden things for those who have no money, as they were for criminals in the days of the Romans. I do not believe that there is a greater hell upon earth than to be penniless in Paris, to be continually at work, amidst all its pleasures, without being able to enjoy one of them. Amidst all this wealth, there is an infinity of poor people who in a whining tone ask for alms."

The poor, the beggars in particular, formed a class apart in the populace of Paris, who lived by their labour, and found the means to lead a comparatively pleasant existence. They set the most store upon amusements of different kinds, and did not mind living in obscure and tortuous streets, and unwholesome, badly-ventilated houses, their furniture, clothing, and food were very simple, and they did not take any thought for the morrow. The husband left his wife to look after the house and the children, the bachelor passed his spare hours in drinking and gambling. When ill, he went to the hospital, and in his old age was not ashamed to ask for charity. He did not tremble at the approach of death, for, in his daily walk across the cemetery of Innocents, he had seen that even the most wretched

Fig. 53.—The German Mountebank ; after Duplessis-Bertaux.

were sure of finding a last resting-place there, between four deal boards, at the bottom of a deep grave, the black and sticky soil in which was composed of human dust.

The people of Paris remained, even in the eighteenth century, what it had been two or three centuries before, brave and social, gay and jovial, fond of pleasure and good living ; the only difference being

Fig. 54.—A French Mountebank in the Place du Louvre ; after Duplessis-Bertaux.

that it had become prouder and more scornful, without ceasing to be just as inquisitive and fond of seeing, hearing, and finding out what was going on in the world. The people abstained from drinking to a certain extent, but continued to be as *badaud* (*cockney*) as ever.

"If this name (badaud) has been specially applied to the people of Paris," says Voltaire, "it is merely because there are more people in Paris than elsewhere, and consequently a greater number of idlers, who stop to stare at the first unusual spectacle, to look at a mountebank, at two women quarrelling, or at a carter whose vehicle is upset, though they will not help to pick it up. There are badauds everywhere, but those in Paris enjoy the greatest celebrity."

It was the evil genius of politics which destroyed the happy indifference of the people of Paris, perverted their best feelings, and stifled their best inspirations. Mercier, in his "Tableaux de Paris" (1783), says: "The Parisians seem to have guessed instinctively that a slight increase of liberty was not worth acquiring at the cost of continuous reflection and effort. The Parisian soon forgets the misfortunes of the past, and one would think that he is too confident of himself to fear being made the slave of an absolute despotism. He displayed much patience, strength, and courage, during the recent struggle between the throne and the laws; many besieged cities have shown less courage and constancy. As a general rule, he is mild, honest, polite, easy to manage, but it would be a mistake to confound his levity with weakness; he is cozened with his eyes open, and I know him well enough to assert that, when driven to an extremity, he can be very obstinate. Don't let us forget the League and the Fronde." Mercier, writing but seven years before the Revolution, was a prophet of evil.

He displayed keener foresight than Chamfort the misanthropical, who lashed the people of his day in the following severe terms: "Playful and fond of gambols as a monkey, and at bottom as mischievous, he is like a hound, born low, cringing, licking the hand of the master that beats him, allowing himself to be chained up, and jumping for joy when he is let loose for the chase."

The country people had neither the defects nor the good qualities of the townspeople, who were always being recruited from them. But the peasants had not the marks of moral and physical degradation which La Bruyère ascribed to them in 1688, when he wrote:

" One sees a set of wild animals, male and female, in the country, black, livid, sun-burnt, attached to the ground which they dig and delve with untiring stubbornness ; they utter semi-articulate sounds, and when they start to their feet they are seen to have a human face ; they are, in fact, human beings. They pass the night in huts, where they live on black bread, roots, and water ; they save other men the trouble of sowing and toiling and gathering in for

Fig. 55.—A Pastoral Scene ; after Boucher.

their livelihood, and thus they deserve to have a share of the bread which they have sown."

This dark picture, which La Bruyère sketched from a study of the peasants in some wretched district, such as Lower Brittany, or the highlands of Auvergne, affords a singular contrast to the glowing descriptions which the literature and arts of the eighteenth century unanimously gave of country life.

Madame de Genlis, in her " Memoirs," gives a more practical explanation of the differences to be noticed in the condition of the peasants : " In our journey of more than 600 leagues through

France, we only found the peasants honest, polite, and obliging in the villages where the chief landowners were amiable and popular; for where the landlords were tyrannical and unpopular, the peasants are uncouth and surly."

Restif de la Bretonne, whose pictures of country life are very true to nature, admits that the peasants were in some cases as depraved as the townspeople. "The human species when massed together in the country districts, becomes depraved as well as in the cities, to say nothing of the fact that the communication which subsists between town and country helps to corrupt the inhabitants of the latter." Pointing out the different degrees of depravation which, in his opinion, exist amongst the various classes of peasants, he says: "The plough promotes morality better than the vineyard, arduous though work in the latter may be; the herdsmen are less virtuous than the vine-dressers, and the shepherds are worse than the herdsmen."

The life of the country people cannot be better depicted than by the following extract taken from Restif de la Bretonne's "Vie de mon Père": "My father by hard work had procured a modest competence, he was held in deserved esteem, his eldest children, boys and girls, were doing well, and he was loved and looked up to by his wife. . . . Each evening, at supper, at which meal the whole family met, he sat, like a venerable patriarch, at the head of a numerous household; for we were generally twenty-two at table, including the ploughmen and vinedressers, who threshed the corn during winter, the herdsman, the shepherd, and two female servants, one of whom assisted in the vineyards, while the other tended the cows and had charge of the dairy. My father sat at one end of the table, near the fire, with his wife beside him, and close to her the dishes, for she saw to the cooking herself. The female servants, who had been at work all day, were seated, and allowed to sup at their ease; then came the children, according to seniority; next to them the oldest ploughman and his comrades, then the vinedressers, the herdsman, and the shepherd. The two maidservants were at the end of the table, opposite to their mistress, who thus had them under her immediate supervision.

"There was only one kind of bread. . . . My father would not allow the odious distinction of white and coarse bread. . . . As my father drank but little wine, what he did take was very good. My mother preferred water, and was with difficulty induced to colour it with a few drops of wine ; all the children drank water. The men had a rough kind of wine which they preferred to that which their

Fig. 56.—A real Shepherd (fac-simile from a print of the period).

master drank, for, like all peasants, they liked something that tickled the throat.

"After supper my father read to us from the Bible, and I never think without emotion of the attentiveness of his listeners, and of the fraternal affection which his words created between us all. During work the next day the subject about which he had been reading formed the staple of conversation, especially amongst the ploughmen. After he had done reading, we all joined in a short prayer ; the young people then recited a lesson from the diocesan catechism, after which we went quietly to bed, for, when the evening prayers had been said, laughter and noisy conversation were strictly forbidden. This was in summer, but in winter when the evenings are longer (there is no difference of season in towns) my father told stories, after the Bible had been read and the catechism repeated. . . This was our recreation. These instructive stories were always looked forward to, and as everybody was at liberty to laugh and make any

Fig. 57.—The Father of the Family, or reading the Bible ; after Greuze.

remarks that might occur to him, this was a great amusement for peasants and children who had never known any other."

The peaceful death of this worthy man was in keeping with his life. When the village priest came to administer to him the last sacraments, " he was followed by all his parishioners ; the old men, in tears, filled the sick chamber, and the remainder, kneeling in the courtyard, prayed for the preservation of his life." The priest addressed to him the following exhortation : " Be of good cheer, my father, you are about to repose in Abraham's bosom, in the company of the just men whom you resemble. But I venture to say that of all these good men none deserves a more glorious recompense than the excellent father who has conferred happiness and inculcated virtue on all around him, who has supplied good ministers to the Church, brave defenders of their country, honest citizens to the State, and exemplary wives to our young men."

Fig. 58.—Evening Stories (scene from rustic life); after Moreau.
" William relates how he made a long journey in Swabia."

This father, this peasant, who left so many touching souvenirs for his descendants, and who was known amongst his contemporaries as " the honest man," did not live to witness the general transformation which took place a few years afterwards in the very nature of the people when the tocsin of the Revolution stirred up the towns and the country against the throne, the church, and the nobility. Count de Ségur, who had been absent from France for ten years, and who returned from Russia in October, 1789, describes in his " Memoirs " the singular impression which the attitude of the urban and country populations made upon him, as he travelled to Paris : "The bourgeois, the peasants, the working men, and even the women,

Fig. 59.—A Winter Assembly (scenes from rustic life) ; after Gravelot.

displayed, in their attitude, their gestures, and especially upon their features, a vivacity and independence which I had never seen before There was an unusual degree of stir everywhere ; groups of men, assembled in the streets, were engaged in brisk conversation ; the beating of drums met my ears in the villages, and I was astonished to see what a number of armed men there were in the towns. When I questioned any of the lower classes, they answered me very brusquely and with a haughty air; wherever I went, I saw the impress of those sentiments of liberty and equality which had become violent passions. In fact, when I left France the people

Fig. 60.—The Fortune-Teller (scenes from rustic life); after Frendeberg.

were peaceable and still bent beneath the yoke of servitude; on my return I found them independent, haughty, and perhaps too ardent, to permit of their enjoying with moderation their newly-acquired freedom."

"Nothing can be more beautiful," says an eye-witness, Marmontel, "than the spectacle of a nation exalted by generous sentiments, but popular enthusiasm is dangerous even when it is caused by worthy motives, for the people, carried away by the passions of the hour, fly from one extremity to the other. At this moment they felt all the value of liberty, but this new-found liberty, intoxicating them, so to speak, soon depraved them, and gave birth to vices of every kind." Yet a few months, and this free people, wild with fanaticism, was destined to plunge madly into the most crapulous excesses.

Fig. 61.--The Bellows Vendor; after Boucher.

CHAPTER V.

THE ARMY AND NAVY.

DURING the last fifteen years of the reign of Louis XIV., there had been several partial renovations of the French armies, which were carrying on the war in Italy, Spain, Flanders, and Germany, with alternate success and reverses. These armies, not very numerous, and disseminated over points of Europe more or less distant from the French frontiers, were as a rule solid and well-disciplined, though composed of heterogeneous and of incoherent elements; the soldier, whatever his origin, became brave and devoted when once enrolled and submitted to discipline. "I will in future judge the nation by its soldiers, their valour has no bounds!" wrote Maréchal de Villars in 1703 to Chamillard, the Minister of War.

But it was not without some difficulty that the general-in-command reduced to discipline the recruits sent to him from Paris and the provinces to fill up the ranks thinned by battle, sickness, and desertion, for these recruits comprised many bad characters and vagabonds who did not like being bound by the military law in war-time, especially in the enemy's country. Marshal Villars, writing to the king in 1703, said, "I have to teach discipline to an army, the loose behaviour of which frightens all the inhabitants away, and deprives us of the commonest objects of necessity. Thank God, my influence over the soldiers increases every day, and I am beginning to get the peasants not to be afraid of them ; but the officers are not accustomed to regular service."

The incapacity of the officers was, in fact, the immediate cause of all the disasters which befell the army during the last years of Louis XIV. The officers, most of whom belonged to the nobility, were not less brave than the men, but their ignorance, their levity and their pride were incessantly paralysing the action of their

Fig. 62.—Types of Soldiers ; after Watteau.

troops. They were utterly devoid of instruction and experience ; their only use was that they could fight. In 1701 and 1702, 157 new infantry regiments were hastily formed out of volunteer militiamen and paid recruits, so that 7000 officers were required forthwith. The way in which these regiments were formed may be gathered from the account of one of the lieutenant-colonels, whose convertible property they became on payment of a fixed sum to the State. He says : " Amongst those who have raised regiments are several unknown and inexperienced adventurers, who thus acquired a position, robbing their king, their officers, their soldiers ! " Louis XIV. naturally reduced his army very much after the signature of the treaty of Rastadt (March 6th, 1714), which ushered in a complete period of peace, and enabled him to finish his reign with a year of unbroken tranquillity. Of the 274 regiments of infantry which had figured with varying success in the Spanish war of succession, from 1701 to 1714, only 121, inclusive of two regiments of guards, were kept up. The king died just as he was upon the point of completely reorganizing the army, and he had already fixed a stated sum for the colonelcy of the regiments which commanded a very high price, and which, with the certainty of a long

Fig. 63.—Types of Soldiers; after Watteau.

peace, the competition of the nobles was likely to raise still higher. "This power to enter by purchase the only gate leading to the higher grades," says Saint-Simon, "is a great cancer in the military system, and keeps away many persons who would make good soldiers. It is a gangrene which has long been eating into all the orders and posts of the State."

Yet there had been no lack of good generals during these last few years. The Duc de Ventadour, Marshals Catinat and Villars, who won more than one victory, knew how to make the most of the insufficient, and often feeble forces at their disposal; they formed many good officers in their school, but they more especially turned out admirable soldiers by setting them a bright example of personal courage. Villars, who sometimes condescended to consult his soldiers, often jumped from his horse and charged, sword in hand, at the head of the grenadiers. " What," he would say to the generals who stood hesitating and undecided around him, " is it necessary then that I, a marshal of France, should show you the way ? Well, let it so be, then ! "

The Regent, Philip of Orleans, who had no wish to involve France in the endless wars of the previous reign, none the less proceeded to improve the material condition of the army and navy. The Council of Regency decided that the equipment and arms of the soldiers should be regularly supplied by the control department of the war office, and this measure effected a large saving. The soldier's pay had at the same time been fixed at what would be equivalent to fifteen pence of our money. Moreover, by reducing the number of companies in each battalion, many superfluous officers were got rid of.

The two principal innovations which showed how solicitous Philip of Orleans was for the welfare of the soldier and the defence of the territory, were the administrative organization of the provincial militia, divided into battalions corresponding to the 121 infantry regiments, and the quartering of the troops in garrison towns.

Hitherto the troops had been billeted upon the inhabitants, except in the fortified towns, and the populations, both in town and country, were much discontented at having to support this oppressive and continually-recurring burden. Louis XIV. had indeed built some barracks in the faubourgs of Paris for the French and the Swiss guards, but they took a quarter of a century to complete. The war council afterwards ordered similar barracks to be built in all towns, the municipalities of which were ready to bear the cost of a building which would put an end to the billeting system. These barracks were erected in all directions, and the soldiers took such a fancy to them that they were called the *palaces of the army*.

The Regent had not, however, succeeded in realising his grand and noble schemes for the reorganization of the army and navy.

INFANTRY ON THE MARCH; AFTER WATTEAU.

His government, so much guided by favour and intrigue, did not reap the fruit of the well-considered reforms which he had endeavoured to carry out. Saint-Simon draws a melancholy picture of the moral and material situation of the military forces at the death of the Duc d'Orléans in 1723 : " The army was disgusted at the penurious economy which reduced it to the extreme of misery, and the pedantic rules which held it in complete bondage, while grades and the cross of St. Louis were indiscriminately awarded, and even made an object of traffic, to the undeserving. The increase of pay had not made the slightest change in the soldier's position, owing to the extreme dearness of the most indispensable objects, so that this part of the State, so important and so numerous, more than ever subjected to the servitude of the bureaux and other despicable creatures, could not but behold with delight the prospect of a change which might lighten its yoke and give a greater opening for real merit. The navy, which had been sadly neglected, naturally resented such treatment, and was ready to welcome any change." The composition of the army was almost the same as at the end of the reign of Louis XIV. These troops comprised the king's household troops, the gendarmerie, the cavalry, the French, and the foreign infantry, and the militia of the kingdom, which represented the reserve or ancient *arrière-ban.*

" The name of *the king's household* was given to the picked troops, horse and foot, which since 1671 had formed the king's guard. In addition to the cent-suisses, the sentinels at the doors, and the provost guards, who were termed the *guards of the inner Louvre* and fulfilled special functions within the palace, there were four companies of body-guards, the first company being Scotch and the others French. The *guards outside the Louvre,* which composed the king's guard, were divided into four categories : the company of gendarmes of the guard, the company of light horse, the two other companies of musketeers, and the two regiments of French and Swiss guards.

The king was nominally captain of each of these companies, which were under the command of a lieutenant-colonel. He was also captain of the four first companies of the gendarmerie of France.

This gendarmerie, composed of thirty-two brigades, eight squadrons, and 1200 gendarmes and light horse, at seventy-five to each company exclusive of field officers, had been created exclusively for the king and the princes; it went on foreign service with them alone.

The French and the foreign infantry, which constituted the real strength of the French army, was raised to 122 regiments by royal decree in 1737, but it did not for all that possess a stronger

Fig. 64.—Colonel-General of the French Guards
(Duc du Châtelet, 1788).

Fig. 65.—Colonel-General of the Swiss and the
Grisons (Comte d'Artois, 1771).

effective than it had with its 101 regiments of ancient date named after the gentlemen to whom they belonged, or the provinces in which they were raised or garrisoned. This effective amounted to 150,000 men, divided into 224 battalions with 175 men to each battalion of French guards, and 582 to each battalion of Swiss guards, including officers and band.

The French and foreign light cavalry, forming fifty-nine regiments divided into 165 squadrons of four troops each, with 160 *masters* or officers, and 200 hussars to a squadron, had annexed to it fifteen regiments of dragoons, serving alternately as cavalry and infantry, and numbering 10,000 men, with 750 officers. Amongst these regiments there were several composed of German, Swiss, and

Spanish volunteers. There were also several free companies of infantry and dragoons which had been created since the Polish war of succession upon the model of the Austrian pandours.

Lastly, there was the provincial militia, which was destined to contribute, in time of war, to the defence of the kingdom and to fill up the vacancies in the permanent army, and which had been disbanded after the Peace of Utrecht. This corps was reorganised in 1719, and divided into as many battalions as there were regiments of regular infantry. The number of battalions of militia was afterwards raised to 123, which were divided into forty regiments, exclusive of sixty companies of arquebusiers. This militia had its colonels, its

Fig. 66.—Colonel-General of Dragoons (Duc de Luynes, 1783).

officers, its uniforms, and its standards, but it did not generally do any active duty, and was only called up to take part in reviews or local ceremonies.

The chief command of the various bodies which composed the French army was exercised by brigadiers of infantry and cavalry, by marshals of the camp, and, over the latter again, by lieutenant-generals, while at the head of the military hierarchy were the marshals of France. A grand-provost-marshal was entrusted with judicial authority over the troops during a campaign.

Many changes of tactical drill had taken place in the early part of the century, and this was a natural consequence of the innovations in the arms of the infantry, when the addition of the bayonet to the musket (the socket for fixing the bayonet is said to have been invented by Vauban), did away with the distinction between musketeers and pikemen. The subjoined table, taken from Marshal de Puységur's comparison of a battalion of Condé's army and one of Turenne's army (see his " Art de la Guerre ") will enable the reader to understand the importance of this transformation.

Thus great changes had been effected in the armament of the troops since the beginning of the century, but the other equipments had undergone few modifications since the complete remodelling of the uniform upon one common system for the whole army in 1703.

Fig. 67.—Marshal of France (Duc de Gontaut-
Biron, 1757).

Fig. 68.—Grand Provost (du Bouschet, Marquis de
Sourches, 1746).

This uniform, very elaborate, very rich, and very highly-finished for the household troops, was for the most part of some bright colour. In Captain Suzanne's " History of the Old French Infantry " we read that " the various regiments were to be distinguished by the shape of their pockets and the arrangement and material out of which their buttons were made, and still more by the colour of the coat-lining, the vests and breeches. Of the French corps, the distinctive colour of those belonging to the household was blue; the regiments of the princes wore scarlet; the other regiments belonging to private gentlemen, and the provincial regiments were distinguished by black, violet, crimson, yellow, and green." The Picardy regiment had a white uniform, and in most of the provincial regiments grey and white predominated.

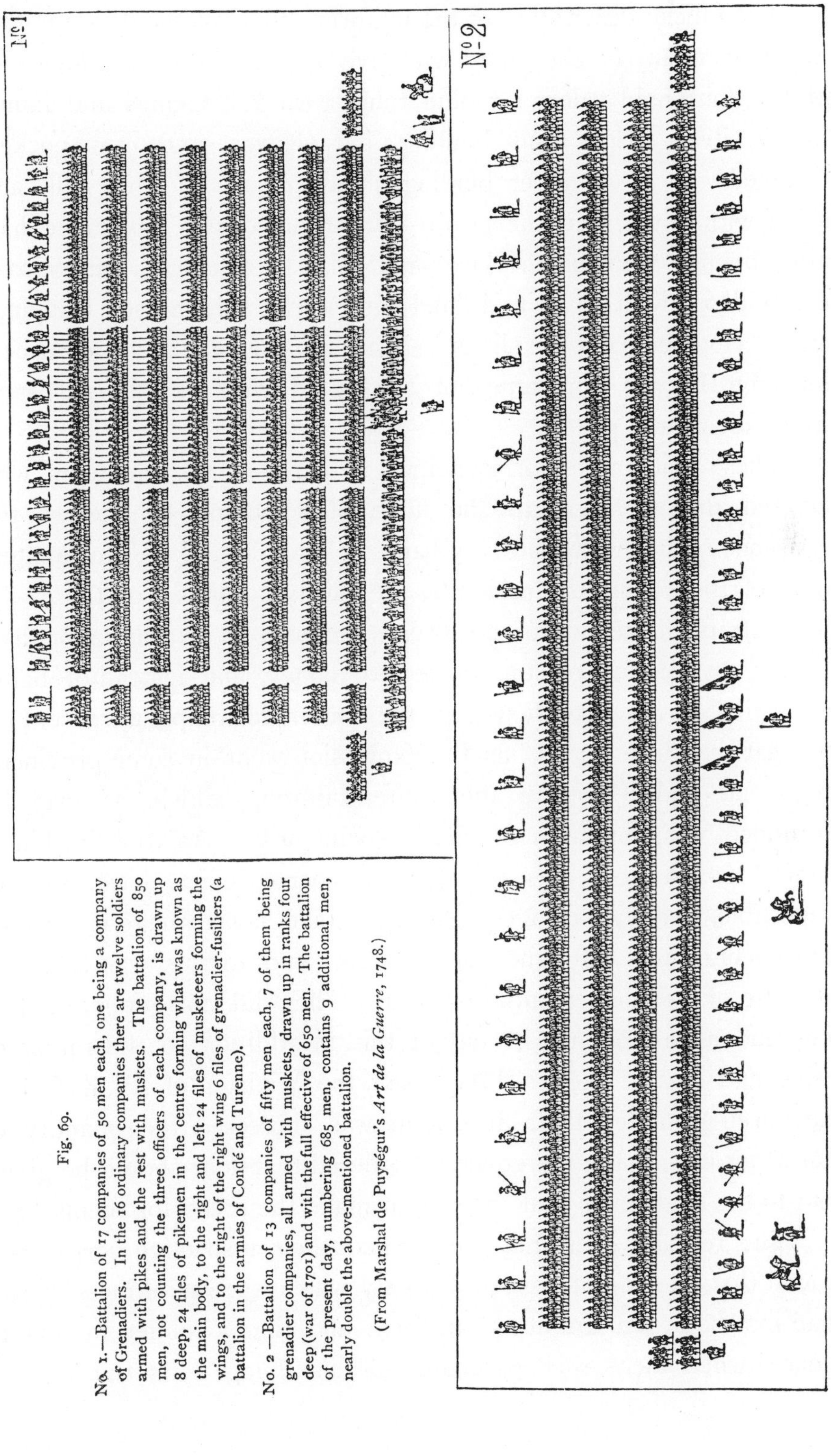

Fig. 69.

No. 1.—Battalion of 17 companies of 50 men each, one being a company of Grenadiers. In the 16 ordinary companies there are twelve soldiers armed with pikes and the rest with muskets. The battalion of 850 men, not counting the three officers of each company, is drawn up 8 deep, 24 files of pikemen in the centre forming what was known as the main body, to the right and left 24 files of musketeers forming the wings, and to the right of the right wing 6 files of grenadier-fusiliers (a battalion in the armies of Condé and Turenne).

No. 2.—Battalion of 13 companies of fifty men each, 7 of them being grenadier companies, all armed with muskets, drawn up in ranks four deep (war of 1701) and with the full effective of 650 men. The battalion of the present day, numbering 685 men, contains 9 additional men, nearly double the above-mentioned battalion.

(From Marshal de Puységur's *Art de la Guerre,* 1748.)

The official description of the uniform and equipment of the first Scotch company of the guard will give an idea of the magnificence of the household troops : " Blue tunic, with red facings and lining, broad silver stripes and binding, big sleeves, and cross-pockets trimmed with broad silver binding, shoulder-belts of white silk and silver with silver lace, the sword-belts trimmed with silver, the hats also bound with silver lace and black cockades, blue cloaks embroidered with silver and lined with scarlet ; the horses' trappings scarlet cloth edged with silver." This Scotch company was armed, like the French companies of the guard, with swords, partisans, musketoons, and pistols.

These brilliant uniforms helped to enrol many volunteers, who entered the service with the hope of belonging to one of the gorgeous regiments which they had so often admired. Unfortunately most of these recruits, dazzled by the illusive promises of those who had entrapped them into the service, received, in exchange for their liberty, a very meagre sum of bounty-money, and instead of being embodied, as they had hoped, in the household troops, were sent off to " eat the king's bread," as the expression went, in some provincial regiment, and " to wear the white uniform," which, as may be imagined, was not often of dazzling whiteness. As to " the king's bread " it was, previous to 1727, so coarse, black, hard, and in-digestible, that the strongest stomachs could not manage it, for part of the bran was left amongst the flour, and to this was added a mixture of horse-chestnuts and oats. They did not get more than one and a half pound per day of this, in addition to the ration of wine and meat. Voyer d'Argenson, the Minister of War, feeling how well-grounded their discontent was, increased the quantity of bread for each man ; moreover, he ordered that flour should be given out to the soldiers so that they might make the bread for themselves.

The recruits, once that they joined their respective corps, soon found that the life of ease and plenty which the recruiting-sergeant had foreshadowed did not await them, and that a soldier, in time of peace, when there was no chance of his living upon the enemy, rarely had enough to eat. The scarcity of food naturally created great discontent, which, in some regiments worse off than the rest, rose almost to mutiny. This was an organic defect of the army, but the complaints of the soldiers did not find any echo beyond the barrack, for they were virtually shut off from the outside world. This explains how it was that the enlisting-agents continued to obtain recruits. These agents were, for the most part, a lieutenant or a non-commissioned officer sent by the colonel of the regiment to populous centres, Paris in particular, to enroll and purchase recruits. In some cases they received a fixed sum during their mission, and in other cases they were remunerated by a premium on each recruit. Other agents, mostly retired soldiers or non-commissioned officers, were employed by a contractor, who afterwards made over, at a considerable price per head, the men who had signed an engagement to serve in return for a few shillings. Men of good stature were in the greatest request, and the scale of payment was in proportion to height. The author of the "Tableau de Paris" says that the current price was a louis for every inch over five feet.

There was no end to the stratagems and unfair proceedings to which energetic agents had recourse in order to obtain their recruits cheaply. The Paris quays, the Quai de la Ferraille in particular, were their favourite haunts, abounding as these quays did in low public-houses to which they could take their victims, who emerged therefrom dead-drunk, and engaged to serve the king for a certain number of years. The recruit, however grossly he might have been deceived, had no hope of redress, for the agents exercised their odious calling under the open sanction of the government. Dressed in handsome uniforms, they erected their bureau in the open air, and, to the sound of military music which attracted the crowd, proceeded to enlist the simple countryman, the starving beggar, and the servant out of place, who could not resist the sight of a few pieces of silver.

These agents were to be met with under every kind of disguise, and they were often to be seen at the gates of the capital, looking out for the new arrivals. They resorted to violence of every kind for which, by the terms of a royal decree issued in 1716, the punishment was absurdly light. Thus they did not scruple to take people by force from the streets and out of their houses. At the same time, no one was eligible for service unless he was sixteen years old, and the engagement, to be valid, must be signed for not less than six years. As a rule, the luckless beings who had unwittingly signed an

Fig. 70.—A Recruiting Agent; from a collection of costumes in the Arsenal Library.

irrevocable engagement, and who saw no way of escape except desertion, which was a capital offence, resigned themselves to their fate, and, once clothed, equipped, armed, and forwarded to their regimental depôt, they became as good soldiers as their comrades. It is hard to understand how an army so recruited maintained so high an effective, for in 1735 the total number of troops, inclusive of a staff of 21,878 officers, was 309,390.

This perpetual enlistment, which went on in Paris upon a specially large scale, explains the instinctive dislike of the Parisians to military service. The capital and its suburbs enjoyed, however, the privilege of exemption from service in the militia, the organisation of which has been described above. Several attempts were made to carry out a general levy in Paris, but with scant success. Thus in February,

Fig. 71.—Cross of the Order of St. Louis, founded by Louis XIV. in 1693.

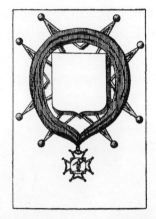

Fig. 72.—Grand Cross of the Order of St. Louis.

1742, a royal decree called up 1800 men for the militia, and males between the ages of sixteen and forty were to take part in the draw-

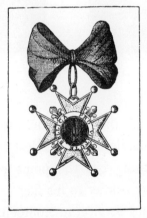

Fig 73.—Order of Military Merit, founded by Louis XV. in 1759, for officers born in a country where the established religion is Protestant.

ing; but the categories of exemption were numberless, and a lot of young men, nicknamed *fuyards* (runaways), took care to absent themselves at the time fixed for the drawing, which gave the king 5000 soldiers, instead of the 1800 he had asked for. It is true that, as the people said at the time, " the king paid for the wine," as the taverns were crowded for several days. In the same way eleven regiments of infantry were drawn from the provincial militia, and, as the royal grenadiers, they soon acquired renown in the German wars. M. d'Espagnac, who commanded one of these regiments, said :— " They showed how much influence the point of honour is capable of exercising ; peasants, fresh from their villages, who had been dubbed

Fig. 74.—Helmet of a Captain of Dragoons.

Fig. 75.—Shako of a Sapper of the Swiss Guards ; after Wille.

grenadiers, at once placed themselves on a level in respect to courage and dash, with the grenadiers of the oldest regiments.

Yet there was nothing but the point of honour, unless it were patriotism, to attach the soldier to his flag. The solid advantages to be derived from military service, in compensation for its perils and privations, were almost null. He had no chance of rising to the rank of officer ; the most that he could expect was to become a brigadier or an ensign. It was very rarely that he was rewarded with the Cross of St. Louis and the pension attaching to it ; as, for instance, for some special act of bravery. When he became old and infirm, his only hope was to be drafted into the 135 companies of invalid soldiers, to be quartered in one of the fortresses, or, if he had influential protectors, to be admitted into the Royal Hotel of the Invalides. In any event, his half-pay was not enough to buy him tobacco.

Yet, with all this, the soldier was proud of his uniform, in peace as in war. He took great care of this uniform, which was renewed once in six years, and which, owing to its showy colour, the abundance

Figs. 76 and 77.—Officers armed with the Spontoon.

of ornaments, the number of pockets, gold and silver stripes, metal buttons, &c., was very difficult to keep clean and neat. The uniform was made simpler when the adoption of Prussian drill led to the abolition of the projecting parts of the uniform, and the substitution of plain braid for open pockets. At the same time the number of buttons was diminished, so as not to interfere with the use of the musket; and the skirts of the tunic, which, falling straight to the knee, prevented the men from keeping step, were hooked back over the thigh. But, while these changes were effected, the colour of the stockings continued either to be white or to match with the breeches, and the hair was still worn powdered and pomaded, plaited and tied in a knot or a pigtail at the back of the head.

There had been more than one transformation of arms since 1701. The pikes (Figs. 78 and 80) were quite done away with in the infantry, but the colonels, lieutenant-colonels and captains still carried a spontoon (Figs. 76, 77, 78, 80), a sort of light lance, seven or eight feet long, which was not without its use when they were in command of the regiment, and which might be very serviceable as a

VARIOUS ARMS USED DURING THE EIGHTEENTH CENTURY.

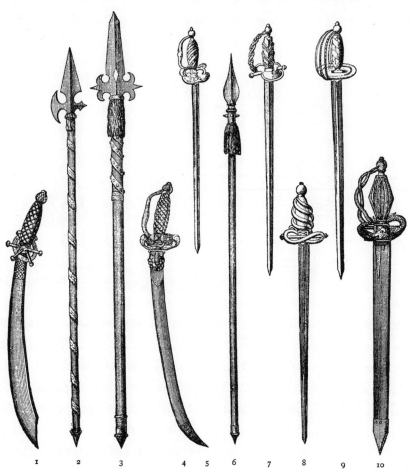

1   2   3   4   5   6   7   8   9   10

Fig. 78.—1, 4, 10, Sabres.—2, Harberd.—3, Partisan.—5, 7, 8, 9, Swords.—6, Spontoon.

defensive weapon. The subalterns, as also the corporals, had a musket with bayonet attached. The sergeants alone carried the halberd (see Fig. 78), and they used it to keep their men in line. All the privates were armed with muskets with fixed bayonets, and each man carried twenty rounds of ammunition. This musket, which measured four and a half feet, and which was very massive and much too heavy, was modified several times in the course of the century (Figs. 79 and 80). Rifled carbines, three feet long, were invented, but as the ball with which they were loaded, had to be

Fig. 79.—A Flint-Lock.

driven down the muzzle with a mallet, they were found too complicated for use.

The field artillery was in its infancy when the example of the King of Prussia, who had increased and improved his artillery in a wonderful manner, induced the French war-office, while still adhering to the model of the French cannon, to found more guns ten and a half feet long, weighing 6200 pounds, and firing thirty-three pound cannon balls. The smaller calibres were reductions of the same model. Though there were four schools of artillery in France, established by Louis XIV. at La Fère, Metz, Strasburg, and Grenoble, the artillery was for a long time very inferior to what it ought to have been. The school of engineering was at Mezières. Until Gribeauval reorganised the French artillery (1775) the most misleading and antiquated estimate was prevalent as to its utility in the open field, though Frederick the Great had already created the horse artillery. Marshal Saxe shared these prejudices, for he maintained that heavy artillery interfered with the march of the army, because it cut up the roads. According to him an army of 46,000 men did not require more than fifty 16-pounders and a dozen mortars of various sizes.

Military music, which is not, of course, so important as the

VARIOUS ARMS USED DURING THE EIGHTEENTH CENTURY.

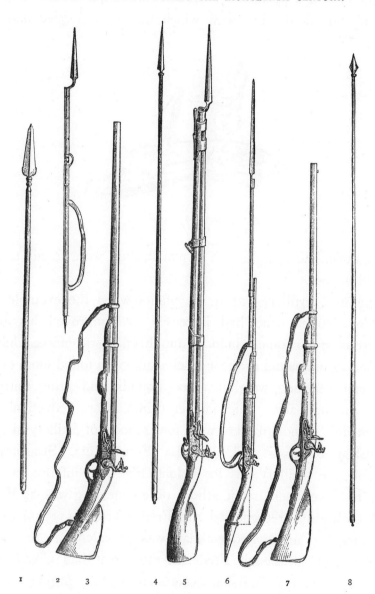

Fig. 80.—1, Chevalier Folard's Partisan.—2, M. de Maizeroy's Gun and Pike.—3, 5, 7, Muskets of different makes;
4, 6, 8, Marshal Saxe's Spontoon : Gun and Pike, nine feet long.

artillery, at all events in war time, was only adopted later in France,
though the German armies had very good bands in the sixteenth

century. In France, the guards attached to the king's household had only six trumpeters and one kettledrum to each company ; the infantry regiments had only drummers, and as the latter were not all subject to a uniform regulation, the drums were beat at different times in different regiments. It was not until 1754 that the drum-major of the French guards was ordered to draw up fixed rules and communicate them to the drum-majors of all the infantry regiments. Ten

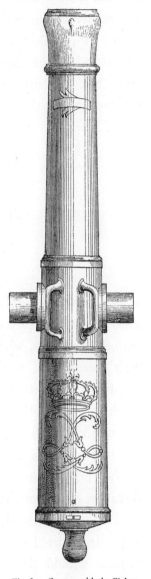

Fig. 81.--Cannon, with the Cipher of Louis XV.

Fig. 82.—Grand Master of the Artillery (Comte d'Eu, 1770).

years later, a band of music, consisting of four clarionettes, four hautboys, four horns, and four bassoons, was attached to the regiment of French guards. This primitive band was very popular, and crowds assembled to hear the music, but the war-office thought that the cost of it was too great for the state to bear, so the colonels were left to provide what music they pleased at their own ex-pense, the war-office paying only for two clarionettes and a fife to accompany the drums.

Upon the other hand, there was no stint of flags and standards, some of which were very gorgeous. No two corps had regimental flags exactly alike. All these flags, of different colours, were covered with coats of arms, devices, and special ornaments, without any regard to one uniform system. It is true that since the reign of Henri IV., while the royal flag was white, the French flag had continued to be azure blue with three golden fleurs-de-lis. Thus in the army the flag merely represented the superior military authority, without having the unique character of a national symbol. But the

Fig. 83.—Military Trophy, after Ozenne.

ensign in the colonel's company of each regiment was invariably white, as if to typify the king's colour. The colours and devices of the other ensigns, which were also remarkable for the richness of their decoration, varied according to the tastes of the original proprietors or founders of each regiment. Their number varied as much as their colour. The first company of the king's guards had six standards, the two companies of the musketeers of the guard had but two flags and two standards; but most of the regiments of French infantry had three flags only, whereas in the foreign Royal-Bavarian regiments, raised in 1709, there were no less than eighteen.

In the eighteenth century, the navy alone possessed a national flag. In 1661 Louis XIV. ordered that the men-of-war and the frigates should fly the white flag (Fig. 85), and it was accordingly hoisted on all vessels of war, except the galleys, which still used the red flag (Fig. 86) until 1748, when the galleys were embodied with the rest of the navy under the authority of the French Admiralty.

Moreover, the French navy, which had played so glorious a part in the great wars which raged during the reign of Louis XIV., had fallen into a sad state of decay at the death of that monarch, who may be said to have created it. France, worn out by these terrible contests, was unable to meet the exorbitant expenditure which the repair of her fleets involved. In 1715 a large number of unfinished

Fig. 84.—Saluting the Flag ; after Gravelot.

vessels were rotting in the docks, and eighty ships of the line, only partially equipped and armed, were lying idle in the ports of the Atlantic and the Mediterranean.

For more than twenty years, whether from indifference or short-sighted prejudice, French statesmen forgot that their country had been a great maritime power, and that she still possessed a navy. At the pernicious advice of Dubois, the prime minister, the council of the Regency seemed to have resolved to annihilate the naval forces of the kingdom. Matters were even worse under the ministry of the Duc de Bourbon and that of Cardinal Fleury, the latter, in

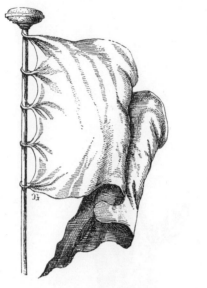
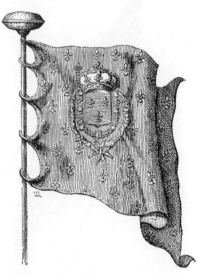

Fig. 85.—The White Flag (the Royal Standard
of the Navy).

Fig. 86.—The Red Galley Flag.

particular, looking upon the navy as a useless luxury. Not a single vessel was constructed, and those fit for service were not kept in proper repair. The number of naval officers was, nevertheless, kept up to full strength, though they were not given any useful work to do.

Yet Louis XIV., in his famous code of 1681, had organised the navy on an excellent basis; the young nobles entered the service freely, but there was an almost complete stoppage of promotion, and many distinguished sailors survived their vessels, so to speak. The body of higher officers of the navy, most of whom had attained their rank since the death of Louis XIV., consisted, in 1735, of one admiral, two vice-admirals, five lieutenant-generals, twelve commanders of squadrons, ninety-nine captains, ten naval controllers, and nine commissary-generals. When England declared war against Spain, our ally, in 1739, we had great difficulty in sending out twenty-two vessels, which were incapable of holding their own against the British fleet. In 1743, there were 35 vessels of the line in the different ports, but only half of them were fit for service. Notwithstanding the bravery of such commanders as La Bourdonnaye, Court, and La Galissonière, defeat and disaster succeeded each other almost without interruption, and the French navy merely existed on paper when peace was signed at Aix-la-Chapelle in 1748.

The army had also suffered reverses and lost battles, but it had gained a few victories, and, in spite of its glorious defeats in the

Fig. 87.— French Admiral (Duc de Penthièvre, 1737).

foreign lands which it had invaded, it had maintained its ancient reputation for courage and daring. It had never been very numerous in the distant expeditions, where its very victories weakened it, by imparting greater energy and cohesion to its antagonists. The campaigns of Bavaria and Bohemia, where it ran short of provisions, received no pay and waited in vain for reinforcements, also exercised a very pernicious influence upon its vigour and discipline. The soldier was obliged to live by pillage, at the expense of the inhabitants, and, following the example of the Pandours and Croats, he committed horrible excesses. During the retreat through Bohemia, Marshal de Belle-Isle wrote to the Minister of War (December 2,

1742): "Desertion and sickness are on the increase, and the bad

Fig. 88.—The *Hercule*, frigate of 58 guns ; after an original drawing by Ozenne.

feeling of the officers is beyond expression. I could not find courage
to tell you all the particulars, for they are enough to disgrace the
nation."

The officers, like the men, were not wanting in courage, and charged boldly at the head of their regiments, but this was all they were capable of. They were utterly ignorant of the art of war, and did not even take the pains to acquire the amount of knowledge required for commanding a regiment. " Honour makes warriors," wrote Abbé Coyer in 1749; "money makes the best officers. A young nobleman who is destined for the army must have the most fashionable tailor and perfumer, the most brilliant equipage and the

Fig. 89.—Cavalry Vedettes ; after Parrocel.

smartest livery ; he must be fond of gambling and dancing, regular in his attendance at the play, and capable of inventing some modification in the uniform of the first corps which he commands."

The heroism of Chevalier d'Assas, a captain in the Auvergne regiment, who sacrificed his life to prevent his regiment from being fallen on unawares by the enemy (1760), might be adduced to show that these great noblemen and officers, who had qualified for service in Paris drawing-rooms and ladies' society, were capable of very valorous conduct on the field of battle. Many similar instances of bravery might be cited. Thus, at the battle of Lawfeld (1747), the

Marquis de Ségur, then only a colonel, had his arm shattered, while endeavouring to rally his regiment, which had been thrice repulsed; but, fearing that his absence would abate the ardour of his men, he remained at his post until victory had been achieved. At the battle of Dettingen, in Bavaria (1743), the young Comte de Boufflers, only ten and a half years old, made his entry into and his exit from life, for Voltaire relates that a cannon-ball fractured his leg, and that he died from the effects of amputation, displaying the greatest courage throughout the whole piece.

Some of the officers, unfortunately, lacked this spirit of courage and self-devotion. Count de Saxe, who took command of the army after the battle of Dettingen, wrote to Voyer d'Argenson, Minister of War: "The disorder and indiscipline are so great, that I have been obliged to make some severe examples. . . . The officers are not ashamed to lie like lackeys. Not a day passes without a murder; horses are stolen, and the officers coolly keep them for their own use. In fact, great severity must be exercised if we would restore order, discipline, and honour." The soldiers, indisciplined as they might be, never failed to do their duty in presence of the enemy. "Frenchmen may have their equals and even their superiors in the open field so far as military training goes," says Voltaire in his "Siècle de Louis XV.," "but they are unsurpassed for those hardy dashes and rapid exploits in which impetuosity, agility, and ardour bear down all obstacles."

Count d'Argenson, who had succeeded the Marquis de Breteuil, as Minister of War in 1743, carried out many useful reforms with a view of restoring the military power of France. He was well seconded by the Count de Saxe, who devoted the whole campaign of 1744 to the moral education and military instruction of his troops at the camp of Courtray. Maurice de Saxe, who had just been created Marshal of France, endeavoured to apply to the French army the severe but somewhat precise principles of the German school. The uniform, drill and arms were remodelled after the Prussian system; but the change was not attended with good effects

A CAVALRY HALT; AFTER PARROCEL.

The author of an " Essay upon the Life of the Marquis de Bouillé " says that "the very constitution of the army was affected by decrees which were conceived under too hasty an appreciation of Prussian discipline. The recollection of the defeats sustained in the last war led to a blind imitation of the system of the conquerors. Thus, dissolution rather than improvement came out of these radical changes."

Fig. 90.—The Soldier, after Leclercq.

Fig. 91.—The Major, after Leclercq.

Louis XV. was not fond of innovations, and would only consent to them under great pressure. So it was that Count d'Argenson was removed from office in the midst of reforms, which he was carrying out with great zeal and perseverance. Soon afterwards, the Duc de Choiseul also inaugurated his appointment to the Ministry of War by fresh reforms which were not so good as those of his predecessor. The latter had founded in 1751 the military school, in which five hundred cadets, without fortune, were to be educated free of cost, for the different branches of the service. In 1750 he created

a military nobility, with exemption from taxes, for officers of thirty
years' service.

The Duc de Choiseul was not content with increasing considerably the army and navy, though this increase did not avert the
necessity of signing a most disastrous treaty of peace at Paris in
1763. In the year 1762 alone, during which period the war
expenses amounted to nearly eighty millions pounds sterling of our
money, France lost thirty-seven vessels of the line and fifty-six
frigates; her navy was gone, and she was obliged to abandon to
England her rich Indian colonies. The Duc de Choiseul took
advantage of the peace to reconstruct the navy, and the towns and
provinces offered to the King seventeen vessels to form the nucleus
of a fresh fleet.

The Duc de Choiseul wrung from Louis XV., almost by force,
the decrees of 1762 which were destined to reconstitute the army;
the field artillery was doubled and raised to seven brigades, which
were afterwards transformed into seven regiments corresponding to
the seven schools of artillery then in existence. Twenty regiments
of French and foreign infantry were disbanded, so as to reduce the
total number of regiments to a hundred; the cost of each regiment
was placed at a fixed sum; many alterations were effected in the
uniform; the administration of the companies was transferred from
the captain to a quarter-master treasurer; and veteran companies,
composed of officers and men whose term of active service had
expired, constituted a permanent garrison in the provincial towns.
Four years later (1766) appeared another decree, regulating the
training and drill of the infantry and cavalry (Figs. 93 to 97).

At this period, Louis XV., reposing upon the laurels won at
Fontenoy, had given up any idea of taking command of the army, in
spite of the flattering insinuations of Doctor Quesnay, who told him
that the presence of the king in the field was as good as thirty
thousand fresh troops. He did not, however, offer any opposition to
the reforms which his minister proposed, but he would not allow him
to construct the navy with which the Duc de Choiseul hoped to

destroy the English fleet and repair the disastrous reverses of the last naval combats.

Louis XVI., when he came to the throne in 1774, was too desirous for peace to think of any warlike preparations. Count de Saint Germain, who succeeded Marshal de Muy in 1775, was very

Fig. 92.—The Musket as carried by an Officer (decree of 1766); after Gravelot.

Fig. 93.—An Officer saluting with his Musket (decree of 1766); after Gravelot.

eager for military reform, and was anxious to make a complete change of the system then in vogue. He had served his apprenticeship in the Austrian army, and he attempted to apply the principles of the Austrian school to France. "The principles of his system," says Baron de Besenval in his Memoirs, "was a good one. He aimed at establishing a gradual and precise flow of promotion, and to see military duties accomplished with due regard to punctuality. Knowing how antagonistic the ideas of the nobility were to these principles, he endeavoured to eliminate them from the army, and to suppress all the privileged corps, the existence of which he considered incompatible with discipline and good order." He augmented the pay and facilitated the promotion of the ablest officers, but as he proposed to apply the German discipline to the French army, and to subject the soldier to the humiliating punishment of being struck with the flat of the sword, he was universally reviled and abhorred. He proposed to admit a certain proportion of non-

Fig. 94.--Infantry Drill (decree of 1766); after Gravelot.

commissioned officers to the rank of officers, but the nobility and the Court protested loudly against this measure, and the minister at once resigned, telling the King that he would not take part in the funeral rites of the army.

The art of war, nevertheless, continued to improve; Count de Guibert published his famous " Essay on Tactics;" General de Gribeauval renewed the artillery-material, and thus maintained in the very first rank a body which had always constituted the most im-

portant element of the French army. Prince de Montbarey, minister
of war, did not pursue the reforms begun by his predecessor, but
Marshal de Ségur, who succeeded him and remained in office from
1780 to 1787, took them up again. In military circles a change of
tactics and the suppression of abuses were the main topics of conversation. Marshal de Ségur began by improving the material conditions of service ; during his tenure of office the soldier was better

Fig. 95.--Loading (decree of 1766) ; after Gravelot.

clothed, better lodged, and better fed. Hitherto, there had been one
bed for three men, but Marshal de Ségur reduced the number of
occupants to two, and there was also an addition to the size and
number of the hospitals. The epaulette, which the Duc de Choiseul
had invented as a reward for good conduct, was as much esteemed
as it had at first been despised by the soldiers, who called it "the
Choiseul rag," though perhaps the increase of pay which was
accorded to those who were entitled to wear it may have helped to
produce this change of feeling. By the exercise of an enlightened
economy, a pension fund was also created for the senior chevaliers

of Saint Louis, and at the same time the rate of military pensions was increased.

Marshal de Ségur had the honour of obtaining the King's assent to the double creation of the light-artillery and the staff corps (1783). His son, the Count de Ségur, states in his " Memoirs," that, " owing to his exertions, the instruction of the officers made great strides.

Fig. 96.—The Cavalry Soldier (decree of 1766) ; after *The Uniforms of the King's Household Troops and all the French Regiments*, by De Monsigny.

The excellent carriage of our troops, their perfect discipline, and the regularity of their manœuvres, excited universal admiration."

With all this, the army, from economical and state reasons, had been gradually diminishing in numbers, while the navy was being enormously increased, and, since the American war (1778), had again become very formidable.

France possessed a magnificent fleet, and her flag had nothing to fear in any waters. The combat of Ushant (1778) had obliterated the recollection of Finisterre (1747), and no one could have expected that such reverses as those sustained by the Marquis de la Jonquière (1747) and Captain Thurot (1760) would occur again. The exploits of du Quesne and Tourville were almost equalled by those of La

Fig. 97.—Poop of the *Invincible* (from the *Monuments erected in honour of Louis XV.*, by Patte).
N.B.—The *Invincible*, with 74 guns, built in the reign of Louis XV., was captured by the English, who, admiring
its construction, built 36 vessels on the same model.

Motte-Picquet and the Bailli de Suffren. But the greater part of the French fleet, on its way to take possession of Jamaica, was again destroyed by the English. Count de Grasse, its unfortunate commander, was execrated from one end of France to the other, and a national subscription was raised to provide the Government with enough money to build twice as many vessels as had been destroyed; but as peace was signed soon afterwards, these new vessels merely served to reconstruct a navy which the Revolution in its turn soon disorganised.

The influence of the Revolution was already making itself felt in the army, then reduced to 172,000 men. The first act of Marshal de Ségur was to make a very unwise concession to the nobility.

The royal decree of May 22nd, 1781, making the grade of officer accessible only to nobles who could show four quarterings, created great discontent in the lower ranks of the army. It was in vain that the minister endeavoured to give personal merit and seniority some channel of promotion; the antagonism and ill-feeling between the officers became more and more accentuated; the spirit of insubordination grew stronger, and the soldier only continued to obey in the hope of soon shaking off his bondage. It is needless to recall the disloyal conduct of the French guards on July 14, 1789, which earned for them the acclamations of the people. Upon that day the royal army ceased to exist, and the Revolution asserted itself.

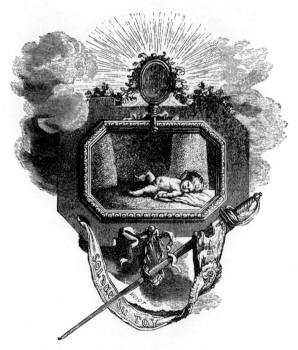

Fig. 98.—A Soldier who has died for his king: an emblematic composition after Marillier.

CHAPTER VI.

THE CLERGY.

Constitution of the Clergy in France.—Their Wealth and Influence.—Religious Quarrels.—The Jansenists.—The *Unigenitus* Bull.—Expulsion of the Jesuits.—The Higher and the Lower Clergy.—The Assembly of Notables and the Clergy upon the Eve of the Revolution.

BARBIER, writing in 1752, said:—" The clergy is very powerful in religious matters in a country where there is such a thing as a religion, and where one is wanted." And yet, at the time that this candid sceptic recognised the influence of the clergy, in despite of the violent attacks which were made upon that body by the Crown, the nobility, and the parliaments, who ought to have been its warmest supporters, the ecclesiastical power was beginning to decline, and was being impelled by its implacable foes to imminent ruin, for, since the beginning of the century, everything seemed to conspire against the authority of the Catholic church and the prerogatives of its ministers. The eighteenth century, which brought into such bold relief the talents and the virtues of the French clergy, was destined to witness, simultaneously with the fall of the monarchy, the temporary eclipse of this great institution, the origin of which in France dated from the third century.

At the end of Louis XIV.'s reign, the clergy held a stronger position in the State than ever before Cardinal Richelieu and Mazarin had raised them to the first place, above even the old nobility, little inclined as the latter were to acknowledge this supremacy. The nobility, it is true, was strongly represented in the ranks of the clergy by younger sons who, elevated to the prelacy, took equal rank with their elder brothers. But the prelates and dignitaries of the Church, who were sprung from the bourgeoisie, and even the people, formed by no means a small proportion of the clergy, and their origin, however low it might have been, was lost beneath their ecclesiastical titles, which put them upon an equality with the most illustrious representatives of the nobility. Thus, it may be said that there was an ecclesiastical nobility, taking higher rank, in many respects, than the highest and oldest part of the temporal nobility.

Those members of the clergy belonging to what was called the *second order*, that is to all the degrees of the clerical hierarchy, they were never required to prove their nobility, and they took equal rank with all nobles. They were exempted from payment of the *taille*, and their only contribution to the Imperial taxes was a pro rata share of the annual or extraordinary sums which the assembly of the clergy presented to the King as a free gift. Thus the wealth of the French clergy was very great, derived as it was not only from the ecclesiastical tithe upon the wheat-crops (consisting of an eleventh part of the produce), but from their landed properties, their money investments, their benefices, their revenues of various kinds, and their parish fees. At the close of the seventeenth century, a large part of the French soil was in the hands of the clergy, and this vast property, instead of diminishing in size or remaining stationary, was still further increased by pious donations or testamentary bequests. The actual value of the ecclesiastical tithes may be estimated as equal to half the taxes paid by the nation to the crown.

The secular and regular clergy, which enjoyed possession of these magnificent revenues, undiminished by taxation, and which declared itself virtually exempt from every form of impost or quit-rent, did not number more than from 420,000 to 450,000 at the end of the reign of Louis XIV. In 1763, the eighteen archbishops at the head of the ecclesiastical provinces of France had under them 109 bishops or suffragans, exclusive of the bishops *in partibus* who did not come within their jurisdiction. In these archbishoprics and bishoprics were 40,000 priests, 50,000 *vicaires* (assistant priests),

27,000 priors or chaplains, 12,000 canons, 20,000 clerks and choristers, in addition to about 100,000 ecclesiastics engaged in the religious orders, employed in the colleges, the seminaries, the missions, the almshouses, or not doing any duty. The regular clergy comprised those who, in fulfilment of the vows they had taken, lived either in or out of cloisters, under different monastic and conventual rules. The monasteries numbered 740, of which 625 were *in commendam*, that is to say, presided over by assistant abbots on behalf of the titular holders ; the rest had the right of electing their

Fig. 99.—Prince Bishop.

own abbots. Sixteen of these abbeys were peopled by heads of orders and of congregations, containing in all but 1200 members. The number of monks employed in the management of the two kinds of abbeys mentioned above, may be estimated at from seven to eight thousand. The monks with or without a private income and belonging to the various reformed and non-reformed orders who formed the population of these monasteries numbered about 80,000, though some of them were not resident there. But for a century past the monkish influence had been decaying, especially in the mendicant orders, which no longer lived on alms, but possessed private property and received pay for ecclesiastical duty. The monasteries did not become impoverished, though at the same time there was a gradual diminution in the number of novices as in that of monks, and many monasteries, which had contained a hundred monks a century before, now had but five-and-twenty.

Upon the other hand, the number of nuns went on increasing, as also did the new congregations and charitable institutions. The benefices allotted to ladies of noble birth, all of which were in the gift of the king, the princes and princesses of the blood, comprised, in 1763, 253 abbeys, 64 priories, and 24 canonical chapters, inhabited by at least 15,000 nuns. The number of those who had taken vows and devoted themselves to monastic life in the convents could not have been less than 100,000. The Benedictine, the Augustine, and the Dominican orders largely predominated, the Ursulines and the *Visitandines*, as also the nuns of St. Claire, had not diminished, but the Carmelites were reduced to a few hundreds. There was little place for nuns who lived solely on alms in a society which discarded religious practices and works of piety for worldly pleasure ; charity had ceased to be a Christian virtue, so to speak, and had become a mere philosophic protest in favour of humanity.

In the early part of the eighteenth century, the clergy was threatened by several secret or disguised enemies who leagued together for the purpose of wresting from it its political power, its moral strength and its material wealth. The politicians and the economists who were as yet only the individual and unobtrusive apostles of a new order of things, both social and political, had already begun their attacks and discovered their purpose. The sceptics and materialists, who hoped to annihilate the state religion, were already in the breach and were quietly preparing to over-turn the altars. This conspiracy went on in the dark, and the threats which its leaders gave utterance to in pamphlets which, printed in Holland and other foreign countries, were circulated in France by the Protestants, left little doubt as to their plan of proceeding. The attacks were first directed against the secular and regular clergy, thus leading gradually up to the dogmas and teaching of the Catholic church. The hostile press of the United Provinces, under the management of the Protestant refugees whom the revocation of the Edict of Nantes had driven from France, carried on an active propaganda, insulting the priests, calumniating the monks, and vexing the souls of the pious.

The clergy, when united, had been invincible. But, unfortunately, their common enemy found an unexpected weapon of attack in the revival of the old Jansenist quarrel, which, it was thought, had been buried in the tomb of the most doughty upholder of the Jansenius doctrine—the celebrated Arnould, who died in exile at Malines on August 8th, 1694.

Fig. 100.—Dresses worn by an Abbot and Abbess out of doors ; from the *Costume Français*, by Dupin.

It is difficult in the present day to understand the excitement which this question of dogma, now definitely decided, created in the eighteenth century.

Solemnly condemned by the Church, Jansenism must now be considered by Catholics as a dangerous heresy, which, though it may have seduced a few honest souls from their allegiance, attacked the very fount and origin of the unity and purity of the Christian faith. But, in the fierce conflict of passions which raged at that period, the truth was not made manifest without long and angry disputes, in which the defenders of the truth, carried away by the strength of their convictions, had not always the upper hand. From an historical point of view, it is worth while to retrace the principal features of this struggle.

A book published by Father Quesnel, " Réflexions Morales," simultaneously with a translation of the New Testament, was the spark which re-lighted a fire that had scarcely died out. Cardinal de Noailles, Archbishop of Paris, had formally approved an edition of this work, published in 1695 ; and he had another edition prepared by no less a person than Bossuet, but it did not see the light. At Rome, where Clement XI. had succeeded Innocent XII. upon the pontifical throne (1700), Father Quesnel's book was denounced as a daring exposition of Jansenist doctrine. The excitement which this book created both at Versailles and Rome, went on increasing for eight years, opinion being divided as to its merits or demerits. The King's confessor, Father Letellier, who had succeeded Father La Chaise, was anxious to bring about the disgrace of Cardinal de Noailles, who was accused of having given his sanction to Father Quesnel's book, and Louis XIV. was on the point of giving way to his confessor. But he had himself read the book, and its contents appeared to him as being very edifying, and he would not do more than promise to apply to the Pope for his sovereign decision. Clement XI. was unwilling to compromise in this affair, the gravity of which he fully appreciated, Cardinal de Noailles, whom he looked upon as one of the greatest of the French prelates, but he condemned the " Réflexions Morales " by a Brief issued July 13th, 1708.

This did not have the desired effect. The King would not accept the brief, which remained a dead letter in France, and Father Quesnel's book continued to find many readers. Attention was drawn to Nicole's declaration that he had never read "a book more worthy of a priest, more calculated to advance the interests of the church, and more fitted for all the world to read," and to that of Father La Chaise, who, in answer to those who reproached him with having read it, said : " How can any one condemn so excellent a

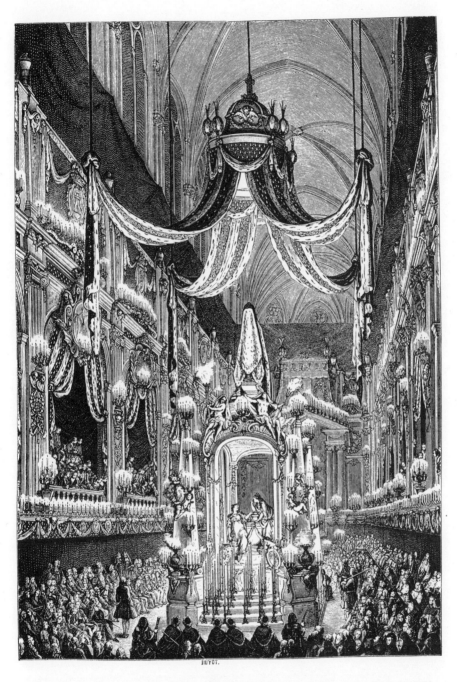

IuYOT.

FUNERAL CEREMONY AT NOTRE DAME CATHEDRAL, PARIS, FOR THE DEATH
OF THE DAUPHINESS; AFTER COCHIN, 1746.

book ? I may tell you frankly that for the last two years I have taken from its pages the subject of my daily meditation, and that I feel much edified by its contents." Thus the opinion of the clergy varied concerning a book which, though condemned at Rome, found support in France. The Jansenists thought this a favourable opportunity for declaring their principles openly ; they thought that they could count upon the indirect and secret protection of the Archbishop of Paris, and they had the hope of bringing the King to look upon them more favourably. Jansenism seemed, also, to have regained possession of its early cradle. The monastery of Port-Royal des Champs again became the centre of the doctrine of Jansenius ; the nuns had again installed themselves there, and it was from this house, rendered famous by so many ardent defenders of Grace and Predestination, that the signal was given for a crusade in support of opinions which had been condemned as heretical in the Formulary of Pope Alexander VII. in 1665. Throughout every class in France, more especially amongst the clergy, there was a general thrill of emotion, which was due to a final and supreme effort of the Jansenists. Cardinal de Noailles endeavoured to moderate the excitement, advising the nuns of Port-Royal and the ecclesiastics who guided their counsels not to precipitate a conflict which must terminate to their disadvantage. "This Cardinal," says Voltaire, "full of virtue and science, the mildest of men, and a sincere friend of peace, protected several Jansenists, though he was not one himself, and he did not like the Jesuits, though he neither feared them nor intrigued against them." His authority was not much obeyed.

The nuns of Port-Royal refused to sign the formulary which condemned the five propositions of Jansenius, and Cardinal de Noailles no longer ventured to defend or justify their conduct. The King, urged on by Father Letellier, expressed his anger at the resistance and rebellious spirit of these nuns, and he gave orders that they should be reduced to reason. They were then expelled from their monasteries and drafted into several convents throughout France

(October, 1709). The church and the monastic buildings were razed to the ground, and even the tombs and funeral monuments were transported to the churches and cemeteries in the neighbourhood (1710).

So these rigorous measures were in part due to a growing antipathy of the public against the Jesuits, who were accused of having instigated them, and this antipathy increased in intensity until it finally effected their overthrow. But at the same time this striking manifestation of their power showed the Court of Rome that, through the agency of his confessor, Father Letellier, they exercised a decisive influence over Louis XIV.

It was at this period that the Jesuits pressed the Pope to take advantage of the condemnation of Father Quesnel's book to publish a Bull, enumerating the propositions condemned in this book, and which, while stigmatising them as attacks upon the dogmas, the morality and the discipline of the Church, should draw up a general constitution, destined to counterbalance the decisions arrived at by the assembly of the clergy in 1682. The King promised to accept this Constitution, to have it registered by parliament, and put in force in all the dioceses of the kingdom. It would be difficult to conceive the difficulties attending the publication, both at Rome and Versailles, of this Bull, which was known as the *Unigenitus* Constitution. In it were condemned, as " heretical, and as renewing various heresies, and principally those contained in the well-known propositions of Jansenius," a hundred-and-one postulates extracted from Father Quesnel's " Réflexions Morales."

The Holy Father announced in this Bull, dated September 8th, 1713, that he had issued it in compliance with the request of Louis XIV., "that most Catholic King, whose zeal for the defence and maintenance of the pure Catholic faith and for the extirpation of heresy we cannot extol too highly." Yet, even when the Bull was once published, there still remained something to be done; it was necessary to get it accepted by the French clergy and registered by Parliament.

Part of the French clergy protested against this Bull, which they represented as the negation of what were called the liberties of the Gallican Church. It created great emotion in France and the provinces, and those who take, as a rule, no interest in theological subjects, joined in protesting against it. The movement extended throughout the whole of French society. "Every salon," to use the language of Duclos, "became a school of theology; the discussion of dogmas formed an important item of conversation; and as the national character never varies in its essential features, a dissertation

Fig. 101.—Grand Almoner of France (Louis de Montmorency-Laval, Bishop of Metz, 1786).

on dogma was interlarded by a theatrical criticism." In a word, the indecision or the disunion of the higher clergy, the resistance of the clergy of the second order, gave rise to great doubt whether the Bull *Unigenitus* could be put into force in France.

However, Father Letellier, who was keeper of the King's conscience, rallied to his side several bishops, notably the new almoner of France, Cardinal de Rohan, who had been appointed to succeed Cardinal de Janson on the express understanding that he would support the Bull and offer unqualified opposition to the Jansenists. Louis XIV. ordered the Parliament to enregister and the Sorbonne to sanction the Bull. The Parliament complied, with certain limitations in respect to the liberties of the Gallican Church, but the Sorbonne still hesitated, and there was a subsidence of the general excitement. Cardinal de Noailles, whose enemies accused him of being on the side of the Jansenists, appealed to the King for protection against what he termed "the mysteries of iniquity." The King himself was puzzled and undecided as to what course he should take. An assembly of forty-eight archbishops and bishops received instructions to examine the Constitution, and, after four months of ardent controversy, forty of these prelates declared in favour of accepting it ; the others, with Cardinal de Noailles at their head, signified their dissent by withdrawing from the assembly.

Thus the Bull was accepted, approved and registered, so that it only remained for the clergy to give way. They did not all do so out of conviction, and Jansenism, in spite of its condemnation, or perhaps because of it, continued to make progress amongst the masters as well as amongst their disciples. The hostile bishops were sent back to their dioceses, by way of punishment ; the ecclesiastics who declared themselves very openly by voice or by the pen against the Bull were threatened with summary arrest (*lettres de cachet*). Still the Constitution did not obtain very rapid acceptance, and Letellier urged the King to protect it with the arm of the secular authority. It is said that Louis XIV. mournfully told him in reply : "You know that I have never understood the real state of affairs, and have implicitly followed your advice. I must leave the whole matter to your conscience, and you will be responsible before God." And the same report says that a few days before his death, the aged monarch, overwhelmed with bitter recollections, declared to his confessor and to Cardinal de Bissy, who had been one of the most active partizans of the Constitution : "If you have deceived me, you have much to answer for, as my only thought has been for the welfare of the Church."

After the death of Louis XIV. the quarrel appeared to be in a fair way of pacification. The Duc d'Orleans was distinctly opposed to anything like religious controversy and dissension, and he was very anxious to bring about an understanding in reference to these dogmatic disputes which might result in an open schism. Thus for the first few months of the Regency, there was ground for hoping that the Constitution would remain a dead letter, and the Jansenists, though the Court held them in detestation, wished to take advantage of the current of public opinion which was running in their favour. Just as Pope Clement XI. was about to inflict a blame upon Cardinal de Noailles, four of his adherents, the Bishops of Mirepoix, Montpellier, Boulogne and Senez, took upon themselves to appeal from the Bull *Unigenitus* to the future Council-general, and many of the Sorbonne professors, in the memorable assembly of March 1st, 1717, adhered to this appeal. This was the signal for fresh discord in the clergy, and amongst their flocks, who in their turn became *appellants*. The Duc d'Orléans ordered the hostile bishops to leave Paris, exiled some of the Sorbonne professors, and prohibited all theological assemblies from calling into question the legality of the Bull. The measures for carrying out these orders were so thorough that the Constitution seemed to be beyond the reach of further opposition. But Jansenism continued its passive hostility, while, upon the other hand, the Jesuits were quietly at work amongst the upper clergy and at Court to regain the ground which they had lost since the death of Louis XIV. Finally, after great efforts, Philip of Orleans was induced to recognize the Bull *Unigenitus*, and his Prime Minister, Dubois, succeeded in getting it registered by the Grand Council. The Bishop of Fréjus, who had been very hostile to it at first, took another view of the matter when he beame Prime Minister, and was a candidate for the red hat, in return for which dignity he allowed the Constitution to be imposed on men's consciences by giving his countenance to the Jesuits in their final struggle against the Jansenists. It was thought that the latter were completely discouraged, if not vanquished and crushed ; but they set powerful agencies at work to defend their doctrines and gain partizans, publishing a polemical newspaper entitled " Nouvelles Ecclésiastiques " and containing an account of the *miracles* alleged to have been worked by the intercession of the *blessed* deacon Paris. The latter, who was a fanatical and uncompromising Jansenist, had lived a most ascetic life, and since his death had been venerated by his followers. The Jansenists, as they could not ask the Pope to canonize him, conceived the idea of beatifying

Fig. 102. —Miracle of the Deacon Paris ; fac-simile after an engraving in the work entitled, *The Truth of the Miracles wrought at the Intercession of M. Paris and other appellants, demonstrated to the Archbishop of Sens* (Languet), by Carré de Mongeron ; 1737, 3 vols. in 4to.

TRANSLATION OF TEXT IN THE ENGRAVING.

La Demoiselle Coirin

is suddenly cured in the night of August 12—13, of her paralysis and cancer. She gets up from her bed and dresses. Her servant, who was bringing her in a bowl of soup, is so astonished to see her sitting dressed in her arm-chair that she cannot believe it is her mistress and takes the soup to her in bed.

him by consecrating his works of piety.   The new saint soon gained

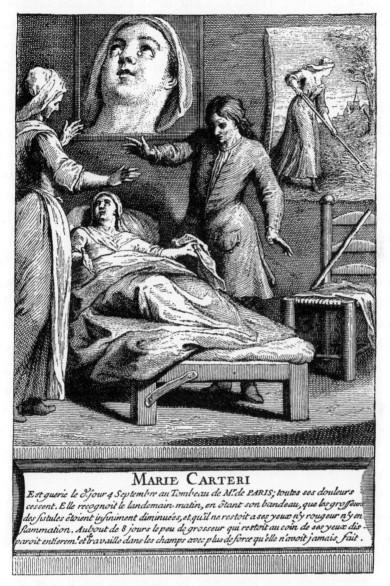

MARIE CARTERI

Est guerie le 8.e jour 4 Septembre au Tombeau de Mr de PARIS; toutes ses douleurs cessent. Elle recognoit le landemain matin, en ôtant son bandeau, que les grosseurs des fistules étoient infiniment diminuées, et qu'il ne restoit a ses yeux n'y rougeur n'y en flammation. Aubout de 8 jours le peu de grosseur qui restoit au coin de ses yeux dis paroit entierem.^t et travaille dans les champs avec plus de force qu'elle n'avoit jamais fait.

Fig. 103.—Miracle of the Deacon Paris ; fac-simile after an engraving in the work entitled, *The Truth of the Miracles wrought at the Intercession of M. Paris and other appellants, demonstrated to the Archbishop of Sens* (Languet), by Carré de Mongeron ; 1737, 3 vols. in 4to.

TRANSLATION OF TEXT IN THE ENGRAVING.

MARIE CARTERI

is cured on Sept. 4th at the tomb of M. de Paris ; all her pains cease.   She discovers on removing her bandages the next morning that the swellings were much reduced and that her eyes were neither red nor inflamed.   In a week's time the swelling had altogether disappeared, and she is able to work in the fields more vigorously than ever before.

a renown amongst the lower clergy and the poorer classes in Paris, which grew greater every day. The most exalted and credulous of his followers founded a small sect which soon gained great notoriety. These fanatics indulged in the wildest acts of penitence and superstition, and received the name of *convulsionists*. They scourged themselves and inflicted various kinds of torture upon their bodies, and, by a long course of fasting, prayer and self-delusion, they fell a prey to hallucinations and catalepsy. These natural phenomena were attributed to the influence of the *blessed* Paris, and the horrible convulsions which accompanied them were looked upon as proofs of his beneficent influence. A few cures of chronic illness were, in fact, brought about by these epileptic seizures, which, on the other hand, gave rise to a far larger number of incurable diseases.

The cures having given rise to polemics, of which the book referred to in Figs. 102 and 103 will give a good idea, there was a perpetual pilgrimage to the cemetery of St. Médard where Paris was buried, and for more than three years his tomb was the theatre of performances at once laughable and scandalous. Men and women of all ages and classes, prostrated themselves or knelt upon a large flat stone which covered his grave, and remained there in prayer until the saint manifested his presence by the convulsions which were to cure their sickness. The tomb was surrounded by infirm and diseased persons, who groaned and wept, while they repeated their prayers, and there were even more sight-seers than pilgrims. To suppress such a public scandal, the police closed the cemetery, and the convulsions, which had not maintained their miraculous and healing powers, soon ceased when they could not be indulged in before the crowd.

The newspaper was less easy to suppress, for it was secretly distributed in Paris, and all efforts to get at the authors, printers, or promoters, proved futile. The most the police could do was to lay hands on a few distributors of the paper, who were unable to give any information, and who, after being kept two or three months in prison, were set at liberty. Yet the Archbishop of Paris,

Christophe de Beaumont, had excommunicated all readers of the "Nouvelles Ecclésiastiques," but the paper, though several times condemned to the flames, arose from its ashes and was to be seen everywhere, even in the ministerial cabinet and the King's chamber.

These facts show what an irreparable blow this civil war of religion had dealt at religion itself. The clergy, who had taken the chief part in these deplorable controversies, were themselves compromised and weakened by their internal divisions. It was something more than a deadly struggle between the Jansenists and the Jesuits, it was the prelude to a rivalry between the Church of France and the Church of Rome, and of a permanent conflict between the temporal and the spiritual powers. The Jansenist quarrel became an inextinguishable brand of discord. The unbelievers, the philosophers, the foes of Catholicism, rejoiced at the blow thus inflicted upon it ; they took part in the quarrel, for the purpose of embittering it ; they made sport of the grave questions of doctrine involved in the Constitution ; they dragged them through the mud, so to speak, by making them the subject of ridiculous rhymes, and the whole nation was there to hear and laugh at these acts of indecent profanity. The feeling of respect, which must be the basis of every religious belief, was gradually being undermined in its hold upon the hearts of the people.

The Parliament issued several orders for putting into force the prescriptions of the Bull *Unigenitus*, and the King, by a declaration which the Parliament enregistered, endeavoured to get the Constitution adopted as a law of the State. Nor was this all, for it was practically imposed upon people's consciences, in the shape of confession-tickets, without which no one could receive the last sacraments of the Church, or be buried in consecrated ground. This obligation was openly imposed for more than twenty years, with a few intervals of comparative moderation, upon the highest and most respectable personages in the land. Hence arose intolerable acts of violence, deplorable scandals, family dissensions, street disturbances, objectionable interference of the secular power in spiritual matters. The church doors were shut to funeral processions, and the coffin, which they were escorting, was laid in unconsecrated ground. Yet the practice of insisting upon confession-tickets was maintained not only in Paris, but in many towns, especially those of Picardy, until the attempt of Damiens to assassinate Louis XV.

The Paris Parliament, apprehensive as to the consequences of the Bull *Unigenitus*, which, as it feared, might become a formidable weapon of offence in the hands of the Jesuits, resolved in 1752 to check the excessive severity for which the confession-tickets were used as an excuse, and its first step was to declare that the Bull had never been a *rule of faith*, and that it was perilous as being likely to create an actual schism. From this moment, the Parliament went entirely over to the side of the Jansenists, for whom it had always entertained a partial sympathy. "Amidst all these troubles," says the author of the "Siècle de Louis XV.," "the King was like a father trying to separate his children when they are fighting. He forbade them to strike or abuse each other, he reprimanded some and exhorted others, he bid them be silent, forbidding the Parliament to interfere in spiritual matters, and advising the bishops to act with the utmost circumspection." Damiens, who, in his attempt upon the King's life, only inflicted a slight wound with a penknife (January 5th, 1757), was a poor wretch whose mind had been deranged by the Constitution. The enemies of the Jesuits insisted loudly that they were responsible for his crime, and this infamous calumny served to ruin them, for they had never been popular, and when they were looked upon as accomplices of the regicide they were execrated throughout the kingdom. Their fate was sealed, and denunciations against them poured in from all directions. The Jesuits had no idea of the interpretation which was to be put upon their statutes, regulations, doctrines, and writings, which were examined in profound secrecy, the result being a decree of Parliament (August 6th, 1761) declaring their doctrine "murderous and abominable," ordering their books to be burnt by the public executioner, and their colleges to be closed during pleasure. This decree was an iniquitous one, for it had not been preceded by a confrontation of accusers and accused. It came upon the latter, who did not even know that their security was being threatened, like a thunderclap.

The sequel soon showed that their condemnation was the result of the conspiracy set on foot by the sect of philosophers to deprive the church and religion of their staunchest supporters. The Jesuits,

Fig. 104.—Confession ; after the *Cérémonies et Coutumes Religieuses de tous les Peuples du Monde,* by Bernard Picart.

no doubt, had committed many faults, but they were, none the less, intrepid defenders of the Catholic faith. It was to no purpose that they put forth all their strength and all their influence to resist this unjust decree ; the King had abandoned their cause. Upon August 6th, 1762, a fresh decree of Parliament ordered them to be excluded from the kingdom "irrevocably and for ever." The clergy, struck dumb with amazement, did not dare to protest, though they felt that in the Jesuits they would lose their main source of strength, while the delight of the philosophers showed them that, once these doughty soldiers of Christ had been driven from France and scattered over all Europe, incredulity would have no insuperable barrier in the way of that social and moral destruction which the philosophers of the " Encyclopædia," after having decided upon it in secret, were openly hurrying onward under the impulse of the vile pass-word " *Écrasons l'infáme* " (let us crush the unclean thing). The Parliament which had thus suppressed the Company of Jesus, was not the last to discover that its decree had outshot its aim and had wounded the Church of France itself. The Jesuits dragged down with them, so to speak, the Jansenists and all their Catholic adversaries. The Constitution *Unigenitus* seemed to fade away amidst universal indifference and contempt; the Bastille and the houses of detention disgorged a host of hostile priests who had spoken or written against the confession-tickets; the people ceased to repeat the lampoons and satiric rhymes in Paris jargon, which the muse of Jansenism had composed so freely. People felt astonished to think that they should have allowed themselves to be so excited by abstract and insoluble questions which they had never understood even when they were most concerned about them. They were soon forgotten, but with them also were gradually forgotten the holiest and most essential articles of belief. This was, in a certain measure, the last war of religion, less terrible and less bloody than the preceding ones, but more fatal perhaps, for it had dealt a mortal blow at religious faith and feeling.

The royalty and the parliaments had more to do with this decadence than the Jansenists and the Jesuits, who had at least in view, amidst all their deplorable quarrels, the interests of religion. The Jansenists had only in view their Church, with its narrow and inflexible doctrine, their principles rather austere and methodical than they were elevated and conciliatory; they had, moreover, combated for liberty of conscience, without taking into account the condition of society. The Jesuits, endowed with more foresight, had arrived at the conclusion that in a political State religion was a tie, which, once loosened, must eventually break; and that modern society menaced, attacked, and laid siege to by philosophical and economical systems, neither more nor less than heresies, could only retain its equilibrium by a docile submission to the sovereign direction of religious authority. At first, the Parliaments had treated the Jansenists as rebels, and afterwards they treated the Jesuits as conspirators. The government of the King had from time to time inclined towards the Jesuits, but without any depth of conviction or religious zeal ; it had invariably made religion subordinate to its

Fig. 105.—Burial in a Church ; after the *Cérémonies et Coutumes Religieuses de tous les Peuples du Monde,* by Bernard Picart.

political interests, and even when it apparently was influenced by the Court of Rome, its sole object was to employ exclusively to its own profit all the forces, all the influence and all the wealth of the clergy.

Since the disastrous struggles which marked the close of the reign of Louis XIV., more than one statesman was painfully struck by the fact that the clergy which, far from having undergone material losses, grew wealthier every day, contributed but the merest trifle to the treasury, whose resources were so greatly diminished while the demands on it continued to grow heavier. The clergy, like the nobility, did not pay the *taille,* but the nobility at all events paid with their blood and their money the military service which they owed to the King. The clergy merely contributed to the Crown, as a *free gift*, a certain sum which they fixed themselves in their general assemblies held once in five years. This sum varied no doubt according to the circumstances, but it never amounted to what the Crown had a right to expect from the generosity of the first and the wealthiest body in the State. Louis XIV., autocrat as he was, would not do anything to lessen the ancient privileges of the clergy which had anticipated his wants and had never been slow to lend him efficacious assistance in his penury. The clergy, moreover, could adduce in support of their immunities the plausible argument that the property at their disposal was only entrusted to their care, and that they only preserved the income accruing therefrom to distribute it amongst the poor. The Regency, at the suggestion of the Duc d'Orléans, discussed the expediency of attaching this property to the Crown domain.

This idea of spoliation, concealed beneath the specious title of " Imperial considerations," was henceforward broached by the different ministers who succeeded each other till the accession to power of Count Voyer d'Argenson. The clergy had always possessed influential and devoted friends at Court, who undertook to protect their interests, but as the requirements of the public service increased, and as the taxation became less and less sufficient to meet them, so did it seem more and more justifiable to have recourse, by their consent or without it, to the enormous revenues which a voluntary or forced contribution would raise. Notwithstanding all this, the clergy, which still clung to the practice of *free gifts*, had not to undergo, previous to 1740, any direct pressure in regard to this contribution, which had always been obtained by fair means. But in the course of that year, the treasury, owing to the disasters in the field, was completely empty, and the increase in taxation did not keep pace with the increase in expenditure. Louis XV. then consented, though with great reluctance, to appeal to the clergy. In the month of July, his commissioners repaired to the assembly of the clergy to ask for some pecuniary assistance, in addition to the *free gift*. This assistance was immediately granted, but as it only

LOUIS XVI. TAKING THE CORONATION OATH; AFTER MOREAU.

amounted to three and a half million livres, the Ministry of Finance refused to accept it as a sufficient payment.

From 1740 to 1761 the clergy defended its manorial privileges and its rights of property and mortmain against the attacks made upon them ; they stoutly refused to pay a twentieth part of their revenues to the King, because this would have been an indirect way of making public the extent of these revenues. Machault d'Arnou-ville and Voyer d'Argenson were the ministers who insisted most strongly, not on the suppression of religious orders, but on the secularization of a part of the monasteries, and a reversion to the State of their feudal privileges. It was said that at this period a third of the property in France belonged to the clergy, who would not agree to anything in the way of a commission of inquiry or a doomsday-book. So the Ministry were obliged to abandon their scheme, and to accept what the clergy thought fit to offer the King, either by way of *free gift*, *liberality*, or succour. This contribution followed an ascending scale, and in 1760 it amounted to sixteen million livres. It was to no purpose that the keeper of the seals urged Parliament to adopt compulsory measures, and the clergy remained masters of the position, continuing to furnish a *free gift* every year, but sturdily refusing to declare the amount of their revenues, which, when roughly valued at the outbreak of the Revolution, were set down at 160 million livres.

These discussions relative to the ecclesiastical property and revenues, took place at each assembly of the clergy, and produced a deplorable effect amongst the people, whose envy and hatred became more and more accentuated. They furnished only too plausible a pretext for accusing the priests and monks of idleness and avarice. It was always on account of their wealth that they were held up to the reprobation of the poorer classes. They were no longer accused of the vices attributed to the monks of the middle ages, for the life of the cenobite had never been held in greater esteem and venera-tion than during the eighteenth century. The number of monks was much smaller, and still continued to diminish, but those who wore the cowl lived a most exemplary life, devoting their whole time to manual and mental labour, and only communicating with the outer world through the gate of charity. We may be sure that such was the case, for the calumnies of their foes had awakened popular suspicion, and yet, closely as their conduct was watched, nothing prejudicial to their good fame was discovered. " After leaving a social meeting, in which he has enjoyed himself to the utmost," says Abbé de Bonnefoy in his treatise on " The Religious State " (1784), " let the same person go straight to see one of the anchorites residing in a monastery. He will be struck by the contrast which the latter's simplicity, modesty, candour, amenity, and serenity, revealing a tranquil and truly happy mind, and giving the impression of deep religious feelings, form with the frivolity of the outside world."

The character and physiognomy of the monastic orders had undergone a complete change ; they still preserved their style of dress and their rules, but they seemed to be moving of their own accord to an inevitable transformation. The Capuchins and the Franciscans gave up the habit of asking alms, the Oratorians devoted themselves to education, the Benedictine monks to important literary works, and the cause of erudition never had better representatives. The example of Mabillon, Montfaucon, and Ruinart had peopled the cloisters with a new congregation of savants, whose researches were directed to profane as well as to sacred literature, and who reflected great credit on French letters. The Jesuits had long enjoyed the distinction of furnishing excellent preachers, such as Bretonneau, Ségaud, Neuville, Lenfant, etc., who, though not equal to Bourdaloue and Massillon (Fig. 106), obtained a deserved reputation for pulpit eloquence. The other orders also produced a large number of noted preachers ; Bridaine, whose impetuous oratory made him a favourite with the people, belonged to the Missions ; Father Elisée was a Carmelite ; Poulle and De Boismont were merely priests. Many religious houses had already been converted into schools, and others into model-farms for the teaching of agriculture and rural economy.

The female congregations, for their part, endeavoured to make themselves useful, and most of the nuns devoted their time to instructing the children of the poor, and to relieving human suffering. Voltaire himself, in despite of his prejudices, could not refrain from bearing testimony to their abnegation and usefulness, for, in his essay, *Sur les Mœurs et l'Esprit des Nations,* he says :—" There is

Fig. 106.—Portrait of Massillon ; after a picture in the Museum of Versailles.

nothing perhaps grander on earth than the sacrifice made by a delicate sex of its beauty and youth, often of its lofty lineage, to relieve in the hospitals that collection of all the forms of human suffering, the sights of which are so humiliating to human pride, and so revolting to our delicacy." And yet the men and women who led a monastic and regular life were not spared by the philosophers and their blind followers ; these pious men and sainted women were accused of absorbing, for the benefit of celibacy, idleness and super-stition, and to the detriment of the people, the property of which they had gained possession. The public were continually being reminded that the Abbey of St. Germain des Prés brought in an income to the Abbot who held it of two hundred thousand livres, and that the Abbey of St. Denis produced almost as much, while the large amount of these ecclesiastical benefices was incessantly being held up to reprobation in the countless books and pamphlets which waged war on the property of the clergy.   Even the clergy belonging to the second order were not disinclined to look with favour upon a reduction, if not a total relinquishment of this property, though they themselves enjoyed their share of it.   It was no doubt with the view of making friends with the higher clergy that the Court nobility prevailed on Louis XVI. to decree that the benefices should only be conferred in future upon nobles by birth—a course which Mercier in his *Tableau de Paris* thus criticises ·—"Who are appointed to bishoprics, rich abbeys and livings ?—the nobles.   What, is it then necessary that, to serve God, one should be a gentleman! Not so; but the Court in this way wins the support of the nobility, and pays them for their military and other less important services at the expense of the Church."   Mercier did not see that the nobility and higher clergy had formed a sort of secret alliance to resist the encroachments of the bourgeoisie, which remained the bourgeoisie, even after it had procured patents of nobility.   The higher clergy, which was the directing power of the whole body, maintained its political functions until the fall of the monarchy, resisting, with a marvellous energy, the ministers, the favourites, the parliaments, and even the monarch. Barbier, who was in a good position to estimate the power of the clergy, having been a witness to their successful struggle with the Keeper of the Seals and Parliament, in reference to the declaration of their property, wrote in 1752 :—"The French clergy are, owing to the religious principles of the people, a very powerful body."   These principles continued to prevail, especially amongst the poorer classes, in spite of all the efforts of the philosophers.   The people were not bigoted, but they were religious, never failing to bow respectfully, and even to make the sign of the cross, when they passed a priest carrying the viaticum to a sick person.   They were regular in their attendance at church, and flocked to witness the religious processions, of which the trade-corporations, with their insignia and banners, often formed part.   They mostly went for

Fig. 107.—A Brother St. Crépin (Member of the Community of the Christian Brothers called *Cordonniers*) in his full canonicals.

advice, in times of distress or difficulty, to the parish priest, in preference to anyone else, and they were very careful in carrying out the directions of the church as to marriages, baptisms, and burials. They felt a great affection for their priests, persevering as were the efforts made to destroy this feeling, for they were sure to meet with consolation and aid from them in the hour of trial.   The people only came into contact with what was then called the *low clergy*, the members of which were often distinguished from the great dignitaries of the church by their intelligence and their virtues.   " The priests of the towns and villages," says Caillot, who has written a treatise on the habits of the eighteenth century, " formed, as a rule, a class worthy of the respect and affection of the people.   Fathers to the poor, though generally poor themselves, consoling the wretched, they divided their time between the duties of their ministry and works of charity.   They inculcated morality from the pulpit, and their practices did not belie their precepts."   Restif de la Bretonne, in a work from which I have already quoted, draws an attractive sketch of the life led by one of these country priests :—"It is fortunate for our age that there are here and there to be found some of those worthy ecclesiastics who remind their brethren by the force of example how the property consecrated to God ought to be employed.   It must be said that these examples are rarely to be found except amongst the priests who are as useful and good as they are badly paid."   Many bishops, too, might be mentioned as fit to compare with such men as Fénélon and Belzunce (Fig. 108); notably the bishops of Verdun (Hippolyte de Béthune), of Mirepoix (Pierre de la Brone), and of Boulogne (Pierre de Sangle), who set an example of Christian charity, and exhausted their resources in alms-giving.   But the Court prelates, the cardinals, bishops, titulary abbots, etc., who resided at Versailles or Paris, gave little heed to their ecclesiastical duties, and did not even wear the dress of their order at Court.

They were courtiers or statesmen, but, except in rare cases, they were not true ministers of the Gospel.   As a rule, the bishops did not reside in their dioceses in the eighteenth century, and it was this fact that suggested to Mercier the witty but exaggerated remark, that "the bishops who carry out the law of residence (and they are a small minority) were possessed of a piety which was turbulent, methodical and intrusive, bordering upon fanaticism, that they worried the inhabitants of their diocese by their obtrusive and ill-timed zeal; whereas the non-resident bishops were intelligent, tolerant, anxious for peace and averse to persecution, so that the only evil, perhaps, arising from their absence is that the money emanating from their province is not spent in it."   Abbé Maury and Abbé de Boismont were not much more indulgent towards the higher clergy than Mercier, for, in some letters upon the religious state of France (1781), they say: "The prevailing fault with the higher clergy is not positive vice, but weakness, cowardice, carelessness, and above all the ambition to be a statesman, has turned the coolest heads. It seems as if our prelates had forgotten to refresh themselves at the springs of the Gospel."

Fig. 108.—Belzunce, Bishop of Marseilles, during the plague of 1720 (fac-simile after Rigaud).

The higher clergy had themselves destroyed the harmony and unity which had constituted their strength, by their imprudence in admitting, if they did not actually initiate, the drawing of a line of demarcation between the noble and the untitled clergy. All the members of the lower clergy expressed their indignation at this act of ostracism, and themselves denounced most imperiously the measure which the higher clergy had wished to impose upon them. They held aloof from their bishops and abbots, or at least they appeared to do so, by associating themselves in a certain measure with the philosophical school. The Revolution had long been germinating amongst the clergy, when it implanted a fruitful grain of liberty and equality in the heart of the Third Estate. The Assembly of Notables considered that the clergy of the first order belonged to the nobility, but that the clergy of the second order, emanating from the bourgeois and the people, were not forgetful of their origin, and the assembly resolved to remain true to them. The same scission, only of a more

pronounced and irreconcilable character, afterwards manifested itself
in the States-General of 1789, where the higher clergy still defended
their privileges with indomitable resolution. It has been argued
that, by making a sacrifice of their temporal property, they would
have saved the King, the Monarchy and themselves, but it is doubtful whether this tardy concession, in the then state of men's minds,
would have sufficed to allay the revolutionary fever.

Fig. 109.—A Holy-Pix in Silver, after Germain.

CHAPTER VII.

THE PARLIAMENTS.

The Paris Parliament—The Provinci 1 Parliaments.—Usages of the Parliamentary Magistracy.—Differences between the Parliament and the Royal Authority.—Resistance to the Edicts on Finance.—Religious Affairs.—Beds of Justice and Exiles.—Chancellor Maupeou and the Reform of 1771.—Return of the Parliament under Louis XVI.—Fresh Conflicts on the Eve of the Revolution.

It was Montesquieu, president of the Bordeaux Parliament, who descanting in 1720 on the grandeur and decadence of the French Parliaments, and foreseeing, no doubt, that their downfall would involve that of the Monarchy, wrote :—" The Parliaments are like those ruins which are trodden under foot, but which always remind one of some famous temple of an ancient faith ; they will confine themselves to administering justice, unless some unforeseen circumstance should restore them their former force and vitality. These great bodies have followed the destiny of all that is human ; they have given way before time, the destroyer of all things, before the corruption of morals which has weakened the whole fabric of society before the supreme authority which has put all things under its feet." It may be added that when Montesquieu wrote these lines, the Paris Parliament was in disfavour and exile for having protested against the financial measures of the Regency.

During the reign of Louis XIV., the Parliaments seemed to have abandoned all idea of taking an active part in politics ; they merely administered justice within the limits of their respective jurisdictions, and, if they from time to time addressed remonstrances to the King, these remonstrances, for all their grandiloquent title, were in reality humble petitions. The Paris Parliament, which since the recent troubles of the Fronde had not ventured to manifest a spirit of revolt and dogged opposition, avoided anything that might seem like an interference in State affairs. Feeling how powerless it was, it had given way in 1655, when the young King entered the chamber booted and spurred on his return from hunting, and ordered its dissolution. This was a punishment for the excesses of which the Parliament had been guilty during the King's minority. It might have been supposed that this Parliament, once so rebellious and turbulent, would abandon all hope of regaining its ancient prerogatives; it had accepted, without protest, the new code which was drawn up, without its co-operation, by the Privy Council, and which, regulating the manner of procedure in civil and criminal cases, and fixing the judges' fees, was made binding in all the Courts of Judicature. Louis XIV., during his long reign, was not troubled by any Parliament or any body dependent upon what were then known as the Supreme or *Sovereign Courts*, though they were altogether subordinate to the decisions of the Crown. The Paris Parliament was even reduced to such passive obedience that, notwithstanding its notorious sympathies with Jansenism, it enregistered the Bull *Unigenitus* (1713) without exercising its right of remonstrance.

These Supreme Courts were not subjected to many important modifications, in respect to the number and the character of the functions belonging to them. The Supreme Courts consisted, taking them in their order of rank, of the Parliaments, the Courts of Accounts, and the Courts of Excise and Exchequer; but the Parliaments, which ranked first, never missed an opportunity of insisting upon their supremacy. They even endeavoured, in their permanent rivalry with the Grand Council, which had under its jurisdiction not only the Supreme Courts, but also all the civil and ecclesiastical tribunals, to assert their ancient privileges, and to maintain their political predominance. The Paris Parliament was the first, as it was the oldest and most illustrious of the French Parliaments; it claimed to be the delegate of a portion of the sovereign power, and was convinced that upon its existence depended that of the Crown, though the King had for many years ceased to consult it upon questions of Government. This Parliament, in which the princes of the blood and the peers, temporal and spiritual, were admitted, with the right of speaking, was composed of a first president, nine presidents-à-mortier, several honorary councillors, and four royal masters of requests-in-ordinary ; of twenty presidents selected from the Chambers of Requests and of Inquests ; of 232 councillors, a procureur-général and three advocate-générals. These officers of the highest rank were disseminated amongst eight chambers, viz :—the grand chamber, which took rank above, and exercised supremacy over all the rest, the five Chambers of Inquests, and the two Chambers of Requests. In addition to these eight chambers, which dealt with civil cases, there was a criminal chamber called La Tournelle, the judges presiding over

Fig. 110.—Duke and Peer (Duc d'Uzès, 1st hereditary Peer of France).

Fig. 111.—Bishop, Duke, and Peer (Duc de Sabran, Bishop of Laon, 1778).

which were, in turn, the five junior presidents of the Parliament, ten councillors of the Grand Chamber, and four of those belonging to the Chambers of Inquests. The Grand Chamber only took cognisance of those criminal processes in which were implicated gentlemen and State personages, such as ministers or other high Government officials. The duties of the Grand Chamber, the other seven chambers, and the criminal chamber also necessitated the creation of a certain number of officials of lower rank, viz :—three chief registrars, four

notaries and parliamentary secretaries, three chief clerks of registration, sixteen procureur-général's substitutes, two chief ushers, and
twenty-nine ushers of the Parliament, and the Courts of Request, four
hundred procureurs, &c. All these officers had under their orders a
multitude of suppôts, copyists, clerks, and subordinate agents, making
a total of more than three thousand persons attached to the Parliament in various capacities, and filling different posts which assured
them a means of existence.

Such was the normal organisation of the Paris Parliament, which,
in the course of the 18th century, underwent several modifications, intended to diminish or augment the number of chambers and
functions which were sold at a price varying according to circumstances, and yielding the holder a fixed income known as *épices* (fees)
or *vacations*. The value of the post of councillor rose or fell, like
the value of real estate ; thus one of these posts, which fetched only
from 25,000 to 30,000 livres in 1712, when the Parliament merely
administered justice, was worth double the latter sum in 1747, when
Parliament insisted upon being recognized as a political body. The
emoluments varied very much, according to the amount of work
undertaken by each member of the Parliament, and also according to
the value which he set on them, which, when very high, made the
fees come very heavy to the parties involved in the case ; for the
law-suits, at that time, were accompanied by a thousand minute
formalities which, by making them extend over a long period
multiplied the costs. This system was responsible for the large
number of individuals who made their living out of the law, and
formed, so to speak, the feudal army of Parliament.

There were also twelve Parliaments distinct from that of Paris,
but yet united to it by the same organic laws and the same esprit de
corps. These Parliaments, which held their sittings at Toulouse,
Grenoble, Bordeaux, Dijon, Rouen, Aix, Rennes, Pau, Metz, Douai,
Besançon and Nancy were, except in a few unimportant details,
composed in the same way, each one having three or four civil and
criminal chambers, with a relative number of presidents, councillors,

lay and clerical, registrars, ushers, procureur-général's and procureur's substitutes, and inferior officials, under the authority of the first president of the Grand Chamber. The eleven Chambers of Accounts,

Fig. 112.—Innocence Proclaimed (decree of the Parliament of Paris, issued in 1786 upon an appeal from the Parliament of Rouen, declaring Victoire Salmon innocent of the crimes of poisoning and theft, for which she had been wrongfully condemned); after Binet.

the five Courts of Excise, the two Courts of Exchequer, those of Paris and Lyons, the three higher councils of Alsace, Roussillon and Artois, also represented a vast aggregate of posts and offices which were comprised under the collective title of Supreme Courts and

Provincial Jurisdictions. It may be safely estimated that more than 40,000 persons were employed in the various courts of Judicature, from the president-à-mortier down to the humble writ-server. To this large number of persons, who peopled the law-courts and formed what was called *the robe*, must be added a host of subordinate agents and satellites, from the verger to the crier, and the man who posted up the decrees. They formed, so to speak, a population apart from the rest of the nation, and, puffed up with self-importance, looked upon themselves as possessing a certain modicum of legal power; a fact which made them obey all the more blindly, not only the orders of their immediate superiors, but the influences of the Parliaments, more especially that of Paris. The Parliaments, having control over so many persons and opinions, always possessed a predominant authority, even under Louis XIV. who had limited their power to the administration of justice. They were certain of recovering their former preponderance, as soon as they could resume their political functions, and this was their constant aim throughout the course of the 18th century. There had for a long time been a permanent rivalry between the Court and the long robe, between the nobles and the Parliamentary class. The latter, it is true, acquired, by reason of their profession, an official nobility which brought them certain honorary prerogatives, but which did not put them on a level with the nobility by birth. Thus this semi-nobility often served to increase the irritation of the haughtiest members of the parliamentary class against the ancient nobility.

The nobility of the long robe never appeared at Court, as they would not have been accorded the rank which they considered due to them, though connected by numerous alliances with the Court nobility, which looked upon them with so much contempt. By way of revenge, they held aloof from the higher bourgeoisie and those engaged in commerce, even when they were related to them by marriage. Nor were they much more intimate with the members of the financial profession, though it had close affinity with theirs, considering that all magisterial posts went by purchase. "Before the Regency," says Duclos, "the ambition of a *fermier-général* (a contractor for the collection of taxes) was to get his son appointed a Councillor to Parliament, and, in order to succeed, he must possess considerable interest."

The Parliamentary families formed, therefore, in the midst of French society, a society apart, which had few relations with other classes. This society, which was a complete corporation in itself, consisted of different groups extending upwards, in accordance with their origin, fortune and position, from the humblest employments to the highest posts of the Judicature. Every new-comer, who had purchased an office, and was *à priori* deemed worthy to hold it, at once became an integral part of the association, and henceforward obtained naturalization into the long robe, breaking off, in a manner of speaking, all family ties. Parliamentary society had always been notorious for its gravity and severity, its formality, its pride and hauteur. Eschewing fêtes, balls, concerts, and theatricals, it was renowned for its dinners, followed by an erudite discussion on matters of jurisprudence, or some quiet game of cards, and the company always separated early, for the magistrates were in the habit of rising before daybreak. The interior of their houses, with large stone staircases, wide vestibules, and richly decorated reception rooms, was in keeping with their character for gloom and severity, and the very servants seemed redolent of the law-courts. Their masters rarely smiled, and assumed a solemn gait, and a majestic, not to say unamiable, exterior. "The ladies of the long robe," says Duclos, "who mix with their peers, have no knowledge of social usages, or, at all events, the little they do possess is erroneous. They are wedded to formality; envy and hatred is their only occupation." It must be said in their excuse that they only appeared in public at the ceremonies of the Parliaments and the Sovereign Court, and it was on these occasions that they imbibed the taste for the minute and unbending formalities observed by the *robins* (as the nobility contemptuously nicknamed the gentlemen of the long robe). The number of bows and their character, from the *révérence en dame* to the mere inclination of the head, were all regulated by a law of etiquette as complicated and as vigorous as that which prevailed at Court.

Still, the young men could not suppress their youth, even when they were seated on the fleur-de-lis, to use the term applied to the Parliament. Nothing could be more dissimilar than an aged judge and young councillor. The latter did not pride himself upon his application to work, though he was obliged to be in Court very early, at six in winter and at seven in summer. Perhaps he did not take so much sleep as his colleagues during the hearing of a case, but, when it came to pronouncing judgment, he always left the decision to his seniors, whose learning and experience he fully appreciated. It was only when his beard began to grow white that he felt himself fully qualified to fulfil the duties of his calling. In the meanwhile he, too, pronounced judgments of another kind in society, where he made himself conspicuous by his affectation and *gallantry*. This latter word was used to imply a taste for what was elegant or *gallant* in the way of dress, equipages, furniture, manners and conversation. " To look at most of our young magistrates," says Noleras de St. Cyr in his " Tableau du Siécle," " one would suppose that they were ashamed of their profession. Some affect an air of giddiness and levity which would make it excusable if any one mistook them for pages. Others set up for dandies and, perfumed like so many women, drove many a coquette wild with envy. Nearly all of them seem to make a point of discarding the decorum which, without being exaggerated into pedantry, ought to distinguish a musketeer from a judge."

The real judge, the real Parliamentarian, was, in many respects, the very antithesis of these young feather-pates. The Marquis de Caraccioli (1772), author of the " Voyage de Raison en Europe," puts into the mouth of an ancient representative of French justice these noble utterances which are, as it were, the public confession of a long life of labour and devotion to the public service : " For nearly sixty years I have dedicated my days and nights to the service of my fellow-citizens. During the day I labour on their behalf, with no other ambition than that of doing my duty. . . . . Hard work made me a skeleton by the time I was six-and-thirty. My body, for which I care nothing, has become hardened to its task, and my mind, which is more to me than all physical gifts, stands me in good stead. The glory of giving succour to the widow and the orphan compensates me

Fig. 113.—The Judge in his Home, and his Suitors ; after a contemporary engraving.

for all my trouble and disappointments. . . . . He only is great who is useful."

This will explain the almost religious respect inspired by the Parliament as a body, in spite of the faults committed by individual members. This respect was never more strongly displayed than on the solemn occasions when there was a formal procession of the Sovereign Courts, in their state robes, the presidents, councillors, advocates-général, procureur-générals, registrars and secretaries of the Court wearing the scarlet robe, some with the mortar-cap of black velvet, and others with the red hood trimmed with ermine; the officers of the Court of Accounts in black robes of velvet, satin, damask or satin; the officers of the Court of Excise in black velvet robes with black hood; the officials of the Court of Exchequer in red robes with ermine hood, and, following them, all the judicial bodies appertaining to the Parliament, each with their respective costumes and insignia, and taking precedence according to their rank. "The people," says Duclos, who had witnessed several of these impressive ceremonies, "have a sort of instinctive respect for the magistrates, whom they look upon as their protectors, though they are, as a matter of fact, their judges."

At the death of Louis XIV. a private understanding was arrived at between the Paris Parliament and the Duc d'Orleans, who wished to maintain his right to the Regency by having the will of the late King declared null. D'Aguesseau, the procureur-général (fig. 114), and Joly de Fleurs, the first advocate-général, both noted for their ability and their probity, negotiated the terms of this compact. Mutual engagements had been entered into by the Prince and the Grand Chamber, which exercised supreme authority over all the Chambers of the Parliament, while the Duc d'Orleans, on his side, expressed his willingness to govern in concert with the Parliament by restoring to it the old-established right of remonstrance, when edicts were laid before it for registration. But he did not mean, by so doing, to restrict the authority of the Crown, or to confer upon the Parliament a degree of power which might some day detract from that of the Sovereign. He did not take into account the traditional ideas of the Parliament as to the political position which it was entitled to hold in the State. St. Simon says that "this company claims, though without any show of reason, to exercise a controlling influence over Kings during their minority, and even afterwards. Parliament pretends that registration is, according to the laws and ordinances, the necessary complement which makes laws, ordinances, etc., but which, in so doing, cannot make them valid or put them in force without the co-operation of the second authority—that which Parliament adds, by its registration, to the authority of the King, and, by its co-operation renders valid.

Fig. 114.—Chancelier d'Aguesseau ; after Vivian.

Without this the authority of the King would be of no effect." This doctrine, breathing a spirit of covert opposition and revolt, was the main motive of the line of conduct adopted by the Parliament, as it was also the cause of the incessant struggles which were carried on during the reigns of Louis XV. and Louis XVI.

The Duc d'Orleans, after having been assisted by the Parliament to become Regent, found that he had burdened himself with councillors who, if they were not altogether his masters, showed themselves very imperious, and who became, in course of time, uncompromising opponents. The first difficulty arose out of a question of etiquette. The Parliament determined to mark its hostility to the nobles by deciding that the Presidents of the Chambers should refuse to salute the peers of France when they came to the audiences covered. The Regent did not take part with either side, and the quarrel became more and more embittered. The young Duc de Richelieu having fought a duel (February 27th, 1716), the Grand Chamber ordered him to constitute himself a prisoner under their jurisdictions, though the Duke, as a peer, claimed to be tried by his proper judges, the peers of France. The latter presented a request to the King, in which they declared: " The Parliament, not content with attacking the outward signs of honours belonging to the peerage, the order of proceedings and the right of expressing an opinion, now deals a blow at the very essence of the peerage, by endeavouring to try a member of our body." The Regent, with a view of putting an end to the conflict, ordered the Duc de Richelieu to constitute himself a prisoner in the Bastille; but this step did not decide the question at issue, and the differences between the peers and the Parliament continued to get wider. The latter body made a violent attack upon the nobles by claiming the right of precedence over them, and the Regent still temporised and adjourned the decision until after the majority of the King.

The Duc d'Orleans endeavoured to adjust matters, so as not to be involved in a struggle with the Parliament, feeling himself under a certain degree of obligation to that body. The Parliament had the presumption to claim precedence over the Regent himself in a public procession, and the latter, not caring to contest the claims of the Parliament, took his place at the head of the King's military household, and preserved his rank as representative of the royalty. The Parliament then resorted to " remonstrances " in order to regain the ground which it had lost since the Fronde, and in doing so it merely made use of an ancient right which the Duc d'Orleans had restored to it. But they carried their remonstrances to such a point that, if acceded to, they would have diminished the authority of the crown. The Regent was at last compelled to declare war upon the Parliament, and to inform it that " he would allow no attacks to be made on the authority of the King during the Regency." The Parliament continued its remonstrances in respect to the money edicts, and endeavoured to resist the new system of finance invented by Law, the Scotchman, and supported by the Regent. Law excited the hatred of the Parliament to such an extent that a proposal was made to have him arrested by the vergers, who would have taken him to the Tribunal of La Tournelle, where he would have been tried, condemned, and executed forthwith. The resistance of the Parliament to the royal edicts created an amount of excitement and effervescence which, lashed to fury by the rhymes and caricatures so freely circulated, threatened to degenerate into civil war. The Regent was not a man to be intimidated, though the people almost in a body sided with the Parliament against Law ; still he felt it necessary to secure the nominal if not the substantial support of the first Body in the State, in order to baffle the intrigues of his enemies who were endeavouring to injure his credit with the King. A decree of the Grand Council, dated Aug. 12th, 1718, prohibited the Parliament from interfering in affairs of State, and this decree, together with the edicts on finance, the Parliament refused to register. The Chambers assembled daily to deliberate on this matter ; great excitement prevailed in Paris, and the public mind was so irritated that there was no saying how the dispute might end.

It was at this juncture that a Bed of Justice was prepared at the Louvre during the night of August 25-26, and early in the morning Parliament, which was sitting with closed doors, received orders to attend it forthwith. The streets and squares of Paris had been filled with troops, which had received orders to put down without hesitation the smallest semblance of rebellion. The Parliament could not disregard the King's summons, and at eleven a.m., a double file of magistrates, 153 in all, wearing their scarlet robes, proceeded on foot from the law-courts to the Louvre by way of the Rue St. Honoré. The spectators who had assembled to see them pass did not make any demonstration. The President attempted, when the Bed of Justice was assembled, to make a speech, but the Keeper of the Seals stopped it by turning towards Louis XV. and intimating that the King counted upon instant compliance. All the edicts were registered, without discussion, and the Parliament returned to its courts of justice, where the members gave free vent to their indignation. The secret deliberations were resumed, lasting four days and four nights. The Regent having made up his mind to put down this reduced imitation of the Fronde, had President de Blamont and two of the most turbulent councillors arrested on the night of August 29th and conveyed, in chariots with six horses, to the State prisons. The Parliament again assembled and determined to suspend the administration of justice; the advocates complied with its resolution, and declared that they would not plead until its lawful claims had been satisfied. But, on further reflection the Parliament deemed it unadvisable to push matters so far, and sent a deputation to the King at Versailles. This deputation was received not by Louis XV., but by de Mesmes, Keeper of the Seals, who merely replied : " The matters which the deputation has come here to discuss appertains to the State and must be considered in silence and secresy. The King has determined that his authority shall be respected."

All this acted as a warning to the Parliament which, though not abandoning its principles and its designs, took care not to drive things to an extremity. It was merely awaiting a more favourable opportunity which soon presented itself when, in 1720, it was called upon to register the edicts relating to Law's bank and the Indian Company. The money had disappeared, and the notes, the traffic in which had enabled so many people to make rapid fortunes, were no longer worth more than half of their nominal value; with this, the price of food had risen enormously, and the popular discontent seemed to presage terrible disturbances. It was at this juncture that the Parliament, called upon to register the edicts, replied that it would have nothing to do with this jobbery in paper which was ruining France.

In the course of Sunday, July 21st, *lettres de cachet* were delivered, by musketeers, to all the members of the Parliaments, ordering them to withdraw to Pontoise and remain in exile there during the King's pleasure. They obeyed the order with dignity, and during their absence all the courts of law in Paris were closed except a chamber which sat specially to dispose of current affairs and minor suits. Thus the administration of justice was not quite suspended. The Paris Parliament had indeed, a narrow escape of being suppressed altogether, for the Duc d'Orleans, whose patience was exhausted, laid at its door all the financial disasters which had occurred and wished to punish it accordingly. Law had suggested to him that he should refund, with bank-notes having a forced circulation, the value of all the functions and offices of the Parliament, and so place these functions at the disposal of the King, who would nominate new officials and enable his subjects to obtain justice free of cost. This bold scheme, owing to the collapse of Law's system, was not carried out.

Barbier, referring to these frequent differences, wrote, "The Parliament is a very respectable body of itself, but it is powerless as a minority and incapable of taking a prominent part in the affairs of State. It is a very large assembly, composed to a great extent of a number of aged men, very learned in legal matters but not possessing the breadth of mind so necessary in delicate questions. Their minds run in the old groove, and they have not habituated themselves to the change which has taken place in the mode of government. The Parliament also contains many ignorant and very young persons, possessed of a considerable fortune, who are after some time transferred to other posts and do not take any interest in the welfare of the company to which they belong ; men of no standing who belong by family ties to finance and to the ministry, who are afraid to hold or maintain an opinion, who are sometimes the spies of the Prince and the Ministry, and who let out the secret." This was what always happened when the Parliament endeavoured to entrench upon the royal authority. It was always obliged to yield, or, at all events, to accept a compromise which preserved its honour intact.　Exiled to Pontoise, it was threatened with a further banishment to Blois, but when Law was obliged to leave the country and his banking system collapsed, the registration of the edicts creating that bank were no longer called for.　The resentment of the Duc d'Orleans had cooled down, and, for political reasons, he was anxious to obtain the registration of the Bull *Unigenitus*.　The Parliament was in reality averse to this measure, but, tired of the exile to Pontoise and not wishing to be ordered to Blois, registered it in order to effect a reconciliation with the Regent and his ministers.

But the Parliament had not abandoned the right of remonstrance, exercising it with greater boldness than ever when the King assumed the direction of affairs in person (Fig. 115) under the ministries of the Duc de Bourbon and Cardinal de Fleury.　A formidable conflict had arisen between the Parliament and the Grand Council; the latter had never been on very good terms with the supreme courts, and when it became the passive instrument for executing the orders of the Prime Minister as to the examination of all the measures emanating from the Parliament, and bearing a political character, the quarrel grew still more bitter.　The Bull *Unigenitus*, which the Paris Parliament had registered in a moment of discouragement, was always the avowed or secret cause of these disputes.　The Parliament was Jansenist, and had against it all the higher clergy. It also held its own against the adherents of the Court and the Ministry.　But its opposition did not go beyond remonstrances to the King, though it was always finding pretexts for presenting them, and, however respectful their form might be, they none the less ran contrary to the policy of the Government.　The Chancellor replied to these remonstrances sometimes, and endeavoured to bring about a compromise of the question in dispute.　But if the Parliament happened to issue a decree infringing upon the King's authority it was immediately annulled by the Grand Council and erased from the Parliamentary register, by order of the King.　The quarrels of 1731, 1737, 1738, 1744, and 1747, arose from different causes, but they all

took the same turn and terminated in the same way. The remonstrances took no effect, and the decrees entrenching upon the prerogatives of the Government were quashed, the Chancellor giving
the Parliament to understand that the King meant to maintain his
mastery. The most turbulent and rebellious members, such, for
instance, as Abbé Pucelle, one of the spiritual councillors, were sent
to the Bastille or ordered to reside at some distance from Paris, but
the Parliament no sooner got out of one difficulty than it involved

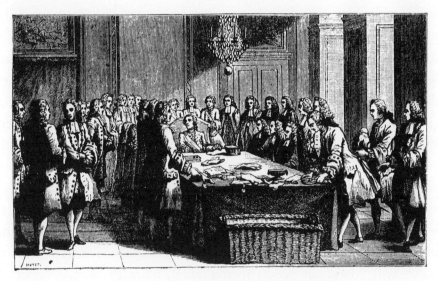

Fig. 115.—Louis XV. holding the Seal in person for the first time, March 4th, 1757.
(From the *Nouveau Traité Diplomatique* of the Benedictines.)

itself in another. The Bull *Unigenitus*, which it had only registered
under compulsion, was the invariable stumbling-block in the way of
the magistracy and the clergy. The controversies and quarrels on
religious questions became more frequent and more virulent. For
more than twenty years the Parliament was at open enmity with the
bishops and clergy, who insisted on refusing the last sacraments and
the right of burial in consecrated ground to Jansenists who had not
recanted their errors.

The King, who, with a view of terminating these differences, had
forbidden the Parliament to interfere in ecclesiastical matters, was

very displeased at the disobedience of the Supreme Courts, and ceased even to reply to their remonstrances. " The more the King insists in one direction, and the Parliament in another," pertinently remarked Barbier, "the greater must be the divergencies, and greater still the danger of compromising the Royal authority."

Christopher de Beaumont, Archbishop of Paris, was the leading opponent of the Parliament : he enjoyed the support of the Grand Council, and could count upon his influence with the King, who readily countenanced him in his disputes with the Parliamentary party. The crisis came when the Archbishop dismissed the lady-superior and the house-keeper of the chief hospital, whom he suspected of Jansenism. The Parliament at once took up their cause against the Archbishop, claiming the secular as the Archbishop claimed the spiritual direction of the hospital. This affair created great commotion, and the King was appealed to. Louis XV., very much annoyed, ordered the Parliament to give way, but that body published a declaration to the effect that : " As the King prohibits us from deliberating, and so interdicts us from exercising our function, the company declares that it is unable and unwilling to fulfil any sort of service." The law-courts were at once closed, and all the Paris Tribunals suspended their sittings. The King, thereupon, sent round an order by his musketeers to all the members commanding them to resume their duties. The magistrates obeyed; but the advocates, who always seconded the Parliament in its resistance, did not appear at the audiences. Thus the course of justice was interrupted by the ill-will of the advocates, who, as their functions did not go by purchase, were free in the exercise of their profession.

It was not until after effecting this coalition that the advocates, forming themselves into a homogeneous body, acquired and preserved a political importance which they had never made any effort to secure. Hitherto, an advocate had given his whole attention to legal matters, but now, having espoused the interests and the passions of the Parliament, he aimed higher ; he looked upon himself as the equal of the Presidents and the Councillors, whom he aided with all his might in their struggle against the Royal authority. The advocates, already puffed up with pride on account of their oratorical triumphs, devoted themselves to intrigue and ambitious schemes; they belonged to the *robe*, and, at this epoch, might aspire to play a part in State affairs.

In 1753, the quarrels between the civil jurisdiction and the ecclesiastical authority extended to every part of France. The Parliament which, in the previous year, had ordered the Bishop's manifesto to be burnt by the public executioner, ventured to address the King with remonstrances more imperious than ever before. Louis XV. would not listen to them, and ordered the Parliament to confine itself to the administration of justice. This order the Parliament resisted, declaring that it could not comply with the royal commands. The King convoked the Grand Council and issued *lettres de cachet* exiling all the Presidents and the Councillors of Requests and Inquests. The Grand Chamber, which was alone excepted from this rigorous, but necessary, measure, protested in its turn (May 10th), and held a solemn deliberation upon the forbidden questions. At daylight the next morning, the members of that Chamber received a *lettre de cachet*, ordering them to transfer themselves to Pontoise and continue their duties there under pain of dismissal. They obeyed this order, but when at Pontoise continued to devote their time to the discussion of religious topics. All France encouraged the resistance of the senators, and the provincial Parliaments sided with that of Paris. The Tribunals were closed, and the public business was suspended. The Government created a chamber composed of six Councillors of State and twenty-one Masters of Requests, to administer justice and replace the Parliament. The provisional Tribunal, which held its sittings in the convent of the Grands-Augustins, met with nothing but disdain, hostility or indifference, though it afterwards sat at the Louvre, and was entitled *the Royal Chamber*. The magistracy had been degraded, and the Parliament, though absent from Paris, still maintained its influence there. It was felt that that this disorderly state of things must come to an end. The Grand Chamber had been transferred from Pontoise to Soissons, but it was still a power in the capital. The King, who had entertained the idea of abolishing the Parliament, did not venture to do so, and he was waiting for some favourable opportunity of pardoning it. The birth of the Duc de Berry, the son of the Dauphin (August 23rd, 1753), furnished him with one, and, after a struggle of eighteen months, the King recalled the Parliament and abolished the *Royal Chamber*.

The antagonism of the Parliament and the clergy soon renewed itself, more violent than ever. It seemed, to judge by the language of the remonstrances which it drew up, that the Parliament was bent upon sharing the royal authority with the King. Louis XV. had on many occasions to condemn these remonstrances very severely, and, addressing himself to a deputation from that body in April, 1755, he said: "I know what are the rights of the authority which I have received from God. It is not for any of my subjects to decide what are their extent or to endeavour to limit them. Let the Parliament conform to my veritable intentions of clemency and moderation." The Parliament, in its fresh remonstrances, persisted in declaring that "it formed one and the same body with the sovereign." Yet the King had accorded a partial satisfaction to the Parliament by exiling its adversary the Archbishop of Paris, though this did not mitigate its opposition to the crown. Under the pretence of uniting its forces against the Grand Council, it formed an association of all the Parliaments of the kingdom, with the name of *classes*, so as to form one homogeneous body acting in unison and governed by the same impulses. Louis XV. foresaw the perils of this Parliamentary coalition, when he said to the Duc de Gontaut-Biron : "You do not understand what they are aiming at : an assembly of republicans. However, I have had enough of all this. No doubt, the present state of things will last my time."

The Bed of Justice held on December 13th, 1756, was not calculated to allay these differences. Two edicts of the King

THE BED OF JUSTICE HELD AT VERSAILLES, IN 1776; AFTER GIRARDET.

circumscribed within very narrow limits the rights and privileges of the Paris Parliament, two chambers of which were suppressed by the terms of a third edict. The King, on leaving the audience-chamber, saw consternation marked on the faces of the people, and, on the same day, nearly all the members of the Parliament sent in their resignations. "That body was resolute and calm," says

Fig. 116.—Chancellor of France (René Nicolas Charles Augustin de Maupeou, 1768).

Fig. 118.—First President of the Paris Parliament (Louis Lefèvre d'Ormesson, 1788).

Voltaire, "but public opinion was expressed in very violent terms." Such was the state of men's minds when Damiens, by his attempt on the King's life (January 5th, 1757), increased the general excitement. We related in the preceding chapter how the crime of this madman was used as a weapon by the various parties, who, in turn, declared Damiens to have been the tool of the Jansenists, the Parliamentarians, and, in the last resort, of the Jesuits; and we also pointed out how this latter calumny, in conjunction with the scandal caused by the bankruptcy of Fathers La Valette and Savy (superior and secretary of the Missions), was mainly instrumental in bringing about the expulsion from France of the Company of Jesus, (edict of May 9th, 1767).

This victory of the Parliament was, eventually, a very dear one, for, just as it deemed itself master of the situation, it discovered that the Court party, which had always stood between it and the

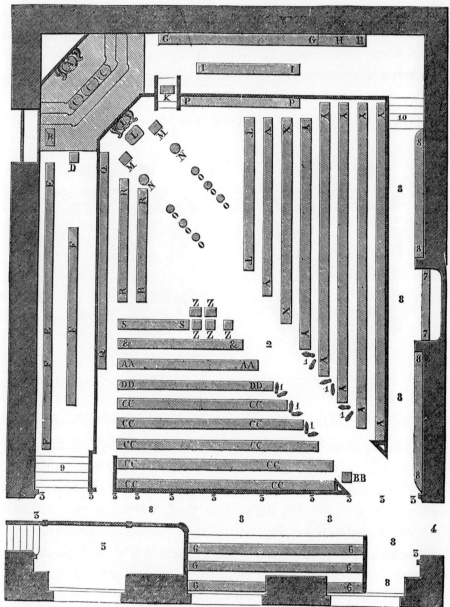

KEY TO THE ENGRAVING.

A The King.—**B.** The Dauphin.—**C.** The Grand Chamberlain.—**D.** The Grand Equerry.—**E.** The Princes of the Blood. —**F.** The Temporal Dukes and Peers.—**G.** The Spiritual Peers.—**H.** The Marshals of France.—**I.** The four Captains of the King's Guard, and the Commander of the Swiss Guard.—**K.** The Provost of Paris, bearing a white wand upon the low step which leads to the king's throne.—**L.** The Chancellor of France in an arm-chair.—**M.** The Grand Master and the Master of Ceremonies.—**N.** The two Mace-Bearers of the King, kneeling.—**O.** The six Heralds, kneeling. —**P.** The first President and the Presidents-à-Mortier.—**Q.** The Presidents of Requests and Inquests.—**R.** The Councillors of State and the Masters of Requests.—**S.** The Secretaries of State.—**T.** The Knights of the Order.— **V.** The Governors of the Provinces.—**X.** The Lieutenants of the Provinces.—**Y.** The Councillors of the Grand Chamber. —**Z.** The Registrar-in-Chief and the Chief Clerks of the Grand Chamber with two small desks in front of them. **&.** The Secretaries of the Court and the Honorary Councillors.—**AA.** The Grand Provost of the Hotel and the Officers of the King.—**BB.** The first Usher of the Grand Chamber.—**CC.** The Councillors of Inquests and Requests.—**DD.** The King's Household.—**1.** The six Guards *de la manche* with their coat of mail and partisan.—**2.** The Grand Major of the King's Guard.—**3.** The King's Guards, shouldering their musketoons.—**4.** The door by which the king makes his entry.—**5.** Gallery for the Queen, the wife of the Dauphin, and Madame.—**6.** Benches for the Public—**7.** Bench for the Inspectors of Menus and the men of the king's furniture-repository on duty.—**8.** For the Public.—**9.** Steps leading to the seats of the Temporal Peers.—**10.** Steps leading to the seats of the Spiritual Peers.

throne, was as strong as ever. Thence began anew the refusals to register edicts, the remonstrances, the deputations to the King, and the exchanges of threats. The Parliament still insisted on its declaration : "That no scheme or edict becomes law until it is registered." It was impossible to avoid seeing that the Parliament, feeling itself very popular, had resolved to obtain a share in the government, and this resolve led Barbier, who was an advocate himself, to remark : "If the authority of the Parliaments and their alleged rights are restricted, there will be no obstacle in the way of a triumphant despotism. If, on the contrary, the Parliaments coalesce to ward off this hostility by making still more extensive claims, such a step can only lead to a general revolution in the State, which would be a very perilous contingency." These bickerings and conflicts went on without ceasing until 1770 ; the Parliaments had acquired a degree of power which held in check that of the King. But, on December 7th, 1770, a new Bed of Justice, held at the instigation of Chancellor Maupeou, who was a determined enemy of the Parliaments, put an end to a state of things which had become unbearable. The King called upon the Parliament to submit, and its members responded by suspending their labours. In the night of January 19-20, 1771 they were requested, by musketeers, to sign *yes* or *no* to letters calling upon them to resume their sittings. They all signed *no*, and were in consequence exiled and their posts confiscated. Justice was still administered by Councillors of State and masters of requests, and the only expenses to the parties concerned in the suits were to be the costs of procedure. By edict of February 22nd, 1771, six new Parliaments were created under the title of *higher councils*, and all the Parliaments of France underwent a radical reform, by which the purchase of places was abolished, as also the *fees* or arbitrary costs. This measure created universal consternation, but order was not disturbed, the public venting their ill-humour in sarcastic rhymes and remonstrances. Not until after the death of Louis XV. and the appointment of a new Chancellor was the ancient Parliament revived ; but Louis XVI. and the Comte de Maurepas restored its privileges, a Bed of Justice being held for that purpose on November 12th, 1774. Louis XVI. even restored to the Parliament that right of remonstrances which had been the source of so much trouble during his grandfather's reign. In order to maintain the popularity of which it was so tenacious, it was necessary for the Parliament to refuse registration of the financial edicts, and place itself in hostility with the Ministry, the Court, and the King. It did not shrink from doing this, and declared that the decisions arrived at during a Bed of Justice held by the King as to the re-establishment of a land-tax, were null and void. It was banished to Troyes (August, 1787), but the Government was weak enough to abandon the tax and recall the Parliament. The ostentatious return of the Parliament to Paris gave rise to disgraceful scenes of public rejoicing. The game was now won, and the Parliament, in its daring attacks upon the King and his Ministers, was led by the only tacticians who had the Revolution in view. Remonstrances were thrust aside as too mild a measure, and the impetuous D'Espréménil, who was only a councillor, drew up an insolent protest against royalty, and undertook to resist it by all legal and physical methods (May, 1788).

The law-courts were all but becoming the scene of a bloody conflict, when d'Espréménil, and several other councillors were arrested one night while taking part in the deliberations of the Grand Chamber. Soon afterwards, the Parliament, having hotly opposed the creation of the Grand-Bailiwicks and the Plenary Court which were intended to replace it, was again exiled and recalled, thanks to the irresolution of the Crown. Upon this occasion, its return was made the pretext for a day's disturbance in Paris (July 29th, 1788). Thus the Revolution began, under the auspices of the Paris Parliament, a year before the storming of the Bastille.

CHAPTER VIII.

FINANCE.

DURING the last fifteen years of the reign of Louis XIV., the finances of the State were in a most deplorable condition, and, as Voltaire remarks in his treatise upon this decline in the public revenues : " A country must be very strong in itself to retain any vigour after such a succession of drains upon its vitality." None of Colbert's successors had the ability to take advantage of the inexhaustible resources of France, without impoverishing and racking the people. Louis XIV. determined to entrust the management of financial affairs to Le Peletier, though Michel le Tellier, keeper of the Seals, assured the King that he was not fitted for such a post, as he was not sufficiently hard-hearted. But the King replied that he did not wish his people to be hardly used. The new Minister had the reputation of being just and benevolent, but he did not understand finance, which was then a conjectural science, and which was not as yet based upon any true principles of economy.

In all financial difficulties—and the treasury emptied itself faster than it filled—provisional expedients, such as increasing the taxes, reducing the standard of money, or borrowing, were resorted to. Thus Montesquieu remarks : " It is impossible for us to put our finances in proper order, because we know that we are going to do something, but we never know what that something is. With us, a great Minister is not the man who wisely controls the public revenues, but the man who is fertile in what are called expedients." Chamillart, who succeeded Pontchartrain, and the controller-general Desmarets, who was the successor of Chamillart, were merely *men of ingenuity*, to use Montesquieu's expression, and were unable to cure a disease which was already past remedy. Still, Chamillart conceived the idea, in 1706, of paying the state expenses, especially those of the War department, in bank-notes, orders for food, etc., but as this paper-money was not received by the treasury in payment of taxes, it was discredited almost as soon as it was issued. Thus it was necessary to return to the system of loans, which was a very ruinous one, enriching the contractors and loading the public debt with enormous liabilities. No measure for raising money was scrutinised too closely, and the tax-gatherers were always ready to make advances to the Government, which conceded them the privilege of re-imbursing themselves, with a large profit to boot, out of the imposts which they undertook to collect.

The King, absolute though his authority was, gave but a reluctant assent to these deplorable expedients which, though they procured a certain amount of ready money, only increased his difficulties in the end. When Desmarets, who was the nephew of Colbert, proposed the impost of a tithe upon the fortunes of private individuals, upon houses, upon all posts and functions in the army, finance and the courts of Justice, as well as upon all other incomes payable in specie, Louis XIV. drew a long sigh, and mumured to himself: "I have not the right to do this!" But the requirements of the Treasury were very pressing, and the contractors, with the money ready to be advanced, were only waiting for the creation of this crushing impost, and the King signed the edict on October 14th, 1710.

What with expedients of one kind and another, the Government managed to tide over the difficulties of the hour, and to avert till the end of the reign, the bankruptcy which seemed immediately impending. When Louis XIV. died (September, 1715) the amount of the national debt amounted to a milliard of francs (£40,000,000). There was also a debt of 580 millions of francs (£23,200,000) immediately due, advances made by the receivers of finance and the contractors, and bills of various kinds, which made a further total of about a milliard and a half (£60,000,000). The only way of gaining time was by resorting to the expedients which had already been employed. This overwhelming amount of indebtedness had been brought about by the frequent wars in which Louis XIV. had been engaged throughout the course of his long reign. So it is a mistake to attribute the financial embarrassments of the State to the King's expenditure on his palaces, his pleasures, and artistic proclivities, for, at the time when he indulged in outlays of this kind, viz., during the ministry of Colbert, the finances were in a very flourishing condition. The Regency of the Duc d'Orleans was on the point of being in-augurated by the bankruptcy of France, for it was openly declared that the young King was not responsible for the debts of his predecessor, and that he ought, in the interest of the nation to leave them to the account of the defunct monarch.

The deficit, it must be admitted, was hard to make up. Louis XIV., during the seventy-two years of his reign, had raised from the nation 18 milliards, which makes an average of more than two and a half million livres per annum, equal, according to Voltaire, to 330 millions (£13,200,000) in 1749. In 1715 the Treasury was empty, and the sources of the public revenue were dried up, the royal notes were discredited, and had lost a fifth of their nominal value. Philippe d'Orleans, who did not scruple to resort to the strangest expedients, was on the point of declaring the country bankrupt, but the Duc de Noailles, President of the Committee of Finance in the Regency Council, offered energetic resistance to a step which would have been the ruin of royalty and of France. He proposed other and more legitimate measures for diminishing the royal debt, and, for the first time since the days of Colbert, insisted upon the necessity of economical reform. In December 1715 was published, at his instance, the famous *visa* edict, in which the deplorable condition of affairs was openly set forth. The King was made to say in this edict: "In such a position, we have not hesitated to reject the proposal for repudiating engagements contracted by others than ourselves ; we have also shunned the perilous example of borrowing at enormous rates of interest, and we have also rejected the mercenary offers of those who would impose on our people fresh burdens." The object of the visa was to control and liquidate all the royal notes in circulation and convert them into one class of note, with a reduction of more than a third, thereby giving the King a profit of 237 million livres (£19,480,000).

"France, at the death of the late King," says Montesquieu in his "Lettres Persanes," "was a body covered with sores, Noailles took up the iron, seared the dead flesh and applied some local remedies, but there still remained an internal disease to cure. A stranger was called in to effect this cure. After many violent remedies, he thought that the patient had recovered his embonpoint, whereas in reality the body was only swollen." This was Law, a talented adventurer, who possessed, by instinct rather than by application, a practical knowledge of finance, and who did so much injury to the country in which he became naturalised, and where he put in practice his wonderful schemes of empiric economy. At this period, political economy was in its infancy. Boisguillebert, in his "Détail de la France," was the first to shadow forth any wise and practical ideas as to the best way of controlling the public revenue. Vauban, who shared these ideas and had perhaps imparted them to Boisguillebert, who was his nephew, bore testimony to the abuses which occurred in the imposition and levying of the *tailles*, the excise and the provincial customs duties, as also in regard to the capitation tax and the *affaires extraordinaires*, as the loans, annuities, royal bank-notes, and other means of raising funds were then termed. So he conceived the idea of substituting for all these taxes, more or less arbitrary and uncertain in their yield, "the establishment of a *royal tithe* levied upon all the fruits of the earth on one hand and upon all that constitutes the revenue of the inhabitants upon the

THE RUE DE QUINCAMPOIX IN 1718.

other," and this scheme appeared to him "the best-balanced of all, the least open to corrupt practices." Vauban's system was made public in 1707 and at once suppressed, though it is not too much to say that it was the basis of all the systems of political economy conceived during the 18th century. But when Vauban elaborated his scheme, there were no financiers in France; nothing but contractors and tax-gatherers (*maltôtiers*).

This term of *maltôtier* was applied to those who were concerned in the assessment and levy of the taxes, and especially of the *taille*, which was the most unpopular of all the imposts. The *contractors* were the successors of the *partisans* whose name had disappeared, accompanied by universal abhorrence. The contractors undertook to levy the royal revenues, under certain conditions which formed the object of a special agreement, but they never undertook any duties which had the most remote relation to a financial system. Montesquieu, in the "Lettres Persanes," says of them : "They are surrounded by wealth on every side; few of them share the fate of Tantalus. Yet they begin this calling very poor. They are despised as so much dirt whilst they are needy, but when they grow rich they are held in relatively high esteem, so they stick at nothing to acquire this good opinion." The most famous and the wealthiest of these contractors, Samuel Bernard, amassed 33 million francs (£1,320,000) worth of esteem. Voltaire, who was personally acquainted with him, said: "He was intoxicated with a kind of renown which rarely attaches to his profession, he was passionately fond of show, and was well aware that the French Ministry repaid with interest anything that was risked on its behalf." Samuel Bernard risked many millions, and he was rewarded not only with enormous wealth, but with the notice which Louis XIV. himself deigned to bestow upon him. The King, on one occasion, required a large sum of money from him, and Samuel Bernard remarked to Chamillart, the Minister who informed him of what was wanted : "When one requires the assistance of any person, the least one can do is to ask him personally." Louis XIV. accorded an interview to the banker, and received him very graciously. He obtained a larger sum than he had counted upon, and rewarded him by ennobling him, and conferring on him the title of chevalier. Montesquieu, in allusion to the honorary distinctions conferred on certain financiers of his day, wrote that : " Matters are indeed at a sad pass when the lucrative profession of contractors has succeeded, by means of its wealth, in being looked upon as an honourable one . . . . All other callings are proportionately degraded, honour loses its value, the slow and natural means of obtaining distinction are discarded, and the very principles of Government are shaken."

Law, less honest and generous than Bernard, but more enterprising and dexterous, was also loaded with honours in his palmy days. The indiscriminating favour of the Duc d'Orleans had brought him into favour, for the Regent was a good judge, and he appreciated the wonderful qualities of this ingenious financier who, merely a lucky speculator in the first place, eventually effected great innovations in the system of finance. The Regent, by letters patent of May 2nd, 1716, accorded him the right of creating a bank, which in a short time ruined all the private banks and became itself a royal establishment. Law had, to use Barbier's expression, " found the secret of placing all the money in the kingdom at the Regent's disposal " and, by way of contrast, while Law was being accorded this banking privilege, and was resorting to the marvellous devices of alchemy which converted paper-money into gold, an *ardent chamber* or *chamber of justice* was being constituted to report upon all the illicit profits made by the contractors, and, by making them disgorge, a sum of 160 millions (£6,400,000) was calculated upon as immediately available. The consternation which this measure had at first excited did not last long, for they found many powerful protectors especially amongst the female sex. A great nobleman went to call upon one of these financiers who had been ordered to refund 1,200,000 levres (£48,000) and offered to obtain him a receipt in full if he would pay a quarter of that sum, but he was met with the reply " you are just too late, I have already settled the matter with your wife who has accepted half the amount you ask for." Some of them

Fig. 119.—Portrait of Samuel Bernard, engraved by Drevet, after Hyacinthe Rigaud.

did not get off so easily, and, amongst others, Poisson de Bourvalais was sacrificed to the popular hatred. But, altogether the *chamber of justice* did a good deal of injury to the public credit and did not bring in more than 15 millions (£600,000) to the Treasury.

The contractors, who were made to refund the public moneys, had themselves to thank for being so universally detested. Nothing could exceed their callousness and their assumption ; they possessed luxurious hotels, domains and equipages. Their luxury seemed to be an insult upon the sufferings of the people ; their dinners, concerts and balls, for which they secured the presence of a few ruined noblemen, surpassed in prodigality the former entertainments of the nobility, and put to a blush the quiet and economical habits of the bourgeoisie. These vain-glorious contractors had been held up to ridicule by Le Sage in his comedy of " Turcaret." The hero of this piece was a lackey who had grown rich out of finance, and who is made to say : " It is not necessary to be very clever to get on in the world ; with the exception of myself and two or three others, the men of finance are not particularly sharp. All that is required is a certain amount of practice and routine which soon comes . . . We see so many people ! . . . We endeavour to copy whatever is worth imitation. That composes the whole of our science." Turcaret and Mondor have become the theatrical types of these contractors, who gradually disappeared or became lost in the world of finance, after the action taken by the chamber of justice and the crushing terms of the edict of 1716, which declared that " the wealth of the contractors was derived from the spoils of the provinces, the subsistence of the inhabitants and the patrimony of the State." The contractors belonged to the reign of Louis XIV : the financiers were, so to speak, brought into existence under the Regency and became more numerous under Louis XV.

Law was one of the most powerful and ingenious of these financiers. His bank was driving a flourishing trade ; its notes circulated everywhere and there was no lack of money. This bank had become the general treasury of the kingdom. But Law's projects did not end there ; he hoped to pay off all the public debt, in the course of a few years, out of the profits of his financial operations, and he founded, in connection with his bank, a Mississippi Company for colonizing Louisiana, for working its mines and concentrating American commerce in that region. This hardy scheme was to result in enormous profits for the holders of shares, which immediately rose very high, as everyone wished to take part in the concern. There was a perfect fever of speculation, and, as Voltaire wrote, " a new and

Fig. 120.—The Contractor, after a caricature by Dumesnil the younger.

reckless game of speculation in which the citizens were playing the one against the other." The Company had its offices in the Rue Quincampoix, and for two years this narrow, dirty street was thronged with people determined to procure shares at any cost. The value of the shares increased from day to day and from hour to hour, yet the Mississippi Company had not paid any dividend or obtained any practical result. Few of the shareholders knew precisely what the Mississippi was. Large fortunes were made very rapidly, and lost still more rapidly.

Montesquieu, who had been a witness of these strange social changes, writing before the catastrophe which he had predicted as inevitable, says : "Those who were rich six months ago are now impecunious, and those who then had to beg their bread are now loaded with wealth. Never did these two extremities so nearly meet. The foreigner (Law) has turned the State inside out, as a clothes-dealer does a coat ; he puts outside what was before hidden from view, and the part that was worn by use he puts on the inside. What fortunes that were undreamed of even by those who have made them ! God could not create a being out of nothing more rapidly. How many servants are waited on to-day by their former comrades, as they will be, perhaps, to-morrow by their former masters. All this frequently leads to strange incidents ; the lackeys who made their fortune in the previous reign now boast of their ancient birth, and they indulge in the same contempt for the speculators of the present day that was felt for themselves a few months ago. They are never tired of exclaiming : ' The nobility is ruined. What disorder in the State ! What confusion in the ranks ! The only rich people are a lot of unknown *parvenus !* ' "

The great noblemen, and even the princes of the blood, set the example of this reckless speculation ; and took shares, when they did not obtain them gratis from Law. Law, carried away by the success of his system, launched out into projects still more daring. The Marquis de Canillac, one of the most dissipated nobles at Court, said to Law one day: "I draw out bills of exchange, get them discounted and fail to meet them. So you have stolen my system." And this sarcastic remark, resented at the time, foreshadowed the end of Law's schemes. The Parliament did all in its power to repress this mania, addressing remonstrances to the King, and refusing to register the Edicts, which it looked upon as fatal to the public weal. It even ordered the arrest of Law, as was explained in the previous chapter, who, for this reason, cherished a grudge against the Parliament, which he proposed to abolish by making a forced purchase of their charges and handing them over to the King. In 1719, his bank became the *Royal Bank*, and he undertook, apart from the wild Mississippi venture, enterprises of a more solid character, and more befitting to the Government which extended to them its protection. The Royal Bank took over the privileges of the old India Company, which, since its creation by

Fig. 121.—Bombario, the Hunchback, who was used as a writing-desk by the brokers and who, in this way, earned £6000 in a few days.
(From a satiric work published in Holland, 1720.)

Colbert, had fallen into decay ; it obtained a monopoly of trade at Senegal, and also of the tobacco manufacture, the post-office, and all the manors in the Kingdom. But a scarcity of specie was soon felt, and in a short time it was entirely superseded by paper-money. The value of the shares in the Royal Bank represented, in 1719 eighty times the amount of specie which there was in France. In three months these shares were absolutely worthless, and Law resorted to every kind of expedient to maintain the nominal value of the bank-notes. The Duc d'Orleans appointed him controller-general of Finance, hoping that in this position he would be better able to sustain the credit of the Royal Bank. But it was not possible to avert any longer a financial crash. The issue of tyrannical decrees only served to accelerate it and make it worse; as, for instance, the royal order that all specie should be paid into the Royal Bank to be exchanged for bank-notes, and the prohibition for any person to retain in his possession more than £20 in cash. This was the signal for a panic on the part of those who possessed only paper-money, and a large crowd besieged the Royal Bank to exchange the bank-notes which had a forced circulation for specie. There was a crush at the cashier's desks, but no money was to be had. Then the most exorbitant rates of interest were charged, and this gave a fresh impulse to brokerage, but without raising the value of the shares or notes. The Royal Bank had been removed from the Palais Mazarin in the Rue Vivienne to the Place Vendôme, which was crowded all day and night by a multitude of people wild with excitement. The specie paid into the bank had already disappeared as if by enchantment; the Prince de Conti had taken away three waggon-loads of it. Most of the contractors, whom the Chamber of Justice had condemned to refund such large sums, had avenged themselves by buying up the specie with paper-money and sending it out of France. Law resorted to schemes of every kind for raising the value of these bank-notes. A royal edict prescribed that the payment of funds and pensions should for the future be effected by the State in paper-money, but this paper-money could not be put in circulation, and the Parliament refused to register the decrees compelling its acceptance. Amidst the general distress, there were still a few people who grew rich; those, for instance, who, following the example of the Government, paid their debts in paper-money which no one would receive.

The Duc d'Orleans felt himself unable to support the originator of such great social calamities any longer. He had sided with him against the Parliament, but he could not resist the people who, almost storming the Palais-Royal, demanded the surrender of Law who had taken refuge there. He did not give him up to the populace, but favoured his flight. It was said, on the one hand, that Law had invested many millions sterling in England, but the more credible version is that he only took away with him 2000 louis which he soon spent at Venice, where he died, poor and forgotten, in 1729. The anonymous author of some *Memoirs* which are generally attributed to Massillon says:—"It will take centuries to eradicate the

A Member of the Stock Exchange.

Law pulling the fish out of the water.

A Stock-Jobber.

Fig. 122.—Caricature taken from the Arc Mémorial dressé au lieu d'enterrement des actionistes consumés.

evil which Law is responsible for, in having accustomed the people to ease and luxury, in having made them discontented with their condition, in having raised the price of food and manual labour, and in making all classes of tradespeople look for exorbitant profits. * * * The only advantage—and that is a very small one to compensate for all the harm done—is that his system unmasked a great many persons of high position at Court, and showed that they were capable of proceedings which no one would have believed possible." For, as Duclos remarks, nearly all the members of the Court loaded with debts took this opportunity of paying them off with paper-money given them by Law. The Duc d'Orleans, and the Duc de Bourbon were the chief offenders, and the latter had received so much specie and paper-money from Law's bank, that the Regency Council was all but order-ing him to refund two or three hundred millions of francs, as if he had been a mere contractor. The Duc d'Orleans, dazzled by Law's promises, had displayed a deplorable amount of weakness, and he was obliged to admit that he had authorized him to issue bank-notes for 1,200,000,000 francs (£48,000,000) beyond the amount fixed by royal decree. The total of the bank-notes issued amounted to two milliards seven hundred millions (£108,000,000), and to cover this there was only the fictitious revenue of the Mississippi Company, and the resources of the India Company, to which the tobacco monopoly had been granted. This was all that remained of the imposing edifice which Law had endeavoured to rear, and which came down with such a crash.

Law was succeeded by financiers of more modest pretensions : the four brothers Paris, who had always been his rivals, and who were partly instrumental in bringing about his fall. The value of a marc in silver, which only averaged from thirty-seven to forty livres in the reign of Louis XIV., had risen to ninety livres, and, during the last few years it had been as high as one hundred and twenty. The brothers Paris staved off national bankruptcy by appointing a Tribunal composed of the masters of Requests and other judges, to make a fresh valuation of all property. More than half a million of people, most of them heads of families, deposited with this Tribunal all they possessed in the shape of shares and royal notes, and these innumer-able liabilities were liquidated at 1631 millions (£65,240,000), which the State undertook to satisfy. The unfortunate lenders did not at that time receive one per cent. on the arrears of interest which was owing to them for the sums they had advanced to the State during the reign of Louis XIV. The State made all the sacrifices possible, and took upon itself all the losses arising from the rise in the rate of interest. At last there seemed to be some chance of extrication from this terrible chaos which the French, light-hearted even in the most depressing circumstances, called *La Comédie de Law.* Duclos in his *Memoirs,* remarks that "the denouement of it was that the

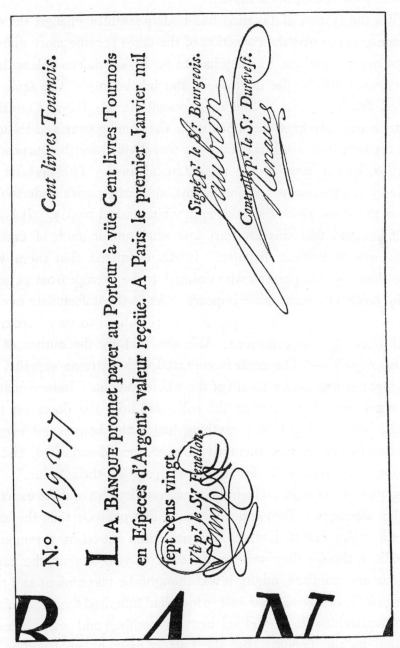

Fig. 123.—A Note of Law's Royal Bank (1719).

swindlers, high and low, had grown rich, that the middle-class, the most honest and useful of all, had been ruined, and that the morality of the nation had been corrupted."

Still the system of taxation had undergone little change, the only difference being that the collection of the taxes became more difficult, if not more vexatious, for they had to be levied nolens volens, however great might be the distress of the inhabitants. The *taille* still formed the main part of the royal revenues ; the Royal Council of Finance annually fixed the amount for the coming year, and the nineteen districts into which the kingdom was divided for the purposes of taxation, had to provide the money in advance. The division was made by the treasurers and intendants, and each parish undertook to collect the sums which the various inhabitants had to pay. It is easy to understand that this arbitrary and often unfair mode of taxation gave birth to endless disputes. It was estimated that there were more than 100,000 persons who claimed to be exempt from payment of the *taille*, and most other imposts. As to the unfortunate persons who could not or would not pay, they were subject to very hard treatment from the tax-collectors. We are told by the author of *La Dixme Royale* :—" The *taille* is collected with extreme severity, and at a cost not less than a fourth of the whole amount. Indeed, matters are often carried so far that the collectors take the doors off their hinges, after having sold everything inside the house, and even in some cases the houses themselves have been demolished, and the building materials sold for a fiftieth part of their value." The peasants went in rags, and left their land untilled to avoid the exactions of the assessors. Two other imposts, less onerous than the *taille*, but still more detested, which had only been raised as a temporary expedient, though they were continued from year to year, the capitation-tax and the tithe, might, it was thought, be taken off at any time. The *gabelle*, or excise upon salt, which had inherited the unpopularity always attaching to it, yielded next to nothing, and was no longer resisted by the people. But the host of persons employed in the levying of taxes generally still made their living out of the savings and labour of the lower classes. The nobility, clergy, and magistracy contributed next to nothing to the State revenues. The higher department of finance was administered by a controller-general and a council, to say nothing of the indirect control exercised by the Sovereign Courts, the Court of Excise, the Chamber of Accounts, and the Court of Exchequer.

The *ferme générale* was an administration apart, sanctioned by

De laquais devenu caissier   Mais la Fortune qui se jǒue
Il fait tant par le tripotage,   De tel qu'elle a le plus chéri
Que l'on appelle agiotage,   Lui fait faire un saut de sa roue
Qu'il se voit très-gros financier ;   Jusqu'à celle du pilori.

Fig. 124.—The Stock-Jobber, elevated by Fortune (fragment of a caricature of the period).

the Council of State in 1720, and enjoying plenary authority by virtue of the privilege which the State conferred on it for collecting the taxes on articles of consumption, such as salt, tobacco, provisions brought into Paris, etc. It contracted with Government leases renewable at stated periods, and gave as security for its carrying out the contract, the undertaking of forty *fermiers généraux* of good fortune. During the first five years of its existence, the administration of the *ferme générale* only paid 55 millions (£2,200,000) into the treasury, but, by the terms of the new lease contracted, in 1726, the sum was fixed at 80 millions (£3,200,000), and it was afterwards increased so much that the number of *fermiers généraux* was raised from 40 to 60. They were all of them millionnaires, for their profits, in the five years from 1726-30, when there were only 40 of them, exceeded 156 millions (£6,240,000). This well explains the aristo-cratic splendour and luxury which they affected. They were nearly all men of good birth, and their patriotism consisted of a feeling of gratitude for the Government to which they owed their fortune. Voltaire, who was on intimate terms with many of the most cele-brated, said that many of them, generally supposed to be actuated by self-interest, were, in reality, men of high feeling. The pecuniary assistance which they afforded to Louis XV., during his disastrous struggle with Germany, was a proof of their honourable sentiments, for they lent him money, borrowed at 5 per cent., at the same rate. When Orry, the controller-general proposed in 1743, with a view of favouring trade with foreign countries, that the export tax upon linen and cotton-goods should be removed, the *fermiers généraux* agreed at once, and would not accept any indemnification. In the scarcity of 1740, when the tax-collectors were accused of ruining Normandy and filling the country districts with beggars, one *fermier général* fed a whole province at his sole expense. It was not until after Samuel Bernard's death that the extent of his charity became known, and Voltaire wrote of him in 1749 : "Not long since, there was a member of the financial body, who had alone assisted the State more than once, and to whom was owing, at the time of his death 10 millions (£400,000) lent to private individuals, half of this sum bearing no interest." Thus, Cardinal de Fleury, when pre-senting to the King the *fermiers généraux* who had just signed a contract with the controller-general, said : "Behold, Sire, the forty pillars of the State." But why should the Marquis de Souvré have added : "Yes, Sire, they hold up the State, as the rope holds up the body of the executed criminal ?" Samuel Bernard, who was present, might have replied : "We hold up the State which enriches us, but we also sustain the nobility which impoverishes us, by borrowing money which it never repays."

The financiers, always being made use of by the courtiers, were none the less a butt for their sarcasms. They knew how to acquire a fortune and to keep it; the nobles, on the contrary, wasted theirs, and were always having recourse to the munificence of the King, or to loans contracted at ruinous interest. The aged Marshal de Villeroy, the Governor of Louis XV., had at all events the frankness to admit that "whoever may be the Minister of Finance, I declare beforehand that I am his friend and almost his relative." Duclos, who, like most men of letters of good standing, was on intimate terms with the financial world, took up the cudgels on their behalf against the nobility, and, in his *Considérations sur les Mœurs*, he wrote: "The fun poked at the financiers behind their back is a proof rather of envy of their wealth than of contempt for their person, for, to their face, people are always paying them compliments. People of condition fancy that this conduct is a mark of superiority, but they deceive no one as to their real motives." In fact, as La Popelinière, one of the most sumptuous of the *fermiers généraux* said, they had only to open their salons to have them filled with the representatives of the most illustrious titles in the French peerage.

Le Sage ridiculed without pity the vices and follies of the contractors in "Turcaret;" and St. Foix in the "Financier," which was applauded by the financiers themselves at the Théâtre-Français (1761), was not too hard upon finance. The financier of his comedy who had just purchased a magnificent country residence, and who spends his money freely, is not spoilt by his good-fortune; he is, moreover, witty and well-bred. The theatrical critic of the *Mercure de France*, writing of the piece just after it was produced, said: "The failings of this financier, like those of most men, are those of the head rather than of the heart, and his want of compassion for the unfortunate does not prove an absence of breeding, but it is rather a vice which opulence often brings with it." It is in the mouth of a valet that the author puts the following criticism upon contemporary manners: "Luxury and wealth have merged all ranks into one." The *fermiers généraux* were at that time on an equal footing

with the greatest noblemen. J. J. Rousseau, who had been introduced to Madame Dupin, whose husband was a *fermier général*,
relates in his *Confessions* the kind reception which he met with from
this lady, who was a natural daughter of Samuel Bernard. He says :
" Her house, one of the most brilliant as it was one of the most
pleasant in Paris (1742), was frequented by people who, though
they were rather more numerous than one might have wished,
formed the *élite* of every class. She liked to see around her people
of notoriety, noblemen, men of letters, beautiful women. Her house
was crowded with dukes, ambassadors and wearers of orders."
Madame Dupin lived in still greater state at the Château de
Chenonceaux, built by Henri II. for Diane de Poitiers, which had
thus become the property of a *fermier général*. Rousseau says that
it was a very pleasant house to stay in, and the Château de
Chevrette, near St. Denis, also belonging to a *fermier général*, La
Live de Bellegarde, was equally renowned for its hospitality. Of
La Popelinière, another of the body, who was a warm patron of the
arts and held open house in Paris, Marmontel says : " One meets in
his reception rooms a continual stream of personages presenting the
most varied types of character and manners. He was intimate with
many of the ambassadors, and it was certainly not one of those
polite diplomatists who, after admiring all the riches of this residence
and being asked by some nobleman present what he thought of it
all, replied : " The only thing wanting is a gallows-tree in the middle
of the courtyard."

Nolivos de St. Cyr, who relates this epigrammatic saying, has
also handed down to us, by way of contrast, the following portrait
of another *fermier général*, Joseph de la Borde, who was banker to
the Court. "*Mont d'or* deserves the esteem and good opinion of all
Frenchmen. Amidst his immense wealth, his heart has never been
perverted by pride, or become hardened, as is too often the case
with men of his calling. All Europe is a witness that his assiduity
to work, his breadth of genius and solidity of judgment have raised
him to his present position. He has certainly been assisted by

fortune, who, perhaps, for the first time, has not conferred her favours with closed eyes. Admitted to the councils of his sovereign, his views have always been guided by the uprightness for which he is so distinguished, and, what is still more remarkable, envy has never marked him for her own, though, at Court, he is said to be the terror of the flatterers."

The bad state of the finances during the reign of Louis XV. was perhaps due, in the first instance, to the disastrous struggles in which France lost her navies and her armies. But it may be truly said that the embarrassments were in a large measure owing to the reckless expenditure of the Crown. All the controller-generals were at their wits' ends to find means of meeting the continually increasing requirements of the treasury; but none of them thought of effecting an economy of expenditure. When Cardinal de Fleury became Minister in 1726, the financial condition of things seemed to be satisfactory; the total revenue of the State was 160 millions (£6,400,000). Twenty years later, this revenue had almost doubled itself, for in 1750 it stood at 300 millions (£12,000,000); but in the meanwhile the expenditure had increased in so much greater proportions, that the Government, instead of abolishing the tithe-tax, as it had long promised to do, was preparing to establish a tax of 5 per cent. on all property, movable and otherwise. The deplorable system of expedients was again resorted to, including the most dangerous of them all—the *acquits de comptant*, which the King signed without the document bearing any mention of the use to which it was to be put. Louis XV. of an economical disposition when hard cash was concerned, never hesitated to sign these *acquits de comptant*, which facilitated the most wasteful expenditure. Barbier says that the expenses were so heavy, and the luxury was so profuse, that people did not know where to turn for money. This was in 1749, when the annual deficit averaged more than a million sterling.

The controller-generals succeeded each other without effecting any improvement in the state of the finances. Machault (1745), one of the cleverest, failed in his attempts to redeem the national debt by establishing the 5 per cent. impost.   Silhouette (1759) signalised his accession to office by a measure which met with great favour, and cost nothing to the State ; he created 72,000 shares of 1,000 francs each, and entitling the holders to half of the profits made by the *fermiers généraux.*   He also reduced the pensions, and

Fig. 125.—Gold and Silver Pieces of the reign of Louis XV.

abolished many of the privileges of exemption from the *taille.* Finally, he proposed a whole series of reforms, which the King seemed inclined to sanction, but the means which he employed to get back the money which had disappeared, were fatal to credit.   Silhouette was a man of strict probity, but no money was to be found, so he was offered as a sacrifice to the public indignation.   The sixty-four *fermiers généraux,* nicknamed *the dauntless,* combined to advance money on the taxes, which were to be raised still higher.   With all this, there was no change in the extravagant habits of the Court.

The economists were in favour, because they were full of wonderful schemes for paying off the debts, and diminishing the liabilities of the State. Louis XV. was still deaf to the remonstrances of the Parliaments, and that of Rouen declared in 1763 that, "if the present condition of the finances, in time of peace, is such as to impose on

Fig. 126.—Portrait of Turgot, after Michel Vanloo.

the people burdens heavier than they have had to bear in time of war, the future is dark indeed." Louis XV. invariably replied: "It will last our time, and after us, the deluge!" Money was always to be had, whoever might happen to be the Court banker; but money cost dear, and the taxes, notwithstanding the daring combinations of the economists, did not grow lighter.

The Duc de Choiseul, during his tenure of office, effected a saving of more than 250 millions (£10,000,000), but after his time the finances were not, to all seeming, better managed than before. Abbé Terray, appointed controller-general in 1769, was imprudent enough to propound the principle that the Government alone ought to be the supreme judge as to the onerous engagements it might have been compelled to contract at periods of pecuniary embarrassment. This was to convert bankruptcy into a reason of State; accordingly, Terray felt no scruples in reducing the interest on the debt to 2½ per cent. He resorted to many expedients of the same kind, gilding the pill as well as he could, even while he was swelling the arbitrary taxes. When it was pointed out to him that one of these financial measures was unjust, he merely replied : " Who said it was just ? " The public indignation affected him as little, for he said : " So much the better ; they treat me as they did Mazarin ; they sing, but they pay." The small holders of national bonds were half-ruined, but Abbé Terray held on his course. Some one ventured to tell him that his system was equivalent to taking the money out of people's pockets, upon which he retorted : " Where else am I to take it from ? "

The economists, with all their schemes, could not bring a penny into the treasury, which was quite empty when Louis XVI. ascended the throne. The latter who prided himself on being something of an economist, called in Turgot to administer the finances (1774). His programme was summed up in these words : " No bankruptcy, no increase of taxation, no loans." This programme could not be carried through without a complete change of the social system, and when Turgot endeavoured to put it in practice by six edicts which were to form the basis of it, he encountered an invincible hostility from the Parliament. He was an honest man with visionary ideas, and he foresaw what would happen when he wrote to the King : " I knew that I should have no help in combating the abuses of every kind and those who made a profit out of them, and that I should be baffled by a host of prejudices which stand in the way of all reform, and which are a formidable weapon in the hands of those whose interest it is to prolong these disorders." Necker, who was called to office in 1777, was merely a banker who knew how to keep accounts. He began by calling in 27 millions (£1,080,000) which the treasurers had retained in their hands as long as they could, so as to obtain the interest on it. He proclaimed himself to be the only man in France capable of administering the finances. He did administer them, it is true, with considerable skill, but he unfortunately published his famous *Compte Rendu*, which was laid before the King in January 1781. "Hitherto," says the Comte de Ségur in his *Memoirs*, "the nation, uninstructed about its pecuniary condition, had been in complete ignorance as to the details of revenue, expenditure and debt, and as to the extent of its requirements and resources."

The public credit was affected by these alarming disclosures. Necker had merely alarmed the country, without lightening its ever-increasing burdens, and, though he had public opinion with him, he was compelled to resign by a coalition of persons attached to the Court. Ségur adds, "The State was sacrificed to the Court, economy to luxury, wisdom to vanity." Two controller-generals, Joly de Fleury and d'Ormesson, who succeeded him, merely displayed their powerlessness, if not their incapacity, to ameliorate the state of affairs. Calonne had the courage to take their place when the treasury was completely drained of specie, and yet Necker had placed on record that the taxes paid throughout the kingdom amounted to 600 millions (£24,000,000). Calonne contracted loan after loan, without paying any heed to the repeated complaints of the Parliament. He had, however, confessed to the King, when he first acceded to office, that the disproportion between the receipts and the expenditure rendered necessary a complete revision of the system of taxation. The remedy was worse than the evil, inasmuch as Calonne proposed to give a fresh constitution to the State, by changing the régime of the finances. He had borrowed such large sums that no more money was to be had, when the King, acting on his advice, convoked the Assembly of Notables before which this reckless minister denounced this enormous deficit which he had so materially contributed to increase. "A deficit," said Mercier, "is a new word, which has unfortunately become naturalised into our language ; it conveys the idea of a dark abyss, and gives rise to vague and gloomy apprehensions." This dark abyss was the Revolution from which was evoked the dread spectre of a deficit and of bankruptcy.

Fig. 127.—A *girandole* of Precious Stones belonging to J. B. F., 1723.

CHAPTER IX.

COMMERCE.

" THE State is a tree," said the Marquis de Mirabeau, "the roots of which are agriculture, the trunk population, the branches industry, the leaves commerce, properly so called, and the arts." This delineation of the social State does not give commerce the high place which it has held in modern life. Montesquieu, after pointing out in his "Esprit des Lois" that "Commerce obliterates baneful prejudices, softens boorish manners, and creates a bond of peace between nations which trade with each other," goes on to describe the evils inherent in commerce. Referring, perhaps, directly to Holland, though his criticisms apply to the France of the 18th century, he says : "In those countries where the spirit of commerce is altogether predominant, all human actions and moral virtues are made the object of traffic ; the smallest matters become a question of money." In an anonymous edition of this great work (1764), Montesquieu's ideas concerning the spirit of commerce, which the economists had exalted too high at the expense of moral and political ideas, are accentuated still more strongly. "Commerce renders men more sociable, or, at all events, less untractable, it makes them more industrious, and more laborious ; but at the same time it renders them less courageous, less discriminating between right and wrong, less susceptible to the dictates of generosity. The commercial system is often reduced to the principle : Let every one labour in his own interest as I labour in mine ; I never ask you for anything without offering an equivalent ; do the same by me." The spirit of commerce, in the opinion of the philosophers of the 18th century, was one of consummate selfishness. This, no doubt, was why the Court, the nobility and even the bourgeoisie (the army and the magistracy above all), looked down with such contempt on the trading classes. Their calling was considered almost a degrading one during the reign of Louis XIV. The merchants and shop-keepers, far from protesting against this contemptuous treatment, kept themselves in the background, and were content to grow rich without attracting attention. Voltaire, who is always a good authority in regard to the leading characteristics of his age, says : " The artizans and traders, whose obscure position protects them from the ambition of the great, are like ants who silently construct their dwelling-place, while the eagles and vultures are tearing each other to pieces." But Voltaire was indignant at the contempt which was displayed for commercial pursuits : " The trader so often hears his calling spoken of with contempt, that he is foolish enough to be ashamed of it. Yet it may be a question which is the most useful member of the State ; the well-powdered nobleman who knows the precise hour at which the King rises and retires for the night, and gives himself great airs while he is slavishly waiting in the minister's ante-chamber, or a merchant who enriches his country, issues orders from his counting-house to Surat and Cairo, and contributes to the prosperity of the world at large."

From the death of Colbert to the end of the reign of Louis XIV., the Government seemed to withdraw from all intermixture in com-mercial affairs, leaving their development or contraction to the initiative of individual traders, but the wise and intelligent measures taken by Colbert to favour the progress of trade and manufacture were still in vigour, and continued to exercise a certain amount of influence. Commerce, left to itself, was mainly carried on with a view to individual interests, but it nevertheless contributed to increase the wealth of the country. The natural products of France, its wines and brandy in particular, its manufacturing products, its woollen and silk stuffs, its linens and articles of luxury and fashion, were a hundredfold beyond the requirements of the country, and formed the basis of an export trade to the most distant countries. This foreign trade, which had been little checked even during the

Fig. 128.—Ancient Merchant-Flag of the French Navy.
(From *Les Pavillons ou Bannières que la plupart des nations arborent en mer;*
David Mortier, Amsterdam, 1718.)

foreign wars, might have been very much extended during the reign of Louis XIV., especially in the Mediterranean and in India, and Piganiol de la Force (1719) relates that a nobleman of the court said : " If God should one day reveal to the Turks the extent of their maritime power and to the French the commercial avenues open to them, the rest of Europe would soon be at their mercy." It was under the empire of this exaggerated idea, no doubt, that the government of Louis XIV. had favoured the creation of several commercial companies to carry on trade in Asia, Africa, and America. But these companies, the last formed in the reign of Louis XIV., the Hudson's Bay and the Guinea Companies, did not prosper, in spite of the many privileges which the King had granted them. They merely helped to found French colonies at certain stations in Africa and North America, by giving a more widely-extended activity to the merchant-navy, and so increasing the effective force of the royal navy, for it is a fact that the best sailors emanated from the merchant service, which was the school of Duguay-Trouin, Cassart, Ducasse, Gardin, and Villestreux.

It is difficult to understand why these great commercial companies, to which the King and the State lent such large sums without interest, and which were exempted from paying duty on the foreign goods they imported into France, decayed so soon after their creation, and eventually abandoned their privileges without having reimbursed their shareholders. Are we to conclude, with the economists of the 18th century, that the French do not possess the commercial spirit which is so strongly developed in the English race? Voltaire in his *Lettres Philosophiques*, says :—" It is solely because the English have become traders that London is a larger and more populous city than Paris." The long struggles which Louis XIV. sustained against England and Holland were, in reality, efforts made by the two latter powers to check the progress of French commerce in the East and West Indies. The companies established in France for carrying on external commerce did not succeed, and at the close of the 17th century, the India Company was compelled to abandon, in return for a very small consideration, to various towns and private individuals the right of trade with India and China. It had only a nominal existence in 1719, when Law, by incorporating it in a new India Company, gave it a fresh lease of prosperity.

If Colbert had been able to overcome the prejudices of Louis XIV. against trade and traders he would undoubtedly have placed commercial institutions upon a more solid basis, by organising a Ministry of Commerce in juxtaposition to the Ministry of Finance. Home and foreign trade were not directly represented in the Royal Council, and the important questions affecting their interests were entrusted in some cases to the Navy and in some cases to the Finance Department. It was not till 1710 that the Government resolved to establish a Council of Commerce, for dealing exclusively with matters of trade, which continued to become more complex and more numerous. This Council was composed of several Councillors of State, six Intendants (overseers) of Commerce, selected from the Masters of Requests, the Syndic of the province of Languedoc, two delegates of the city of Paris and nine other delegates from the chief commercial towns. The Council was presided over by the Secretary of the State for the Navy and the Controller-General of Finance, the latter of whom summoned to assist at the Council, when necessary, two commissioners of taxes. The duty of the six Intendants of Commerce, a post which had been created in 1708, was to superintend the various branches of commerce, divided into six special categories, so it was necessary for them to be well versed in the subjects coming before the Council for discussion. As to the delegates of the commercial towns they were, no doubt, selected from amongst the leading traders in those cities where commerce was at once most extensive and the most flourishing.

The members of the Court, the nobility, and even the financiers, some out of contempt, others out of jealousy, had opposed the introduction of traders into a council which formed an annex, so to speak, of the Council of State and of the Ministerial Departments of Marine and Finance. At the death of Louis XIV. the Council of Commerce was suppressed, and its functions were discharged by the two newly-created Councils of Marine and Finance, themselves subordinate to the Council of Regency. Still the Duc d'Orleans did not absolutely abolish the Council of Commerce, for he selected several members of the two Councils of Finance and Marine, and deputed them to transact business with the six Intendants of Commerce and the delegates of the commercial towns alternately. But, though the latter had not the right of vote at these meetings, a spirit of antagonism soon manifested itself and deprived them of all influence, their rôle being merely a passive one. The six posts of Intendants of Commerce were done away with in 1715, and the Council of Commerce was thus reduced to three Councillors of State, and three Masters of Requests, who, after considering and reporting upon the questions at issue, submitted them for final decision to the President of the Council of Finance or the President of the Council of Marine. The trade inspectors, appointed by the President of the Council of Finance, received their commissions from him, with the exception of the Inspector at Marseilles, who was named by the President of the Council of Marine.

Such was the administrative organisation of commerce during the Regency, and yet this Council, in which the most competent and respected of traders had a seat, sanctioned the most reckless innovations of Law. This latter, full of resources, but too impatient and rash, had founded a bank to which, by means of ingenious combinations, he had attracted all the specie in the kingdom, issuing in exchange bank-notes which speculation had raised to a fictitious rate of value. Law felt that he must give this bank a solid foundation by offering some personal and real security for the paper-money circulated with such reckless profusion, and it was to commerce and agriculture that he appealed, at least in appearance, for the consolidation of his financial system. The Louisiana Company, which had not given any satisfactory results since its creation, passed into the hands of Law, and became, by letters-patent of the King, dated September, 1717, the Western Company. The principal object of the new company was the plantation and tilling of the districts watered by the Mississippi, and it was for them to succeed where Crozat, one of the wealthiest and most competent of the traders, had failed. With a view of recruiting the prosperity of this decaying colony, it was proposed to develop the maritime commerce and work the gold mines of the country. Unfortunately these mines only existed on paper. The schemes and efforts of the Western Company, the shares in which were quickly taken up, obtained great notoriety. In May, 1718, six vessels, conveying colonists and labourers, started for the Mississippi, which was soon to become, as every one believed, the centre of a flourishing colony. The value of the shares in Law's bank became higher and higher, he having obtained from the King the monopolies of the Canada fur trade, that of negro traffic in Senegal (see Figs. 129 and 130), and that of navigation and trade in all the Eastern seas, from the Cape of Good Hope to China. It was then that by an edict of May, 1719, the Western Company was transformed into the Company of the Two Indies, incorporating the ancient India and China Companies, which had been gradually decaying, encumbered with debt. The King conceded to the new

Fig. 129.—Negro Traffic (the sale of a slave); after Eisen.

company the lands, islands, forts, dwelling-houses, stores, moveable and fixed furniture, rights, incomes, vessels, banks, ammunition, provisions, negroes, cattle and merchandise possessed by the two ancient companies, on the condition that it discharged all their debts and paid the King an indemnity of fifty million francs (£2,000,000).

Law's bank had then become the state bank, and was, subsequent to 1720, managed by the India Company. The enormous enterprises which Law had embarked in were not carried into execution, for the ancient India Company never sent more than a few ship-loads of its products to France, and the unfortunate Mississippi colony furnished next to nothing.   Law, in fact, had not the time to carry out these schemes, for his enemies and rivals, the leaders of French finance, and the foreign—the English and the Dutch more particularly—had drained the royal bank of all its specie, leaving only paper money in exchange.   The catastrophe, which was inevitable, came with terrible suddenness.   Money had disappeared : the value of bank-notes and the shares of the India Company had fallen to nothing.   The only means of avoiding a general bankruptcy was to reduce their number and value.   The royal bank and the India Company were merged into one financial and commercial institution.   The unfortunate shareholders had lost two-thirds of their capital ; they had to give up all idea of the premiums and dividends which had been promised to them, receiving no other compensation than an infinitesimal share in the tobacco monopoly, and they looked forward to the prospect of the loss being made up to them when the India Company, better managed and freed from its incumbrances, should realize the hopes of its promoters.

Freed, since 1725, of its banking business, the India Company, though it had been deprived of a part of its privileges, still preserved enough to make large profits, representing, as it did, the maritime commerce of France with the East and West Indies, and with Africa. It enjoyed a monopoly of tobacco, coffee, tea, and spice, upon which, when imported into France, it paid but a nominal duty ; it imported from China silks, and other wearing material, porcelain, and curiosities.   All the debts were liquidated by the emission of 48,000 shares, the dividend of which was fixed at a hundred livres, and yet the shareholders did not receive even this small sum.   Crozat and Samuel Bernard remained at the head of the company, the vice-protector of which was the Duc de Bourbon, then Prime Minister, and the honorary directors, the Duc d'Antin, Marshals de Grammont and d'Estrées, the Marquis de Lassy, the Duc de Chaulnes, the Marquis de Mézières, and M. de Vendôme.   Public opinion was decidedly

THE PORT OF ROCHEFORT: AFTER JOSEPH VERNET.

hostile to them, and they were openly accused of having ruined the unfortunate shareholders by their unscrupulous greed. Nevertheless, the traders and men of business were flattered at finding themselves indirectly associated with princes and great noblemen. There were, also, eight other directors, selected from amongst the principal bankers, and it was they who made the company a great power in

Fig. 130.—Negro Traffic (compelling the slaves to work) ; after Eisen.

Asia, counting its trading stations, its agents, and its vessels by the thousand, increasing its business and its imports every day, and yet, with all that, not paying its shareholders or its creditors. The latter did not lose confidence, and were content to go on lending their money whenever it was asked for. The Government alone derived a profit from the commercial and political extensions of the company, which had its principal seats at Pondicherry and Chandernagor.

The Government, warned by the disasters which had attended

Law's schemes, affected to interfere very little in commercial affairs, confining itself to giving a general protection to trade, and to seeing that the treaties concluded with foreign nations were duly executed. The selfish principle was adopted of leaving the trader to protect himself, and make the most that he could of the liberty accorded to him. The Council of Commerce, established by royal decree in January, 1717, had been superseded (June, 1721) by a mere committee of eight members. Two years after (June, 1723), it was increased by four Intendants of Commerce, who were privy councillors, to superintend and protect home trade as well as foreign trade on dry land. The twelve delegates of the chief commercial towns of the kingdom took part in the discussions, each having his special department, and they were also called upon to give their advice in all matters relating to maritime commerce abroad.

The Intendants of Commerce were either Councillors of State or Masters of Requests; but notwithstanding this fact, there was still a sort of social degradation connected with trade. The royal decree, due to Colbert (1669), declaring trade and nobility to be compatible, had remained a dead letter. Nor had the edicts which authorized the nobles to take part in wholesale commerce without forfeiting their dignity been of any more effect. The magistracy looked down upon commerce even more than did the nobility, and those traders, who were ashamed of their calling, dubbed themselves financiers. Several large manufacturers, such as Robais and Cados, obtained letters of nobility, but they were not looked upon precisely as traders, though their fabrics contributed to the commerce of the country. Louis XIV. recompensed Samuel Bernard's services by conferring upon him the title of count; but in the letters of creation he was spoken of as a financier, and not as a trader, and this is why Bernard never assumed the title. Nothing could eradicate this prejudice against commercial pursuits, and it was only the nobility of the islands and colonies which could embark upon them without loss of dignity. It was in vain that the economists and philosophers, who had so much influence over men's ideas and actions in the 18th century, recommended trade to the poorer classes of the nobility as an honourable means of utilizing their abilities, and of serving their country as well as if they had girt the sword. They made few converts, and though in after years the order of St. Michel, in despite of its statutes, which required that all members should be noble from at least two generations, was given to a few eminent merchants under the guise of financiers, the Govern-

Fig. 131.—Pictorial Signboard of a Dealer in Toys (communicated by **M.** Bonnardot).

ment none the less adhered to the principle laid down by Montesquieu in his *Esprit de Lois :*—" It is contrary to the spirit of the monarchy that the nobility should engage in trade. The English custom of allowing the nobility to embark upon commercial pursuits is one of the causes which have served to weaken the monarchy."

It is true that in commerce, as in the nobility, the bourgeoisie, and the magistracy, there were many different classes. There was a commercial aristocracy and democracy. The great traders were men of rank as compared to the small shopkeepers, and many financiers were traders in disguise. The Marquis de Mirabeau, in his *Ami des hommes*, endeavoured to establish a fraternal union between commerce, industry, and manufacture. " In a State constituted as France is, a trader should be laborious, enterprising, frank, independent, and simple-minded, and should be proud of these qualities ; let finance merge itself in trade, instead of oppressing and despising it ; let the artisan be industrious, wide-awake, regular in his habits, and abstemious." Duclos, in the *considérations sur les mœurs*, thus estimates his preference for the trader, as compared to the financier. " The traders are the prime sources of plenty, financiers are but the channels through which money circulates, and is often swallowed up. . . . The traders are entitled to honour for the origin of their wealth, the financiers fancy that they will impose esteem by their ostentation." At this period, the latter were very conspicuous in society, while the traders had little notoriety, passing most of their time in their counting-houses, and living very simply in despite of their fortune. It is Duclos, also, who said : "the traders grow wealthy by increasing the resources of the country, and their riches are a proof of the services they have rendered. They are not seen so much in society as the financiers, because they are too much occupied to waste their valuable time in frivolous amusement." There was then a marked difference between the trader (*commerçant*), and the shopkeeper (*marchand*), as also between the trader (*commerçant*), and the merchant (*négociant*). Abbé Coyer gives the following definition of the *négociant* in the *Noblesse Commerciale :* " A merchant, thoroughly versed in all the science of trade, knows the shape of the seas, coasts, and provinces, the length of the voyages, the dangers of the various routes, the natural requirements and interests, the manners and customs of the peoples, the local products, the preparation and exchange of all the fabrics in vogue, the value of the different kinds of money, the variations in the rate of exchange, the condition of public credit, and the proper rate of the circulation of gold in the veins of the State. Such a man is always engaged in applying, meditating, and contriving schemes." Towards the close of the reign of Louis XV., when the calling of a merchant was thought a more honourable one, Joseph de la Borde, the great *fermier-général* and Court banker, took pride on having, in his early life, been exclusively engaged in commerce. In some memoirs that have never been made public, he writes : " I have always preserved a great liking for commerce ; it is the calling of a true citizen. A

Fig. 132.—A Dealer in Tin Ware, after Christoph Kilian.

merchant operating on a large scale, sets in motion all the parts of the State machinery, each receiving its share of profit. Agriculture, manufactures, artists, and workmen of different kinds all derive benefit from the operations of the merchant. I have had as many as twenty vessels fishing off the American coasts, in the East and West Indies, and at Guinea. To how many people did this give employ-ment, and how much money was thus circulating, benefiting rich and poor alike by giving them an outlet for their products."

The Paris shopkeepers, who were divided into different classes, had in many instances justified the unfavourable opinion which La Bruyère has left us as to their probity. In the 8th edition of *Les Caractères* (1694), he says :—" The shopkeeper puts his best articles in the window, and sells inferior goods, he manages to have a false light, and he trumps up his merchandise to sell it for more than it is worth ; he has a lot of false marks, which make people think that they are buying at a fixed price, he gives short measure when he can, and has a pair of scales to see that the money paid him is full weight. Cotolendi, in his Sicilian letter already referred to, does not give the Paris shopkeepers a much better character, for he makes his Sicilian traveller say :—"If you ever should come to Paris, take care not to put your foot inside any of the shops which sell fancy articles. In the first place, the shopkeeper describes his goods in very attractive terms, and then, by employing some flattering language, induces you to make a purchase, and at last he talks so much that he quite deafens you. When you go into his shop, he begins by showing you things that you cannot possibly require, and, when he has done that, he produces what you had asked for, but he uses his tongue to such purpose, that you spend all your money, and buy his goods for more than they are worth. This constitutes his profit on the civility which he has displayed, and his trouble for showing, a hundred times a day, goods to people who come in without buying anything." This, no doubt, may have held true of many shopkeepers too greedy of gain, but, as a rule, the Paris tradesman, and the provincial tradesman as well, made it a point of honour to sell good articles, and not to take in the purchaser. Hence arose the title given to many houses which were established in the 18th century, and which were known as *maisons de confiance.* Many of them had been in the same family for two or three centuries, and had been resorted to during that period by the same families. The shopkeepers, moreover, formed part of the corporations and companies in which their reputation for honesty was acknowledged by election to honorary posts, sufficient to satisfy their modest ambition, and enabling them to aspire to the dignity of churchwarden, judge of the consular, tribunal or member of the city council of notables.

As a rule, the shopkeepers led a very laborious and simple life. They were engaged in their shop from early morning, and whenever they retired late to rest, it was because they had been busy with their

Fig. 133.—Pictorial Signboad of a Fan-Dealer.

TRANSLATION OF EXPLANATION IN THE ENGRAVING.

Wholesale and retail manufacturer of fans of all sorts, at all prices and to suit all tastes, for home and abroad. He undertakes all kinds of repairs, supplies the wood and the fancy designs for making them up, at a most moderate price.

accounts. They lived very economically, and made their wives and children assist them in their business, assistants being at that time looked upon as a cause of ruin and waste in a well-ordered establishment. Mercier writes in his *Tableau de Paris* that, "The wives of small shopkeepers assist their husbands in their business, and it suits their purpose to do so. There is a perfect equality of functions ; the household is fortified by it. A woman is the life of a shop." The fortunes made by saving habits were only to be sustained by an equal degree of economy. There were many rich shopkeepers, but they were only all the more parsimonious, setting their family an example of simple and orderly habits. The week was devoted to work, Sunday to rest and recreation, after religious duties had been attended to. The most expensive amusement which a well-to-do tradesman indulged in—and that but rarely—was the theatre. The religious festivals were celebrated by intimate gatherings of neighbours or colleagues. The *Ami des Hommes* contains the following description of these gatherings :—" At Christmas, the family has met together, the pan is ready for roasting the chestnuts in white wine, then comes the Réveillon, &c. Then at Epiphany, there is the haricot bean, and the traditional cry of ' Le Roi boit !' At Easter, there are the eggs which the head of the family formerly distributed to all the household, inclusive of the servants, the ham, &c. At Whitsuntide there are the early fruits. Meetings of this kind awaken the sentiments, cause people to forget the troubles of the past, or to dread those of the future, bring young people together under their parents' supervision, promote suitable marriages, and call up the recollection of past affection and forgotten kinship."

The shops were still as small, dark, and dirty-looking as in the previous century, quite devoid of ornament, and with no indication outside other than a painted signboard. Most of them were half open to the street, or were closed by two or three movable shutters. They generally had folding doors closing with a latch. A few articles placed on a slab in the window showed what was the nature of the trade carried on by the shopkeeper, who, as a rule, provided wooden benches or stools for his customers. He generally lived over his shop, with an aperture which enabled him to see what was going on without being himself visible. By habit more than anything else, certain streets were the centres of particular trades, which gave their names to the localities. Thus the drapers predominated in the Rue de la Vieille-Draperie ; the goldsmiths on the Quai des Orfèvres, and the shoemakers in the Rue de la Cordonnerie, &c. It was not until after the Regency that the various trades became gradually

Fig. 134.—A Dressmaker's Shop (communicated by M. Bonnardot).

disseminated throughout the city, and that in the Rue St. Honoré,

Fig. 135.—A Furrier's Shop (from the Encyclopædia).

near the Palais Royal, were established brilliant shops with every article of luxury that could tempt the fancy of wealthy customers.

Everybody was either rich, or endeavoured to appear so at that time, and those who dealt in fancy goods never made larger profits.

From this period dates the ostentation of certain enriched shop-keepers who, discarding the habits of their ancestors, endeavoured to imitate the financiers and the higher bourgeoisie: "All the leading tradesmen," wrote the Marquis de Mirabeau in 1755, "have their country-houses, where money flies at a fine pace." The Baron de Besenval, however, states that there was not nearly so much luxury amongst the shopkeepers at first, and that they were the last to taste the sweets of the good things out of which they had grown rich. The Marquis de Mirabeau, who speaks in very severe terms of the profuse expenditure in which all classes indulged, remarks with in-dignation upon "the shopkeeper who lies in bed half the morning, and employs a shopman to do his work. His wife wears coloured silks, ribbons, lace, and diamonds, instead of the simple black dress with which she was formerly content; they burn candles, drink coffee, and have their game of cards every evening, so that the shopkeeper, obliged to supply his better-half with all these luxuries, and himself to keep up appearances, charges the extra expenditure upon his goods."

A shopkeeper of this kind, who had made his fortune by an accumulation of petty profits, offers a strong contrast to the trading merchant whom Bedos (1779) represents as controlling the destiny of maritime commerce, "analysing the information sent him by his correspondents, looking over his various liabilities, verifying the sums standing to his credit, taking an inventory of his goods in stock and on their way home, valuing the cargoes of his vessels which are loading and unloading." Unfortunately, these *patriotic merchants* had experienced irreparable reverses during the war, and the Govern-ment had done next to nothing for the protection of the merchant vessels which were furrowing every sea. A great many had been captured by the English, who were incessantly increasing their navy with the view of destroying our commerce and wresting from us our colonies which the joint efforts of agriculture and trade had rendered so prosperous. The Indies Company, flourishing as were its establishments in Canada, Bengal, Madagascar, and St. Domingo, could only maintain itself by having recourse to loans; and it employed all its resources in paying its troops and fitting out vessels of

Fig. 136.—Pictorial Signboard of an Instrument Maker, after Eisen.

war to protect its commerce. Dupleix, who was governor of this company at Pondicherry, and Mahé de la Bourdonnais, who was governor of the Mauritius and Bourbon Islands, were very jealous of each other, and their mutual enmity neutralized the success which they had obtained. The English continued their efforts to destroy the Indies Company, and Comte de Lally, reduced by starvation, was obliged to open to them the gates of Pondicherry (January 15th, 1761). France lost, one after another, all her colonies in the East Indies, and a portion of those in America. Her foreign trade was almost annihilated, notwithstanding the increasing prosperity of St. Domingo, where the crops of sugar, coffee, cotton, indigo, and cocoa yielded more reliable and lasting returns than the gold mines of Mexico and Peru. The Indies Company, loaded with debts which it had no means of satisfying, was no longer in a position to take advantage of the privileges accorded to it at its creation, and, in presence of the freedom of trade which was the base of the new code of political economy, its existence became an anomaly. It accordingly transferred all its rights and property to the Crown, which undertook to discharge the liabilities and compensate the shareholders (February 17th, 1770). But, fifteen years afterwards, it was discovered that this unrestricted freedom, so strongly advocated by the economists, was very prejudicial to the import and export trade; and that while a reckless accumulation of merchandize of the same kind at one point led to a ruinous fall in its value, there was a scarcity of the same article somewhere else. The supply of the country being, therefore, so capricious, the principle of monopoly and protection was resorted to afresh. The King instituted a new Indies Company (April 14th, 1785), which was invested, but only for seven years, with the exclusive right of trade, by land and sea, from the Cape of Good Hope to India, China, and Japan. Lorient was to be the French port to and from which all the expeditions were to sail. The great successes of the French navy in the Indian seas justified the hope that the new company would make amends for the reverses which England had inflicted on the maritime commerce of France, but the Revolution, which was already dawning had for its axiom : " Let the colonies perish rather than a single principle !" So freedom of commerce was re-established, and the India Company abolished.

In the course of the eighteenth century, the balance of trade had been in a great measure paralysed or displaced by the theories of the economists, who treated commercial questions *à priori*, and attempted to bring about an organic change in all the rules and customs of business. The merchants, as it fortunately happened, did not read the countless pamphlets in which these reforms were advocated ; they were too much occupied with their daily business. The corn trade, in particular, was the subject of controversy, and it must be admitted that the jobbery which went on justified the angry

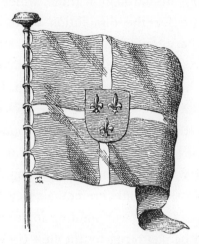

Fig. 137.—New Flag (spotted with fleur-de-lis) for the French Merchant-Navy.
(From *Les Pavillons ou Bannières que la plupart des nations arbore en mer*;
David Mortier, Amsterdam, 1718.)

comments of the reformers. Dealers were in the habit of buying up all the grain and creating an artificial scarcity, without regard to the wants of the population. The famine, whether artificial or real, kept up or prolonged by unscrupulous speculators, was calculated to prove that freedom of trade, as Montesquieu had remarked, was very different from the freedom of the trader. It was said that at a time when the people were in want of bread, while the granaries of specu lators were full of grain, Louis XV. himself had derived a profit from this source. The freedom of the corn trade was not carried into effect until 1774, under the reign of Louis XVI., and at the instance of Turgot. The economists and philosophers applauded this measure, which they had so long been advocating, but in practice the theory was not found to work, and, after the system had been tried for some time, it was found that the corn trade, of all others, needed official supervision. It was not till 1787, at the instance of the Assembly of Notables, that was re-established the system of free trade in corn, which, practicable and even advantageous in good years, is very fatal when bad crops bring in their train scarcity and disturbance.

The abuse of the economical systems did not stop here, and their application was most disastrous for trade, which was further injured by Turgot's measure for the dissolution of the trade corporations and councils (February, 1776). The people, ever blinded by partiality, were delighted by the sudden abolition of these commercial institutions upon which they had looked with hatred and jelaousy for many centuries, and the economists also welcomed this arbitrary measure. Six months afterwards, it was found necessary to re-establish these bodies which had given a great impulse to industry and commerce, and whose insignia had so long held an honourable place in the public festivals and ceremonials (see Fig. 138). The new edifice, reared in great haste, was wanting in solidity, and it was easy to see that it would be shattered by the first convulsion of the social fabric. It would have been better to have improved, by means of wise and graduated reforms, the commercial situation of the country, reconciling agriculture and commerce, abolishing the various disparities of weights and measures, equalising the customs duties, recovering the moneys which had become deteriorated in value, adopting uniform rules for the different provinces of the kingdom, modifying the taxes, limiting privileges, and curbing the excesses of competition and speculation. For the home trade was still subject to the tyrannical exactions of local customs, and each province was shut in by a barrier of arbitrary taxes and exclusive regulations ; thus, Languedoc, as a producing, and Provence, as an exporting province, were divided by contending interests. The cloth manufactured in Languedoc underwent a discount of 40 per cent on its arrival at Marseilles, which city enjoyed the monopoly of selling this cloth in the Levant sea-ports. The cost of transit from one province to another was in many cases as great as the actual value of the goods.

The visionary ideas of political economy and the wonderful projects of commercial science, had not resulted in any practical good. New theories of trade were expounded right and left, the

Fig. 138.—Games, Dances, and Sword Exercises, executed by the Bakers at the defile of the Strasburg Corporations before Louis XV., October 9th, 1744.
(From the representation of the fêtes given at Strasburg, to celebrate the convalescence of the king and his residence in that city, by J. M. Weiss.)

academies and the learned societies proposed essays on these special subjects, which were never treated by specialists. Even the women discoursed gravely as to the circulation of coin and the supervision of the markets. But trade, properly so called, continued to decline. The Government, in order to gratify the prevailing fancies, had concluded with most of the European Powers a number of treaties, many of which were not favourable to the true interests of France. Yet it was expected that trade was to make France rich and powerful. Louis XVI. had intended to create a Ministry of Commerce, for he had not much reason to be pleased with the system of Turgot, who remained Controller-General of Finance, and who, in spite of his popularity, fell before he had had time to complete his work of organization, or rather of disorganization.

Though the higher commerce was depressed, and though colonial troubles had interfered with the weighty operations of exchange and maritime transport, the trade in articles of luxury had assumed proportions which contrasted very strongly with the financial embarrassments, and which did not appear to be diminished by the scarcity of money. All undertakings connected with dress, food, and furniture, with the comfort and ease of life, increased in prosperity. The export trade of the numerous fancy goods which were monopolised by France had never been more active and flourishing. Inventors and manufacturers concentrated their attention upon objects of this kind, which were sought after by the whole world. The manufacturers of decorated papers, painted cloth, glazed metal, silk, artificial flowers, tulle, gauze, embroideries and lace, could not keep pace with the demand. Paris, as a matter of course, was the centre of this fashionable trade. The shopkeepers, by giving unlimited credit, tempted people to indulge in the most reckless expenditure. The shops were transformed into handsomely decorated saloons, brilliant with mirrors and gilding, illuminated at night like so many fancy palaces. The commercial quarters of Paris underwent a complete metamorphosis ; the ancient Galerie du Palais (see Fig. 139), to which the shop-windows of the booksellers, the hatters, and the mercers, formerly attracted large crowds, were deserted; the St. Germain and St. Laurent fairs were only visited by provincials and the lower orders; the charnel-houses in the Cemetery of the Innocents, where the linendrapers and milliners had so long plied their trade in proximity to the dead, were forgotten, and in the Palais Royal, built by the Duc d'Orleans in the garden of his private palace (1782), were concentrated all the articles which went to make up the fancy trade. As Mercier remarked at a time when the shops there were let before they were finished : " This spot is a true Pandora's box ; it is chiselled and highly wrought, but

Fig. 139.—The Galeries du Palais, Paris, after Gravelot.

every one knows what were the contents of the box presented to Prometheus by the woman of clay." It was Mercier, too, who wrote : " The high rents, run up by blind competitors, ruin the shopkeepers. There is a never-ending series of failures. The effrontery of these shopkeepers has no parallel throughout France ; they do not scruple to sell you copper for gold, and paste for diamonds ; their stuffs are but showy imitations of the real article. They seem to imagine that the high rents they pay justifies them in cheating without remorse." This was the prelude of what was innocently termed freedom of commerce, and from this temple of commercial fraud was about to issue, as from Pandora's box, political discussions and agitation, the clubs, riots, and the revolutionary bourgeoisie, with Camille Desmoulins mustering the idlers in the gardens and cafés of the Palais Royal for the siege of the Bastille, encouraged by Philippe-Egalité.

Fig. 140.—Pictorial Signboard of a Surgeon-Dentist, after Maillier (communicated by M. Bonnardot).

CHAPTER X.

EDUCATION.

Public Education.—The University.—School and College.—The Louis-le-Grand College.—The School of Law and the Students.—Private Education.—Education for Girls.—Infant Education.—Reforms and Visionary Ideas.

IT would have been surprising if the philosophy of the 18th century which, under pretext of reform, endeavoured to subvert everything, had not laid an unsparing, and in some cases, a sacrilegious hand upon the ark of public education. The university had been for five or six centuries the faithful guardian of this sacred ark, and now it had to meet the uncompromising attacks of the modern philosophers who were bent upon the destruction of everything that served as a basis to ancient society. Not only did they point out the defects of education, such as it had been organised by the habits and customs of the time, but they were determined to transform it completely, and the wildest and most insensate systems were submitted one after the other to the public, which did not adopt any of them in its entirety, though it used them as dangerous weapons for sapping and destroying the edifice which our forefathers had constructed with so much wisdom and foresight. Even in the reign of Louis XIV. moralists had anticipated that the system of education would eventually fail to produce satisfactory results. La Bruyère declared that "it is expecting too much from parents to count upon them to educate their children completely ; but it is equally absurd to expect nothing from them." He was obliged to admit that education does not change people's hearts or characters, and that, for the most part, "it does not penetrate below the surface."

Great doubts were felt as to the advantages and good results of public education, and they were strengthened by the authority of Montesquieu, who, in the *Esprit des lois* (1748), says : " At present we receive three different or opposing kinds of education, given us by our parents, our schoolmasters, and the world.   The third upsets all the ideas taught us by the two first."   He adds : " It is not the public schools for children that, in monarchical countries, form the chief centre of education ; education begins, in the main, when a lad makes his entry into public life.   There is a school of what is called *honour*—a master whose teachings should always be in our mind."   Duclos, concurring in the criticisms of Montesquieu, indi cated in the following sentences the reforms which he wished to see applied : " We possess a good deal of instruction, and very little education.   Savants and artists abound ; each branch of literature, science, and art is successfully cultivated by processes more or less desirable.   But no attempt has yet been made to form men, that is to say, to bring them up with due regard the one to the other, to place upon a general basis of education all the special subjects of study. . . . . We all of us carry in our hearts the germs of virtues and vices, and it is necessary to develop the former and crush the latter.   All the faculties of the mind are summed up in thought and feeling ; and our pleasures consist of love and knowledge, so that we have only to regulate and exercise these inclinations to make men useful and happy by the good which they would do and the satisfaction which they would themselves feel.   Such is education as it ought to be, general and uniform, and preparing the way for instruction which should vary according to the position, inclination, and abilities of the individual."   Duclos was merely repeating what Rollin had already said in his admirable work upon education, published in 1726.   The latter pointed out that the aim of instruction and of study of every kind is to make men better, "this is the aim of good teachers.   They have little regard for the sciences where they do not conduce to virtue ; they set no store by the deepest erudition when it is not accompanied by probity.   They prefer an honest man to a man of learning." The numerous visionaries who aired their unwholesome theories about education in the course of the 18th century, had not, as a rule, made themselves acquainted with Rollin's book, and it may be taken for granted that Rousseau, who casually refers to it in one passage of *"Emile,"* had not read it.

Fig. 141.—Portrait of Rollin, after Baléchou.

Education differed very much at that period, according to the birth, condition, fortune, and disposition of the children. It was forth-coming, as must be admitted, to every one who chose to avail himself of it, and though very costly in cases where the family were willing to pay a large sum, it was gratuitous, for those who had not the means to pay, from primary instruction up to classical studies. It

was in matters of education, above all others, that the teaching con-
gregationists vied in liberality with the members of the clergy, and,
as remarked by Rollin, who had been in the priesthood before he
became rector of the Paris University, "The aim of our labours,
the end of all our teaching, should be religion : though not always
talking about it, it ought ever to be present to our mind." The
philosophers, therefore, directed their first attacks upon ecclesiastical
education, as being the watchful enemy which arrested and baffled
their destructive schemes.

The education of the people was thus concentrated in the hands
of the church, which entrusted the task to the priest and his coad-
jutor the school-master, who was generally the churchwarden or the
clerk of the parish. Moreover, in all the religious establishments
there were schools in which girls and boys received, from their earliest
infancy, an education in keeping with their position. Marmontel
does not scruple to confess in his " Memoirs " that he learnt to read
in a convent, the sisters of which were friendly with his mother. He
says : " They only took in girls ; but an exception was made in my
favour. A lady of good birth, who had been living here in retirement for some time, was kind enough to take charge of me. I cannot
nurse their memory too fondly." He was then sent to a school kept
by a priest in the town, who, without payment and from predilection,
had devoted himself to the education of youth. " Only son of a
shoemaker, who was a very honest fellow," adds Marmontel, " this
worthy priest was a true model of filial piety. Abbé Vaissière (for
that was his name), after having completed his duties in the church,
gave up the rest of the day to teaching us." Marmontel learnt with
him Latin, and made such rapid progress with it that when only 11
years of age he passed fourth at the College of Mauriac.

Abbé Vaissière was a well-instructed priest, capable of teaching
his pupils Latin ; Berthier, the school-master of Nitry in Burgundy,
whom Restif de la Bretonne alludes to in his *Vie de Mon Père*, was
only a layman, who gave young children the first elements of instruction, and who treated the older lads and girls to homely lectures

upon social and moral duties. Restif says : "As he was the father of a numerous family, his advice seemed to bear with it the weight of his experience, yet it was in reality dictated by the priest. Our schoolmaster made a rough draught of the work, and our pastor completed it. These simple lessons were surely as worthy of admiration as the discourses of the Vicaire Savoyard in Rousseau's 'Emile.'"

Fig. 142.—A Schoolmaster, after an etching by Boissieu.

Restif goes on to say : " How much do you suppose we pay this excellent master a month (for we have never had free schools here, as they have in several places) ?—Three sous for the pupils who do not learn writing, and five sous for those that do. This is the cost of his fatherly care. The community added to this an annual contribution of 30 bushels of wheat and an equal quantity of barley, worth from 70 to 72 livres. Thus the honest fellow had scarcely enough to live upon, yet he never complained."

University education in Paris and the chief cities was, no doubt, far more costly, but it did not take the patriarchial form of a rustic education. There was a great number of colleges, of small ones in particular, throughout France, and the education imparted at them would pass muster, though these colleges did not all depend upon the thirteen universities, of which that of Paris was the oldest (1200), and that of Nancy the youngest, (1769). But the Regents who presided over the classes all belonged to the universities and the Church, and they were not much better paid than the schoolmasters, though they were masters of arts or graduates ; for, as their fees were not fixed, they only received what the scholars were able to give them. Until the year 1719, they had to pay the principals of the colleges for the right of teaching, but at that period the State, in compliance with the remonstrances of the Parliaments, devoted to the payment of the teaching staff the twenty-eighth part of the gross revenue of the post-office, though this endowment was not estimated at more than 14,000 livres, which was very insufficient for defraying the costs of gratuitous instruction. Children were not, as a rule, sent to college until after they had been confirmed, or, in other words, when they were from eleven to twelve years of age. Hitherto, they had been educated either at home or at preparatory schools. These latter, kept by aged ecclesiastics, under the super-intendence of the university were as a rule intended for a special category of pupils, either nobles or bourgeois, though the primary education for each of these classes did not differ very materially. There were, however, a few schools of this kind which aimed at something higher. The Marquis de Dangeau, Grand-Master of the Order of St. Lazare, founded one of these schools for nobles in the Rue de Charonne (Paris), where he brought up, at his own cost, twenty young boys of noble birth, all of them Chevaliers of the Order. Duclos, though of plebeian birth, obtained admittance to this establishment, for the founder had consented to the admission of boys belonging to the better class of bourgeoisie (the parents paying for their education), with the view of exciting the emulation of the young nobles. The bourgeois lads excelled the nobles, for "the latter being too young for horse-exercise and lessons of arms, the base of instruction was reading, writing, Latin, history, geography, and dancing." The supremacy in intellectual studies was not always on the side of the nobles, who even came off second best, at times, in physical competitions. Duclos was a warm advocate of these school republics, and he states that " the young bourgeois, who posssessed greater strength than the young noble, made the latter feel it, and that

Fig. 143.—After School, from St. Aubin (taken from *Les Petits Polissons ae Paris*).

the pupils who got on best with their studies were most respected." These schools, most of which were situate in the outskirts of Paris, with plenty of fresh air and large gardens, were as comfortable as private houses, and the children sent to begin their education there were content to remain until they entered college. Bury, in his " Historic and Moral Essay upon French Education" (1776), bears testimony to the wholesome effects of this preparatory education. "The masters of these schools treat the children very kindly, the teaching is imparted gently, with intelligence and measure. The children lead a very regular life. The hours of rising and going to bed, the hours for study, meals, and recreation never vary. The food given them is simple but excellent."

This, unfortunately, was not the case with the colleges to which boys were transferred from the schools in which they had received so much care. College life was very different from family life. At college, the pupils were badly looked after, badly fed, badly lodged, badly clothed, and often maltreated. The principal of a college seemed to pay no heed to the bodily health of his pupils, as if his only duty was to superintend their moral and intellectual culture. There was no distinction between the boys who took part in the lessons : noble and bourgeois, rich and poor, each enjoyed equal rights, and had to fulfil the same duties when they took their place in class. Yet, as a matter of necessity, the privilege of fortune asserted itself ; and the sons of rich people had private tutors, who accompanied them to the college, and who remained with them in the intervals between classes. These privileged lads lived in a manner apart from their school-fellows, not only being watched over by their tutors, but taking their meals and studying in private apartments. Yet equality was the principle of public education, and when the young noblemen, returning to the Louis-le-Grand College after the vacation, stepped from their coroneted carriages, wearing a sword, and preceded by a servant in livery, who proclaimed their style and titles, they at once deposited their sword in the professors' ante-room, and were not allowed to carry it until the term was over. All the Paris colleges, like those in the old provincial towns, were old buildings deficient in air and light, whose barred windows, massive doors, and enormous bolts, gave them the gloomy aspect of the prison. Everything in these colleges was cold and repelling, the school-rooms, the dormitories, the refectories, and the play-grounds. So people looked back with horror and disgust to the years of restraint and discomfort passed at the Colleges of Navarre, Plessis, Montaigu, or Cardinal Lemoine.

The system of education was almost identical in all the colleges, whatever might be the teaching body selected to carry it out. All the

Fig. 144.—The Governess, after Chardin.

Regents had taken their degree at the Sorbonne or the provincial universities ; they were all doctors of divinity or masters of arts. Their methods of teaching were accordingly very much the same. They taught principally the classics and rhetoric, the course of study being terminated by lessons in philosophy. The poets and prose-writers of Roman antiquity were recited and translated, and the boys had to do Latin themes and verses, but they only learnt the elements of Greek, with a slight admixture of classical geography and archæology. The French language was scarcely touched, the sciences, including even mathematics were utterly neglected, and nothing but Latin and Greek was taught to the scholars who, for five or six years lived, thought, and acted, so to speak, with the Romans and Greeks. Religious instruction alone divided the supremacy of Greek and Latin. The scholars of every class, in addition to their regular prayers, had to recite a certain number of verses from the Bible, " so that the other studies," to quote the rules of the Paris university, "might be seasoned as it were by this divine salt." Rollen commends this practice in the following terms : " It is easy to perceive that the intention of this *alma mater* (the university), is to consecrate and sanctify the studies of the young by means of religion, and that he only retains them such a long time, in order that they may be born again in Jesus Christ." Marmontel, philosopher though he was, recalled in his old age with feelings of emotion the religious habits which he had contracted at the Collége de Mauriac." " One advantage possessed by this college, even more precious than emulation, is the spirit of religion which is carefully cultivated. There is no better safeguard for the morals of the young, than the obligation of attending the confessional every month. The shame of being obliged to confess the most secret faults, perhaps, prevented the committal of more sins than the most holy motives would have done." Even Voltaire, who had been a pupil of the Jesuits at the Louis-le-Grand College, gave a respectful adherence to the rules of religious education.

The Louis-le-Grand College was deservedly looked upon as the best model of classical teaching, and amongst its pupils were many scions of the old nobility, who went from it to the military schools in which they prepared themselves for the army. The Jesuits were at this time in high favour at Court, and they naturally urged the claims of the Louis-le-Grand College which, until the middle of the 18th century, was almost exclusively patronised by the nobility. The magistracy, on the other hand, took care to send their children to colleges where their Jansenist opinions would not be eradicated ; but the financiers and wealthy bourgeois liked to place their sons at a college where they would associate with the scions of the nobility. The course of instruction at the Louis-le-Grand College was not more severe than elsewhere, and was in some respects more paternal and homely. The masters often took part in their pupil's games, and even became their friends and companions, without relaxing in any

Fig. 145.—Tutors returning from the Tuileries, after Cochin.

way the order and discipline which was strictly carried out, with no distinction of rank. The Marquis d'Argenson relates that having ventured, in his second year of rhetoric (1711), together with the young Duc de Boufflers, colonel of the regiment which bore his name, to shoot peas at his professor, Father Lejay, he and his accomplices were brought up before the master and flogged before all the class. Flogging was even inflicted upon the scholars who were learning philosophy, when they had transgressed the rules. There was a whole arsenal of punishments, varying in severity, from the proverbial *pensum* and restriction to bread and water, to flogging either in public or private. Notwithstanding these punishments, which were administered with thorough impartiality, the pupils never forgot their masters and schoolfellows, after having completed an education which left behind it pleasant recollections. Voltaire, after having become the deist which the professors, with whom he still remained friendly, declared he would be, did not scruple to avow in a letter to one of them (1735) that they had taught him " to love virtue, truth, and literature." Writing to Moncrif in 1746, he says : " The Jesuits should know that I have been attached to them since my youth ; assure them that it is not in me to forget my masters and those who have brought me up." Voltaire did not display his ingratitude until after their expulsion, which at first he opposed as unjust and inexpedient.

The instruction was nowhere so solid and so brilliant as that imparted at the Louis-le-Grand College. No efforts were spared to develop the intelligence and zeal of the pupils. They were taught to speak before a numerous audience, and carried on discussions which thus accustomed them to debate on subjects of various kinds. The theatrical representations, which were given with great pomp at the distribution of prizes, and on other special occasions, also had some influence upon the minds of the scholars who assisted at them as actors or spectators. These plays always attracted a large attendance, though they were written in Latin. Father Porée considered that this practice developed the mind of his pupils, and Voltaire was one of those who derived the most profit from them, as he admits in the following letter to another Father (February, 1746) : " I was brought up for seven years by men who spare no effort to form the mind and morals of the young. . . . Nothing will ever make me forget Father Porée, who is beloved by all who ever studied under him. No one ever rendered study and virtue more attractive. The hours for his lessons were always looked forward to with delight, and I wish that he had settled in Paris instead of Athens, so that, even when past boyhood, one might attend his lectures. I should have been a frequent visitor. I had the good fortune to be taught by more than one Jesuit like Father Porée, and I know that he has successors who are worthy to take his place. In a word, during the seven years that I passed with them, I was a witness to their laborious, frugal, and regular habits; all their time was taken up in teaching us and in attending to the duties of their austere calling."

Not only did the Jesuits lead a frugal life themselves, but they made their pupils fare with equal simplicity. The books of the time

Fig. 146.—Pulling up a horse on the snaffle (from the *Manége moderne dans sa perfection*, by Baron d'Eisenberg, engraved by Bernard Picart, 1727).

contain many angry or humorous references to the food supplied by the refectory, to say nothing of the compulsory fastings at certain seasons. The bread was tough and sometimes mouldy; the wine was lost in the flood of water; the meat was never well cooked; and the coarse vegetables, such as lentils and beans, served up with it, swam in a sickly sauce. The dormitory was not more luxurious; the bed being hard, with no superabundance of clothes, and a frequent suspicion of vermin. The class-rooms were also very dirty, and there is no denying that this was the chief defect of the colleges managed by the clergy, both in Paris and the provinces. At this period, the cultivation of the mind was carried on at the expense of the body. Thus the standard of education was very high, and the smallest provincial college, which did not take boarders, devoted the closest attention to the teaching of its pupils, as is related by Marmontel, who passed six years (1732-38) at the Collége de Mauriac in Auvergne : "A custom which I have never seen adopted elsewhere," he says, "gave a redoubled emulation to our studies towards the close of the year. Before being put up a class, there was a severe examination to be gone through, and one of the subjects was learning a piece of Latin by heart. According to the class, it was Ovid, Virgil, or Horace, of the poets, and Cicero, Livy, Quintus-Curtius, or Sallust, of the prose writers. The quantity to be learnt by heart involved a considerable degree of labour." But at Mauriac, as in all other colleges, the *corrector* was the bugbear of the scholars. This redoubtable personage, armed with his birch, was as a rule the brother-porter or the brother-inspector. Marmontel and he had more than one bone to pick with each other, notably when, with several of his schoolfellows, he was accused of having altered the hands of the college clock. He says in his *Memoirs :* "At the hour for evening-school the prefect sent for me, and on reaching his room I found ten or twelve of my schoolfellows standing in a row against the wall, while in the middle of the room was the prefect, who called them out one after another to be flogged by the *corrector.*" Marmontel had already reached the rhetoric class, and, unwilling to submit to the humiliation of a flogging, he ran out of the room, leaving one of the skirts of his coat in the hands of the *corrector.* The infliction of corporal punishment had more than once led to serious disturbance, and even to bloodshed, but the force of tradition and habit prevailed over the dictates of good sense and decency, and the *corrector* figured in all colleges till the expulsion of the Jesuits. This was one reason which made parents averse to sending their sons to the colleges, for even the day pupils were liable to corporal punishment. The consequence was that the children of many noblemen and wealthy bourgeois were educated at home. Their education, entrusted at first to a governess (see Fig. 144), and, as they grew older, to tutors, was far from producing the good results which were looked for. It was very difficult to find a tutor capable of fulfilling duties which were onerous, and which were of a very delicate character. As a rule, the

Fig. 147.—A Fencing-School (illustrated poster), communicated by M. Bonnardot.

tutors were badly paid, and they were not treated with the deference and attention to which they thought themselves entitled.

It must, however, be admitted that these tutors were not particularly remarkable for their good qualities or their abilities, being, in many cases, little better than lackeys, without experience, instruction, probity, or knowledge of the world. But there were a few honourable exceptions, for the grammarian Dumarsais, the poet Danchet, and J.-J. Rousseau, had been tutors. More was asked of them than they could well perform, and their employers expected that their children were to be taught grammar and catechism by men of genius. Madame Cornuel, so celebrated for her witticisms, wrote to a provincial dame, who had asked her to recommend a tutor gifted with all the qualities and talents imaginable : " I have not yet found such a person, but I will continue my inquiries, and, when I light upon him, will not fail to make him my husband." This will account for the high esteem which d'Alembert professed for the tutors, who, called on to take the place of the head of the family towards the children entrusted to their care, devoted all their time to this ungrateful task. One of these tutors, the learned Abbé Blanchet, contemptuously remarked to several fathers : " You have begotten but men ; it is for us to make citizens of them." But in some cases the tutors were dull and ill-conditioned, fond of ill-treating their pupils, and avenging upon them the mortifications with which they had to put up themselves. So Rollin was justified in remarking in his *Traité des Études :* " It is often necessary to entrust the education of children to young tutors, devoid of experience and almost devoid of instruction. As long as they are zealous and docile, gifted with some degree of cleverness and judgment, fond of work, and above all regular in their habits of life, there is no great reason to complain."

J. J. Rousseau was not a tutor of this stamp. He was, during the year 1740, entrusted with the education of the two sons of M. de Mably, and, by his own admission, he did not fufil his task so well as the future author of " Emile " ought to have done. He says, " as long as matters progressed smoothly, and when I saw that the trouble which I took was not thrown away, I was an angel ; but when things went wrong I was the very reverse. When my pupils were careless, I got into a passion ; and when they were inclined to be saucy, I could have killed them. This was not the way to make them good and attentive. . . . I was not wanting in assiduity ; but my temper was not equable enough, and I was particularly wanting in prudence. I only employed three instruments, all equally useless, and in many cases pernicious with children ; sentiment, reasoning, and anger." Mercier must have forgotten this avowal, which Rousseau made in his *confessions*, when he took the part of the tutors, as a class, against the children and their parents. "How much you are to be pitied, poor tutors, and how unjust people are towards you! If your pupil does not derive benefit from your assiduous attention, his parents throw the blame on your shoulders; if, on the other hand, he makes good progress, they attribute it to

Fig. 148.—The Dancing Lesson, after Cazot.

his ability and not to yours. You may count upon being paid in the coin of ingratitude."

After the classical education, which terminated in the Latin humanities, either at college or under the paternal roof, the young people took different roads to the completion of their professional education. The nobles, who were going to embrace a military career, entered the military schools, after they had furnished authentic proof of their nobility; the bourgeois, who aspired to become magistrates, advocates, professors, physicians, &c., or to take the degrees of master of arts, bachelor, licentiate, or doctor, attended the lectures at the university, the Sorbonne, the Schools of Law and Medicine. The two classes again met at the academies of fencing and dancing, and at the riding-schools. They all carried a sword, which they knew how to use when the occasion arose. Duclos, in his youthful *Memoirs*, tells us that he was as turbulent and quarrelsome as any of his companions at the School of Law : " I inscribed my name at the schools, but, instead of following my course, I spent on the fencing-master what was intended for the professor of law. It is true that in this I only did like most of my comrades. And so I may mention that the lectures of the school of law were more neglected than any of the others, though the professors and the lecturers are very clever, and selected by competition." The students of law and medicine were no longer the intractable and daring scholars of the Middle Ages, but they did not deny themselves the satisfaction of creating a disturbance in the streets when they met at the university. Duclos mentions one of these pranks in which he took part. Some archers had apprehended, near the Pont St. Michel, a man who cried out for help ; he had been arrested for debt. A lot of young men who had made each other's acquaintance at the fencing-room, resolved to rescue the prisoner. They drew their swords, and being joined by the crowd, the archers abandoned their prey, without having resort to their arms. When the guard from the palace and the Châtelet arrived, order had already been restored, and the debtor had taken refuge in the Rue de la Harpe. The lectures at the schools were not very regularly attended by these dashing youths, who preferred their lessons in dancing and fencing. The room in which the lectures were given was cold in winter and intolerably hot in summer. Voltaire, who never cared much for the calling of the long robe, did not remain long at the Paris School of Law, and, as he says himself in his " Commentaire Historique," he was so shocked by the way in which jurisprudence was taught there, that that fact alone sufficed to make him turn his attention to literature. The provincial schools of law were even worse. Bury, in his "Historical and Moral Essay upon French Education," relates how a young man who had passed his examination in one of these schools, and who was himself astonished at his own success, betrayed his ignorance by insolently stating to the

Fig. 149.—A Good Education, after Chardin.

professor who had examined him : "As it is so easy to be made an advocate, I should be glad if you would pass my horse." The professor's rejoinder was : "That is beyond my power, for we only receive jackasses here."

The children of the people and the lower bourgeoisie did not often receive their education in the colleges. It was only when they evinced great application to study that they were selected by the masters of the parochial or monastic schools where, before they had been confirmed, they received elementary instruction. Those who were thus selected obtained admittance to the colleges as bursars. The other children were only taught, exclusive of their religions, reading, writing, and arithmetic. Sometimes they received a further amount of education at home, or from the employers to whom they were apprenticed. But this primary education was never very complete, and the lad, as he grew to a man, without making any greater progress in reading and writing, entered upon his career with nothing but his native wit to depend upon, entirely devoid of culture, and insensible to the ambition of perfecting his knowledge. The most simple notions of science were a closed book for the workmen and shopkeepers, who knew nothing but the catechism, and who were content so long as they could write out and sign an account of work done or goods supplied. Amongst the lower classes, the parents did not attempt to give their children a better education than they had received themselves, as the latter were to follow the same calling, and had no chance of attaining a higher social position than their ancestors. Hence, in the towns as in the country, the people were profoundly ignorant, and even in districts where the majority knew how to read, write, and count, they were utterly unacquainted with history and geography, as also with the most necessary elements of general knowledge which, notwithstanding the native wit and inherent curiosity of the French character, they made no effort to master.

It must be said, too, that true education, that which consists in polished manners and knowledge of the world, was only imparted after leaving school and college, and it was for the most part attained at home or in society. These qualities, rightly looked upon as social duties, as the necessary complement of all education, were taught by example better than by precept. Vicomte de Ségur, in his book entitled "Les Femmes," says: "In the time of Louis XV., and his successor, a young man entering upon life made what was called his *début*. He cultivated the art of pleasing, and his father indicated and assisted him in this labour, for labour it in reality was; but the mother alone could impart to her son that supreme degree of politeness, grace, and affability, which completed his education. . . . . To this was due the rare politeness, the finished taste, the guarded habit of talking and joking, the elegant carriage, and, in a word, the general features which made up what was called *good company*, and which

Fig. 150.—The Delights of Maternity, after Moreau.

always distinguished French society at home and abroad." The young man of that period, excepting a few libertines and bad characters, did not frequent the cafés and the gaming-houses. Amongst the bourgeoisie, as amongst the nobility, it was the habit to give friendly parties, in which young people of a similar age and position met to enjoy themselves. "I have been present on many such occasions," says Bury, " and I can affirm that friendships were contracted between young people which lasted all their life."

Female education was often neglected, when the mother did not undertake it herself, and handed her daughter over, without control, to the care of strangers. It was not easy to procure a good governess, even by paying a high salary, and insisting upon an excellent character. The governess was generally more or less uninstructed, and, as Fénelon remarks in his book on " Female Education," " it was not too much to ask that such a person should at all events possess a right understanding, a tractable temper, and a thorough fear of God." When the education was only superficial and incomplete, people might be thankful that it was not absolutely bad, and, even in the latter event, the fault lay rather with the parent than with the governess. To quote Fénelon again :—" Confusion and change prevail in most houses ; they are crowded with servants who are as perverse as their master and mistress are disunited. What a terrible school for children ! In many cases, a mother, who spends her time in gaming, at the play, and in indecent conversation, complains that she cannot get a governess fit to educate her daughters."

The convent education produced excellent results, especially from a moral point of view, and the girls brought up in them, though not better instructed than those who had been taught by governesses, were better prepared to become wives and mothers, even when their writing was full of faults, and their orthography imperfect. But, in many cases, especially amongst the bourgeoisie, great efforts were made to give a high standard of education to girls, in obedience to the theories of the philosophers. Lessons of Greek and Latin were given to young girls, who became as learned as the prizemen of the colleges, and who often turned out intolerably pedantic. Such was the origin of the *bas-bleu* in England. In France, they had long since been turned to ridicule by Molière, but his comedy, " Les Femmes Savantes," did not correct this failing, and in the 18th century the teaching of the encyclopædia was still adopted by some mothers, as is proved by the subjoined letter written by Laurette de Malboissière, ¿

marvellously clever woman, who died at the age of nineteen :—" To-day, after having studied Locke and Spinosa, done my Spanish theme and Italian translation, I took my mathematical and dancing lessons. At five o'clock my little drawing-master arrived, remaining an hour and a quarter. After he had gone, I read twelve chapters of Epictetus, and the last part of Shakespeare's " Timon of Athens."

Fig. 151.—The Nurse's Visit, after Eisen.

The philosophers and economists, who were bent upon re-casting society in a new mould, began their efforts at public and private education, and for fifty years there was a deluge of pamphlets and treatises on this head. The influence of J.-J. Rousseau was not devoid of good, for in that paradoxical work, " Emile," he inculcates the duties which are incumbent upon a mother during the infancy of her children, and though his ideas were perhaps carried too far, they have been found powerful for good in our day.

The system of teaching in the colleges had long been denounced by the theorists of national education, when the Society of Jesuits was dissolved, and the flourishing colleges which they had founded and organised were handed over to the keeping of their rivals and enemies. The Parliament had merely gratified the grudge of the Jansenists in ordering the colleges, that of Louis-le-Grand in particular, to be closed. The nobility and the Court endeavoured, but in vain, to save the Jesuits, who had educated their children ; the King was reluctantly compelled to confirm the decree of the Parliament (1762). These measures quite upset the order of public instruction, just as the *educographs*, as they styled themselves, were launching their anathemas against university education. The publication of Rousseau's "Emile" coincided with the decree which deprived the Jesuits of the education of the young twenty-two years before this. J.-J. Rousseau, in a letter to M. de Mailly, had expressed his views as follows: "The object to be aimed at in educating a boy should be the forming of his heart, his judgment, and his mind, taking them in the order given. Most schoolmasters, the pedants in particular, looking upon the wholesale acquirement of learning as the one end and object of a good education."

The university was near being involved with the Jesuits in their fall, but the Government accorded it its protection, so that the whole edifice of learning might not come down together, but, at the same time, accepted rather inconsiderately most of the reforms which were proposed. One of the most implacable enemies of the Jesuits, La Chalotais, President of the Brittany Parliament, brought forward a "plan of general education," and some of his ideas were adopted, though nothing was done to avert the anarchy, which visionary schemes were about to entail on education.

The expulsion of the Jesuits was followed by a general liquidation of the accounts of all the Paris colleges, all of which received bursars for the cost of whose maintenance the college revenues were insufficient to provide. The property of the Jesuits made up the deficiency. An edict of 1763 adjoined to each college a lay board, which, besides supervising the establishment, nominated the principal and the professors. The position of these latter was considerably improved, their fees were fixed at a reasonable rate, and they were promised a retiring pension, being also exempted (decree of 1764) from all municipal liabilities. But as the number of professors continued to diminish, a staff of aggregates, chosen by competition, were appointed in 1768, from amongst whom the teaching body might be recruited. The Benedictines and the Oratorians had in part accepted the succession of the Jesuits, in respect to public teaching, but the philosophers endeavoured to wrest it from them, being determined to deprive the clergy of all share in education. They had been only too successful in 1789, when Father Bonnefoux, Superior-General of the Priests of the Christian Doctrine, wrote : "Unquestionably, the gravest scandal, and that which will entail the most fatal consequences, is the almost absolute abandonment of religious teaching in the public schools." This was foreseen by the assembly of the clergy fifteen years before, when that body, denouncing to the King the deplorable projects of the reformers, said : "We know that the enemies of religion consider as essential to the success of their pernicious doctrines the deprivation of the clergy of the right of educating the young."

The author of "Emile" is mainly responsible for the disorder and confusion which prevailed in regard to education. The university lost credit and authority every day, though the 500 colleges attached to it, and governed by its rules, contained over 70,000 pupils. But, in many families, an effort was made to put in practice the reveries of Rousseau. The Duc de Chartres set a bad example, by entrusting the education of his three sons to Madame de Genlis, who had already acted as governess for their sister. Louis XVI., when asked for his advice, contemptuously replied : "Governor or governess! You are free to do as you please, and, moreover, the Comte d'Artois is not childless!" The Duc de Chartres did not follow the example of the Dauphin and his wife, the father and mother of Louis XVI., who would not confide the education of their children to strangers. Bury, in his work on French education, relates that "all the Court has seen these two illustrious personages presiding at the education of their children ; they had them brought before them, asked them questions as to the lessons they had been doing, and made them re- peat what they had learnt by heart." It was in this way that the Duc de Penthièvre had brought up his numerous family, and Louis XVI. himself was the principal tutor of his eldest son whom he was anxious to teach the duties of a citizen before those of a king. The last lessons which the Dauphin received from his father were given in the Temple prison, and they were interrupted by the scaffold of the Revolution.

Fig. 152.—The Singing Lesson, after Chodowieski (communicated by M. Eug. Sauzay).

CHAPTER XI.

CHARITY.

Charity and Benevolence.—The Hospitals.—The Hôtel Dieu.—Reforms effected by Piarron de
Chamousset.—La Peyronie, Godinot, Tronchin.—Charity Marriages.—Charity of Louis XVI.,
Marie Antoinette and their Children.—The Philanthropists.

IF charity has existed since the gospel was first preached, benevolence, in the modern sense of the word, does not date beyond the
first part of the 18th century. Charity was a christian virtue ;
benevolence is, so to speak, a rule of philosophy. It was thought
at one time that the very word *bienfaisance* had been invented
by the Abbé de St. Pierre, but he merely employed a well-
known term to designate something which the philosophers distinguished as apart from charity, benevolence being in their
opinion the action of doing good out of love for humanity. A characteristic phrase, which the Abbé de St. Pierre uses in his
Mémoire pour la diminution des proces, proves that he looked upon
benevolence as nothing more than a social quality :—" The laws
should tend to inspire perseverance, work, economy, temperance,
equity, and *benevolence*."

We may say, in fact, that the 18th century was the century of
benevolence. No doubt French charity, which inherited such noble
traditions, continued, during this century of selfish enjoyment and
religious indifference, to give many proofs of its fruitful influence and
generous energy. Then, as in the time of Louis XIII., as in the
Middle Ages, there was no lack of devoted persons who, at the
bidding of the gospel, and impelled by catholic principles, passed
their time in relieving the sick and the distressed, and there still

existed, as there will always exist, abnegation, self-sacrifice, the love of doing good. Hospitals, homes of refuge, and charitable establishments were founded, endowed and protected out of feelings of devotion. But it must be admitted that the spirit of philosophy had advanced the practice of benevolence, which was a manifestation on the part of civil society, and which became a form of political economy. A poor priest, Vincent de Paul, was the apostle of charity in the 17th century; a rich nobleman was the founder of benevolence in the 18th.

Montesquieu, in his *Lettres Persanes,* was the first to describe the system of benevolence when he writes :—"Whatever may be a person's religion, supposing that he has any at all, he must believe that God loves mankind, inasmuch as he has established a religion to make them happy. He must also believe that, if God loves mankind, one is sure to please Him by loving them also, and exercising towards them all the duties of charity and humanity." A philosophic definition was in time given to benevolence, and those who practised it, and Duclos asserts that " the benefactor is the man who does good, and the acts which he does may be considered under three acts : acts of kindness, acts of forgiveness, and acts of service. The *kindness* is a free act on the part of the doer, though the object of his kindness may be worthy of it. . . . The true benefactor obeys a natural inclination which leads him to do a kindness, and in satisfying this inclination, he finds a satisfaction which is at once the chief merit and recompense of his good action, but all acts of kindness do not proceed from benevolence." This is cold and lifeless as compared to true christian charity, which was prompted by the love of God, while benevolence has its origin in affection for humanity. It is hard to understand how this latter feeling acquired so much influence in the 18th century, for the philosophers had not attempted to give it an attractive shape, even when Moncrif, with a view of recommending it to the favour of the frivolous, wrote :— " Charity is perhaps the only virtue the possession of which is not disputed."

The sufferings of the people at the end of the reign of Louis XIV., the scarcity, the epidemics, and the lack of work, would have been sufficient to revive the spirit of charity, even if it had died out. The alms entrusted to the enlightened dispensation of the clergy

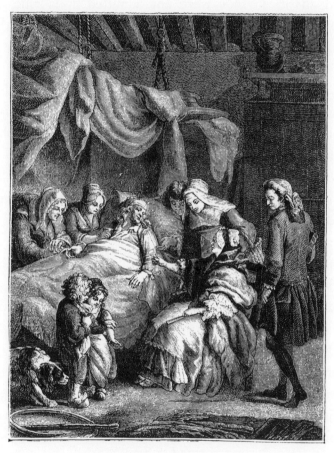

Fig. 153.—The Sister of Charity, after Eisen.

amounted to a very large sum in Paris and in the provinces, and as the religious orders made a very generous use of the ecclesiastical property, the poor were saved from starvation. Food was distributed every day at the monastery gates, and this ancient practice, so touch-ing and worthy of respect, which the philosophers looked upon as degrading to humanity, was carried on until the Revolution. "A crowd of beggars in rags assemble each morning," wrote Mercier in 1782, "at the doors of the monastery. A monk opens the gate, and, without letting them in, pours an allowance into the bowl with which each beggar is provided, there being a general scramble as to which shall get the most." The poor had no fault to find with these old-established charities ; they were not admitted, it is true, into the monasteries to swallow their soup, but when they fell ill they were assured of finding a refuge in the almshouses and hospitals, in which they were carefully tended by the monks and nuns. Even the bishops were not above giving their personal attendance to the distressed. During the great scarcity of 1704, Gabriel de Caylus, Bishop of Auxerre, assembled all the poor of the town and the neighbourhood in the court-yard of his palace, presiding in person at the distribution of soup and bread. He exhausted all his resources, and at last sold his silver plate to provide food for the hungry crowd. He distributed alms throughout his diocese, and on arriving one day at Gien, after having given away all his money and having gone without food the whole day, he could only reply to a crowd of poor people who had gathered around him : " My children, I have nothing left to give you." They replied that they had come not to ask for further help, but to thank him for what he had already done, and falling upon their knees, they received the episcopal benediction.

Such was christian charity ; and the Bishop of Auxerre was but following in the footsteps of his colleague, Pierre de la Broue, Bishop of Mirepoix, who, devoting all his income to good works, said : " It is my duty to give to the poor that which is theirs by right." Many other bishops, amongst others Pierre de Langle, of Boulogne, sold the silver plate belonging to their see, to feed the poor of their dioceses during the famine of 1709. The example of charity which the higher clergy set the nobles gave a stimulus to the contributions of the latter, and the appeals which the bishops and clergy made from the pulpit were freely responded to. J.-B. Languet, Curé of St. Sulpice, who, after selling his furniture, pictures, and works of art,

DISTRIBUTION OF FOOD TO THE PEOPLE AT STRASBURG IN 1744.

to relieve the poor, possessed only three small dishes and a bed lent him by a lady of his congregation, collected such a large amount of money that he was enabled to found the institution of the Infant-Jesus, in which 1400 young ladies, belonging to noble but unfortunate families, received a free education (1741).

The charitable foundations were very numerous in Paris until the middle of the 18th century, but after that period nearly all the new institutions were "benevolent." In addition to the Infant-Jesus community, founded by Father Languet (1732), we may cite the orphanage of the St. Enfant-Jesus and of the Mother of Purity (1711), the Sisterhoods of St. Michael and of Our Lady of Charity (1724), the Home of the Good Shepherd (1717), &c. In the second half of the 18th century, the tendency of public benevolence was to establish branch-houses attached to the Hôtel-Dieu, and out of money given either by royal or municipal subsidy and by private subscription, five or six hospitals of this kind were established which still preserve the name of their principal founders: the Hospital of the Military Household of the King (1765), the Necker Hospital (1779), the Cochin Hospital (1780), the Royal Maison de Santé (1781), the Beaujon Hospital (1784), &c. The Hôtel-Dieu, though twice burnt almost to the ground, in 1737 and 1772, had continued to flourish and to improve, in spite of the carelessness and the stubborn routine of the department of Public Assistance.

The individual who first undertook the reform of this time-honoured institution was a true type of "benevolence." Humbert Piarron de Chamousset, born at Paris in 1717, devoted himself from an early age to the relief of human suffering. His panegyrist, Abbé Cotton des Houssayes, gives an allegorical description of how Benevolence in divine form took him by the hand, and addressed him as follows : " The Author of all things has created you to exercise the difficult and precious art of vanquishing death and prolonging life. He has endowed you with the happy sensitiveness, the determined desire, the rapid and accurate judgment, the profound respect for human life, and the heroic force necessary to him who would triumph over the spectre of human misery." Chamousset had inherited a large fortune, nearly the whole of which he spent in charity. He was a master of accounts, but he made himself physician, surgeon, and apothecary; he possessed a luxurious residence, but he converted it into a hospital. All his thoughts and efforts were concentrated upon one purpose : the foundation of philanthropic establishments. His first scheme was a co-operative home, " in which each member, on payment of a small subscription, could claim assistance in case of illness." This useful scheme was approved of by the economists and philosophers, as also by the Ministry and the Provost of Paris, but the inventor did not obtain a sufficient amount of support to enable him to put it into execution. He then proceeded to call public attention to the urgency of a general reform of the Hôtel-Dieu. This was a very indispensable measure, and Chamousset did but echo the opinion of the public when he declared that " the necessity for a remedy reveals the extent of the evil."

The description which he gave of the interior of the Hôtel-Dieu stirred the indignation of those who had never visited this abode of misery. " Let people picture to themselves," he wrote, " a room in which patients suffering from every kind of disease are massed together, and, for want of space, often obliged to sleep three, four, five, or six in the same bed ; the dying and those on the road to recovery lying next to one another ; the dead beside the living ; the air tainted with the emanations from so many diseased bodies, and carrying with it the germ of many fresh diseases. The air breathed in this room would be vitiated even if it was inhabited by as many people in perfect health." Yet each patient who was admitted to the Hôtel-Dieu, whether he left it dead or alive, represented a cost of 50 fr. to the management, and a quarter of the patients were condemned to certain death. Thus, in the interval of ten years, from 1737 to 1748, 251,178 patients were admitted, and out of this number there were 61,091 deaths. Thus, as Chamousset points out, " it would be better to leave the poor in their own hovels, with no other assistance than what they might obtain from their neighbours." Chamousset draws a comparison between the Hôtel-Dieu and various hospitals in Paris and the provinces; such, for instance, as the Charité Hospital which, where the inmates were separated and breathed good air, did not lose an eighth of its patients, and the Versailles Hospital for the poor, where the mortality was even less.

The system proposed by Chamousset was that the administrative body of the Hôtel-Dieu should merely concern itself with the financial affairs of the hospital, leaving the care of the sick to a benevolent society which, in return for a grant of 50 livres for each patient cured, should take upon itself all the expenses of food, attendance, and medical treatment. The wealthy and powerful body with which he had to deal paid no heed to the well-conceived reforms which he advocated, and, until 1781, stood out against the entreaties of the poor and the wishes of all good citizens. But Louis XVI., in his letters patent of April 22nd 1781, declared "that henceforward 2,500 patients should have a separate bed, and that 500 should sleep in a double, divided with a partition running down the middle. There will be exercise courts and special rooms for the convalescent; infirmaries will be established in the hospitals devoted to out-patients; many parishes will be provided with alms-houses, and the accounts of the managing body of the Hôtel-Dieu will be regularly communicated to the public."

These were the measures of reform which Chamousset had in vain urged, not only for the Hôtel-Dieu, but in respect to all the hospitals in the kingdom. He had been dead since 1774, and the last years of his life were spent in various efforts to amend the system of Public Assistance, which only resulted in absorbing a considerable part of his fortune. He founded an establishment for the sustenance of infants, and he was anxious to substitute for hired nurses a mixture of barley-water and fresh milk. He also attempted to supply the various quarters of Paris with filtered water, and to extirpate mendicancy by concentrating the resources of the different hospitals and creating provincial alms-houses. For two years he was inspector of military hospitals, but he was baffled in his attempts at reorganisation by the hostility of the heads of departments and their subordinates. He also wished to establish in Paris a registry for servants and workmen, a home for servants in ill-heath, and other benevolent institutions; and he also found time to visit the prisoners twice a week, and to go round every day to several needy families whom he was in the habit of relieving. His whole life was devoted to benevolence, and he was unable to sleep, racked as his brain was to discover new methods of charity which were not, like those of Abbe de St. Pierre "the ideal dreams of a good man," for they were all easy of application, and most of them have since been put into practice. He might have said, with Fénelon: "I love humanity better than my country, my country than my family, my family than myself." His family were the poor and the distressed.

Benevolence became a habit in all classes of society, perhaps because people agreed with the maxim laid down by Moncrif: "Benevolence may be looked on as an investment, which always yields a return, direct or indirect." Chamousset's example did not lack followers, the Provosts of Paris being not the least conspicuous. While M. de Vastau held this post "the poor did not feel their poverty," to borrow the happy expression of a councillor of the city who pronounced his funeral oration, in which he said: "The poor were provided with rice and money, large quantities of wood were distributed during winter in the public squares, and the men were set to break the ice and do other useful work, which enabled them to earn good wages." Under the administration of Michel-Etienne Turgot (1729-45) the poor suffered but little from cold or hunger. By increasing the revenues of the city by one-half, he found funds for relieving the needy, and when a fire broke out in the Hôtel-Dieu (1737), his first step was to remove the patients to the Cathedral of Notre Dame. " Now that they are safely removed," he told the firemen, " let us try and save the building itself." His example was also followed by La Peyronie, first surgeon to the King, who converted his house into a hospital for hundreds of patients who, when they were cured, he dismissed with a present of money. " I have made my fortune out of sickness," he would say, " so it is but right that I should share it with the sick." Each town had its own benefactor. Thus, at Rheims, a canon called Godinot devoted all his fortune to providing his native city with fountains, promenades, and public monuments. He concealed his identity under the pseu-

Fig. 154.—The Fashionable Doctor (Tronchin) running over his rivals (allegorical composition), communicated by M. Bonnardot.

donym of M. de Pouilly, who was president of the Municipal Council, and the latter, stimulated by this mysterious liberality, gave more than 500,000 livres (£20,000) of his own fortune to charitable works in the city.

Paris also derived considerable benefit from the benevolence of Tronchin, when that celebrated physician came from Geneva to reside there (1766). " He became the fashionable doctor (see Fig. 154), and was consulted by people of every country in Europe . . . . Very warm-hearted and benevolent, he devoted two hours of each day to what he called his bureau of philanthropy, or, in other words, he gave his advice gratuitously to the poor, and supplied them with money to buy the necessary medicines." (Haag Brothers, " Protestant France.")

The King, the Queen, and the Princes of the blood were always the first to relieve distress. Louis XIV., on his death-bed, impressed upon his future successor, then a child, that his happiness would depend upon his submission to God, and his efforts to ameliorate the condition of his subjects. Louis XV. never forgot this advice, and when at the siege of Menin in 1744, a general told him that, at the sacrifice of a few lives, he could advance the capture of the town by four days, the King replied :—" Never mind the four days, I would sooner wait that time than lose one of my subjects." In 1751, the city of Paris celebrated the birth of the new Duc de Bourgogne. A sum of 600,000 livres (£24,000) had been set apart for fireworks on the Seine, but the King requested that the money should be divided as a marriage portion amongst the 600 poorest girls in Paris. The King's example was generally followed throughout France, and in all the chief towns many marriages were celebrated under the same conditions. As Louis XV. remarked :—" Fireworks afford the people a few minutes' amusement, but a dowry and a husband endure for many years, and do not afford less pleasure ; I shall be glad, too, to pay for sweetmeats at the christening feasts." The city of Bordeaux endowed 116 girls ; Rheims, 20; Chateauroux, 6, &c. The Court took up the fashion of arranging similar marriages (see Fig. 155), and the King continued to give them his approval.

Queen Marie Leczinska was not less charitably disposed than her royal husband, having inherited the sentiments of her father, King Stanislas of Poland, who, like Chamousset, was called " the benevolent philosopher." She spent most of her savings in alms-giving, and her generosity was never appealed to in vain. She was always engaged in making lint for the military hospitals, and in preparing linen for the poor.

Charity and benevolence kissed each other in the royal family. The Duc d'Orleans, son of the regent, died in retirement at the Abbey of St. Geneviève, after having spent most of his fortune in good works. " He is a happy being," said the Queen, when informed of his death, " but he leaves many unhappy beings behind him." The grandson of Marie Leczinska, the Duc de Bourgogne, who was almost a saint at the age of nine, had an innate love of bene-

Fig. 155.—Dowry for marrying ten poor girls, after Gravelot

volence. The first time that he received the monthly allowance which the King had set apart for his pocket-money, he put aside half of it for the poor, saying, " This will give me as much pleasure as the rest."

The Dauphin's second son, brought up under the care of his grandmother the Queen, and his sainted mother, Marie Josephine de

Saxe, had been from his early youth taught to feel that benevolence is one of the noblest privileges of royalty, and he prepared himself, by the exercise of it, to be worthy to wear the crown. After the terrible catastrophe which occurred during the rejoicings at Paris on his marriage with Marie Antoinette (May 1770), he was much affected on learning that so many people had been crushed to death in the Place Louis XV. He had just received the monthly allowance of 6000 livres (£240) which the King allowed him as pocket-money, and he immediately sent it to the lieutenant of police with the following autograph letter :—" I have just learnt of the accident which has taken place, and of which I am indirectly the cause. It has grieved me deeply. I can only dispose of the pocket-money which the King has this moment sent to me, but I send you that, and beg you to distribute it amongst those who need most immediate assistance." His bride had almost anticipated him by giving all the money she had about her for the families of the victims, and their joint example excited amongst all classes a friendly competition of benevolence, which found vent in anonymous donations and plentiful collections for the poor.

The reign of Louis XVI. may be termed the reign of benevolence, and though the treasury was only too often empty, money was always forthcoming for the relief of distress. Amongst all the expensive tastes in which Marie-Antoinette was, with good grounds, accused of indulging, her charity-giving ought to have been taken into account. In the preceding reign, the King and his family had always been ready to give, but their gifts, which were matters of daily occurrence, were necessarily limited in amount. Louis XV. provided pensions out of his privy purse for many retired officers and impoverished noblemen, while during the famine of 1740 he distributed bread to the people in the courtyard of the Louvre, and in 1762, when the St. Germain Fair was burnt down, he sent 100,000 livres (£4000) to be distributed amongst the shopkeepers who had suffered the most. In the reign of Louis XVI., the gifts were more numerous and much larger in amount. In the terrible winter of 1784, the King ordered the controller-general to devote a sum of three millions (£120,000) to the relief of the people. M. de Calonne, who held this post, offered the Queen to hand over to her, out of this sum, one third, to employ as she thought fit. The Queen concealed her indignation, and replied to the Minister that "the whole sum must be distributed in the King's name, and that, for the whole of the year, she would forego all her pleasures, so as to devote to the relief of the distressed any savings she could make." Madame Campan, who mentions this fact, adds, that she had put some money on one side, and "spent in good works a sum of between two and three hundred thousand francs (from eight to twelve thousand pounds), some of which her hand-maids distributed themselves, the rest being sent to M. Lenoir (lieutenant of police), the curés of Paris and Versailles, and the sisters of charity." The Queen, as Weber relates, made it her duty "to implant and cherish in the heart of her daughter the noble qualities which she herself possessed; respect for virute, gratitude for services rendered, love of humanity, compassion for the unfortunate, moderation amid greatness, charity, kindness and indulgence." She never failed to impress on her how terribly the poor had suffered during that winter of 1784. Her daughter had saved up a sum of about £400 for charity, and a part of this she distributed "for the people who were cold, because they had no warm clothes." On New Year's Eve, during that trying winter, the Queen had arranged a number of playthings in her boudoir, and sent for the Dauphin and her daughter to come and see them. When they had looked at them all she said:—"You must be content with having looked at them; I cannot give them to you. The cold weather is so trying to the poor that all my money has been spent in buying blankets, clothing, and firewood for them." The two children both said that, beautiful as the toys were, they did not wish to have them under the circumstances.

The charity of the King and Queen was never displayed more strikingly. Louis XVI. wrote at the foot of a letter in which the lieutenant of police drew a most gloomy picture of the misery in

Paris :—" I authorise you to give all the relief required to temper the sufferings of the poor." The controller-general, M. de Calonne, pointed out that three million francs had already been spent, and that the finances were not in a flourishing condition ; but the King replied that all other expenses must be made subordinate to this solemn duty. The Queen, who had already given away a great deal, sent 500 louis to the lieutenant of police, and a similar sum to the Archbishop of Paris, for the relief of the most urgent necessities. Soup-kitchens were established in the convents, churches, and barracks. Large fires were also kept burning at the doorways and in the courtyards of large houses. Louis XVI. was to be met with at Versailles every evening, walking about in the snow to see that the fires were kept alight, and distributing alms with his own hands. Such an example could not fail to produce a good effect, and everyone joined in aiding the poor, according to his means. After two months of suffering, which had been mitigated as far as possible, the people who lived in the St. Honoré district erected a pyramid of snow opposite the Louvre, upon which popular poets pasted numerous songs in honour of the " august benevolence " of Louis XVI.

The French, and the Parisians more especially, had always been noted for piety and charity ; their kindness of heart prompted them to relieve the necessities of their fellow-creatures. This natural disposition became still more marked during the reign of Louis XV. At this period, according to contemporary evidence (Pr. de Vergy, 1662) :—" the alms were devoted to the hospitals, which, in spite of their wealth, had not sufficient funds to answer the calls made upon them." The managers of these hospitals were in many cases accused of enriching themselves at the expense of the poor. This state of things was little changed twenty years later, when Mercier wrote in his *Tableaux de Paris:*—" There are enough charitable institutions to provide for a third of France. How comes it that, such being the case, there is so much distress ? Does the fault lie in the distribution of charity ? The most difficult task is not to do good, but to do it effectually. The people, oppressed with suffering, lay the fault upon the managers of the charities, accusing them of growing rich out of the money intended for the poor."

Yet, in the course of these twenty years, incessant progress had been going on in the system of public benevolence. Mercier

Fig. 156.—Marie-Antoinette's Charity, after Moreau.

himself states that "benevolence is ample and universal, dictated by a spirit of charity which is very contagious; our ancestors did not understand the active and prompt charity which combats human ills, and endeavours to neutralize suffering as soon as it manifests itself. The Parisian, easily moved by compassion, is always an *alms-giver*, and that in the true sense of the word." He also dwelt upon the fact that " in no century has benevolence and charity been more widely practised." He attributes it to "the publications which have recommended benevolence, making it the basis of all other virtues. We owe much to the word *humanity*, which writers have been never weary of reproducing in every conceivable form."

It was to this sentiment of humanity, to these benevolent ideas, that the reign of Louis XVI. owes two of the best charitable institutions of the 18th century. Abbé de l'Epée founded the Deaf and Dumb School in 1778, and Haüy that for Blind Children in 1784. Abbé de l'Epée's method for teaching the deaf and dumb had been tried at public meetings, patronized by Marie-Antoinette and her brother the Emperor Joseph II. of Austria, and Haüy's system for teaching the blind reading, writing, arithmetic, and music was specially encouraged by Louis XVI., who took a deep interest in the scheme. The King and Queen gave material help towards the establishment of these two schools, which served as a model for similar institutions in other countries. The public took up new institutions of this kind with great vehemence, but, in this as in everything else, an excess of zeal engendered abuses, and, under the veil of humanity, the rich were appealed to for funds in support of institutions of the most visionary kind.

But benevolence, having been looked upon as a vulgar term, was pompously converted into philanthropy. The philosophers were partly to blame for these absurd exaggerations, for they said that the mention of charity and alms reflected upon the dignity of man. Still simple Christian charity was not so easily discouraged, and a sum of more than £700 was discovered one day in 1788 in the poor-box at the church of St. Roch. Prejudice and malevolence, however, insisted that the civil element should be omnipotent in the new charitable institutions, and the monks and sisters of charity were scarcely allowed to tend the sick. A catholic writer (Abbé Bonnefoy in his Treatise on Religion) ventured to point out that these worthy persons " in acquitting themselves of their duties with zeal, belong to

the benefactors of humanity, and, as such, are entitled to public gratitude." The political events of 1788, and 1789 diminished this flow
of benevolence, which ceased altogether during the period of the
Revolution, in the course of which, however, the hospitals were
organized on a better system, excepting that the sisters of charity
were excluded from them.

Fig. 157.—The statue of Benevolence, erected in a hospital (allegorical composition, after Marilliei).

CHAPTER XII.

JUSTICE AND THE POLICE.

Justice.—The Right of Pardon.—Organization of the various Jurisdictions.—Purchase System for the Judicial Posts.—Criminal Justice.—Torture and Capital Punishments.—The Police.—The Lieutenants of Police.—The Municipal Police.

IN the Marquis de Mirabeau's *L'Ami des Hommes*, there is a passage in which he compares the system of justice to the circulation of blood in the social body, of which the Supreme Courts form the principal members, the tribunals of the second order, the arteries and the veins, while the Monarch represents the principle of life. This ingenious comparison harmonized, in fact, with the opinions held by the supporters of absolute monarchy, as they maintained that the Parliaments should be merely docile instruments for carrying out the royal will. This was the idea expressed by the Chancellor René de Maupeon in his reply to the energetic remonstrances addressed by the Rouen Parliament to the King in September, 1753 :—" The plenitude of justice resides in the person of His Majesty alone, and it is from him only that the magistrates derive the power of administering it to his subjects."

Justice was therefore administered in the name of the King, who, however, was never responsible for it in the eyes of his subjects, for, in reality, he merely reserved to himself the right of pardon, of which he often made immoderate use. Upon one occasion, Louis XIV. ordered Chancellor Voysin (1714) to put the seal to a letter commuting the sentence of a criminal who did not deserve the royal pardon. Voysin obeyed in silence, and after having executed his task, placed the seal before the King. Louis XIV. bid him take it back, to which he replied :—"Sire, it is soiled, and I do not wish to resume possession of it." Louis XIV. treated his dignified objection as it deserved, for he put the letter of pardon into the fire, and the Chancellor remained at his post.

There were not many pardons granted during the 18th century, for while this privilege had been indulged in to excess by the sovereigns who preceded Louis XIV., a commutation was not easily

Fig. 158.—Provost of the city, the provostship and viscounty of Paris (Marquis de Boulainvilliers, 1766).

obtained after his reign. Louis XV., when only thirteen years of age, could hardly be got to sign the pardon of Count de Charolais for murder. It was urged in excuse for him that he was intoxicated when he committed the crime, and that, moreover, he was almost a lunatic. Returning from the chase, he had shot an inhabitant of the village of Anet who was standing at the door of his cottage. The next day he went to see the Regent, and expressed his regret at what he had done. The Duc d'Orleans, who was indignant at his crime, told him " The pardon for which you ask is due to your rank and your title of prince of the blood ; the King grants it to you, but he will grant as much, and far more readily, to anyone who will do the same by you." The impunity thus accorded him excited the anger of the courts of justice, and the Marquis de Mirabeau relates that, at the trial of a certain gentleman of rank, one of the judges, knowing that the prisoner's sentence would be commuted, said to his brother judges :—" Let us adopt severe measures, and let the nobles feel our authority." It must be said, however, that the fear of seeing influential persons protected from the decrees of justice by the exercise of the royal clemency had little influence on the decisions of the tribunals, which administered the law without regard to the rank and position of the accused. The judge seemed always to bear in mind the noble maxim which Voltaire so well defined :—" If Justice has been pourtrayed with her eyes veiled, Reason must act as her guide."

Justice was administered in the King's name throughout the country, but it was exercised simultaneously and contradictorily in a number of different jurisdictions, which were the one subordinate on the other, and which did not occasion any confusion or inconsistency, notwithstanding the complication of their attributions and customs, and the fact that they did not emanate from the same authority, apply the same laws, or inflict the same kinds of punishment. Above the Parliaments, which were the Supreme Courts of appeal, and which claimed a political place in the State, there were special tribunals, under the jurisdiction of the King's court, to try privileged cases, suits instituted by direct order of the King, or withdrawn from the ordinary tribunals. These special tribunals were the Privy Council, the Royal Chamber of Requests, and the Grand Council, or Council of State. Ranking below the Parliaments were the presidial courts, which were grand tribunals for preliminary process or courts of appeal of the second rank, and there were also many inferior tribunals, such as the bailiwicks and the seneschal courts, the provostships, and the municipal and consular jurisdictions. These latter comprised the feudal and seigneurial courts which, as a matter of fact, had only a nominal existence, though the ancient *fourches patibulaires* (a species of gallows), which represented the right of high feudal justice, still existed, and were used for the execution of those who had committed a crime upon the property of the lord. But these seigneurial courts, numbering from 70,000 to 80,000, sometimes presided over by a seneschal or a bailiff girt with the sword, only took cognizance of feudal affairs, and their intervention in criminal proceedings was limited to a preliminary enquiry into offences at common law.

These were not the only tribunals which took cognizance with wonderful precision, of civil and administrative affairs, of criminal and petty offences, without encroaching in the least degree upon each

Fig. 159.—Gabriel de Sartine, lieutenant of police (1759-74); after Vigée.

other's functions. The courts of accounts and excise which, like the Parliaments, enjoy the title of Supreme Courts, dealt with all matters of finance, taxation, accounts, waters and forests, salt-taxes, &c. These tribunals, sitting in the various districts, were special jurisdictions, under the direct authority of the Supreme Courts, and they did not in any way interfere with the exercise of the feudal and seigneurial justice of the King, as represented by the three great jurisdictions attached to the marble table in the Paris law-courts, viz., the constableship, the admiralty, and the higher tribunal of waters and forests. The constableship, which was a court of appeal from the French Marshalseas, revised the decisions of ninety-eight provost courts, and the admiralty of fifty courts appertaining to the Parliaments. The higher tribunal of waters and forests, which had the authority of a Sovereign Court, was a court of appeal for cases that had been tried in the twenty tribunals of second order, which were under the jurisdiction of the wardenship of waters and forests. Moreover, amongst the seigneurial courts which had retained most of their privileges, must be included the numerous ecclesiastical tribunals which tried matters connected with Church discipline, under the supreme control of the sovereign assembly of the clergy ; they were the eight ecclesiastical chambers, the primatial, archiepiscopal and diocesan courts, the university tribunal, and many other small jurisdictions, such as the bailiwicks of the bishoprics, abbeys, and chapters.

The royal seneschal courts and bailiwicks, which subsequent to the decrees in council of 1719, were no longer presided over by hereditary seneschals and bailiffs, numbered 930 in the first half of the 18th century, but they had dwindled down to 480 in 1789. The most important of them were made one with the presidial courts, the minor ones were called provostships, *vigueries* or serjeantships, and *governments*. In this case, they were but ordinary police courts. Moreover, in all large towns, Paris more especially, the police formed an important legal body, invested with different degrees of juris-diction. The head-quarters of the Paris police were at the Châtelet, which comprised all the jurisdictions of the ancient provostship of the city, divided into four tribunals : the *Parc civil*, presided over by the civil lieutenant, the presidial court, and the council chamber, alternately presided over by special lieutenants, and the criminal chamber, presided over by the criminal lieutenant. The provost of the city, the provostship and the viscounty of Paris, was the titular chief of this great tribunal, in which the lieutenant-general of police, who was supposed to preside in person, was generally represented by one of the special lieutenants (called gentlemen of the short robe) at these audiences, at which trifling affairs and *royal cases*, that is to say highway offences, infractions of the usury laws, fraudulent bankruptcy, adultery, &c., were summarily disposed of. The courts of justice

La reception des Forcats faite a Gruet a la Tournet·

gruet Soit bien venu

Gruet sen brauade vous jr'ce soir -   Ŧ Tous le ton de la riuier ler lan lanla bis
Voir Vos Camarade vous alée bien boure Ŧ Pour estre forcats

Fig. 160.—Gruet at la Tournelle, with the convict chain. Fac-simile of a popular engraving of the period.

N.B.—J. Fr. Gruet, mounted usher at the Châtelet, collector of the capitation tax in Paris, was condemned by the Chamber of Justice (Dec. 7, 1716) to do penance for having misappropriated the public money, after being pilloried on three consecutive market-days (see Fig. 162), then to be sent to the king's galleys for life.

appertaining to the provostships of Paris numbered at least 1600 officers or agents, and all the posts which they held went by purchase, as in the Parliaments and Supreme Courts. Some of these officials, such as the presiding judges, the commissaries of the Châtelet, the inspectors of police, &c., also heard cases and pronounced sentences, which were valid unless reversed on appeal, but without receiving fees. The other officials of the Châtelet, the registrars, criers, receivers, notaries, procureurs, mounted ushers and vergers, all had their places in the complex and varied operations of this vast civil and criminal jurisdiction. The lieutenant-general of police, who was at the head of this body in the 18th century, and who, in course of time, arrogated to himself a degree of power almost equal to that exercised by the keeper of the seals, became the real representative of the royal authority in Paris, leaving the provost to represent, in a minor and more limited degree, the political principle of the Parisian municipality, and the provost of Paris, who was always styled "the first personage in the city after the King and the gentlemen of the Parliament," to represent in the fullest sense urban and popular justice.

It would be a mistake to suppose that this minute subdivision of justice was prejudicial to the due execution of the laws. Justice, no doubt, became more complicated in its modes of action, but it was also more precise and exact in its results. The only fault to be found with it was its intolerable slowness. All suits had to go through an infinity of forms, most of which were very costly, and a case, in which any technical error had been made, had to wait still longer before it could be brought up for trial, and even then the judges often held it over for months and years. As the author of *Amusements sérieux et comiques* well remarks :—" Quibbling is more to be feared than absolute injustice. The latter, even when it inflicts ruin upon you, leaves you at least the consolation of having a right to complain, but quibbling makes you out, by means of its technicalities, to be in the wrong, while it deprives you of your rights." All that Louis XIV. had done with a view of reducing the costs of procedure and the law's delays came to nothing, and the costs increased rather than diminished. Dufresny points out that though there is nothing durable in this world, lawsuits seem to be interminable, and lawyers make it a duty to keep the vestal flame burning.

There were, beyond doubt, many differences and conflicts between the various jurisdictions, each of which had its code of rules, and in many cases they could not agree as to precedence, but these were incidental questions settled by a decision of the Grand Council. In the beginning of the 18th century, the philosophical school of the

Abbé de St. Pierre advocated an uniformity of laws, and unity of justice, but these were reforms which could not have been carried out without making a complete change in the conditions of French society, and which were better in theory than they would have been in practice. The great body of enlightened jurisconsults were

Fig. 161.—Desrues, the poisoner, put to the question (the boot). Fac-simile of a rough popular engraving of the period.

strongly opposed to this proposal. As President Hénault remarked :—" Customs differ at Dunkirk and Toulouse, Paris and Marseilles, Normandy and St. Malo, and the nobleman, the bourgeois and the shopkeeper cannot justly be governed by the same procedure. . . . . To make uniform laws, what rule could be followed ? To what order of citizens would preference be accorded over the rest ?" Thus no efforts were made in the way of legal reform or judicial re-organization during the reign of Louis XV.; and the hesitating experiments made by the Government of Louis XVI., in attacking the secular constitution of the Parliaments, only served to weaken the edifice of justice, which was destined to crumble into ruins in 1789. Admitting that some of the criticisms levelled against the legal institutions were well founded, it is none the less true that the magistracy, as a rule, was worthy of its high calling. "Of all callings," says the Marquis de Mirabeau, "it is that in which the ancient spirit of unselfishness which the French possess has best maintained its traditions. No other calling does more for the State and at so little cost (I refer of course to the magistrates, and not to all the quibbling clique); it contents itself, too easily in my opinion, with its own self-respect." In another passage, he dwells upon the personal qualities of most magistrates, saying that he has seen amongst them "men who are eagle-eyed in business, of great probity, possessing elevated ideas of honour and justice, a profound knowledge of laws, customs and public rights." He mentions as a case in point :—" I have only been engaged in one lawsuit during my life, but it went through many stages, and this is quite enough when one loses one's case. I must none the less aver that I found the judges to be affable servants, patient and attentive masters, who followed and paid great attention to what I had to say, and, when I left the court, I could not help admiring them."

A modern writer, M. Paul Boiteau, in a clever but too one-sided work (*État de la France en* 1789), criticises the ancient magistracy, condemning the principle on which it was founded. He says : "A great deal has been said as to the system of purchase, which created an aristocracy of justice. Certain regulations fixed the age of appointment, and in some cases the maximum price which was to be paid for an appointment ; but, excepting the limits of age, all these regulations were eluded. In defence of this system, people talk about the *esprit de corps*, the powerful influence of family traditions upon the magistracy, and even of the small cost to the state of officials, who were content with a moderate interest upon the capital which they had invested for the purchase of functions, a few honorary titles, some moral influence and certain privileges." In reality, these preponderating motives, which militate in favour of the ancient magistracy, were in harmony with the ideas, customs, and habits of the 18th century. The magistracy formed an hereditary corps, so to speak, in which the grand traditions of justice were perpetuated, and the magistrates were, for the most part, worthy of

Fig. 162.—Gruet at the pillory of the Halles. See Fig. 160. Fac-simile of a popular engraving of the period.

De tous les corps de métiers   C'est lui qui pour une pistole
Voilà ce fléau redoutable.   Faisant deux cents écus de frais.
Qui, malgré le temps misérable,   A quel diable ce drôle allait-il à l'école
Obligeait deux fois à payer.   Pour savoir de si beaux secrets?

Couplets sung by the people, who were delighted to witness the punishment of a man who had defrauded them.

the respect which they enjoyed. The price of the various charges had also diminished by two thirds since the 17th century; that of President of the Paris Parliament, which had been worth 1,800,000 livres (£72,000), was only worth 500,000 livres (£20,000); that of councillor had declined from 335,000 livres (about £13,500) to 40,000 (£1,600). It was only reasonable that these functions should represent the normal interest of the money invested. Hence arose the fees, which were paid by the parties to a suit, and which amounted, for the whole of the French magistracy, to about £2,000,000. Thus the State had only to pay the small disbursements of justice which, for the Paris Parliament of 1759, did not amount to £3,000. The fees were generally fixed at a very low rate, and as they would have been insufficient to enable a magistrate who had no private fortune to live in becoming style, the company to which he belonged made up the deficiency by obtaining for him, through the chancellor, a private allowance from the King.

The criminal justice, which was administered altogether gratuitously, was more speedy in its operation than the civil courts. The judges who dispensed it needed to be fully impressed with the solemn nature of the duties imposed upon them, for the laws were very severe. Little had been done to temper the barbarous punishments of the Middle Ages, and the executions still preserved a character of monstrous ferocity. It was in vain that the philosophers protested, in the name of humanity, against the penal laws, and they were carried out, in all their rigour, to the eve of the Revolution. The judges themselves recoiled from carrying out the law, especially at the close of the reign of Louis XVI., when the best features of philosophy began to obtain favour. "Out of 100 malefactors condemned to the galleys," wrote Mercier in 1782, "a third owe their lives and their exemption from punishment to the humanity of their judges." It must not, however, be supposed, as he would have us believe, that the indulgence of the judges could be purchased; the criminal judges were above corruption. Upon the other hand, it is said that in certain *civil* cases, the presiding magistrate had not been content with the fees which the tribunal allotted to him, and had accepted a bribe from the parties. The suit which Beaumarchais instituted against Madame Goëzman (1774), wife of a councillor of the Parliament, for the recovery of 15 louis which he had given this lady for her husband's secretary, and which she refused to hand over on the ground that she had never received them, brought great disgrace on the higher magistracy, hitherto so respected, and did it

JUSTICE MILITAIRE.
Iustice militaire est la punition qu'on
fait des soldats coupables de deser
tion ou. de quelque autre faute —
contre le devoir de la discipline. un
des Prevosts de l'armee est chargé
de les interroger, d'instruire leur pro-
cès, de le raporter dans le conseil de-
guerre, de dresser la Sentence et—
de la faire executer. Toutte la procé=
dure, se termine en très peu de temps
et l'executeur pour l'ordinaire est—
quelque voleur au quel on aura—
fait grace.

Fig. 163.—Military Justice ; from the *Jeu de la Guerre*, a sort of *Game of Goose*.

EXPLANATION OF TEXT IN THE ENGRAVING.

Military Justice is the punishment inflicted on soldiers who have been guilty of desertion, or some other offence against discipline ; one of the provost-marshals proceeds to interrogate and try them, lay the case before the court-martial, draw up the sentence, and see it carried into execution. The whole process is a very summary one, and the executioner is generally some thief who thus earns his pardon.

more harm than the horrors of the rack and all the cruelties of criminal justice.

These latter practices were a " survival " of the ancient penal laws, a legacy of Roman and barbarian jurisprudence. The most virtuous and estimable of the magistrates had never thought of protesting against these judicial excesses : they applied the law, neither more nor less, without any regard as to the atrocity of the punishments. They enumerated the various details as they passed sentence, and assisted impassably at the terrible spectacle of putting a prisoner to the "question." Montesquieu himself, philosopher though he was, does not dwell very strongly upon the frightful nature of the punishments resorted to. In his *Esprit des lois*, after pointing out that capital punishment is the remedy for social disease, he merely adds : "other sorts of punishment will arrest some of the consequences of the general disease, but they will not correct the disease itself." Voltaire, on the contrary, neglected no opportunity of inveighing against the system of torture, though he admitted that "punishment is unfortunately necessary ; for criminals must be made to tremble." But he never failed to advocate the mitigation of corporal punishments, and he insisted that the practice of putting prisoners to the question should be abolished, except in cases "where the safety of the State was at stake." But his arguments, and those of all the philosophers failed to take effect, and the question was applied not only to condemned criminals, but in some cases accused persons, from whom it was thought possible to extract a confession. This was the "preliminary question," which was either ordinary or extraordinary, according to the good pleasure of the judge. The "previous question" followed, almost as a matter of course, after the delivery of sentence to death. The "extraordinary question" was accompanied by a refinement of torture, which was resorted to only in exceptional cases, as for instance, after Damiens had attempted to assassinate Louis XV. The boot and cold water were the usual forms of torture. The victim was laid upon his back, and the contents of four or five tin pots, called *coquemars*, holding about fifteen pints of water, were slowly poured down his throat. His feet were tied tightly together, the kneecaps and ankles being first kept apart by two stout planks, between which wedges of wood and iron were driven in with a mallet. The number of wedges was twelve for the "extraordinary question," and six in other cases. The executioner who conducted this terrible operation received a sum of 20 livres.

The executioner's ability and strength were, however, most

highly tried when the punishments were inflicted in public. They took place in the market-places, the public squares, and the street corners. The old pillory at the Halles (see Fig. 162) was still used, and, from time to time, fraudulent bankrupts and other wrong-doers were placed there, with a placard setting forth their misdemeanour

Fig. 164.—Desrues doing penance at Notre-Dame.
Fac-simile after some popular drawings of the period, entitled *Détails historiques et véritables des crimes atroces, commis de dessein prémédité*, by A. Fr. Desrues.

and the nature of their punishment. Persons condemned to the pillory had a fleur-de-lis and certain letters branded on their shoulder with a red-hot iron, and in these cases the executioner received from thirty to thirty-five livres per head. In the provinces, the persons placed in the pillory were often made to wear a grotesque-looking straw hat, and to hold a distaff in their hands. The infliction of flogging was not resorted to very frequently in the jurisdiction of the Paris Châtelet, and when resorted to the punishment was administered in private. There were, however, certain offences visited with flogging in public during the eighteenth century; thus the pickpockets were flogged at the *cart-tail*, to use the customary expression. The punishments which culminated in death were always carried out on the Place de Grève, since the ancient gibbets erected outside the city, that at Montfaucon amongst others, had made way for new streets.   The modes of execution which were in vogue until the Revolution consisted of drawing and quartering, breaking on the wheel, and hanging.   Decapitation, notwithstanding the feudal privilege which conferred on nobles condemned to capital punishment the right of being put to death in this way, had fallen into disuse, and the executioners had quite lost the secret of severing the head with one blow of the sabre (the axe had been discarded since the reign of Louis XIII.), as was only too clearly shown at the execution of Count de Lally (1766).   The custom of burning criminals was entirely abandoned, even in the case of coiners, but the Paris parliament made up for it by burning a great number of books by the public hangman at the foot of the grand staircase of the law courts.

Hanging went on as usual, but the gibbets were not permanent erections, being set up in the public squares for each execution, and taken down as quickly as possible.   As a general rule, and from motives of economy, three or four persons, or even more, were hung at the same time; for under these circumstances the hangman was only paid twenty-five livres for each criminal, and he had to furnish the rope, which cost six livres, and was only allowed to be used twice.   The punishment of drawing and quartering was a more complicated and expensive affair, on account of the horses and men whom the hangman had to assist him in his work.   He himself tied the criminal by his arms and legs to the four horses, which were then driven in opposite directions, until, after excruciating agonies, the body had been torn asunder.   The most general punishment for criminals condemned to death in the eighteenth century was the wheel.   The victim was laid out and bound to a large wheel, the executioner breaking the bones of his arms, legs, and thighs with a heavy iron bar, his dexterous manipulation of which was always applauded by the crowd.   In recompense for his unthankful task he received a fee of twenty-five livres.   This was only one of the perquisites of his post, to which was attached a fixed income of 6000 livres (£240) for the provinces, and 18,000 (£720) for Paris.

A capital execution was always looked forward to with delight by the people, especially in Paris. The most celebrated of these executions on the Place de Grève during the eighteenth century

Fig. 165.—Desrues being led to execution.

Fac-simile after some popular drawings of the period, entitled *Détails historiques et véritables des crimes atroces, commis de dessein prémédité,* by A. Fr. Desrues.

were those of Cartouche and his confederates, the highwaymen; of Nivet and others, who were broken on the wheel (1729); of the infamous Deschauffours, who was garotted previous to being burnt (1733); of the female, Lescombat, who was hung (1755) for abetting in the murder of her husband; of Damiens, who was drawn and quartered for attempting to assassinate Louis XV.; of Desrues, the poisoner, &c. The date of execution was announced beforehand by the public criers, who sold copies of the printed decree; and quasi-pilgrims, wearing a cross and scapular, to distinguish them from the persons who went about singing doggrel rhymes, marched slowly through the streets, reciting in a nasal tone the new ditty relating the crimes which the condemned culprit had committed. The latter was taken in a cart, on the day appointed, to the place of execution, where an enormous crowd had assembled to witness his death agonies. The women and children were not the least eager and impatient to witness this spectacle, which often lasted more than an hour. The executioner, surrounded by his assistants, looked like a nobleman surrounded by his servants; he was curled and powdered, dressed with great elegance, and gave himself great airs. The people followed all his movements with deep interest, and the executioner enjoyed the distinction of exciting as much curiosity as the culprit. The latter was also made to feel whether the people were in a good humour or not, the crowd expressing their feelings towards him by cries of pity or rage, by applause or hooting.

In a city like Paris, the duties of the police were far more important and complicated than those of justice. The lieutenant-general of police being the supreme head of the vast administration which was entrusted with the maintenance of public order and security, not only in the streets but in private, occupied, beyond doubt, the most difficult and delicate function in the state. It was not only in his capacity of magistrate sitting at the Châtelet that the lieutenant of police took part in the administration of justice, he also had the right to give final judgment in many cases of great importance, and nearly all of them were heard by him in secret, and without any other judges. Montesquieu, in chap. xxvii. of the *Esprit des Lois*, says: "With the police it is the magistrate that punishes rather than the law. . . . Police affairs are of momentary occurrence, and as a rule, little more than formal importance. The action of the police is prompt, and extends to matters of daily recurrence, so it is not necessary that it should be entrusted with the application of severe punishment. It has to do with matters of order rather than of law." Fontenelle, in his eulogy of Argenson, who was a model lieutenant of police, draws the following picture of the police at the close of the reign of Louis XIV.: " To ensure the regular supply of a vast city like Paris where many unlooked-for accidents may at any time combine to check its regular flow;

to prevent the shopkeepers from tyrannizing over the public, and at the same time to give an impulse to their business; to purge society of the dishonest people who can so easily conceal themselves in a large city where there is such a scope for their fraudulent enterprises; to moderate those evils which it is impossible altogether to repress;

Fig. 166.—Punishment of Desrues, broken on the wheel on the Place de Grève.
Fac-simile after some popular drawings of the period, entitled *Détails historiques et véritables des crimes atroces, commis de dessein prémédité,* by A. Fr. Desrues.
N.B.—He is accompanied, according to custom, by a Doctor of the Sorbonne.

to wink at what it is inexpedient to punish, and to inflict a salutary measure of punishment when repression becomes inevitable; to penetrate into the interior of families, and to keep the secrets which have been discovered so long as it is not necessary to make use of them; to be present everywhere without attracting notice; to regulate the movements of a tumultuous population, to be the ever-busy and hidden prompter of their action : such are, in the main, the functions of a police magistrate."

Marc René d'Argenson, who had succeeded La Reynie as lieutenant of police in 1697, was the real organiser of the civil and political police. He held his post until 1718, after the death of Louis XIV., whom he had served very diligently, though without bringing himself prominently forward. He was, none the less, the terror of the people, by whom he was nicknamed the *damné*, because, says the Duc de Richelieu, he looked the name. St. Simon, who is frequently so severe upon his contemporaries, did not share their dislike for this redoubtable lieutenant of police, for he says : " With a face which reminds one of the three judges of the infernal regions, he was witty and amusing, and had adopted so well-conceived a system that he could be informed at a few minutes' notice as to the habits of every resident in Paris. He had an exquisite degree of discernment as to when to be severe and when lenient, always inclining to the latter, though he could, when he chose, make the innocent tremble. Amidst these functions of so hardening a tendency, he was full of humanity." To give an idea of the wonderful intelligence of the police under his administration we may cite the following case : A wealthy shopkeeper from Rouen had occasion to go to Paris on business, and before starting paid a visit to one of his friends, telling him of his intention and adding that he was taking a large sum of money with him. His friend said that if he would defer his departure for a few days he would accompany him, but when the time came he told the shopkeeper that he would not be able to go after all, and asked him to take charge of a very important letter, and deliver it at its address on his arrival. The shopkeeper undertook the commission, but on arriving at the gates of Paris, a police agent ordered him to get down from the diligence, and accompany him to the office of the lieutenant of police. The latter told him : " You have got compromising papers about you and you must hand them over to me ; it is a matter of life and death for you." The shopkeeper declared that he had only a lot of business documents, but the magistrate said : " You have others about you ; I repeat that you are putting your life in danger." The shopkeeper suddenly remembered that he had his friend's letter, and on opening this at d'Argenson's orders, he read as follows : " Seize the bearer of this letter and despatch him immediately. I am following close behind him, and we will share the spoil." The shopkeeper fell senseless with fear, and when he came to himself d'Argenson said to him : " I was informed of the whole business, and the two culprits are now in my clutches. You have nothing to fear, but be more cautious as to whom you trust, and if you remain in Paris till next month you may have the pleasure of seeing your Rouen friend and his accomplice swinging from the gallows."

Fig. 167.—Desrues' widow, after having been flogged and branded, is taken, with a halter round her neck, to the hospital where she is to be confined for life, as an accomplice in the crimes of her husband, March 9, 1719.
Fac-simile from a popular engraving of the time.

D'Argenson employed two categories of agents, who formed a small army responsible only to him. Upon the one hand the *exempts*, the archers, and the sergeants, mounted and unmounted, all of whom were armed with swords, pistols, and in some cases, muskets. " Upon the other," says the editor of the Duc de Richelieu's *Memoirs*, " there was an invisible army of detectives, of all ranks and both sexes, who secretly pervaded society, penetrating into every house, moving in all societies and places, not even excepting the Parliament. In this way d'Argenson was kept informed of everything that took place ; servants, guests, and visitors all contributed to supply him with information." This secret organization of the police, as founded by d'Argenson with marvellous ingenuity, lasted until 1789, and the most able of his successors, Hérault (1725), Berryer (1747), De Sartine (1759), Lenoir (1776), and De Crosne (1785), could not improve upon it, and were content to follow in his traces. The only difference was that they endeavoured to exercise a greater influence over the morality of the lower classes. It was by the police that the Marquis de Mirabeau proposed to regenerate society. "The improvement of morals is at once the most delicate and most important function of the police and of the law. Just as enlightened charity seeks rather to prevent poverty than to succour the distressed, so the duties of the police, properly understood, consists not so much in punishing crime, as in drying up the sources of vice, and fostering the growth of virtue." Unfortunately, the police of the eighteenth century, though always dealing with questions of morality, was not very moral itself, and rumour has it that their secret reports were drawn rather with the view of gratifying the prurient curiosity of Louis XV. and his favourites, than of promoting the public good.

The powers of the lieutenancy of police had grown larger and larger throughout the century. The number of persons in its employ had become so preposterous, that Lenoir told a public writer, whom he had sent for to rebuke on account of some indiscreet remarks which he had made in a café before two people: "Remember, that wherever you are, there I am also." It is said that at this period there were at least 30,000 people in the secret service of the lieutenant of police. Amongst these *mouches* (detectives), who were recruited from all ranks of society, there were, beyond doubt, many bad characters and evil doers, but the lieutenant of police might have answered like d'Argenson, when he was blamed for employing rogues : "Will you find me some honest people who will do the work ?" The armed police were also increased in numbers, and it often happened that amongst the archers were discovered released convicts, who, however, did their duty as well as their comrades. The *watch*, previous to d'Argenson's time, consisted of 150 men, commanded by the *chevalier of the watch*, and it was gradually increased by 120 mounted and 160 dismounted men, to whom were afterwards added the Garde de Paris of 930 infantry and 128 horse soldiers. The Guard and the Watch were under the control both of the Lieutenant of Police and the Provost of Paris.

Fig. 168.—Cartouche at the Hôtel-de-Ville before his execution ; after Bonnart.

The extent and variety of the functions exercised by the lieutenant of police may be gathered from a summary of the services promiscuously apportioned amongst the eight divisions of this vast administrative body. The first division comprised the Bastille, Vincennes, the State prisons, the censorships of books and plays, and the Mont-de-Piété ; the second division embraced charitable establishments and chimney sweeping ; the third comprehended the open-ing of letters and the transaction of urgent business ; the fourth had to do with the food supply of Paris, the lighting and cleansing of the streets, the hawkers, the theatres, the fairs, the fire brigades, the hire of nurses, &c.; the fifth comprised the King's orders, and the houses of correction ; the sixth was concerned with arts and trade ; the seventh comprised the bureau of commerce, manufactures, money changers, lotteries, Protestantism, &c.; and the eighth exercised con-trol over the Jews, furnished apartments, the public safety, and the correspondence with the marshalsea, and the other jurisdictions of the kingdom.

There was only one lieutenant of police, though there can be no doubt that three or four different magistrates were required to supervise the three or four distinct functions which the police had to fulfil : political, judicial, municipal, and moral. The administration of the prisons alone, employing a very large staff of officials, was enough to occupy the whole time of one magistrate, whose duty it was to have the *lettres de cachet* put into execution, to keep himself informed as to the situation of the prisoners, and to exercise a strict though occult supervision over the prisons, though the internal management of them was nominally entrusted to gaolers and governors of prisons. The Bastille and the fortress of Vincennes, like all state prisons, were under the command of a military governor. The lieutenant of police exercised a more direct authority over the houses of correction and the *locks-up*, in which beggars and vaga-bonds were confined. He also had nearly exclusive control over matters connected with the press and seditious talk. Barbier, in his *Journal Historique,* says : " The rumours and information collected by the spies in places of public resort and private drawing-rooms, were laid before the lieutenant of police every evening, and the latter forwarded to the ministry any facts which he considered worth notice." The manuscript sheets of news which circulated in Paris and throughout France were revised by the police before publication, unknown even to the editors. The prohibited books and pamphlets sent from abroad rarely escaped the police, except when they had received an intimation to ignore the circulation of these clandestine works. The censorship over the press and literature generally was exercised in a most arbitrary manner, accompanied by unblushing

Fig. 169.—Lenoir, lieutenant of police (1776–85); from Bligny.

favouritism. The only appeal from the censors was to the bureau of the library. In 1785 a royal censor authorized the publication of a " Précis historique sur le Chevalier de Bonnard," who had been one of the tutors of the Duc d'Orleans, and the book, written by Garat, was published, without the author's name, by Didot the younger. The Duc d'Orleans complained to the lieutenant of police, and requested him to take proceedings against the publisher. This that functionary refused to do, but the Duke obtained a decree in council prohibiting Didot from using his presses for a month.

The police which exercised control over social matters was more complicated in its organization, but less severe. The inspectors, who were in too many cases disreputable and open to bribery, kept watch over the gaming-houses, the tables d'hôte, the lodging-houses, the inns, the cafés, and all places of public resort, and they drew up a daily report, which was submitted to the chief of police. The judicial police kept up a correspondence with the marshalsea or mounted county police in every part of the kingdom. Mercier says that in 1782 "there are more than 10,000 brigands and vagabonds; but the marshalsea, composed of 3,756 men, is ever on the watch for these malefactors who frequent the public highways." Thanks to the activity of the military agents of the police, the malefactors had great difficulty in executing their misdeeds in the streets of Paris, where, during the regency of the Duc d'Orleans, people were robbed and murdered in open daylight, and which, patrolled by the police, were now as safe at night as they were by day. Moreover, a company of lantern-bearers was organized about 1780, and the men belonging to it accompanied belated or drunken inhabitants to their homes when the nights were dark.

The municipal police were also very active and useful, giving special attention to the food supply of the capital. They exercised a strict supervision over the markets, and were very zealous during periods of epidemic, which were then far more frequent than they now are, and also during the inundations, which were constantly occurring (1709, 1768, 1774, 1788, and 1789). During severe winters they took steps to prevent the bridges from being carried away by the action of the thaw; and they were always prompt to lend assistance in cases of fire, which, with so many old wooden houses, broke out very frequently. They were effectual in circumscribing the ravages of the terrible conflagration of the Chamber of Accounts (1737), of the Pont-au-Change (1746), of the Foire St. Germain (1762), of the Opera (1763 and 1781), of the Hôtel-Dieu (1737 and

1772), and of the Palais-de-Justice (1776). The administration of
the public roads was not created till the middle of the reign of
Louis XIV., when it was organized by La Reynie; but since its
institution it had continued to improve, doing a great deal in the
way of cleansing and paving the public streets, keeping the sewers
in proper order, and inspecting the dwelling-houses. In 1729 the

Fig. 170.—The Commissaire and the Sergeant of the Watch ; from Jeaurat.

names of the streets were indicated, but the houses were not numbered until the end of the century. Though the mud and the
rubbish were removed once a week, the streets were still very dirty,
on account of the gutters, which were a receptacle for dirty water,
and even for the blood from the slaughter-houses. The police did
their best ; but they had only a limited budget to go upon, and it
was no easy matter to keep 5,772 lanterns lighted with tallow candles.
This was the state of things in 1729, for oil-lamps were not adopted
till the end of 1745, and there were only 3,500 of them in 1769.

They were continually at loggerheads with the proprietors and tenants of the houses abutting on the streets, as the latter were always encroaching upon the pavement, which was looked upon as crown property. It took centuries before the public streets and highways were placed under the exclusive charge of the municipal police, which, in its relations with the inhabitants, acted the part of the father towards his children, experiencing great difficulty in promoting concord and justice, but never tiring in its efforts to ensure their security and comfort.

CHAPTER XIII.

THE ASPECT OF PARIS.

The Population of Paris.—Parisian Customs.—The Drawbacks of Paris.—The Badauds.—The Vagabonds and the Beggars.—Street Cries.—Accidents.—Paris Improvements previous to the Revolution.

In the early part of the 18th century Montesquieu put the following description of Paris in the mouth of one of the characters in the " Lettres Persanes." This personage is supposed to have arrived there in 1720, and, writing to his friend Ibben, he is made to say : " Paris is as large as Ispahan ; the houses are so high that one would suppose they were inhabited only by astrologers. You may imagine that a town built in the air, with six or seven houses the one on the top of the other, is densely populated, and that when all the inhabitants come down into the street there is a nice crush. I have been here a month, and I have not yet seen a single person walking at a foot-pace. There is no one in the world like a Frenchman to get over the ground ; he runs and flies. The rate at which Asian carriages travel, and the measured paces of our camels, would drive him mad. For my part, accustomed as I am to walk leisurely, I sometimes lose all patience, for, to say nothing of being splashed with dirt from head to foot, I cannot put up with being elbowed at every turn. Some man coming up behind me compels me to turn right out of my path, and then somebody else, coming in another direction, drives me back to the place from which the former had pushed me ; before I have walked a hundred yards I am as tired as if I had been ten leagues." Paris was still the populous, noisy, sombre, and dirty city which Boileau had described 60 years before in his celebrated satire " Les Embarras de Paris." The general aspect of the capital and the character of its inhabitants had not changed in the least degree for more than a century. It may be said that it remained stationary under Louis XIV., who had made no effort to enlarge or improve its normal condition, though he had planted avenues along its ancient walls ; created handsome squares, such as the Place Vendôme, the Place Louis-le-Grand, and the Place des Victoires ; erected triumphal gates, such as the Porte St. Denis and the Porte St. Martin ; created new districts, such as the Quartier du Temple and the Quartier de la Butte St. Rach ; raised handsome public buildings, such as the Observatory and the Invalides, and proceeded with the completion of the Tuileries and the Louvre.

Germain Brice, who was reputed to be the best stranger's guide in Paris during the reign of Louis XIV., thus describes the physical appearance of the city in 1698 : " It must be remembered that throughout its vast area there is not a single spot which is not densely populated and covered with houses, each inhabited, for the most part, by several families. This is not the case in the other large cities of Europe, for the inhabitants like to have a house to themselves, and these cities do not contain houses with seven stories such as may be seen near the Grand Châtelet and the Halles, and the smallest corners of which are let very high." Twenty years later, Germain Brice declared that Paris, though it had not yet undergone any marked change, was gradually losing its physiognomy as a city of the Middle Ages, and beginning to lend itself to the modifications required by the altered customs of its inhabitants. The city then numbered 80,000 houses, which formed about 900 streets, and there were 4,000 other houses built within the courtyards and secluded from the streets. About 4,000 of these houses, with a carriage entrance to their courtyards, were let on the average for 2,000 livres (£80) ; 20,000 of them, having only small doors communicating with the street, were let at from 600 to 700 livres (£24 to £28), and the rest could not command more than half this amount. Germain Brice goes on to say that "the rent of all the houses in the city will bring in 20 millions (£800,000) a year; which is an unprecedentedly high sum." According to the present

Fig. 171.—Parisian types.—The Commissionnaire ; from St. Aubin.

value of money, the twenty millions would be equivalent to ten times the sum.

There was. no official census of the population, but certain statisticians had reckoned it, in 1710, at 700,000, " notwithstanding the ravages, during recent years, of war, epidemics, and famine." Out of this number there were 150,000 servants. Vauban arrived at the conclusion, after the study of authentic documents, that the township of Paris comprised 856,938 souls. The annual consumption of food at this period was estimated at 50,000 head of cattle,

700,000 sheep, 125,000 calves, 40,000 pigs, 350,000 hogsheads of wine, in addition to considerable quantities of beer and cider, and 150,000 hogshead measures of corn. There were about 12,000 carriages, and the number of draught-horses was put at 25,000. In proportion as the population of Paris increased, so did the Parisian element decrease, its place being taken by cosmopolitan elements. So the generally unfavourable opinion passed on the Parisians did not apply to the native and more or less degenerated race of the city, so much as to the chance inhabitants who found their way to the capital from every province of France and every country in Europe. " There is no other people so imperious and so daring," wrote St. Evremond in 1698. " They consider themselves entitled to forget to-day what they promised yesterday, and they think that they are the only persons in the world who can break their promises without dishonour." Referring to their want of good sense and morality, he says : " People are always ready to promise and not perform, to accept a service and forget all about it ; there are a great many lunatics in the streets, and a few under lock-and-key. But modesty and good sense are rare ; and so, too, are timidity and scrupulousness, nor can one ever find in Paris repose, retirement, or a true friend."

Montesquieu attributed their singularities and inconsistencies to levity and pride. In the " Lettres Persanes" (1721) he says, " Liberty and equality reign in Paris. Birth, virtue, and even war-like triumphs, however illustrious, are not enough to distinguish a man from the crowd amidst which he is confounded. Jealousy of rank is a thing unknown there. The first personage in Paris is thought to be the man who has the best horses to his carriage." St. Foix, in his " Essais Historiques sur Paris," in order to disculpate the true Parisians of the accusations of levity, want of gratitude and inconstancy, also uses the argument, already mentioned above, that a large part of the population was not Parisian by birth.

This incessant invasion of Paris had been going on for a long time, for it had been complained of even in the reign of Henri IV., but it had increased to such an extent during the eighteenth century, that the economists apprehended the depopulation of the provinces. Strangers did not come in any great quantities until the Regency, but since then their numbers had continued to increase. "Knock at all the doors, from the highest to the lowest," wrote the Marquis de Mirabeau, "and you will hear people talking in every language and

Fig. 172.—Parisian types.—The Baker; from Boucardon (Cris de Paris).

every idiom. I will be bound that you will not find more than three per cent. of the population natives of Paris." People could not understand what became of the native inhabitants of Paris, and wondered whether they in turn did not leave their homes to seek their fortune elsewhere; and the Marquis de Mirabeau, in reference to this point, says: "Everybody marries, but what becomes of their children?" And he arrived at the conclusion that the offspring of the great cities is a pure loss for humanity, and that they die off without its being possible to say what becomes of them.

Yet, with all this, there was a population essentially Parisian in its characteristics, which, if not born in Paris, had acquired the habits and tendencies of the natives. Whoever took up his residence in Paris rapidly became a Parisian. Dufresny, in the "Amusements sérieux et comiques," draws the following picture of the native or naturalized Parisians : " They are always restless and active ; their movements are so rapid that they take up a thousand things before having finished one, and finish a thousand others without having even commenced them. They are incapable of exercising attention or patience ; nothing is more prompt than the effect of hearing or of view, and yet they will not give themselves time to listen or see. The Parisians do not give thorough attention to anything but pleasure and ease ; they grow more luxurious every day." But the distinguishing characteristic of the Parisians was their insatiable curiosity, whence originated the old proverb, *il n'est badaud que de Paris* (Paris is the home of the cockney). One of the characters in the " Lettres Persanes" complains in the following terms of the badauds : "The curiosity of the Parisians is carried to a most extravagant pitch. When I arrived people stared at me as if I had dropped from the sky. Old men, young men, women, children, were all anxious to look at me. If I went out everybody rushed to the windows ; in the Tuileries gardens I had a circle round me in no time, and what with the women who came to stare at me, it seemed as if I was surrounded by a rainbow. At the play I had a hundred glasses levelled at me ; in fact, there never was anyone so stared at as I have been. . . . I had no idea there was anything so remarkable about me, and though I have a good opinion of myself, I should never have thought that I was destined to excite the emotion of a large city in which I was a stranger."

After Montesquieu's Persian, we must hear what Dufresny's Siamese has to say. The latter author writes :—" We will suppose that my Siamese is set down in the midst of this vast and tumultuous city, which hardly rests even during the night. To begin with, the whirl of the Rue St. Honoré deafens him, and makes him giddy. He sees an infinity of machines which men set in motion. Some of the men are above, and others behind; some are carrying and others are being carried; one draws and another pushes; one strikes and another cries out with pain; some are running away, and others are

Fig. 173.—Crossing the gutter after a thunderstorm; from Garnier.

pursuing. I ask my Siamese what he thinks of all this, and his reply is, ' I admire and tremble. I admire because I see so many animals and machines, moving in opposite and different directions and within so narrow a space, threading their way without confusion. It proves how adroit the French are. But their temerity makes me tremble, when I see them rushing over the rough and slippery stones, amidst so many dangers, where one false step would put them in peril of their lives.' "

The Parisian was, beyond all doubt, a great adept at threading his way through the streets. He preferred, as a rule, walking to riding. "The Parisian," says Mercier in his "Tableau de Paris," "learns when quite young to keep his footing on the pavement, to get out of the way of horses and carriages, to diminish his bulk like a true Gascon, to jump over the gutters, to run up seven storeys without losing breath, and to come down like a flash of lightning; but he cannot accustom himself to riding. It is true that the most practised horseman might well be uneasy at finding himself shut in by the carriages at the street corners; and, quoting Mercier again, "it is a curious sight to look down from an upper window upon the mass of carriages of different kinds which are going to and fro; to watch the foot-passengers who, like birds when they see some one coming with a gun, flutter off in all directions, one putting his foot in the gutter and splashing himself from head to foot, and another getting the dust driven in his eyes." These unfortunates could not have been Parisians to the manner born, for the true Parisian had long had the reputation of being able to walk about all day without dirtying his feet, black as was the colour of the mud. St. Evremond makes his visitor from Sicily say : " Even when there has been no rain one often finds the streets muddy. As rubbish of all kinds is deposited in the streets, the authorities are unable to keep them clean. Yet the ladies walk about with nothing but *mules* (slippers very low at heel) on their feet. In former days the men always wore top boots, and a Spaniard, on arriving in Paris, enquired if all the inhabitants were going off as postilions." It was remarked in the 17th century that half the population lived in the street and that all the animation of the city was concentrated upon the Pont-Neuf, between the Samaritaine and the Statue of Henri IV. (Figs. 174 and 175). The Pont-Neuf was no longer a fashionable place of promenade in the 18th century, though, owing to the width of the roadway and the pavement, it was still much frequented. The increase of population had augmented the crowd and increased the difficulties of locomotion in the central streets and business quarters. These difficulties arose from the block of vehicles.

When these blocks occurred, there was no respect of persons, and the ladies, whose carriages happened to be entangled in them, had their ears assailed by the most frightful oaths. The coachmen and

Fig. 174.—The Statue of Henri IV. on the Pont Neuf.

N.B.—The statue, the work of Dupré (with the exception of the horse, which was by Jean de Bologne), is represented as it stood at that period, upon a pedestal decorated by Francheville with bronze figures, which are now at the Invalides.

waggoners indulged freely in invective and often in a duel of whips. Victory did not always remain with the most foul-mouthed, the most adroit, or the most reckless of the automedons. The most dilapidated fiacre would have remained where it was until nightfall sooner than have made way for a court-carriage. Mercier says : " A procureur, for his piece of 24 sous, stops the Keeper of the Seals ; a recruiting-sergeant checks the progress of a Marshal of France, and an opera-dancer would not yield the pas to an archbishop. All these different conditions of men are drawn up in a row, and the coachmen indulge in their energetic language before the Robe, the Church, and the great ladies."

The confusion was all the greater at this period, as the streets were crowded with costermongers, street-porters, vagabonds, street-musicians (Figs. 176 and 177), idlers, and small tradespeople. The police occasionally made a raid on the beggars and other ragamuffins, but they were not kept in confinement very long, and, though released on the condition that they would work for their living, they at once returned to their former habits. A certain number of beggars, the infirm, the halt, and the blind, were authorized by the police to ask for alms. St. Evremond's Sicilian traveller says : " I never saw so many blind people ; they perambulate the whole city without guides, several of them walking together, threading their way amidst carriages and carts as deftly as if they had eyes in their feet. They pester people at the church doors, holding a copper bowl for alms in one hand and a stick in the other." Twenty years afterwards, notwithstanding the improvements effected by Voyer d'Argenson, the blind beggars, though not quite so numerous, were quite as artful, and Montesquieu makes his Persian say, after a visit to Le Marais, which is the most remote part of the city : "A man offered to show me the way. He extricated me from all difficulties, and, when we had nearly reached our destination, I asked him who he was. He replied : ' I am a blind man. But here is your street, and I must leave you to attend the service at this church where you see the people going in. You may be sure that I shall trouble them more than they will incommode me.' "

These relatively harmless persons were nothing by comparison with the vagabonds who, in every disguise and under every pretext, helped to swell the crowd on all occasions. They were not to be easily recognized by their gait and dress. Mercier said that " the callings from which the greatest number of beggars are recruited are those of tailor, boot maker and cook ; but the most incorrigible is the beggar by birth, for, though he may be locked up a dozen times, he always returns to his natural avocation." It was still more difficult to detect, from amongst the idlers and beggars, the dexterous thieves (*filous*), who, to quote St. Evremond, are so adroit that, if one did not feel ashamed of being robbed, it would make one feel proud of having fallen a victim to them. These pickpockets are always punished by the judges, but they are only caught when their hand has lost its cunning." As a general rule, the pickpocket was not taken red-handed, and the depredation was not discovered until he had got well off. As a preservative against these marauders, the

Fig. 175.—The Pont-Neuf ; fac-simile after Rigaud.

N.B.—The Pont-Neuf was the general rendezvous of the dentists and quack doctors (the most celebrated of whom was the Grand-Thomas) until 1783, when the king's physician had them dislodged.

purse was kept in an inside pocket, instead of being attached to the belt, as was the case half a century before. It was indispensable, moreover, to use one's elbows very freely to get through the crowd, which never dreamt of making way. "When we consider this immense crowd," writes Madame de Sartory in her "Petit Tableau de Paris" (1783), "it is a wonder that there are not ten fires and twenty murders every day, and the surveillance over nearly a million people is to my mind the perfection of human skill."

The carriages and horses, the coachmen and the waggoners contributed very materially to the perpetual tumult which reigned in the

streets and which rendered conversation impossible in such streets as
the Rue St. Denis, or the Rue St. Honoré. Another contribution
to the din were the church and convent bells, which were always in

Fig. 176.—Parisian types.—Michel le Clerc, street musician; after Ingouf.

motion, and which inspired Voltaire with his first poetical ideas,
when, addressing the ringers, he says : "What a pity that the rope
you hold in your hand is not round your neck!" The Sicilian
traveller says : "Add to the clashing of the bells the shouts and
cries of the perambulating dealers in vegetables, milk, fruit, rags,
sand, brooms, fish and water." The water-carriers of themselves,
numbering some 20,000, each of whom distributed from 30 to 40

pails a day, were sufficient to account for the infernal concert which
went on from dawn to nightfall in every part of Paris. This was a
legacy of the middle ages, and the small hucksters had even pre-

Fig. 177.—Parisian types.—Charles Minart, street musician ; after Ingouf.

served in their integrity the street-cries, which were terribly discordant. For the most part they were incomprehensible, consisting
merely of guttural sounds, out of which the most practised ear could
make nothing. It was only by habit that people learnt to distinguish
by their cries the dealers in old iron, broken glass, etc. In the
course of a century there had been few additions to the stock of
street cries. The people of Paris, caring little for musical discord,

did not object to the noise, for they were in the habit of talking very loudly themselves. "The common people," says Mercier, "are naturally noisy, and their voices are terribly inharmonious." So the louder the hucksters cried, the better they were pleased.

The author of the *Tableau de Paris* has compiled some of the modern cries which are characteristic of the 18th century, when the people prided themselves on being witty even in crying their goods for sale. He says : "You hear shrill, piercing and deadened cries in every direction, as, for instance, *Live mackerel, just arrived! Fresh herrings, fresh herrings! Baked potatoes! They are piping hot!* (this referred to cakes quite cold). *Voilà le plaisir des dames, voilà le plaisir!* (gingerbread). *A la barque! a la barque! a l'écaille* (these were oysters). *Portugal! Portugal!* (oranges). Add to these cries those of the dealers in old clothes, the sellers of parasols, old iron, and water-carriers. The men cry like women and the women as if they were men. There is one perpetual yelling, and it is impossible to describe the sound and the accent of all these multitudinous voices when they are raised in chorus." The street-cries did not stop altogether as evening set in, or during the night. The wafer-merchant, the *oublyer* as he was formerly denominated, had not quite disappeared, and his doleful cries awoke the echoes of the solitary streets, though his trade was rapidly dwindling away. The public criers did the best business with their sale of official decrees on the eve of a public execution, for they found customers at every house. Later in the night might be heard the cries of the lantern-bearer escorting people to their homes. At daybreak, in winter as in summer, the cries began afresh, one of the first heard being that of the milkmaids from the country, who, owing to the quantity of café au lait consumed by the Parisians, drove a brisk trade.

Paris in the 18th century differed little, physically and materially, from the Paris of the previous century, when Voyer d'Argenson, the successor of La Reynie, took upon himself several of the municipal duties hitherto within the attributions of the Provost of Paris and the Town Council. The police orders, issued in large numbers,

A PAINTER REMOVING; AFTER JEAURAT.

were very judicious in their conception, but they were not carried

PARIS STREET CRIES, by Bouchardon ; 1737—1742 (Figs. 178 to 221).

Fig. 178.—" Carpe vive ! "

Fig. 179.—" La lanterne ! " in winter ; " L'eau " in summer.

Fig. 180. - " Café ! Café ! "

Fig. 181.—A Wood-cutter.

out with strictness and they soon fell into disuse. Thus, during the
reign of Louis XIV., it was proposed to cleanse the streets, light

them at night, affix their names, construct sewers, get rid of foul air,

Fig. 182.—Water-carrier.

Fig. 183.—Fruit-seller.

Fig. 184.—A higgler.

Fig. 185.—An Auvergnat tinker.

and keep watch over the purity of food and water; but though the whole system was beautifully conceived in theory, the spirit of routine was too strong, and nothing was done at that time to carry

Fig. 186.—" Bellows or buckets to mend !"

Fig. 187.—" All hot ! All hot !"

Fig. 188.—" La vie ! La vie !"

Fig. 189.—" Oysters in the shell !"

it out. Thus, the streets of Paris had not changed in outward appearance during the Regency and the reign of Louis XV. The façades of the houses were, as a general rule, dirty and dilapidated ;

Fig. 190.—" Stoneware for sale

Fig. 191.—The cobbler.

Fig. 192.—The Provençal.

Fig. 193.—The print-seller.

and most of them, being at least from two to three hundred years old, though built of wood faced with plaster, displayed yawning cracks, and were half-tottering to their fall.   To most of these

Fig. 194.—"Brooms! Brooms!"

Fig. 195.—"My beautiful pinks!"

Fig. 196.—"Baked apples!

Fig. 197.—"Who'll buy spoons ana larding-pins!"

houses were superadded, at every available point, hoardings in wood
and large iron signs, for the inhabitants always encroached as much

as possible upon the public highway; and nearly every window had

Fig. 198.—" Fresh salad!"

Fig. 199.—" The list of the winners in the lottery! '

Fig. 200.—A cooper.

Fig. 201.—" Death to the rats!"

its flower-pots or birdcage. Inhabited by the shopkeepers and
lower bourgeoisie, they were as ill-cared for inside as they were out.

The court-yards were small, gloomy, and close, and the staircase, to

Fig. 202.—A well-cleaner

Fig. 203.—Bill-sticker.

Fig. 204.—" Cottrets !"

Fig. 205.—The organ-player.

which access was gained through a dark passage with a cellar at
the end, was ill-lighted and unsavoury. The *concierge* was a still

unknown luxury, and the people, who had a great aversion for the

Fig. 206.—A sweeper.

Fig. 207.—A lantern-merchant.

Fig. 208.—A chimney-sweep.

Fig. 209.—A magic lantern.

magnificent *suisses* in full livery and armed with halberds, who
mounted guard at the entrance to the hotels of the nobility and the

financiers, never thought it necessary that each house should have

Fig. 210.—" Green walnuts."

Fig. 211.—Knife-grinder.

Fig. 212.—" Rabbit skins !"

Fig. 213.—Woman dealing in old hats.

its resident porter to act as door-keeper. The door was closed at
nightfall, and all the persons living in the house had their key, or

were acquainted with the secret spring which enabled them to go in

Fig. 214.—"Who'll buy a windmill?"

Fig. 215.—"Scissors, knives, and combs!

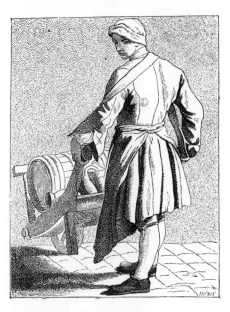

Fig. 216.—A strolling vinegar-merchant.

Fig. 217.—A blind man from the Quinze-Vingts Infirmary.

and out at all hours. The highway was not kept in better order
than the houses adjoining it, being only repaired at rare intervals;

and it was, indeed, difficult to ascertain when the roadway wanted

Fig. 218.—A milkmaid.

Fig. 219.—A hurdy-gurdy player.

Fig. 220.—" My fine boot-laces !"

Fig. 221.—"Good ink !"

mending, concealed as it nearly always was beneath a layer of dung, rubbish, or thick mud. The drain formed in the middle of the street to carry off the water from the houses formed a stagnant pool, which was stirred up by the carriage-wheels and horses' hoofs. Mercier (*Tableau de Paris*) says : "When it rains there is a wide stream, swollen by the outflow from the shoots, and over this a movable bridge is laid. The man in charge of this construction lifts it up to let carriages pass, and expects to be paid a *liard* for his trouble. You will see this at the corner of the Rue Tiquetonne any day after a heavy storm. If the plank which forms the bridge happens to break, foot passengers must be carried across, if they do not want to get their feet wet." (See Fig. 173). There were high stone pillars, some of them hooped with iron, to prevent the wheels from grating against the walls of the houses, and behind these the luckless pedestrian was often glad to take refuge. The carriage-way was at many points narrowed by the flights of steps leading up to the houses, and by mounting-blocks, which were no longer used now that the physicians, lawyers, and wealthy bourgeois had given up the habit of riding about on mules, on account of the crowd of vehicles. For the same reason sedan-chairs were rarely used, except in some remote districts, such as the Marais and the Louvre.

Accidents were much more numerous than at present, notwithstanding the precautions of the police ; but, as in other matters, routine was too strong for them. There was no improvement in 1789, and Father Manuel, in his "Police de Paris dévoilée," did not exaggerate when he wrote : "It is surprising that the police allowed so many abuses to exist—the absence of pavements, the shoots pouring the rainfall on to the people's head, the overhanging gables, the houses built on the bridges (see Fig. 222), the lamps left unlighted, the infiltrations from the cesspools, etc." No account was kept of the number of people run over in the streets. There were certain points where one or two people met with such accidents every day. Whether killed or wounded, they were conveyed to the dead-house of the Châtelet, where also were deposited the bodies picked up in the Seine, without any effort being made to recall them to life. The Town Council gave a silver medal to any one who had saved another from drowning; but a regular system of aid was only established in 1782, at the cost of a former councillor called Pia, who erected on the banks of the river several huts which were supplied with everything that might be instrumental in restoring animation. In many cases charitable persons volunteered to care for

Fig. 222.—The Pont St. Michel; after Martinet.

N.B.—The houses built on this bridge were demolished in the reign of Louis XVI.

those who had been wounded in a street accident, and to take them to the Hôtel-Dieu without waiting for the arrival of the commissioner of police, who took formal evidence of the accident. At the public ceremonies there were always many persons more or less injured in the crush; but this was not looked upon as a matter of much importance. When death was evidently the result of crime the police took more active steps, for nocturnal attacks on foot-passengers were not so frequent as might have been expected, and, thanks to the vigilance of the watch, the streets of Paris were almost as secure at night as they were by day. This was not the case during the last years of the reign of Louis XIV., when it was dangerous to cross the Pont-Neuf after midnight, and during the Regency the poet

Vergier, who was a naval commissioner, was assassinated on his way home from a supper party by some of the Cartouche band, close to the Rue Montmartre.

Most of the streets were very dark when there was no moon, for, with the exception of a few lamps suspended from private houses (see Fig. 244), they were only lighted by occasional lanterns, con-

Fig. 223.—A street-porter ; after Bouchardon.

taining a candle, which swung twenty feet above the ground. In 1745 these lanterns were lighted with oil made from the intestines of the animals killed in the slaughter-houses, but they were never all kept burning, and on moonlight nights they were sometimes not lighted at all. The fears of the belated passengers were often excited by the spectral-looking signboards, many of which projected far into the streets. Each house had its signboard, which answered the purpose of a number, and some of them were eight or ten feet in diameter, painted or gilded, and covered with inscriptions, the grammar and orthography of which were not always unexceptionable.

It was only after long efforts that these signboards could be prevented from projecting on the streets, and that the system of numbering the houses could be carried into execution.

There was no rule as to the whitewashing or colouring of the house-fronts ; most of them were begrimed with smoke, but a few were painted or whitewashed at intervals, though this did not

Fig. 224.—Hotel lamp, in ornamental wrought iron.

prevent the bill-stickers from availing themselves of any walls that they found ready to their hand. To this was owing a marvellous display of posters of all colours, many of these posters containing sarcastic references to political and other topics, which were greatly appreciated by the scandal-loving public. It need hardly be said that the seditious posters were not placed on the walls by any of the forty sworn billstickers of the Châtelet, the authors of which incurred the risk of a heavy fine, and even the pillory.

However compact and noisy might be the crowd of foot-passengers and vehicles in the street, they immediately made way for a

funeral procession, the approach of which was always heralded by the
chant of the priest who accompanied the body. There was a moment
of silence as the cortége passed by, and everyone, uncovering and
bowing in the presence of death, muttered a prayer and made the
sign of the cross. The same respectful attitude was maintained by
the crowd when the tinkling of a bell announced the passage of a
priest on his way to administer a dying person. A feeling of devotion still prevailed amongst the people, who, in spite of their natural
roughness, never failed to greet with deference the members of the
clergy whom they met in the streets, or to kneel in humility before
the viaticum. But as the Parisian must always be inquisitive and
badaud, he would follow the priest and the viaticum to the house of
the sick person, just as he would follow the funeral to the cemetery.

There was much luxury in Paris during the last years of the
seventeenth century, and the Sicilian traveller (1698) is made to say :
" There is so much luxury here that whoever would wish to enrich
300 cities has only to destroy Paris." He added, it is true, that the
chief developments of this luxury were in respect to good living,
wearing apparel, and equipages. The luxury of the rich was concentrated upon their homes ; they did little to improve the general
condition of the city. Voltaire complained in 1749 of the selfishness
of the Parisians in this respect, and in his treatise on the beautifying
of Paris he asks : " Whose duty is it to improve the city, if not of
those inhabitants who enjoy within its walls all that opulence and
amusements can procure ? We need public markets, fountains
giving pure water, roomy crossways, and theatres. The narrow and
squalid streets should be widened, so as to open up the view of the
public buildings which are concealed from sight, and to permit the
erection of new ones." Voltaire enumerated all that was most
lacking in Paris, which, as he said, contained wherewith to ransom a
kingdom. Upon the one hand was the Louvre, the façade of which,
a monument to the greatness of Louis XIV., the zeal of Colbert,
and the genius of Perrault, was concealed from view by buildings
only worthy of Goths and Vandals ; while upon the other were

rudely constructed theatres, difficult alike of ingress and egress. The public markets were situated in narrow and dirty streets ; many large districts had neither public squares nor statues, and the centre of the city, with the gloomy houses all huddled together, was repre-

Fig. 225.—The psalm-singer ; after Cochin.

sentative of a barbarous epoch. Voltaire was right, but his advice was not immediately followed, though it was backed up by the Marquis de Mirabeau, who, writing six years later, declared :— "Excepting the quays and some of the bridges, what is there ? There are three theatres, two of which are tennis-courts, whilst the third is a monument of Cardinal de Richelieu's paternal affection for a play which he had adopted ; they have neither size, nor accommodation, nor proper ingress and egress. The town-hall is fit for a third-rate provincial city; there is no place for public festivities, no fountain that would be thought sufficient for a small village. In a word, the beauties of this great city are so disseminated that they do not reflect lustre upon each other."

These remonstrances produced some effect in the end, and,

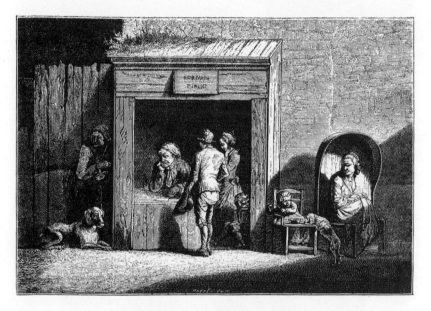

Fig. 226.—The public letter-writer; after Boissieu.

N.B.—The ordinary letter cost 5 sous; a petition to the king or his ministers was charged 12 sous, "because it was necessary to make it more stylish."

dating from 1770, new houses, new streets, and fresh districts, were gradually built. Building became the fashionable mania. Yet with all this the population did not increase. The author of "Petit tableau de Paris" in 1783 says: "There are 32,000 apartments, and houses are being built in all directions. This is the mode in which luxury now develops itself." Much money was also expended upon carriages and horses at this period, and the writer of "Diogenes in Paris" (1787) says: "The gentleman of quality who would formerly be content with six or eight horses, now has thrice the number; many bourgeois have ten or a dozen carriage horses and several hacks, with which they career through the streets." The circulation in the streets was not so often impeded, for though the number of carriages was much greater, the police had been able to enforce better regulations. Paris had never been safer, by day and by night, or better lighted; the public health had never been better cared for; the city had never been more brilliant and magnificent. The dome of the church of St. Geneviève was being completed, and, as Mercier prophetically declared in 1782, "there was some talk of pulling down the execrable Bastille."

Fig. 227.—The little boot-cleaner ; after Bouchardon.

CHAPTER XIV.

THE FÊTE-DAYS AND THE AMUSEMENTS OF PARIS.

The Amusements of Paris.—Holidays and fixed Fête Days.—Guinguettes, Cabarets, and Cafés.—The Places of Resort in the Suburbs.—The Paris Promenades; the Champs Elysées, the Tuileries, the Palais Royal, and the Boulevards.—The St. Germain, St. Laurent, and St. Ovide Fairs, or Bazaars.—The Quacks and the Amusements of the Fairs.—Dancing Places.—Wauxhall and the Colisée.—Horse Races and Reviews.—Balloons.—Fireworks and Illuminations.

MONTESQUIEU, writing in 1745 to an Italian prelate, said, " I shall not go to Paris for a year at least, for I have not the money to spend in that city, which eats up the provinces and claims to amuse, because it makes one forget that one lives." In his "Lettres persanes," written five-and-twenty years before, he declared : " Paris is perhaps the most sensual city in the world, and the one in which pleasure is carried to the highest pitch ; but at the same time it is the city in which one leads the hardest life." For, in fact, excepting strangers on a visit to the capital, everybody in Paris worked hard, though, after their work was over, they endeavoured to amuse themselves as much as possible. During the week the wealthy alone could find time for pleasure. Their reception-rooms were open every day, their carriages were brought to the door and their table was laid ; they paid and received visits, drove, dined, had friends to supper, passed their evenings at play or in conversation at their clubs, or went to one of the theatres. But the industrial classes and the working population had only Sundays and fête-days for their amusement. Paris was, nevertheless, looked upon as the most lively city in Europe, and it was for this reason that foreigners flocked to it from all parts of the Continent. " Paris is the finest theatre in the world," says Bastide in " Les choses comme on doit les voir" (1787), and he adds : "Marvellously decorated in harmony with its size, it attracts the mind by the pleasures of vision, presenting scenic effects in which the Frenchman and the foreigner, grouped together, display every variety of genius and taste, depicting to all nations their habits, vices, duties and pleasures." Yet it must

Fig. 228.—The cocoa-seller ; after Poisson. "All fresh ! Who'll buy a drink? Two goes for a *liard!*"

be added, that, in spite of the number of strangers agglomerated amongst the population of the capital, Paris was not a cosmopolitan city, and that everything in it was essentially Parisian.

The Sundays and the fête days, which the people of Paris devoted specially to their amusements, represented in reality a third of the whole year, for the holy days, of which the Church authorized or tolerated the observance, added to those which were obligatory, were so frequent that the economists and philosophers might plausibly argue that the ecclesiastical authorities should be called upon to reduce the number. In his circular to all the magistrates of the kingdom, Voltaire, who was opposed to this multiplicity of holy days, stated (1756), "Twenty fête days too many in the country condemn to inactivity and expose to dissipation twenty times a year ten millions of working-men, each of whom would earn five pence a day, and this gives a total of 180,000,000 livres (£7,200,000) lost to the State in the course of a twelvemonth. This painful fact is beyond all doubt." The Marquis de Mirabeau, though in milder terms, makes a similar complaint in his "Ami des Hommes," stating that "Skilled artizans, such as jewellers, goldsmiths, &c., spend a great deal on Sundays and holy days in repasts, at which there is no stint of foreign wines, &c. Their wives and daughters take part in these festivals. The lower order of working men frequent the *guinguettes*, licensed places of dissipation, which, it is rumoured, the authorities tolerate because of the taxes levied on them. They all go home tipsy and are unfit for work the next day. Employers of labour will tell you that their men work half time on Saturday and on Monday sleep off the effects of their dissipation ; they are not up to much on Tuesday, and if there should happen to be a saint's-day in the middle of the week they do not see anything of them the other four days."

The people were, as a rule, very regular in their attendance at mass on Sundays and holy days, though they did not, on that account, deprive themselves of amusement in the after part of the day. Mercier admits that the people were good Catholics, for, writing in 1782, he says, "The people still attend mass, but they are less regular at vespers, this because they are obliged to remain standing or else pay for the hire of a chair, and the demand of six sous for the use of one during the sermon is very much resented. The churches are empty, except on solemn occasions. During the octave of the Corpus-Christi there are large congregations at evening prayer and for the elevation of the host." This proves that the churches were crowded on Sundays and holy days, even at so short an interval from the Revolution which attacked all the principles of religious faith.

The French clergy, in compliance with the incessant remonstrances of the economists, had agreed to the suppression of fourteen obligatory fête days ; but this concession had little effect, and was not well received by those whom it affected the most, for the artizans and lower classes did not object to the large number of fête days, each of which brought them a suspension from work.   The trade corporations, 180 in all, had their patron-saints, in honour of whom they observed at least one day in the year, the ceremony beginning in the church or chapel dedicated to the particular saint, and terminating with a banquet and other amusements.   Some of these fêtes were made an excuse for excursions to the localities on the outskirts of Paris, the trade societies walking there in procession with their banners and insignia.   Though the company on these occasions did not, as a rule, indulge in wild excesses, the temptation to drunkenness and disorder was very great.   Mercier tells the story of a cobbler who, picking up a drunken man out of the gutter on a week day, exclaimed with a sigh, " And to think that I shall be in this state on Sunday !"   There was little drunkenness in the streets previous to the Revolution, and all intoxicated persons were taken to the watch-house, from which they were only released on payment of a fine.   The regulations were still more severe in the reign of Louis XIII., when all drunken persons were imprisoned and kept on bread and water, and, if it was a second offence, flogged.   The writers of the 18th century bear unanimous testimony to the relative sobriety of the people.   The Marquis de Caraccioli in his " Voyage de Raison " (1772), says, " The amusements of the people are not of a baneful tendency, and the artizan enjoys himself in a fairly innocent manner.   In this respect he is much above the middle classes in London and Amsterdam.   This is due to the influence of a well-conceived education and to the natural good humour of the French. Every nation that is fond of laughing is sociable."

The *guinguettes* differed from the cabarets (taverns), to which people resorted for eating and drinking, and which were transformed into wine-shops.   The guinguette was much smaller, and the frequenters, taking their refreshments at tables, were regaled with dancing and singing. These establishments were especially numerous in the faubourgs, and at the approaches to the barriers, as at these places the wine and spirituous liquors did not pay octroi-duty. The guinguette merely consisted, in most cases, of a large tent, around the inside of which were long rows of rough deal tables, a place being left vacant in the centre of the tent for the dancers, whose orchestra was made up of a squeaky violin and a discordant flute. The guinguettes outside Paris were more frequented, on account of their rustic aspect; they were arbours, hidden in greenery, standing in a garden or shrubbery. This is why they were called *Courtilles*, which means plots of ground planted with trees. There was the Grande Courtille at the end of the Faubourg du Temple, on the road to Belleville, and the Petite Courtille, near the Porcherons, on the road to Clichy. The most celebrated of these guinguettes was that of the *Tambour Royal*, kept by Ramponeau at the Courtille des Porcherons. This tavern-keeper was immensely popular in his day; and M. Victor Fournel relates that "his sense of humour, his witty remarks, his good-tempered, fat face, his Silenus-like neck, and the gorgeous signboard upon which he was represented astride a hogshead, contributed, not less than the reputation of his cellar, to make his tavern a favourite resort of choice spirits. All Paris went to see his establishment, and brilliant equipages might be seen at his door. The great people went there, just as they went to the markets and the Quai de Gesvres, to hear in all its native beauty the slang which the works of Vadé had made fashionable, and to which the younger scions of the nobility had become accustomed during their dances with the young women who sold fish and butter at the markets (see full-page engraving). The nobles and the great ladies occasionally condescended to come and taste Ramponeau's white wine, and join in the amusements of the people. The latter were always well represented at this tavern, where the wine was good, and to be had for 3½ sous a pint, which was a sou less than elsewhere. The Porcherons and Courtille dancing-places retained their renown until

THE MARCHÉ DES INNOCENTS; AFTER JEAURAT.

the Revolution, and Marie-Antoinette was taken there more than
once by her brother-in-law, the Comte d'Artois, her incognito being
respected by the visitors who happened to recognise her. The
Queen often said that she had never enjoyed herself so much

Fig. 229.—Ramponeau's tavern at La Courtille ; view from outside.   Fac-simile from a popular drawing.

as on the night of Shrove-Tuesday, when she was present at the
course in the Grand-Salon des Porcherons.   The *course*, which
brought the ball to a close, was a wild farandole, in which five or
six hundred people, joining hands, whirled round the room at full
speed, treading under their feet those who had the misfortune to fall
down.

   A different, though often not less noisy class of people were to
be met with in the cafés which had become so numerous since the
Regency, and which continued to multiply.   The success of the Café
Procope (in the street now called Rue de l'Ancienne-Comédie)

proved the popularity of these establishments, to which people repaired to take a cup of coffee, but still more to rest themselves and hear the news. " I think that I may safely assert," says the author of " Diogenes at Paris " (1787), " that it is to the establishment of so many cafés in Paris that is due the urbanity and mildness discernible upon most faces. Before they existed, nearly everybody passed his time at the cabaret, where even business matters were discussed. Since their establishment, people assemble there to hear what is going on, drinking and playing only in moderation, and the consequence is, that they are more civil and polite, at least in appearance." The cafés (of which there were 600 in the reign of Louis XV.) were the daily rendezvous of the unoccupied, of people who were fond of talking, of domino, chess, and draught-players, and of newspaper-readers. Billiard-rooms were not added until the Revolution, and no one would ever have ventured to smoke there. The fondness for tobacco led to the creation of *estaminets* and tap-rooms, which were classed much below the cafés. In the latter, there was little or no drunkenness, coffee, and other refreshing drinks, being almost the only things supplied. They were, for the most part, plain and devoid of decoration, some of them quiet and even silent, while others were noisy, and each had its peculiar physiognomy. The Café de la Régence and the Café du Quai de l'Ecole had inherited the renown of the Café Procope. Bachelors, both young and old, men of letters, retired officers, foreigners, and news-reporters, formed the regular customers of the Paris cafés.

The young men, who seemed to care less and less for the manly sports and exercises once so popular, needed more exciting amusements than were to be had in the cafés. They still learnt fencing and riding, but the lower classes had the monopoly of bowls, skittles, and archery. St. Evremond's Sicilian traveller, in reference to Paris during the last few years of the 17th century, is made to say : " The young people are very fond of bodily exercise, especially of tennis, but the elderly people spend their time on dice, cards, and scandal. Paris at this time had a large number of tennis-courts, which were

A FASHIONABLE GROUP AFTER AUGUSTIN DE ST. AUBIN.

much frequented, but at the close of the 18th century there were only five or six left." The Marquis de Mirabeau accounts for the decline of tennis as follows : " A man who has just had his hair curled and perfumed does not care to risk having it disarranged, because he intends the operation to carry him over a fortnight, so, instead of playing tennis, he takes his ease in an arm-chair." The sons of the bourgeois and the shopkeepers no longer frequented the Arsenal playground, where the young nobles had so enjoyed themselves during the Fronde, and the trade-apprentices had quite given up their games of football and running-matches which formerly enlivened the exterior Boulevards. The mode was in favour of more sedentary amusements ; but in excursions to the country, where young men and women were assembled together, little provocation was required to get up a dance. They also indulged in prisoner's base and rounders, and the *Parisienne* was also very clever at battle-dore and shuttlecock. There was little bathing in the summer months, for few young men knew how to swim, and those who did bathe were content with the baths at the Porte St. Bernard, without going higher up the river. When, as often happened, the Seine was frozen over, there was a great crowd on the ice and plenty of sliding, but not a single skater, unless it were a stray Dutchman anxious to display his national gift. The chief amusement of the Parisians, rich and poor, young and old, alike, was the promenade, which the wealthy indulged in every day, while the lower-classes were restricted to Sundays and holy days. Dufresny (1705) says : " We have two sorts of promenades in Paris ; the one to which people go to see and be seen, the other to be seen by nobody." The latter were known as lovers' walks, and the young men and women belonging to the lower orders and the middle-classes frequented them very much of an evening, extending their walks, during summer time, to the fields outside Paris. The extra-mural resorts, such as Bicêtre, Gentilly, Belleville, Ménilmontant, Vincennes, and St. Mandé, were always crowded on Sundays and holy days, the excursionists halting at most of the *guinguettes* on the way. The *badauds* and the people out of employ frequented, on week days, the public squares, most of which were very animated, particularly the Place Dauphine, where the quacks, the street musicians, and the pedlars drove a roaring trade. The Sicilian traveller, writing in 1698, says : "Some of these quacks offer to replace teeth that have fallen out, others to fix glass-eyes, and all of them are able to cure hopeless diseases. Another has a secret for beautifying the visage, and for imparting perpetual youth, while a third effaces wrinkles and makes wooden legs." The successors of the notorious Tabarin retained the secret of impressing upon their audiences a belief in their powers.

The public promenades had each its special physiognomy and type of frequenters. The author of the "Amusements Sérieux et Comiques" says : "From the Bois de Boulogne we come to the Cours-la-Reine (which then formed part of the Champs Élysées). It is a forest avenue in which horses but not men are allowed to take the air. In a neighbouring climate, called the Tuileries, the air which one is allowed to inhale is thick with a blinding dust which prevents the fashionables from being seen and admired. The worst of these promenades is that they are infested with insects, flies in summer, gnats in autumn, and newsmongers at all seasons."

The Bois de Boulogne, the Champs Elysées, and the Place Louis XV. (see Fig. 230) were, as a matter of course, reserved for carriages and equestrians. The pedestrians went for their walks as far as possible from their respective places of residence. They frequented for the most part the Jardin des Plantes, the Place Royale, the Luxembourg and Tuileries gardens, and the Palais Royal. The Parc Monceau (see Fig. 231) was not at that period open to the public. The Marquis de Caraccioli states that the Palais Royal, previous to the removal of the original garden, was the fashionable promenade, the Luxembourg that of the thinkers, and the Tuileries the popular one. He also complains that in a garden so much frequented as this latter, there should be so few flowers and trees, and he adds that the din of conversation was deafening. Half a century before he wrote, our old friend from Sicily praises the Tuileries

Fig. 230.—The Place Louis XV. (1763) ; after Moreau.

N. B. This square, laid out by Gabriel, chief architect to the King, contained a statue of Louis XV., by Pigalle.

gardens in no measured terms : " In this charming spot people gossip and banter, talk about love matters, general news and war intelligence. Matters of all kinds are debated and settled, there is no end of badinage ; but for all that everybody is in good humour." The beauty of the ladies and the display of dress was the chief attraction, as is remarked by Restif de la Bretonne, who, in his " Tableaux de la bonne Compagnie" (1786), says : "What can be more charming than these serried ranks of beautiful women who line the noble avenue of the Tuileries on a summer evening, and during the fine days of spring and autumn! The groups of people, all possessing some special variety of attraction, exchange a continuous series of ideas which charm the mind, as the beauty of those who give utterance to them delights the eyes."

There were certain days and hours which the fashionable world had selected for their promenades. It was not usual to appear in full dress at the Palais Royal except before and after the opera, and the ladies seated themselves beneath the shade of the chestnut-trees, which was the fashionable spot previous to the construction of the galleries. The newspaper readers had their head-quarters under the Cracow tree, so called because of the false news propagated beneath its branches. The burning of the opera (1783), and the alterations effected in the garden by the erection of galleries, though not reducing the number of visitors, brought about a complete change in the character and appearance of this resort (see chromolithograph, No. 10).

The tide of popularity afterwards flowed towards the northern boulevards, which, long deserted, regained their former animation. Dulaure, in his description of Paris curiosities (1786), said : " The old Boulevard combines all the attractions sought for by the loungers ; varied sights, splendid houses, and delightful gardens, down even to the cafés and wineshops, which, with their flowers and shrubs, have quite a fairy appearance. On the afternoons of Sundays and Thursdays the boulevard is patronized by the prettiest women in Paris, and the long strings of carriages are an ever-varying

THE WALK UPON THE RAMPARTS OF PARIS; AFTER AUGUSTIN DE ST. AUBIN.

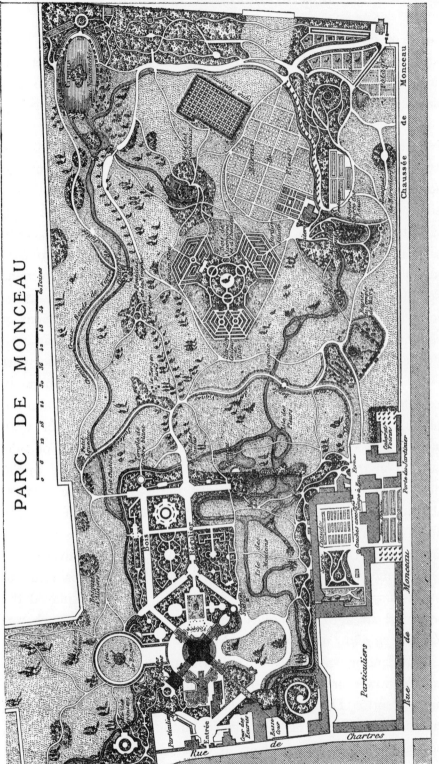

PARC DE MONCEAU

Fig. 231.—Plan of the Parc de Monceau (1778), executed by Carmontelle for the Duc d'Orleans.

source of curiosity." The Boulevard du Temple, in which were four or five popular theatres, and several other places of amusement, was still more gay. But of all the people who flocked to this quarter of an evening the great majority belonged to the working-classes, who looked upon this boulevard as its special property, preferring it even to the St. Germain and St. Laurent Fairs. These two rival fairs also had a great number of places of amusement, but though they were always open as bazaars, they were not fairs in the usual sense of the term for more than three months in the year. The St. Germain fair was held in the winter, and the St. Laurent fair in the early part of the summer. The former never recovered its popularity after the fire which destroyed the wooden constructions used during the fair (1763), though by the erection of new galleries, more elegant than the old ones, there was added to the attractions of the fair a dancing-saloon, the winter Wauxhall, which was well attended for a time. The St. Laurent fair, held in the upper part of the faubourg of that name, was larger and more elaborately decorated than the St. Germain fair, but it had no Wauxhall, and the only amusements for frequenters of its Chinese Redoubt were swings, and other foreign games. In the very centre of new Paris, upon the Place Vendôme, then bounded on one side by the church and convent of the Capucines, the St. Ovide fair was established in August, 1764, and it was held there every year at the same period until transferred to the Place Louis XV., where it did not last long, though it had originally been made fashionable as the *gingerbread fair*. It was at this fair that Nicolet, previous to establishing his theatre *des grands danseurs du Roi*, displayed the wonderful strength and agility which gave rise to the proverb "*de plus fort en plus fort, comme chez Nicolet*."

But dancing was always the favourite amusement of the Parisians, and the lower orders could only gratify this passion in places of public resort. This they never failed to do, and all the provincial dances found a home in Paris, thanks to the ardour of the dancers, who undertook to teach them to their partners. The Auvergne

THE ST. OVIDE FAIR.—PLACE LOUIS-LE-GRAND.

bourrées, the Basque steps, the Poitou jog, the Picardy jig, were especially popular.   It was the fashion amongst the upper classes to give balls during the winter only, generally during the carnival, and the dances in fashion were of a very stiff and ceremonious kind. The ball was generally opened by a minuet, which was not often seen at the balls of the bourgeoisie, where less formality prevailed.

Fig. 232.—Visiting the fair ; fac-simile after Gillot.

The latter were generally given for the amusement of the young people, beginning about three in the afternoon.   Bury, in his essay on French education, says : " These balls were of a very unpretending kind.   Deportment was taught in what are called *les belles danses*, after which there were some round dances. . . . This lasted till eight o'clock, when a plain supper was served.   The parents and the young ladies sat at one table, and there was a separate one for the lads, who waited on the ladies.   The whole entertainment was very quiet."   The young men, craving for more excitement than was to be had from these parties, which only took place during the carnival, frequented the public balls where dancing went on at all seasons of the year; in the open air during the summer, and in handsome saloons during winter. The Wauxhalls were imitated from England, and a clever Italian named Torre, who had erected on the present site of the Rue Lancry a building in which pantomimes accompanied by fireworks were represented, afterwards converted his theatre into a ball-room (1768). This was the Wauxhall Torre, afterwards called the Summer Wauxhall, but the splendid *fêtes de nuit* given there drove away the dancing public. Another Wauxhall, still more splendid, was erected at the western end of the Champ Elysées, and called the Colisée (1770). It was a large rotunda, 78 feet in diameter and 80 high, intended for dancing, but the middle classes did not like it so well as the old winter Wauxhall, and the large sum (more than £80,000) spent upon the Colisée was lost to the investors.

The Colisée was quite deserted by 1780, and this was the fate of many places of amusement called Wauxhalls, redoubts, gardens, and circuses, which were opened in quick succession all over Paris. They had cost a good deal to erect, and being only open once or twice a week, the receipts did not balance the cost of keeping them up. The Parisians, fond of change in this as in most other things, thronged a newly opened place, and then left it for some other novelty.

The Parisians were, moreover, economical in their amusements, and for less than two shillings they could gain admittance to a public garden, in which were provided a variety of amusements, illuminations, fireworks, and dancing. Where an Englishman would readily have paid his guinea, the Parisian thought twice before he laid out a few pieces of silver. What he delighted in most of all were gratuitous amusements, such as were to be had on public festivals. To take part in them, he did not regard fatigue or loss of time. In rain, wind, or dust, he would tramp from one end of the city to the other, and stand for hours to see the illuminations, fireworks, and other amusements. He did not even hesitate to take his wife into the seething crowd, and though they might return home half dead

THE ROYAL STATE CARRIAGES IN 1783   AFTER MOREAU.

with crushing and hunger, they were content if they could only say they had seen the sights. To *see*, was, in fact, the one aim and

Fig. 233.

Fig. 234.

Fig. 235.

Fig. 236.

Figs. 233—236. —Acrobatic Feats.

object of the Parisian badauds. The public holy days were never too numerous for them, and, in addition to the festival of St. John and the Royal fête day, there were the solemn processions of the churches and convents, the Corpus-Christi day, the parade through the streets of the shrine of St. Geneviève at times of drought, the festival instituted by Louis XIV., &c. These processions, which defiled through the streets, hung with flags and emblems, were made attractive by the attendance of official persons in full costume, and the ecclesiastical processions were specially magnificent. They formed a topic of conversation for a week afterwards.

The Parisians crowded to witness the Parliament, with its members arrayed in their scarlet robes, repair to a Bed of Justice, or to see the *bœuf-gras* at carnival-time on its way to the Palais de Justice, just as the bourgeois also collected to see the state entry of an archbishop or an ambassador, the funeral of a distinguished personage, the erection of a statue, or the opening of a church. More than once, during the 18th century, the whole population turned out to witness the trial of some singular invention, such as a man crossing the river without wetting his feet, which feat was performed more or less successfully by the aid of an apparatus attached to his boots, while on another occasion Count de Bacqueville gave notice that he would fly from his residence in the Rue des Pères across the river to the Louvre. This experiment was not very successful, for the new Icarus fell into the Seine, and coming into collision with a barge broke his leg. He was hissed for his pains by the crowd, which showed itself more indulgent to the *sorcerer* Bleton, who undertook to discover with a magic wand springs of fresh water in various parts of Paris. The crush was so great that many people were half suffocated at the Luxemburg, when he pointed to a spring of bubbling water in the hitherto dryest part of the garden.

Even when admittance to a place of amusement was by payment, more than half of the audience consisted of " free admissions." The river jousts, authorised by the police in 1768, and carried on with great success for many years, attracted enormous crowds. The promoters of this entertainment erected on the banks of the Seine, near La Râpée, stands to which admission was by payment, but more than 100,000 people got a gratuitous view of the jousts, by

REVIEW OF THE SWISS AND FRENCH GUARDS HELD BY THE KING ON THE PLAINE DES SABLONS; AFTER MOREAU.

taking possession of the banks. These aquatic sports did not last long, and the people took even more kindly to the combats of different animals which the police tolerated in 1781. Even women crowded to the Barrière St. Martin to see a donkey or bull done

Fig. 237.—Charles, the engineer and professor of physics, inventor of the hydrogen gas for inflating balloons from a very rare drawing.

to death by savage dogs. Horse-races were a more reputable form of amusement, which the lower orders cared little about, when that sport was introduced from England. At first they had attended a few of these races, which were merely private matches made by great noblemen. In 1726, the Comte de Saillans had wagered with the Marquis de Courtauraux that he would ride in half an hour from

the gates of Versailles to the Invalides ; in 1753 an Englishman had
bet the Duc d'Orleans that he would ride from Fontainebleau to the
Barrière d'Enfer (one of the gates of Paris) in two hours, only
changing horses three times.   Horse-races were not in reality
established until 1775, when a number of noblemen subscribed to get
up races for horses bred in France.   The Parisians did not much
affect these races, which took place at Vincennes, and they did not
attend them when they were held in the Plaine des Sablons, and
made excuse for heavy betting.   The ladies of the Court, who saw
in these races an opportunity for displaying their dress, gave the ton
to this kind of amusement, which, essentially English in its character,
had little charm for the bourgeois, who infinitely preferred the yearly
review, by the King, of the French and Swiss guards, also held in
the Plaine des Sablons (see Plate).

Upon the other hand, the bourgeois and the lower orders were
passionately fond of the balloons, which at the time of their invention,
excited great hopes.   It was reported in Paris that a means had been
discovered for travelling in Paris by the aid of fire.   Montgolfier's invention was in the mouth of every inhabitant, few of whom, however,
knew what it really consisted of.   The first experiments were made
at Annonay in the Vivarais, and they were repeated in Paris before a
large assemblage in August, 1782.   The silk balloon rose to a great
elevation, and the people watched its rise with feverish interest.
The brothers Montgolfier then had made in the paper-manufactory
of Réveillon in the Faubourg St. Antoine, a machine in linen and
paper, 70 ft. high and 44 ft. in diameter ; but it was destroyed by the
wind and rain.   A new balloon was made in great haste for a trial
which was to be made at Versailles on the 19th September before
the King and Queen.   This balloon, made of varnished cotton-cloth,
was 45 ft. high by 41 ft. in diameter, and it was filled with carbonic
gas.   It rose very quickly, having in the car a sheep, a cock, and a
duck, but it only remained ten minutes in the air.   The success of
the experiment seemed conclusive, and more than twenty savants
contended for the honour of making the first ascent.   Professor

Pilatre de Rozier gained the day, having on two or three occasions ascended in the presence of two or three thousand spectators. The captive balloon did not, however, rise more than a few hundred feet,

Fig. 238.—Ascent of a Montgolfier balloon ; from an engraving of the period.

as the straw used for furnishing the gas gave only a limited quantity. Soon afterwards, Pilatre de Rozier and the Marquis d'Arlander ventured to ascend in a balloon that was not attached to the ground, and they rose from the Parc de la Muette more than 2,000 ft. above, and effected a safe descent near the Gobelins manufactory. All

Paris witnessed with delight this successful experiment. Another ascent, December 1st, raised the enthusiasm of the people to a still higher pitch. A balloon made of silk, to which was suspended a gilded gondola, containing Professors Robert and Charles (see Fig. 237) ascended in the Tuileries gardens, and came down in Picardy, at nearly 50 miles from where it had started. After this, there were many notable ascents, but the novelty gradually wore off, though there was always a large crowd present at the departure of the balloon.

The people prized very highly the public festivals given for their amusement. They did not even care so much for the gratuitous distribution of wine and eatables as for the illuminations and fireworks. The tocsin of Notre Dame, sounded day and night for twenty-four hours, invited to the festival, so to speak, the inhabitants of Paris. In addition to the celebration of the king's fête day, which was kept with the same rejoicings year after year, there were special ceremonies given in connection with christenings and other occurrences connected with the royal family. Sometimes the Parisians were treated to a festival by some private individual, and, in May, 1722, the Duc d'Ossuna, ambassador of Spain, gave illuminations and fireworks which cost nearly £8,000 in honour of the betrothal of the Infanta to Louis XV. There were a hundred illuminated boats, each with a band of music in it, rowing up and down the Seine. Barbier says that " no such crowd was ever assembled before in one place." The makers of fireworks obtained permission in 1741 to give a display of fireworks every year on St. Louis' day, and they constructed on the banks of the river, between the Pont-Neuf and the Pont-Royal, a number of raised seats, which were not occupied because the price of admission was considered to be too high. But as the crowd which assembled to witness the spectacle did not contribute to the expense the firework manufacturers found the experiment a very costly one.

It is impossible to mention the public rejoicings held during the reigns of Louis XV. and Louis XVI. They were not all alike

FIREWORKS ON THE PONT-NEUF, PARIS, IN 1745.

successful, but the entertainment offered to the King on the marriage of Madame Elizabeth of France with the Infant of Spain in August, 1739, has remained famous (see Plates). That which took place at the first marriage of the Dauphin was not so popular, for dancing-saloons had been constructed in the different parts of the city, and the bourgeois would not condescend to dance in public, and the people themselves kept away. The fireworks were very liable to be spoilt by bad weather, and at the fête given by the city of Paris

Fig. 239.—Set piece of the firework display given in honour of the Dauphin, at Meudon, Sept. 3, 1735.

to celebrate the inauguration of the King's statue and the con-clusion of peace (June 22nd, 1763), a sudden thunderstorm came on while the Tuileries gardens were crowded with spectators. Barbier adds that all the fine clothes were spoilt, and that there were no fireworks in the evening. The most tragic occurrence was that which occurred, as mentioned in a previous chapter, during the fêtes given in honour of the marriage of Louis XVI. (as he afterwards became) with Marie Antoinette. The fireworks had gone off to perfection, but there was a crush in the Rue Royale, and in the panic that ensued more than 300 persons were trampled to death, while 1000 were severely injured. About 133 corpses were found lying in the street the next morning. This was looked upon at the time as an evil omen for the young couple, whose marriage had been the in-direct cause of so much suffering; but the warning was forgotten when the time came round for the illuminations in the following year. The last fête celebrated at Paris in honour of the King was in 1791, but there was little enthusiasm about it, and the tragic events which occurred on the 10th of August prevented its renewal in 1792.

CHAPTER XV.

THE KITCHEN AND THE TABLE.

Old French Habits.—Breakfast, Dinner, and Supper.—The Court Repasts in the Reign of Louis XIV.
—Progress of the Culinary Art under Louis XV.—The Prince de Soubise and his cook Marin.—
Celebrated Gourmets.—Luxuriousness of the Table Service.—The King's Repasts in Public.—
Suppers.—An Eccentric ; Grimod de la Reynière.

THE most brilliant epoch of French cookery may be considered
to have been during the Regency. Hitherto the French had fed
largely, a good deal too largely perhaps, but they did not understand the art of eating. The dishes of the 17th century were very
plentiful, very varied and very complicated, but they were neither
delicate in flavour, wholesome, nor appetizing, though the author of
the " Cuisinier Royal," published in the middle of Louis the Fourteenth's reign, declared that " though Europe is celebrated for the
cleanliness, judgment, and adroitness with which food is prepared for
table, France bears away the palm in this as she does in point of
politeness and a thousand other qualities." Yet it must be said
that Frenchmen were naturally sober and moderate in their tastes,
and, though fond of the table, they did not like taking their meals
alone. The hours for eating had not changed at all during the last
years of Louis XIV.: breakfast between 7 and 8, dinner at noon.
Supper at about 7 p.m. The breakfast was a very light meal, consisting for the most part of soup, which was still the national dish.
Chocolate, coffee, and tea were, however, becoming popular, and
they already threatened to dethrone the soup-bowl.

In the time of Louis XIV., all Europe imitated French cookery,
which, though but a perfected reproduction of the kitchen laws

codified by Taillerent, the cook to Charles VII., also owed a good deal to the Italian school of cookery of the 16th century. The defect was that not sufficient discrimination was exercised in selecting the ingredients of ragoûts, and that the meat lost a large quantity of its natural goodness by the predominance of grease and the amalgam of different kinds of animal food not suited to go together. The result was that, as the doctors declared, the strongest stomachs had great difficulty in digesting their food. Louis XIV., always the largest eater at Court, was obliged to take opening medicine once a month, to purify the blood and stimulate the appetite. Like all heavy feeders, he was not a refined gourmet, though he generally took his meals alone, and eat slowly. He ordered each morning the *petit-couvert* or *très petit-couvert* according to how he felt, but both of them consisted of several dishes, three services, without fruit. Dinner was at one o'clock, but it was often put back when the council of Ministers prolonged its sitting. The King returned to his apartment, and a square table, all ready served, was placed opposite to the centre window. When the King was seated, the principal courtiers and sometimes members of the royal family came into the room, and one of them handed him the napkin, while the Chamberlain served the dishes. The dinner lasted about an hour, during which time the King continued to eat steadily, scarcely speaking, except in a few broken sentences to one or two favourites. The quantity of food he consumed during dinner is something beyond belief, and though he was more sparing at supper, a *night repast*, consisting of cold meat, pastry and sweetmeats, was placed in his bed-chamber, in the event of his waking up hungry. The *grand couvert* was rarely laid, except on state occasions and at Fontainebleau.

After looking down the list of dishes which represented a court dinner at this period, it is difficult to understand how the strongest stomach could digest such repasts, if indeed the guests did not content themselves with tasting only a few. The longest dinner did not last more than two hours, and that would not have given people time even to taste the whole series of dishes. There is no ménu

BANQUET GIVEN AT THE SPANISH EMBASSY, PARIS; AFTER SCOTIN, 1707.

extant of the king's private dinners, for the Versailles cooks kept their secrets as to the quantity and nature of the royal repasts, but there are a great number of contemporary menus for all seasons of the year, and we can guess what the king's table was likely to be from what we know of the habits of princes of his family and great noblemen. Taking, for instance, as a point of comparison, the banquet given by the Marquis de Louvois, at his Château de Meudon, to the Dauphin, to Monsieur, the King's brother, Madame, and their son the Duc de Chartres, we find that there were eleven soups, eleven entrées, and thirteen hors-d'œuvres, for the first service; twenty-four roasts for the second service; twenty-four entremêts, and eleven vegetables, omelettes, creams, foies-gras and truffles, and dessert in proportion. This banquet, which must have been a very costly one, was given on August 25th, and it will be noticed that there was no fish.

In contrast to this repast may be given an ordinary dinner of Louis XV., who never took his meals alone, like Louis XIV., being, on the contrary, fond of sharing them with his family in public. The following menu is selected haphazard in the year 1744, and contains no fish, which was rarely eaten, except on fast days : two grand soups of partridge and capon; two ordinary soups, bisque of pigeons and cock's-combs; four side soups of hashed capon, partridge and lentils, stuffed chicken, and boiled capon; quarter of veal and pigeon pie as grand entrées; fricassée of chicken and salmi of partridge as ordinary entrées; six side dishes of roast partridges, braized pigeons, grilled turkeys, truffled chickens, whole and in hash; two large dishes holding fat capons, chickens, pigeons, partridges, and pies; two dishes of woodcock, teal, young capons, and partridges. The list of vegetables, salads, creams, rissoles, and beignets, is not given, and the dessert does not appear in this account of the king's table, who spent the sum of 399 livres, 18 sous, 11 deniers (about £16), for his three meals of breakfast, dinner, and supper. This is comparatively little, and it is certain that the great noblemen and wealthy financiers spent much more in proportion when they received their friends at dinner or supper. The wealthier of the nobility always kept open table, but the bourgeoisie were more economical in their habits, as may be gathered from the following description by Laurette de Malboissière (from her "Letters," published by the Marquise de la Grange in 1866) of a dinner at the house of a retired banker at Montmartre (May 20th, 1764): "Our repast was simple and frugal; a good honest soup with lettuce, sorrel, and leeks, a nice piece of *bouillé* (the meat which has been boiled in the soup), fresh butter and radishes, some well-cooked cutlets without sauce, a well-roasted chicken, a delicious salad, a pigeon pie, a frangipani, and some green peas à la bourgeoise. These were all the dishes on the table. For dessert we had some cream cheese, echode-cakes, preserve, bonbons, and dried apricots; and, as a fitting crown to the edifice, some coffee made by the host himself." This dinner, which Mdlle. de Malboissière speaks of as "simple and frugal," was the kind of dinner served in the provinces for a party of ten, as we learn from Brillat-Savarin in his "Physiologie du Goût." Good cheer was to be had everywhere, even at the Bastille, and Marmontel thus records a dinner served him while confined there in 1761: "An excellent soup, a slice of tender beef, the leg of a well-boiled capon, a small dish of artichokes fried in marinade, one of spinach, a mellow pear, some fresh grapes, a bottle of old Burgundy, and some exquisite Mocha coffee." Voltaire, who had not found the hospitality of the Bastille so attractive thirty-five years before, complained in 1749 of the excessive luxury indulged in at table, and he did not anticipate that a *lettre de cachet* would ever be equivalent to an invitation to dinner in the king's prisons; and he says, "Money must be plentiful indeed when people spend so much money on repasts which undermine the health, and eventually numb all the faculties of the mind."

This was an unfair accusation, and cookery in the reign of Louis XV. deserved the praises bestowed upon it by Meusnier de Querlon in his preface to the "Dons de Comus," the work of the famous cook Marin (1748): "The ancient system of cooking was popularized by France throughout Europe, and was generally fol-

Fig. 240.—Large dining-room fountain in lead gilt rom the hotel of Le Normand d'Etioles, farmer-general, Ruc de Sentier, Paris. (Collection of M. L. Double.)

lowed until within the last thirty years. Modern cookery, based upon the same principles though less complex and formal, has as great variety, while it is more simple, cleaner, more delicate, and perhaps still more erudite. The ancient system of cookery was very complicated and full of details; modern cookery is a sort of chemistry." Connoisseurs assert that French cookery was at its apogee towards the close of the reign of Louis XV., though some gastronomists maintain that it continued to progress towards perfection all through the reign of Louis XVI. Mercier, not himself an authority on the subject, can merely repeat what was told him by Grimod de la Raynière, who subsequently wrote the "Almanach des Gourmands," and in his "Tableau de Paris" (1781-82), he says: "The dishes of the present day are very light, and they have a peculiar delicacy and perfume. The secret has been discovered of enabling us to eat more and to eat better, as also to digest more rapidly. . . . The new cookery is conducive to health, to good temper, and to long life. There is no doubt that we are healthier and better fed than our ancestors."

The 18th century was in truth the century of grand cookery and eminent cooks. The latter were even to be found in war time at the head quarters of the army, and it was to no purpose that Louis XIV., in his military code, enjoined upon the officers on active service frugality in their repasts, and prohibited, under severe penalties, anything like excess. Rollin relates in his "Traité des Etudes" that after the last war of the reign of Louis XIV. "the officers residing in Paris talked of scarcely anything else than the good living which they had enjoyed during the campaign." Louis XV. was compelled to insist afresh upon the regulations of the military code in reference to the officers' fare during a campaign, and by an ordinance of April 1st, 1750, forbade "the lieutenant-generals who entertained company from having any other dishes than soups and roast joints, together with entrées and entremêts of plain meat, to the exclusion of side dishes and hors-d'œuvres." These regulations did not prevent the Prince de Soubise, who commanded an army corps at the beginning of the Seven Years' War (1757) from taking with him to Germany his full kitchen and table services, and the campaign was more noted for the general's good dinners than for his victories. He was defeated at Rosbach, but the victorious army did not capture his silver plate or his cook Marin. Nearly everybody belonging to society was more or less of a gourmand at this period ; but the pleasures of the table could not have been very much abused, as the voice of scandal, which spared nobody, is silent on this point. There is, however, a story told of one Verdelet, a resident in the Bourbonnais, who spent 1200 livres (£48) on a dish made of two or three thousand carps' tongues, and who eat so much of this dish that he died of indigestion, which was the scourge of heavy feeders. Dufresny, the comic writer and rival of Regnard, was one of the victims. Upon one occasion, after receiving payment for a comedy which he had written, he spent the money upon a dinner composed only of two dishes—a soup made of the liquid yielded by fresh eggs after they have been boiled, and a dish of the *noix* of several shoulders of veal. The Prince de Soubise, whose means allowed him to gratify the most costly whims, often had served him a royal omelette, which Marin had invented expressly for Louis XV., and which was made with cock's-combs and the roes of carp. This dish cost as much as a hundred crowns.

There were so many eminent cooks in Paris, that few of their names have been handed down to us. Marin was the most talented and inventive, and his book, the " Dons de Comus," was long considered the standard work on cooking, even in preference to the " Vieux Cuisinier." The many treatises by Menon, author of the " Cuisinière Bourgeoise," did not detract from its reputation. Mouthier, who was private cook to the king while Mdme. de Pompadour was in favour, claimed to be an hygienic professor, and to have discovered the secret of delicious dishes which would strengthen the constitution and prolong the life of those who partook of them. In the reign of Louis XVI. the palm for good cooking was unanimously awarded to Messelier, who, without inventing sanitary dishes and writing treatises, formed many celebrated pupils, chief amongst whom was Laguipière. Before the beginning of the century St. Evremond wrote: "There is no end to the new sauces and ragoûts, and the French have discovered a mode of making an exquisite dish." For it was with the bones of poultry and game, pounded and boiled down, that the cooks obtained their best gravies.

In great houses, under the immediate control of the chef de cuisine, were several assistants and subordinate servants, each of whom had his particular duty assigned to him. These various duties will be best understood by an enumeration of the offices in the royal kitchen during 1775: a controller, four half-year and eight quarterly attendants (*écuyers*); four master-cooks, four overseers of the roast meat; four soup-boilers; four pastry-cooks; four porters; four kitchen-boys; four plate-cleaners; two ushers, two table-bearers, six dish-removers, and four scourers. The sauce-department had been abolished, but the fruit-room, with all its functionaries, was still in existence, and so too was the pantry and the wine-cellar, in which more than fifty people were employed. In large private houses the staff was not, of course, so numerous, but even in them, besides the assistants of the cook, there were six distinct classes of servants: the maître d'hôtel, the head-cook, the roaster, the pastry-cook, the confectioner, and the cellarman. The maître d'hôtel had under his control all the table service, and the Abbé Coyer represents one of these important personages as "richly clad, wearing a sword, with a diamond ring on his finger, and playing with a gold snuff-box. He was asked whether he was not some great personage, to which he replied: 'I am content to serve a great man; I am his maître d'hôtel.' He went on to say that in going over his accounts for the preceding year, he found Monsignor had spent a hundred thousand crowns." The table expenditure was even greater at the houses of certain noblemen and financiers, for a single dinner given by the Prince de Soubise to the King and the Court cost more than £3000. Describing the kitchens and offices of one of these great houses, Abbé Coyer says: "I was taken to the kitchens, and requested to observe the good taste of the master of the house. It is the only part of the establishment which is shown to visitors. Elegant, commodious, scrupulously clean, solidly constructed, nothing is wanting in this vast workshop of Comus, a modern work of art in which the

Fig. 241.—A supper ; after Masquelier.
(From the collection of the *Chansons de Laborde*, 4 vols., in 8vo.)

architect has displayed all the resources of his genius." Abbé Coyer omitted to describe the furnaces, which were the ever-smoking altar of gastronomy, the ceaselessly-revolving spits, and the rows of copper and iron saucepans which adorned the walls. To show the extent of the kitchen utensils in a large house, it may be mentioned that, to prepare a banquet given by the Marquis de Seignelay at his residence at Sceaux to Louis XIV., thirty-six cooks and assistants used sixty small saucepans, twenty round saucepans large and small, twenty boilers of various sizes, and thirty spits.

So many additions had been made to the luxuries of the table since the time of Louis XIV., that Duclos declared in his "Memoirs" : "If the people who lived sixty years ago could revisit Paris they would not recognize it in respect to the table. Formerly, only houses of the first class kept men cooks, and more than half the magistrates were content with female cooks." There was a general tendency, even amongst the lower middle classes, to *se ruer en cuisine* (spend a lot of money on their tables), as the term went, and the latter imitated the great people as well as they could with the help of a female cook and a cookery-book. Marin, in 1748, was very sarcastic on this ambition of the bourgeoisie, and all famous men-cooks looked down with contempt upon artists of the other sex. The women-cooks were held in better esteem towards the close of the century, for Mercier, writing in 1782, says : "Some people prefer female cooks, asserting that men cooks have their palate destroyed by the time they are forty. The Picardy women are considered the best." However this may be, there can be no doubt that female cooks were looked upon for a long time as incapable of preparing a luxurious repast; and, strange to say, they were never allowed to make pastry. A certain contractor declared, on one occasion, that women were only fit to wash the dishes, though it may be remarked that very delicate hands are necessary to clean the table service when it is in gold or silver, or in Dresden, Austrian, Chinese, or Japanese porcelain. These services were often of enormous value. Those in foreign china were only to be seen since the year 1700, when Louis XIV. sent all his plate to the Mint to be melted down. Nothing but common chinaware was at that time manufactured in France, and the first experiments in the making of porcelain were not at all successful. The German porcelain was very expensive, though less so than that imported from China and Japan, for which fabulous prices were paid. The use of plate, both in solid silver and gilt, soon became general again, and was never more fashionable and abundant than during the Regency. That belonging to Cardinal Dubois, who, according to St. Simon, "always kept a splendid table, though of naturally moderate habits himself," was said to have been the most handsome of the period.

The Regency, though not perhaps the most brilliant epoch of cookery, was undoubtedly that during which the table services were most luxurious. A contemporary says that eating was the chief

Figs. 242 and 243.—Part of a silver table service, belonging to Father Germain. (See also Figs. 244 to 251.)

occupation of the time. While the Parliament was exiled to Pontoise (1720), there were always two tables laid at the residence of the first President, at one of which he did the honours in person; while the other, at which the inferior officials of the Parliament took their seats and, as Barbier who was one of them records, fared excellently, was presided over by his secretary. Barbier adds, "The first President has five-and-twenty people to dinner and supper; he has a head cook and eight assistants. President Pelletier, and Bernard the Councillor, also entertain. Roland de Meslay gave a dinner the other day to the first President which cost him nearly £300." When the Parliament was ordered from Pontoise to Blois, the king's decree arrived just as that body were about to sit down to

a splendid repast, which the first President was about to give in
celebration of St. Martin's Day. Barbier says, regretfully, " The
roaster had left upon his hands 15,000 lbs. of meat, which he sold on
behalf of his master."

These large joints of butcher's meat, and the pyramids of poultry
and game, were placed in the centre of the table, which was sometimes round, sometimes square, and sometimes oval, upon large

Figs. 244 to 247.—Pieces of the silver table service, belonging to Father Germain (see Figs. 242 to 251), except the candle-
stick on the right, in bronze, gilt, and moulded. This was made by Martincourt for the marriage of Marie Antoinette
and is now in the collection of M. Double.

dishes, which were styled *dormants*, a name given to them because
they were not handed round. Thus, wild boars, sides of veal, garnished with three chickens and six pigeons, a leg of venison, surrounded by game of all kinds, a large sturgeon, garnished with red
mullets, &c. The meat was generally cooked slowly in large boilers,
with bunches of herbs and onions ; the poultry and the game were
also cooked slowly for twelve or fifteen hours. The gravies for the
soups and entrées were made separately, but all roast joints, large or
small, were placed upon spits one over the other, so as all to receive
an equal amount of heat from a clear fire. In course of time the

sight of these enormous masses of meat became distasteful, and in the new system of cookery their place was taken by smaller dishes, containing all the essence and aroma of the larger ones. The table service simultaneously underwent a complete transformation, for the large dishes formerly used were replaced by a permanent ornament, also called *dormant* or *surtout*, and consisting as a rule of a glass stand, with a frame in silver or gold. This stood in the centre

Figs. 248 to 250.—Pieces of the silver table service, belonging to Father Germain. (See Figs. 242 to 251.

of the table, and from it branched a number of vases and salvers, filled with flowers and sweetmeats, the whole being intermixed with statuettes and candelabra in silver or silver-gilt. The *surtout* in course of time became so surcharged with ornaments that it covered the whole table, and the dishes had to be handed round to the guests one by one. These *surtouts* gradually became objects of art, and as it was impossible to change them at each repast, and as people got tired of always seeing the same piece, no matter how magnificent it was, it became the fashion to decorate them with flowers ; as a means of varying their appearance, a cake of potter's earth was placed upon the cloth, and the florist placed in this a lot of cut flowers, which represented a bed. Statuaries, designers, and painters, were also employed to decorate the table, the centre of which was often covered with statues and emblematical groups, with temples, amphitheatres, bridges, and columns, made of paste. In some cases the artist would represent a landscape, the ground being covered with snow. A man called Carada invented artificial hoar frost, which melted in the heat of the room, and during that process the guests saw the thawing of the river, the budding of the trees and the flowers as spring succeeded winter. There were also *sableurs* who, by means of coloured sand, designed very ingenious figures upon the tablecloth, some of them representing Persian carpets, powdered marble, ground glass, bread crumbs, and other objects, beautifully coloured. Delorme, Pan, and Richard, who were the most celebrated of these *sableurs*, executed their work with wonderful rapidity, and half an hour sufficed them for the production of these charming designs, which, however, were so fragile that a breath or a drop of water would spoil them.

This mode of decoration was especially fashionable throughout the reign of Louis XVI., and it harmonized very well with the services of Sèvres porcelain which had taken the place of the Dresden, and even of the Chinese porcelain. Silver plate was relegated to the sideboard, where it set off the room, though it was not so convenient as porcelain for use. This plate, with the arms and initials of the owner, was very massive, and became even more so when only made for show. The luxury of the table had diminished, for the number of dishes was reduced by half, and they were brought in one by one to the dining-room, where the maître d'hôtel whispered them in the ear of each guest. People ate and drank less, and meals were got through as rapidly as possible. Still the master of the house prided himself on having a good cook, a numerous staff of servants, and on offering his guests the varieties of the season and the choicest wines. The ladies, absorbed in their passion for dress, and caring more for frivolous amusements than repose, set no store by good living. They attended dinners and suppers, but they ate or drank scarcely anything, playing with a few sweetmeats, or sipping a little sweet wine, and in their hurry to rise from table they prevented the male guests from doing justice to the good things provided for them.

The state of affairs at Court during the reign of Louis XV. was very different, when people allowed themselves time to eat, though the repasts were neither so copious or so long as they had been in the previous reign. The ladies, however coquettish they might be,

Fig. 251.—Part of the silver table-service belonging to Father Germain. (See Figs. 242 to 250.

did not abstain from taking part in them, for fear of getting too stout. Louis XV., who nearly always dined in public, made it a rule never to remain very long at table, and he had got into the habit of eating very fast. He was not indifferent to good cooking, and, being very fond of fresh-water fish, trout from the Lake of Geneva were sent regularly to Versailles every fast-day. Louis XV., gourmand as he was, often had boiled eggs served at his table, one reason, perhaps, being that he was very adroit in striking off the crown of the egg with his fork. He then dipped two or three sippets of bread into the egg, much to the delight of the worthy burghers of Paris, who returned from Versailles full of what they had seen at the King's dinner-table. Louis XV. generally supped with his family, especially with his three daughters, Mesdames Adelaide, Victoire, and Sophie-Elizabeth, whose lively conversation always drove away his melancholy.

Marie-Antoinette, when she became Queen, would gladly have escaped the tyrannical custom of dining in public, but Louis XVI. adhered to the royal usage, and the *grand couvert* was laid at Versailles every Sunday. The Queen made an excuse for not appearing as often as possible, and on these occasions she dined in her private apartments, served by the ladies of her chamber. She declared that she could not accustom herself to be stared at by a large crowd ; it prevented her from touching any food, and she was also annoyed that the King's large appetite and somewhat slovenly way of eating should be commented upon by the whole populace.

As a general rule, the King and Queen, with the Comtes d'Artois and de Provence and their wives, dined together without ceremony or etiquette. These family dinners were only given up when the Queen formed the habit of dining with the Duchesse de Polignac, who was the governess of her children, and even then the whole party met for supper in the apartments of the Comtesse de Provence. "This custom, hitherto without precedent," says Madame de Campan, "was due to the initiative of Marie-Antoinette who kept it up with the utmost perseverance."

The King and the royal family sometimes took part at the state banquets, given in their honour at the Hôtel-de-Ville in Paris on certain special occasions. These banquets, which cost the municipality a large sum, did not often go off very brilliantly, for there was generally some break-down in the arrangements, owing to the confusion inseparable from the assembly of so many guests in such a small space. In addition to the royal table there were other tables for the King's household and the people invited by the municipality. An exception may be made in favour of the fête offered to Louis XV. on Sunday, August 15, 1744, on his return from Metz, for though the illuminations were spoilt by the rain, the banquet given within the Hôtel-de-Ville was splendid. The dessert, with the sugar ornaments which formed the centre pieces, was particularly admired. As usual, there were several tables, at all of which the service was renewed five times, each service consisting of two soups, nine entrées, a roast, entremets, and dessert with wine and liquor of every kind. Barbier, who was present, says that "it is wonderful the quantity of things that were consumed!" It may be supposed, however, that the King did not enjoy these formal banquets as he did the suppers prepared by the two excellent cooks of the Duc d'Orleans and the Prince de Soubise at the entertainments which

Fig. 252.—Surtout de table ; after Meissonnier.

they gave him at the Château de St. Ouen (August 1750) and the Château de St. Cloud (October 1752). Louis XVI. was not so delicate a feeder, and he never ate so largely as he did on public occasions when all eyes were fixed upon him. The entertainment given by the provost of the merchants and the burghers of the city to celebrate the birth of the Dauphin (January 22nd, 1782), was a terrible failure, and the King was the only person who did not perceive this. Half the dishes were cold or spoilt, at the table of seventy-eight covers which was reserved for the King and the Queen, his brothers, the Princesses, and the ladies of the Court. The other tables were even worse off, and that at which the dukes and peers were seated was not supplied at all, except with butter and radishes, off which they had to make their dinner.

The dinners and suppers of the 18th century were not held in such high esteem for the mere gratification of the appetite; they were still more celebrated for the brilliancy of the conversation, which was their greatest charm. The houses which were most frequented were not always those in which the table was most luxurious. In fact, the fare was very indifferent in many houses where the hostess was much sought after because of her wit, and though women as a rule were very fond of good living from the Regency to the time of Louis XVI., those who prided themselves on their learning were an exception. Longchamps, Voltaire's secretary, draws the reverse of an attractive picture of Madame du Châtelet's house. He says: "She only took one meal a day, viz., supper, and this nearly always out of her own house. She breakfasted on a cup of café au lait and a roll, so her maître d'hôtel and cook had little to do. I don't think she gave more than ten or twelve suppers (during her stay in Paris), and then only to a few guests who had little to eat and less to drink. And what wine! Burgundy made in Paris, and champagne of the same brand!" Madame Geoffrin's suppers, so celebrated on account of the guests who were present at them, had little to recommend them from the gourmand's point of view, for Marmontel records that they consisted for the most part of a chicken, some spinach, and an omelette. But the company made up for the indifference of the supper at these intimate gatherings, which took place every evening. She also gave two dinners a week, on Monday to artists, and on Wednesday to men of letters. Mdlle. Quinault, an actress at the Comédie-Française, less wealthy than Madame Geoffrin, but more beautiful and still more clever, gave much better suppers. The dinners given by Quesnay, Baron d'Holbach, Helvetius, and Buffon, were pretexts for collecting under one roof several men of talent, and engaging them in a general conversation which could not fail to be brilliant and animated, and to which each, while discussing his repast, contributed his share. But these hospitable and brilliant gatherings gradually declined during the reign of Louis XVI., and the table ceased to exercise its once irresistible attraction.   One

Fig. 253.—Funeral Supper, given by Grimod de la Reynière the younger, at his hotel in the Champs Elysées, Paris, Feb. 1st, 1783. (From a very rare engraving, communicated by M. Fontaine.)

Grimod de la Reynière, who was a finished but eccentric gastronomist, attempted to renew the tradition of the past, by giving an entertainment during the carnival of 1783, to two-and-twenty of his friends.   The entertainment began by a sort of funeral ceremony, and terminated in a magnificent supper of nine courses, each of which was composed of only one kind of meat cooked in twenty-two different ways. This singular supper, which resembled a funeral feast, was the talk of Paris for a fortnight afterwards.

Fig. 254.—A candelabrum.

CHAPTER XVI.

THE THEATRES.

The Stage at the end of the Reign of Louis XIV.—Mdme. de Maintenon and the Young Ladies at
St. Cyr.—Revival of Theatrical Tastes during the Regency.—The Opera ; the Comédie Française ;
the Théâtre-Italien ; the Opéra Comique.—Actors and their Relations with the Public.—The Pit.
—Costumes and Scenery.—The Theatres at the Fairs.—Private Theatres.

LOUIS XIV., in marrying Madame de Maintenon, as if to do
penance for the errors of his youth, had to submit to the dictation
of the widow of Scarron (the author of " Jodelet," and " Don
Japhet d'Arménie), who was the irreconcilable enemy of the stage
and of actors. The King thus expiated his former passion for the
stage, refusing to attend representations at Versailles by the royal
company, not only of new pieces, whether comic or tragic, but even
of those belonging to the ancient repertory. Madame de Maintenon
twice offered him in compensation, a reminiscence as it were of the
dramatic performances once held in such high favour, when Racine
wrote at her request " Esther " and " Athalie " for the young ladies
educated at St. Cyr (1689 and 1691). These two tragedies were
not very attractive when compared to the earlier pieces of Racine
and Molière's comedies, as played by the leading actors of the
theatres of the Palais-Royal and the Hôtel de Bourgogne. Madame
de Maintenon, who did not like to appear in public, had the theatre
brought to her own apartments, and St. Simon says that the King
often came there to witness religious plays such as " Absolon,"
" Athalie," etc., the principal characters being represented by the
Duchesse de Bourgogne, the Duc d'Orleans, the Comte and the
Comtesse d'Ayen, the young Comte de Noailles, and Mlle. de

Melun, under the direction of Baron.   There was only room for
forty spectators at these dramatic entertainments.

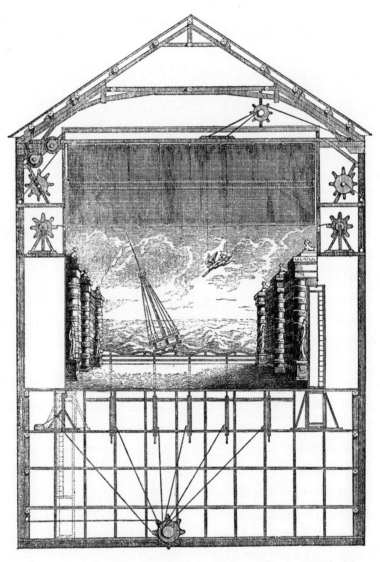

Fig. 255.—Section showing the height and breadth of the Opera built at the Palais-Royal, by
Moreau, after the designs of Radel, stage-machinist of the Paris Opera.

Paris possessed only two theatres at this date, the Royal
Academy of Music and the Théâtre Français.   The representations
of the Italian comedians, who had settled at the theatre of the Hôtel

de Bourgogne, in the Rue Mauconseil after the two royal troupes had become incorporated into one at the theatre in the Rue Guénégaud (1680), were prohibited after the production of a piece called " La

Fig. 256.—The Italian Theatre ; after Lancret.

Fausse Parade," which was considered to be a satire on Madame de Maintenon.   This was in May, 1697, and on the members of the troupe appealing to Louis XIV. to withdraw the decree they were received very coldly and dismissed by the King, who said to them : " You have no reason to complain that Cardinal Mazarin tempted you from Italy.   You came to France on foot, and you have made enough to return in your carriages."   The Comédie-Italienne was much more popular than the Comédie-Française, as is attested by St. Evremond, who makes his Sicilian visitor say : " The general public likes a hearty laugh, and this is why the Italian actors are preferred." The Marais Théâtre, which had long been a rival of the Hôtel de Bourgogne, ceased to exist in 1673, and the speculators who had frequently endeavoured to establish permanent theatres upon the St. Germain fair field, were invariably closed, as trenching on the privileges of the Comédie-Française, which moved in 1689 from the Rue Guénégaud to the new theatre, built for it upon the site of the Etoile tennis-court, in the street then called Rue des Fossés-St.-Germain (now the Rue de l'Ancienne Comédie).

The example set by the Sovereign was generally followed by the courtiers and nobility, though the Royal Academy of Music, which gave three representations a week at the building in the Palais-Royal where Lully had established it, was still patronized by many of the wealthy who were able to afford the luxury of a box taken by the year. Upon the door were engraved in gold letters the name and arms (when he had any) of the renter, and the princes of finance set great store upon having one of these boxes, for their vanity was gratified by being able to appear with their wives in full dress and to have their names called out by the *Suisse* of the theatre, as their carriage drew up to the peristyle after the performance. It was customary for the renter of the box, when he did not intend to go to the theatre, to send the key to one of his friends. The Palais-Royal theatre did not hold more than 1500 people, and a great many seats in the galleries and parterre (pit) were reserved without payment for persons belonging to the King's household. The other places, not taken by the year, were scarcely numerous enough to accommodate the foreigners who never thought of leaving Paris without paying a visit to the opera. Thus, the receipts were not so heavy as might have been guessed after a glance at the crowded theatre, and Francine, the director, to whom the King continued the privilege granted to Lully, his father-in-law, had great difficulty in meeting the expenses of management. His liabilities having reached 300,000 livres (£12,000) in 1712, the creditors formed a committee, which carried on the theatre until 1721 in the name of Francine.

Lully's music, though it had been given almost exclusively for the last thirty years, still maintained its supremacy, though it must be said that musical taste was scarcely in existence at that period of French history. But the lyric tragedies of Quinault, with the accom-

Fig. 257.—Gardener.—Captain.—Sportsman.
Costumes tirés des *Nouveaux dessins d'habillements à l'usage des Ballets, Opéras et Comédies;* by Gillot.

paniment of music and singing, were as popular as the tragedies declaimed in rhythmical periods by the actors of the Théâtre Français. The new pieces occasionally interpolated into the ancient repertory were, moreover, very inferior to the works of Quinault and Lully. The verses of Lamotte, Danchet, Roy, Abbé Pellegrin, and the musical compositions of Destouches, Campro, Lacoste and Bertin, were about on a level of mediocrity. The opera-ballets were not much better, but the ballet proper had much improved since the death of Lully (1687). As regards scenery, dresses, and stage effects, the Royal Academy of Music was unrivalled. As Dufresny wrote in the "Amusements Sérieux et Comiques," the opera was "an enchanted spot and the land of rapid transformations. In the twinkling of an eye, the men become demi-gods, and the goddesses change into weak mortals. There is no need to travel in foreign countries, for they are brought before your eyes, and, without moving from your seat you can go from one end of the world to the

Fig. 258.—Dumirail, as a peasant ; after Watteau.

other, and from the infernal regions to the Elysian fields. If you are distressed at the sight of some arid desert, a signal lands you in the abode of the gods ; another signal and you are in fairyland." The opera was the very temple of heathen mythology, and yet it was tolerated by the moralists, who were very severe as a rule, while gentlemen and ladies of high birth were entitled, in accordance with the privilege granted to Lully and Molière by Louis XIV., to sing in public without loss of rank.

The old Court party never went to the play, and the courtiers took care not to be seen there, for fear of losing favour with Madame de Maintenon and the King. Even the Princes and Princesses scarcely ventured to attend the theatres, and when they did it was almost in secret. The Duc d'Orleans, who was much more at Paris than at Versailles, was the only exception. Notwithstanding the

Fig. 259.—Poisson, as a peasant ; after Watteau.

altered habits of the Court, theatrical representations were always being given at the Château de Chantilly, residence of the Princess de Condé, and by the Duchesse de Maine at Sceaux. The theatre of the Rue de l'Ancienne Comédie also maintained its vogue, owing to the marked liking of the public for tragedy and comedy. This theatre possessed many good actors, and produced several new pieces which were very successful. This was the epoch of Regnard, Dancourt, Dufresny, and Boursault, while the dramas of Jolyot de Crébillon took their place beside those of Corneille, Racine, and Molière. Still the receipts were but small, especially during Lent, and at the great festivals of the Church.

The situation improved as soon as the Duc d'Orleans became Regent. The old Court party did not attend the theatre any more than it had done during the last years of Louis XIV., but the younger Court party was only too anxious to make up for lost time. And thus the Regency made the fortune of the theatres, which were nearly ruined by the austerity that marked the close of the previous reign. The Court of the Palais Royal set the fashion, and the Regent, or some of his household, assisted nearly every evening, in state or in private, either at the Opera or the Comédie. The Théâtre-Français was never more popular, and obtained several brilliant successes, as with Voltaire's "Œdipe" in 1718, Lamotte's "Macha-bées," and Legrand's "Cartouche" in 1721 ; but, however successful new pieces might be, they were never played more than a limited number of times. The ancient repertory, which was gone through every year, still continued to attract the largest and most remunera- tive audiences. The Royal Academy of Music also gave very brilliant representations, but as the frequenters of this theatre insisted upon very costly scenery and stage effects, the contractors who under- took the management found their resources insufficient.

In the first years of the Regency, the Duc d'Orleans allowed the Italian players to return, and, again settling at the Hôtel de Bour- gogne (April 25th, 1718), they regained the popularity which they had enjoyed previous to their expulsion. But as the Italian language was not familiar to the wealthy parvenus, without whom a theatre cannot hope to prosper, the Italians, amongst whom were several good comic actors, such as Romagnesi, Dominico, Biancolelli, and Riccoboni, gradually resorted to pieces written in French. This was the origin of the good fortune which, while preserving its title of *Théâtre-Italien*, was in turn a formidable rival for the Opera, the Comédie-Française, and the Opéra-Comique. The origin of French comic-opera may be traced to the temporary theatres at the St. Laurent and St. Germain fairs, where it was first played in 1713 by permission of the Royal Academy of Music, which had the right of prohibiting the performance. Thanks to this arrangement, the fair theatre became the Opéra-Comique, which had a career not less prosperous than the Théâtre-Italien, with the charming vaudevilles, with interludes of ballet, which Le Sage, Dorneval, and Fuzelier gave

Fig. 260.—Mdlle. Clairon, the celebrated tragédienne ; after Schénau (1766).

there for more than thirty years. The only theatres in Paris up to 1719 were the Opera, the Comédie-Française, the Comédie-Italienne, and the Opéra-Comique. The three last had each a special vein of comedy which is well-defined by St. Foix : " Thalia, at the Théâtre-Français, has a noble and dignified bearing : she likes ingenious plots, well-developed situations, delicate and almost impalpable satire, maxims which are neither gloomy nor ponderous, a style as devoid of tragic gravity as of the vulgarity of the strolling-player. At the

Théâtre-Italien, the muse is not less faithful to the fashion which she has initiated there. Nearly always gay and sportive, she scarcely touches on subjects of morality. A new fashion, an art-dispute, any occurrence which has been the talk of the town for four-and-twenty hours form subjects for her pencil, and the fund of such is inexhaustible. The Opéra-Comique is perhaps most analogous to the character of the nation. I don't say that this style is the loftiest and the best, but I do assert that it harmonizes better than any other with the vivacity of the French, who are (why should we attempt to deny it ?) a singing and a dancing people."

The Théâtre-Français, though possibly outdone by the Comédie-Italienne and the Opéra-Comique in the way of receipts and popularity, was still the first theatre in France and in Europe, because it was the highest and most complete expression of French dramatic art. The company of this theatre scrupulously maintained the traditions of high dramatic art, and was composed of the best actors both of tragedy and comedy. Entitled to call themselves *Comédiens ordinaires du Roi*, they constituted, as in the time of Molière, an association which had the royal authorization to manage the theatre itself, all questions of general interest being decided by a majority of votes in this assembly. The adjunction, in the reign of Louis XV., of the four first gentlemen of the chamber, subjected the Comédie-Française in a certain measure to the arbitrary authority which, until the Revolution, exercised sovereign control over the internal affairs of this and all the other theatres of Paris. The opinions expressed by these four gentlemen were as good as law, for nothing could be done without their sanction. Not only did they act as arbitrators between the public and the actors, but they also intervened in cases of misunderstanding between the actors themselves, they saw that the regulations in regard to the theatre were carried out, granted retiring pensions, ordered the début of a new actor, sanctioned the programme for each evening, and sometimes reprimanded any actor who failed in his task. The finance department alone was left by them to the management of the Sociétaires. In addition to the authority of the gentlemen of the chamber, that of the inspectors of *menus*, though less meddlesome and harsh, was specially exercised whenever there was to be a state representation, and these regulations lasted until 1789.

The actors of the period, previous to the Revolution, were the

Fig. 261.—The " Glorieux," comedy by Destouches ; after Lancret.

N.B.—The actor in the centre is Grandval, who played the part of the "Glorieux."

victims of injustice and prejudice, being looked upon, from a social point of view, as inferior beings. Excommunicated by the Church, and excluded from society, they were also obliged to submit to any humiliations and insults which the public might think fit to inflict upon them when they were upon the stage, and if they ventured to face the storm and resent the insults levelled against them by the pit, they were hauled off to prison and confined there until they had apologised to those who had ill-used them. Many actors, rather than submit to such indignity, withdrew from the stage, after having undergone a term of imprisonment at For-l'Évêque, whither they were consigned by order of the gentlemen of the chamber of the Lieutenant of Police. This was the case with Mdlle. Clairon, of the Comédie-Française, who was lost to the stage when she was at the very height of her talent (1765). Actors, though they were made a butt of by the frequenters of the pit, were at the same time treated with great condescension by many persons of quality, by whom their society was much sought after. Mercier, in his "Tableau de Paris," says: "The actors who have made their fortune by copying the manners of people of quality are often imitated by them in the end. I have seen the mannerisms of Grandval (Fig. 261), Bellecour, and Molé, copied by many noblemen who practised before their looking-glasses. When an actor's tricks have been copied all round, he loses his vogue, and, though he is the only person not to see it, he becomes antiquated and out of date. His patrons look out for other models, even if they have to carry their researches down to second-rate theatres."

The presence of spectators on the stage, and their consequent intercourse with the actors, accounts in a great measure for the familiar, if not intimate, footing on which they stood to each other. At the Comédie-Française, there were four rows of seats, railed off by an iron balustrade, on each side of the stage. On special occasions, a fifth row of seats was placed in front of the balustrade, and about fifty people were allowed to stand, ranged in a semi-circle at the back of the stage. This arrangement spoilt the scenic effect, for the spectators were often mistaken for the actors, and when the latter came upon the stage, they had to make their way through the crowd, while their voices were often drowned by the hum of conversation going on around them. Still it was a long time before this reprehensible practice was forbidden, for we find that it went on until 1759. When Racine's "Athalie" was revived on December 18th, 1739, the stage was so encumbered with seats and people that it was impossible to go on with the representation. Upon a similar occasion, Baron, turning towards the spectators on the stage, silenced them by repeating, in a meaning voice, the lines which he had to declaim, and, at last, upon the urgent remonstrances of Voltaire, and at the request of the Comte de Lauraguais, who offered to bear the expense of making the necessary alterations in the theatre, the seats on the stage were removed, during the close of the theatre at Easter, 1759. They were replaced by a row of seats, taken from the pit, and facing the stage, which accomodated about 180 people.

Fig. 262.—Portrait of Lekain, in "Mérope;" after Huguier.

The pit, at this period, was not provided with seats, and at the representation of a favourite piece, the spectators in this part of the theatre were half suffocated by the crush. They were compelled to stand on tiptoe or look over each other's shoulders to see the actors, and, what with protecting their pockets and holding their canes, swords, cloaks, and hats—for there were no cloak-rooms then—they had enough to do. It was difficult to establish silence in this surging crowd, for the disputes often reached such a point that the police were compelled to interfere. The pit was surrounded by a file of soldiers with fixed bayonets, and the officer in command had the power of arresting or ejecting the insubordinate spectators.

This precaution soon worked its effect, but the pit still preserved its privilege of hissing the piece, or any particular actor, but when the disapprobation was expressed in too offensive a form, the police, aided by the soldiers if necessary, quickly restored order. Mercier, in the " Tableau de Paris," criticises very severely the conduct of the soldiery. He says: "The public are irritated by the parade of

Fig. 263.—Costume of Idamé (in the " Orphelin de la Chine," by Voltaire), designed by Leclerc, and supplied by Sarrazin, costumier to the royal princes.

armed men. . . . The theatre looks like a prison, but when the pit gradually works itself up into a state of fermentation, it is difficult to prevent the explosion." The disturbance sometimes rose to such a height that it was necessary to turn out half the people in the pit. These scandalous scenes were not so frequent at the Comédie-Française as in the other theatres. One of the most stormy evenings on record was in April, 1765, at the final representation of Du Belloy's tragedy the " Siege of Calais." All the other actors refused to appear in the piece with one Dubois, on the ground that he had misconducted himself, but the pit endeavoured to force them to do so, by refusing to listen to the actor charged with his part. The company persisted in their determination, and, at last, the theatre was cleared and the money paid back at the doors. The actors were confined at For-l'Evêque for twelve days, though they

Fig. 264.—Madame Vestris in the character of Irène. Costume designed at the Théâtre-Français, and communicated to Moreau for his picture of the crowning of Voltaire's bust (Jan. 30, 1778).

were sent to play their parts at the theatre, and brought back to the prison after the performance, Lekain, Dauberval, Molé, and Mdlle. Clairon being amongst those arrested. At last Du Belloy withdrew his tragedy from the bills; Dubois retired from the troupe; Mdlle. Clairon renounced the stage for ever; while Bellecour, on behalf of his comrades and himself, apologised to the pit; and so peace was re-established.

Actors, as well as authors, had some supporters amongst the pit audience. At first these partisans were personal friends and admirers, who were granted free admission, on the strength of which they applauded loudly. But in the course of time it became the

Fig. 265.—Monvel, as Memnon, in the tragedy of "Irène." (See Fig. 264.)

custom to hire persons to applaud, and in 1786 military recruiting agents undertook, on payment of a fixed sum for each representation, to *back up* an actor or a play. It is true that the influence of the *claqueurs*, as they were called, was counterbalanced by the presence of a group of disinterested connoisseurs who occupied one corner of the pit. Lekain, after being applauded even more enthusiastically than usual one evening, left the stage with a very disconcerted air, and, on being asked by a brother-actor how this was, he replied : " It is true that I was applauded, but the applause did not come from the *little corner.*" In this corner were the most noted dramatic

Fig. 266.—Leaving the Opera ; after Moreau.

critics, some of them very hard to please, such as the Chevaliers de Mouhy and de la Molière, who could command the success or failure of any piece or actor. The supremacy of the pit did not long out-live the placing of seats in that part of the theatre, a change which was effected in 1782. It is said that this alteration had an unfavourable effect on dramatic art, and Mercier, amongst others, relates that the pit, when seats were provided, went from one extreme to the other, and from being over-excitable became lethargic and indifferent.

The royal actors paid no rent for their theatre, which, together with the cost of keeping it in repair and the stage furniture, was defrayed out of the King's privy purse, which also contributed to pay the costumier's bill. The costumes, very rich and showy, were often

Fig. 267.—Dresses of Juno, the King, and Night.
(From Gillot's " Designs of Costumes for Ballet, Opera, and Comedy.")

eccentric and even ridiculous, for the actors took no trouble to make them harmonise with the piece. Lekain and Mdlle. Clairon were the first to inculcate a regard for historical accuracy in this respect, and on August 20th, 1755, Voltaire's tragedy, " L'Orphelin de Chine," was played in Chinese costume. Mdlle. Clairon discarded the panniers which had hitherto been looked upon as an indispensable complement to tragedy-costume, and Lekain abandoned the plumes and tinsel which former actors had worn so as to increase their stature by a foot or two. Since then the costumes were made to conform to the subject and date of the piece, without losing any of their original splendour. Lekain spent more than £2,000 on his wardrobe, which was sold for about a tenth of that sum at his death, and Bellecour's wardrobe, which had cost £1,200, fetched but £168 after his decease.

Fig. 268.—Mademoiselle Sallé, a celebrated danseuse; after Lancret.

It was necessary that the costumes should be made of brilliant colours, and set off with spangles, as the stage, only lighted with tallow candles, which were snuffed between each act, was almost in obscurity. In 1784 the tallow candles were replaced by oil lamps and wax lights. This reform, long demanded, was accompanied by the largest increase in the prices of admission which had taken place during the century. In 1699, the price of admission to the pit of the Comédie-Française cost eighteen sous, and up to 1782 it was only increased by two sous. A seat in the orchestra and first tier boxes cost four livres, in the amphitheatre and second boxes two

Fig. 269. –Pas de deux, danced by Dauberval and Mlle. Alard, in the opera of " Sylvie," 1766 ; after Carmontelle.

livres, but in 1782 the prices were raised to forty-eight sous for the pit, six livres for the orchestra and first boxes, though no extra charge was made at the first representation of a new play.

More important reforms had been effected at the Royal Academy of Music, which, in the course of the 18th century, witnessed many changes resulting from the increased expenditure, and not a few revolutions in the musical art. This great theatre, though it enjoyed certain administrative privileges, was under the complete control of the King's household, but as its expenses always exceeded its receipts, the deficiencies had to be made good by the treasury. As a rule, the management of the Opera was confided to financiers, it being thought that they were best able to bear the enormous expenses, but the wealthiest and the most enterprising resigned after a very few years, to avoid complete and inevitable ruin. Thus

Fig. 270.—Costume of Neptune; after Martin.   Fig. 271.—African costume in " Aline, Queen of Golconda ;" after Martin.

it was that the contractor, Claude Gruer, succeeded the musician Destouches, who managed the theatre in the name of the King (1730). Gruer was dismissed in the following year, and he was succeeded in turn by Lecomte (1731), under-farmer of excise ; Thuret (1733), ex-captain in the Picardy regiment, and Rebel and Francœur (1744), directors of music in the King's household. Each of these administrations had increased by about £20,000 the debt, which amounted to many million francs, and which was never paid off in full. In 1749, the opera was made over to the City of Paris, and the Provost of the Merchants personally undertook the duties of director.

As may be supposed, he soon got tired of filling this onerous post, and he leased the theatre to Rebel and Francœur, who had held it for the King. The city found it necessary, in 1767, to resume the system of letting the opera by contract, and it was managed by

Fig. 272.—Ballet-dress (a zephyr); after Martin.

several directors, all of whom ruined themselves in the undertaking. The two fires (1763 and 1781) which destroyed the Palais-Royal Theatre and the opera built in its place, scarcely interrupted the performances which seemed indispensable to the prosperity of the capital.

The financial disasters associated with the Royal Academy of Music had little effect on the popularity of the theatre, in which music and the ballet always received the same enthusiastic welcome.

In the new house at the Palais-Royal, Gluck and Piccini divided the musical honours, and Noverre effected a complete change in the style of the ballets. Moreover, the opera called *seria-buffa*, which was given alternately with French opera three times a week,

Fig. 273.—Ballet-dress (a demon); after Martin.

initiated the public into the beauties of Italian Music. After the fire of 1781, the theatre was removed from the Palais-Royal to a provisional building, erected in sixty-five days, on the Boulevard St. Martin, where the masterpieces of French, Italian, and German music were produced. Grétry, Piccini, Sacchini, and Salieri, were amongst the composers, and Gardel was the chief ballet-master. The vocal talents of Sophie Arnould and Rosalie Levasseur, of Larrivée and Legros, were seconded, if not eclipsed, by those of

Laïs, Chardini, and St. Huberty. At this date, the expenses were twice as large as they had been in the middle of the century. In 1760, the cost of carrying on the theatre did not exceed £16,000, and the receipts would have sufficed to pay this sum, if they had not

Fig. 274.—The theatre of a fair. (Representation of " Harlequin, King of Gérendib," at the St. Germain fair (1713); after Bonnart.

been wasted in useless expenditure. The staff of persons belonging to the theatre, which in 1760 numbered 150, consisting of actors and actresses, dancers and danseuses, symphonists and musicians, inspectors and subordinate *employés*, had more than doubled twenty years later, and this exclusive of the pupils who were learning singing and dancing in the two schools attached to the opera in the Rue St. Nicaise.

The three leading theatres of Paris, the Royal Academy of Music, the Comédie-Française, and the Théâtre-Italien, resisted as long as they could the establishment of fresh theatres. Three times, in 1718, 1745, and 1762, they had succeeded in depriving the Opera-

Fig. 275.—Volange, as Jeannot, in "Les Battus payent l'amende;" after Wille the younger.

Comique, the success of which excited their jealousy, of the privileges conferred upon it. In the end, the Opera-Comique and the Théâtre-Italien were incorporated, when two theatrical managers, Audinot and Nicolet, each obtained permission to erect two new theatres, one at the Foire St. Germain (Fig. 274), the other at the Foire St. Laurent. These two small theatres, at which very amusing pieces, with interludes of singing and dancing, were given, became very popular. Nicolet's best actor was a monkey which imitated the acting and mannerisms of Molé the comedian. Nicolet's monkey earned him enough money to enable him to build a theatre on the Boulevard du Temple, whither his popularity followed him. His privileges, of which the leading theatres endeavoured to deprive him, were increased and confirmed, and Louis XV. condescended to become the sponsor of this theatre, which in 1772 was named the "Spectacle des grands danseurs du Roi." Audinot, who had made a fortune at the Foire St. Germain, also removed to the Boulevard du Temple, and his small theatre, at which light comedy was played by children, took the title of *Ambigu-Comique*. The construction by Louis of a new theatre at the Palais-Royal, which, built after the fire of 1781, was originally intended for the opera, was converted, after the Opera-House was erected on the Boulevard St. Martin, into the *Théâtre des Variétés Amusantes*. The right of playing all pieces except *tragedies* and *arietta-comedies* was conceded to MM. Dorfeuille and Gaillard, and the theatre was crammed for three or four hundred nights running to see Volange in his wonderful impersonations of "Pointus" et "Jeannot." This was the theatre which, after the Revolution, was occupied by the troupe of "Comedians of the Théâtre-Français of the Rue de Richelieu," to which Talma belonged.

The drama had never been so popular in France as now. All the chief provincial cities possessed theatres which were worthy to compare with those of Paris, and that built by Louis at Bordeaux was even larger and more magnificent than any in the capital. Pieces composed by inhabitants of the district or even of the town itself were produced at these theatres, and there were also, as in Molière's days, strolling companies which gave performances at small towns which had no theatre of their own. These companies were an excellent school for young artists who, after they had acquired a roving reputation, came to play at the Paris theatres. Every year, during the Easter fortnight, the café in the Rue des Boucheries was the general meeting-place of actors in search of an engagement. The theatres, as their numbers increased, found that

THE VARIÉTÉS AMUSANTES (NOW THE THÉATRE-FRANÇAIS) IN 1789.

the spectators, upon whom they were dependent for their success, had increased in like proportion. Just before the Revolution, all the theatres were thronged, night after night, by the Parisians, who cared more for the theatre than for any other form of amusement. This tendency of the French mind was observable throughout the whole of the 18th century, and the origin of the taste for the drama may perhaps be ascribed to the teaching of the Jesuits, who taught their

Fig. 276.—A tailpiece.

pupils to play tragic and comic parts in representations which naturally impressed them with a liking for the theatre. Madame de Maintenon, even, had encouraged the taste, by asking Racine to write a tragedy for the royal institution at St. Cyr, as also did the great noblemen and the members of the Royal family. We have already mentioned that the Duchesse du Maine had a private theatre in her Château at Sceaux, in which only mythological and romantic pieces were played.

After the Regency, it became the fashion amongst the wealthy financiers and the leading bourgeois to have their private theatre.

When Voltaire settled in exile at Ferney, he determined to have a theatre, and it was so well arranged that there was no exaggeration in saying that tragedy was played there better than at Paris.   Louis XV., morose as he was, was prevailed upon to permit the construction of a private theatre at Versailles, and to take a part in one or two pieces (1747).   Little is known concerning these private theatres until the reign of Louis XVI., during which the theatres of the Comtesse de Montesson and Madame de Genlis, were little inferior to the regular theatres of Paris.   Marie-Antoinette was not exempt from the dramatic mania, and she even played before her royal husband, the part of *Suzanne* in " Le Mariage de Figaro," that wonderful comedy which had within it the germ of the Revolution.

CHAPTER XVII.

SOCIETY.

Society at the end of the Reign of Louis XIV.—The Hôtel de Sully.—The Duchesse du Maine at
Sceaux.—The Prince de Conti at the Temple.—The Marquise de Lambert.—Madame d'Houdetot.
—Madame de Tencin.—Madame Geoffrin.—Madame du Deffand.—Embroidery, Purfling, and
Puppets.—Madame Doublet de Persan.—Political Salons.—The Last of the Salons.

THE intimate gatherings which had offered so many attractions
to polished society during the early part of the reign of Louis XIV.
gradually died out with the witty and charming persons to whom
they had owed their renown. The death of Mdlle. de Scudéry in
1711 closed one of the last of these celebrated *salons*, though the
latter years of his long reign were still saved from utter gloom by
the receptions at the Hôtels de Bouillon, de Nevers and de Sully in
Paris, and by those of the Duchesse du Maine at the Château de
Sceaux.

The Court was dull to the last degree, and this perhaps will
account for the fact that after Louis the Fourteenth's death there
were few additions to the list of salons mentioned in the preceding
sentence, which preserved the traditions of the Hôtel de Rambouillet.
The Regency of the Duc d'Orleans did not conduce to those habits
of propriety and delicacy which are the charm of intimate receptions.
Many salons were opened by members of the nobility, of the financial
order, and even of the bourgeoisie, but the receptions were noisy, the
talk frivolous, and the company very mixed. Licence had taken the
place of decorum and tact. The art of conversation and the talent
for listening were also lost. The Marquis d'Argenson, writing in
1740, said : " People complain that there is no such a thing as con-

versation now-a-day in France; the reason is simple enough; nobody has the patience to act the part of listener."

Thus, amidst the wild follies of the Regency, the salons in which people knew how to talk, because they knew how to listen, were very few and far between. It was neither at the Palais-Royal, nor at St. Cloud, nor at the Luxembourg, that the finished model of French urbanity and polish was to be found, but rather at the Hôtel de Sully, where wit, taste and ability were allied with nobility and knowledge of the world. François Barrière, one of the most trustworthy appraisers of the genius of the 18th century, says of the Hôtel de Sully : " No society could be more select or more varied ; the temperaments of its frequenters were different, without being opposed to one another ; there was a display of learning devoid of pedantry, of liberty of speech tempered by decorum. They say that M. de Sully shows that he has been in the habit of associating with wits, just as a flask retains for a long time the smell of the perfume which it has contained."

Amongst the brilliant circle in the reception-room of the Hôtel de Sully were magistrates, such as President de Maisons and Lamoignon ; financiers, such as M. de Caumartin; writers and philosophers, such as Fontenelle and Ramsay ; poets, such as Chaulieu in his decline and Voltaire in his glory. The company was completed, as François Barrière remarks, by many young noblemen then known as *Petits-Maîtres* who were "more conspicuous for polished manners than for originality of mind, for impetuosity than wit, for petulance than impetuosity." Petulance was, as d'Argenson declared, the defect of the day, and people " mistook it for gaiety."

The society which frequented the Hôtel de Bouillon, composed of much the same elements as the sceptical and light-hearted group which had its head-quarters at the Temple, was less ceremonious and refined. Literary tastes prevailed there, and men of letters were often invited, to bring them in contact with the leaders of fashion. Le Sage, who went little into society, was invited on one occasion to read his comedy, " Turcaret," before an assemblage in which, as he was assured, there would not be a single financier. He arrived very much behind time, and when the Duchesse de Bouillon haughtily remarked, " You have made us lose an hour," his reply was, " I will make you gain double the time!" and with that he left the house. This, and several other occurrences of a like kind, show

Fig. 276.*—Reading ; after Chodowieski.
(Communicated by M. Eug. Sauzay.)

that many men of letters, whether from pride or indifference, gave up their visits to the receptions of the nobility, preferring to meet in the cafés. There was no lack of poets and men of letters, however, at the receptions of the Duchesse du Maine at Sceaux, but they were Court poets, such as Malezieu, Abbé Genest, and St. Aulaire, who wrote love sonnets when he was eighty. In these salons, so famous for their masquerades, comedies, concerts, and fêtes-de-nuit, which were known as " Les Divertissements de Sceaux," there was little leisure for conversation, though the Duchesse du Maine, who excelled in the art herself, gathered round her a large number of men and women belonging to the highest and most gifted classes of French society.

Mdlle. de Launay (afterwards Mdme. de Staal) says in her "Memoirs," speaking of the Duchesse du Maine : " Her pronunciation is very distinct, accurate, and rapid, and she speaks in a singularly noble and natural tone. She does not employ subtle metaphors to express what she means, and her mind reflects her thoughts as faithfully as a mirror does the object placed before it." It must be admitted that the Duchesse du Maine was a better talker than she was a listener. Madame de Staal, who had been a lady of the chamber to her, says in another part of her " Memoirs," " Her banter is delicate and free from malice ; she has a wonderful memory, and she expresses herself eloquently, but with too much vehemence and prolixity. She is difficult to converse with, for she will talk but not listen, and thus she cannot gain any insight into the qualities of her friends." But the duchess was even fonder of reading and play, passing whole days at the game of biribi with her household, and parts of her nights in hearing stories read.

In the reception rooms of the Duc de Nevers, who was also an exceptional type of fashionable society, the old Court party, grave and serious, formed a striking contrast with the wits and rakes of the Regency. The duke, in fact, had one foot in the salons of the Duchesse du Maine, and another in the Hôtel Bouillon and the Temple. The little Court at Sceaux was still governed, even at its most extravagant period, by the influence of Mdme. de Maintenon, being noted for its decorous conduct, its pure conversation, extreme delicacy, and faultless propriety. In the salons of the Temple, on the other hand, etiquette and reserve made way for wild fancy and caprice. There was a full flow of wit, as of wine, during the famous suppers, at which the ordinary guests were La Fare, J. B. Rousseau, Hamilton, Quinault, Vergier, and, previous to them, the Marquis de Coulange and La Fontaine. Thus the salons of the Hôtel de Nevers were a sort of neutral ground on which the adherents of Sceaux and the Temple were enabled to meet.

But in this same palatial residence, constructed by Mazarin between the Rue de Richelieu and the Rue Vivienne, there was another salon not less distinguished, though less brilliant and less conspicuous, in which the waning traditions of the Hôtel de Rambouillet were still perpetuated. This was the salon of the Marquise de Lambert, who, after the death of her husband in 1710, had taken, on a lease for life, part of the large hotel inhabited by the Duc de Nevers, and constructed a separate entrance from the Rue Colbert, which runs at right angles with the Rue de Richelieu. For more than twenty years she occupied this residence, upon the alteration of which she had spent more than £4000, receiving every Tuesday the most distinguished of the nobility and the leading men of science. She was very fond of metaphysics, and Voltaire accuses her of talking about what she did not understand. On Wednesdays she received men of letters, academicians, and artists, and on these occasions the conversation took a lighter turn. It was here that were held the first meetings of the so-called *bureau d'esprit* which afterwards became so fashionable.

The principal habitués of this severe salon were the academicians, Sacy, who was the friend and adviser of the lady of the house, Fontenelle, Lamotte, St. Aulaire, Mairan, &c. There was neither music, cards, nor even chess, but the flow of conversation never ceased, and a speaker, even when he was indulging in the most subtle dissertations, could always count upon attentive listeners. Yet it was after the image of this salon, the chief defect of which was its excessive pompousness and austerity, that were formed those of Mdme. Geoffrin and Mdme. d'Houdetot, which were the most complete and living embodiments of French wit.

In the reign of Louis XV. there was no lack of salons frequented by good society, but manners had lost much of their original polish. Society was, moreover, invaded by amphibious creatures, who were brought to life in the stagnant waters of the nobility and clergy. These were the abbés and chevaliers who, succeeding to the marquis so often depicted by Molière, managed by dint of audacity and impertinence, and a certain amount of mother wit, to make their way into society. In the reign of Louis XIV. persons of this kind were called *nécessaires*, and in that of Louis XV. they became *indis-pensables*. Some of the chevaliers gave themselves out as officers on leave, others as the sons or the nephews of provincial gentlemen. The abbés, of course, had no abbeys, and though they wore eccle-siastical dress, they did not even belong to the church, taking their degrees, as they jokingly remarked, in society.

In some of these salons, frequented by women as well as by men, the conversation assumed a very high tone, but as a general rule it was empty and frivolous. "It consists," says the Marquis d'Argenson, "of epigrams, idle anecdotes, and ill-natured remarks, sometimes made in the presence of the people against whom they are levelled. What is still worse, the talk is all on commonplace topics, which add nothing to our knowledge. People are too indolent to argue, for no one listens to what is said; and the age is one of ineradicable prejudices, undiscriminating contempt, and unreasoning criticism. Listen to the twittering of the birds among the branches, they all warble together, to the destruction of melody."

The habit of talking in a loud tone, and even trying to drown the voices of those with whom one is arguing, became common even in good society, and no doubt was introduced from Germany or Italy, where it had been contracted by the officers who had been fighting in those countries. This practice became very general, and was indulged in even at Court. The Marquis d'Argenson relates that what he calls this Babel of tongues was such even in the royal presence, that "the King himself could not put in a word." In the course of time people took to yawning without the slightest disguise when some great talker took up the conversation. Certain salons, especially those in which the female element predominated, were exempt from this flagrant defect, and there at all events people did not all talk at once. The conversation was embellished with witty remarks and the airy trifles which were then in fashion, and which, amongst those who moved in the same circles, carried a meaning not understood by outsiders. In salons such as these, frequented by the flower of French dandyism, the men were not above taking part in ladies' work; some of them did tapestry work, and others frame embroidery. These manual occupations were, to a great extent, governed by the laws of fashion, and some of the gravest and most

Fig. 277.—The Comet (drawing-room game); after Eisen.

venerable personages in the state might be seen displaying their patience and dexterity at *purfling*, an operation which consisted in unravelling, thread by thread, the silk and the metal in a piece of gold or silver tissue. In many cases the tissue was brought by the gentlemen, and the ladies divided the spoil amongst themselves.

In 1728, the fashionable employment was the cutting out of drawings; which, after they had been extracted from books and almanacks, were pasted on to screens, lamp-shades and boxes. These drawings were sometimes coloured or varnished, and pasted into groups which, by a skilful arrangement of the component parts, represented complete scenes of various kinds. Simultaneously with this fashion was introduced that of mechanical puppets mounted on wire.

Poinsinet, in his Comedy of the "Cercle, ou la Soirée à la mode," played at the Théâtre-Français in 1764, thus satirizes the lacka-daisical manners of the young councillors, the young colonels, and the young abbés who frequented these *salons* : Ismène and Cidalise, tired of their game of *tri* and at a loss for topics of scandal, determine to do some work. Araminte happens to be embroidering a flower, and Cidalise, taking up a piece of gold thread, draws a frame up to her chair. Yawning the while, she embroiders a piece of dress-trimming, while Ismène, stretched upon the sofa, works at a Marly flounce. There is a neighing of horses, a bell rings, and a lackey announces Monsieur le Marquis, who, as he comes into the room, exclaims : " How delighted I am to find you at home, ladies! And what lovely work! How beautifully grouped those flowers are ! And how even the threads of this embroidery seem to be ! It is the work of the Graces and the fairies, or rather of you!" He then takes a small tube from his pocket, selects a gold-needle, and begins to embroider. The ladies admire his dexterity, and he, after having examined Araminte's work, goes to the frame at which Cidalise is working, and finishes the flower which she had begun . . . . From her he moves to the sofa, and, seizing one end of the flounce, assists Ismène, to whom he pays special attention, to complete her task. You can fancy how delighted the three ladies are.

Ladies took with them of an evening workbags, often very large, which they filled with a host of articles, not forgetting the patchbox and the rouge-pot, the fashionable novel and the latest arietta. The men also had their workbags, of smaller dimensions, which were afterwards termed *ridicules* (reticules) and which contained a whole arsenal of cutlery and fancy-articles such as boxes of different shapes filled with lozenges, bonbons, snuff, and scent.

People were so apt to suffer from what is inelegantly but expressively known as "boredom," that they were always on the look out for some novel mode of amusement. For a short time, charades, riddles and word-puzzles were all the rage. Many of these puzzles were published by the *Mercure de France*, but the wits of the day endeavoured to invent new ones for the salons in which they were invited guests. In addition to the general receptions, many ladies admitted a few intimate friends to chat with them while they were at their toilette (Fig. 278). The conversation, on these occasions, was of a very sentimental turn, and often, as the Abbé Coyer wrote to an English lady, wandered away to questions of toilette.

As a variation to the calumnies and scandals which formed the staple of fashionable talk, coxcombs invented *persiflage*, or the art of poking fun at persons who were often entitled to more consideration than was paid to them. This was considered *bon-ton*, but, as Duclos remarked, "it needs a great deal of wit to make this *persiflage* acceptable, and as most of those who indulged it are shallow-brained simpletons, it becomes in their mouth insupportable jargon."

The attractions of scandal and *persiflage* were not strong enough to dissipate the weariness with which female society was oppressed, and hence arose the fashion of "vapours." All ladies of fashion made a point of being affected with these "vapours" as an excuse for their yawning and headaches. "You feel your head heavy," says the doctor in " Le Cercle " to one of his lady patients, " you feel disinclined to do anything which requires effort. . . . I understand, there is a certain amount of giddiness and *fibrous* impatience. These are all 'vapours,' the nervous fluid is electrified by the heat . . . the nerves contract, and you feel spasmodic thrills." Abbé Coyer, writing to an English lady, says : "You may be forgiven for not suffering from headache, but it is unpardonable not to have 'vapours,' for only market-women have the right to be in robust health."

"Vapours" found no place in the so-called *bureaux d'esprit*, of which there were many more since Madame de Lambert had set the fashion. Most of these salons, in which things of the mind always held the first place, were opened under the auspices of distinguished ladies who, though not often young and beautiful, were well informed and devoted to literature. Madame de Tencin had written several interesting novels, before forming a literary circle which lasted until her death (1749). To this circle, which was occasionally visited by politicians and statesmen, were admitted talented men of every kind, and they received a hearty welcome, which was none the less pleasing because the suppers were very renowned. Fontenelle and Montesquieu often met to discuss on various subjects with Panard and Collé, but, if Madame de Genlis is to be believed—though she only spoke from hearsay—Madame de Tencin treated her literary guests with a somewhat contemptuous familiarity. She called them *mes bêtes*, and though everybody knew she meant just the opposite, the nickname was not a flattering one. Still Madame Geoffrin was only too glad to win them over to her own salons, and when she came to see Madame de Tencin on her deathbed, the latter said : "The cunning little woman has come to see whether she cannot inherit my property."

All the frequenters of Madame de Tencin's salons passed over to Madame Geoffrin, who was more remarkable for her intelligence, taste, and polish, than for her cleverness. According to Marmontel, whose "Memoirs" contain the subjoined portraiture of this lady, her chief quality was her *savoir-vivre*. "Her temperament," he says, "is difficult of pourtrayal, for it was made up of semi-tones, and had few broadly marked characteristics. . . . Her mind, though cultivated only by her mixture in society, is refined, just, and discerning. Her native intuition always enables her to find the right words to express her thoughts. The master-mind in this celebrated salon was her intimate friend d'Alembert, around whom were grouped Mairan the astronomer, Marivaux the dramatic writer, St. Lambert the poet, the Marquis de Chastellux, who was a humble

disciple of the philosophers, Abbé Morellet, a very caustic con-
versationalist, the pompous Thomas and the talented Helvetius.
Amongst all these eminent men, there was one woman who was

Fig. 278.—A Morning Visit; after Eisen.

looked upon as at least their equal, viz., Mdlle. Lespinasse, who was
a recruit from the salons of Madame du Deffand. The Comte de
Guibert, who also belonged to the coterie of Madame Geoffrin, says
of Mdlle. de Lespinasse: "She had the talent of adapting her
conversation to the intellects of her listeners, and she seemed to form
an instinctive judgment of the characteristics of those in whose

society she might be thrown. . . . She talked for the most part on plain subjects, but she did not express herself in a common way, and this art, which seemed to be a second nature with her, never obtruded itself upon notice, and never led her into affectation."

Madame Geoffrin's salon was frequented too by a number of charming women, many of them belonging to the very highest class of society, as for instance the Duchesse d'Egmont and Madame de Boufflers, the latter of whom, according to Mdlle. de Lespinasse, " was better versed in the small talk of the day than any other lady in Paris." So it was that these receptions acquired an European celebrity. All persons of distinction, of either sex, who came to Paris, made a point of procuring admission to a house in which they were certain of meeting the élite of French litterateurs. The fame of her salon extended to herself, and the Empress Katherine II. of Russia did all she could to induce Madame Geoffrin to visit St. Petersburg, with a view of showing her courtiers at the Hermitage a specimen of French polish.

Madame du Deffand's salon formed a striking contrast with that of Madame Geoffrin ; it had been opened earlier than the latter, as it also survived the rival which had eclipsed it for a time, as Madame du Deffand died at the age of eighty-three, three years after the death of Madame Geoffrin (1777). Madame du Deffand was, to borrow an expression of the time " a monster of wit," who did not enjoy any personal popularity, though, for the matter of that, she did nothing to court it.

Yet she affected at times an air of good nature, and practised with success the maxim *ars est celare artem.* She was not deficient of general information, and she was a pleasant talker ; but though her salon was filled with philosophers and men of letters, the conversation did not often run on philosophy or literature. She received many famous writers, Fontenelle, Diderot, Montesquieu, Voltaire, and President Hénault among the number ; distinguished foreigners, such as David Hume, Gibbon, and Horace Walpole, and amongst the women of fashion, the Marquise de Châtelet, the Duchesse de Chaulnes, and the Duchesse de Boufflers. And yet Madame du Deffand, almost blind, discontented with herself and the world around her, jealous of all who were young and beautiful, and concealing her peevishness and bitterness of spirit beneath a mask of kindness, can write to her friend Horace Walpole : "Society is made up of persons incapable of knowledge, thought, and feeling, and of clever persons puffed up with vanity, jealous and envious ; the latter one cannot but hate or despise."

It was only natural therefore that men of letters should prefer other salons in which they might count upon a better welcome, and in which they were also sure of finding that etiquette did not necessarily exclude cordiality. Such were the receptions of Madame Dupin and Madame de Forcalquier, which rivalled the select gatherings of Madame d'Houdetot. St. Lambert, the devoted friend of the latter lady, assisted her in doing the honours of her salon, and Marmontel in his " Memoirs of a Father " asserts that : " Never was there a more perfect harmony of thought and feeling between two minds and two souls. They also resembled each other by the hearty manner in which they received their friends, displaying an amount of unaffected and considerate politeness, which touched the hearts of those towards whom it was manifested, just as it most unmistakably came from the hearts of those who displayed it." This salon, or *bureau d'esprit*, was very similar, both in regard to its composition and intellectual physiognomy, to that of Madame Dupin concerning which J.-J. Rousseau, one of its frequenters, has left such a graphic record : " Madame Dupin, though very amiable, was serious and rather cold. Her house, one of the most brilliant in Paris, was the rendezvous of a company which, if its numbers had only been fewer, would have represented the élite of every class of society. She liked to be surrounded by people who were distinguished, whether for their high birth, their literary genius or their beauty. Her salons were filled with dukes, ambassadors, and titled personages. The Princesse de Rohan, the Comtesse de Forcalquier, Madame de Mirepoix, Madame de Brignoles, and Lady Hervey were amongst the number of her female friends. M. de Fontenelle, the Abbé de St. Pierre, Abbé Sallier, M. de Fourmont, M. de Bernis, M. de Buffon, and M. de Voltaire were amongst her guests. Though her reserved manners did not attract many young people, the society which frequented her drawing-rooms was, for that very reason, all the more dignified." It must be mentioned that the indispensable accompaniment of every fashionable salon were dinners and suppers.

There were certain salons which may be looked upon as more exclusively literary and philosophical, as, for instance, that of Falconet, the King's consulting physician. His gatherings were called " The men of letter's mass," the reason being that they always took place on Sunday mornings, until his death in 1782. By the variety and extent of his learning, he imparted to the conversation an interest at once agreeable and instructive, which was wanting at the receptions of Baron d'Holbach and Helvetius, though these salons were, for the most part, frequented by the same people. But the receptions given by Helvetius, being more formal and very numerously attended, did not admit of a general conversation, while, at the house of Baron d'Holbach, the talk typified the ideas and opinions of the Baron and his friends by turning upon the most delicate points of philosophy and politics. It was more than a salon, it was an arsenal, so to speak, in which were forged the weapons with which to attack and overthrow the principles and the laws of society, religion and government.

Another celebrated salon was that of Madame Doublet de Persan, who never left her apartment, where she received every day a small circle of men of letters and fashionables, whose fondness for scandal attracted them to the house of this old lady, who was at once well-informed and discreet. From her apartment were issued the *nouvelles à la main*, manuscript sheets which circulated widely throughout France and abroad for more than forty years. It was said that there were two registers constantly open on the table of the salon: one for authentic and reliable news, the other for doubtful

A SALON IN THE TIME OF LOUIS XVI.; AFTER LAWRENCE.

information.   Petit de Bachaumont, who was a dilettante, especially in regard to artistic matters, composed out of these two registers the official journal of the day's news, which his pupil, Pidansat de Mairo-

Fig. 279.—Winter ; after Lancret.

bert, continued even after the death of Madame Doublet de Persan (1771).   Her intimates had comprised St. Palaze, Mairan, the Abbé de Voisnénon, Piron, Falconet, Foncemagne, Perrin, Devaur, d'Argental, and the Chevalier de Mouhy.   The latter was on such friendly terms with the police, that he no doubt kept them well-informed as to what took place in this salon, though, for the matter of that, the admission of four or five women, Madame du Boccage and Madame d'Argental amongst the number, was an assurance that secrecy would be preserved no longer. As a matter of fact, their indiscreet talk contributed in no small degree to bring about the suppression of these news-sheets.

Madame Doublet had, however, some imitators, though they were not so clever or so well-informed as she was. A year before the suicide of Mairobert (1779) had dispersed the members of this coterie, Patrin de la Blancherie started, on his own account, a weekly sheet called *Nouvelles de la République des lettres*, a sort of general correspondence similar to that which bore the name of Bachaumont, but more moderate in tone. The materials for this sheet were collected at a meeting which Blancherie convoked at a garret of the College de Bayeux in the Rue de la Harpe. Mairobert's journal records that " there were no chairs, and the members of this conference (which was the prototype of literary and artistic gatherings) had to remain on their legs till six in the evening."

At this epoch, each salon had its special and distinct characteristics ; the encyclopedists and the philosophers affected the salons of the Duchesse de Choiseul and the Maréchale de Luxembourg ; the economists, those of Madame de Marchais and Turgot ; the artists, that of Watelet the financier and a member of the French Academy ; the lovers of music, those of Rameau and Abbé Morellet ; the literary people, those of Suard and Panckoucke, editor of the *Mercure.* There was no end to the number of salons in which the conversation was of a frivolous kind, dealing with such topics as magnetism, free-masonry, fashions, ballooning, horse-racing, theatres, and the favourite amusements of the hour ; but there were everywhere unmistakable signs of a complete metamorphosis in French society, which was losing its national traditions, and become more noisy and careless of ceremony. In shaking off etiquette, politeness had disappeared with it.

And yet agreeable conversation, varying from grave to gay,

was still to be enjoyed in certain great houses : such as those of the Princesse de Beauvau, the Duchesse de Grammont, the Duchesse d'Anville, the Comtesse de Tessé, the Comtesse de Ségur, the Comtesse de Boufflers, Madame de Puisieux, and Madame de Montesson, who had been secretly married to the Duc d'Orleans.

Fig. 280.—The dance ; after Chodowieski.
(Communicated by M. Eug. Sauzay.)

The Comte de Ségur, from whose book this information is derived, adds : "We find there an undefinable mixture of simplicity and elegance, of grace and reasoning, of criticism and urbanity. Their frequenters learnt, beyond all doubt, to understand the history and politics of their time, and studied with eagerness all the fresh productions of the transcendent talents and genius which then shed such lustre upon France. Discussions, which rarely degenerated into disputes, were carried on with moderation, and as discerning foresight made people proficient in the art of pleasing, wearisome topics were avoided by mutual consent. The most distinguished representatives of literature were admitted into the houses of the old nobility. This intermixture of courtiers and men of letters developed the intelligence of the former and improved the tastes of the latter.. Never did Paris more nearly resemble ancient Athens!"

These aristocratic salons had ceased to be more than brilliant exceptions which became fewer every day, as the passion for liberty and equality gained hold of the middle classes of the nation, and impelled them to introduce into France English ideas and habits. Polite society was the first victim of this foreign imitation. Political meetings were held at which the most delicate political questions were discussed by a noisy and brawling multitude, and other sections of society met to hear scientific papers read or to witness experiments in physics and chemistry. Under the pretence of being serious, society became heavy, pedantic, and unbearable.

These noisy and tumultuous crowds were but the vanguard of the Revolution, which was beginning to destroy French society. The nobles did not take part in the destruction, but, by adopting the customs of England and America, they allowed it to run its course. But, with all this, people still prided themselves on belonging to good society and on their *savoir-vivre,* and the taste for conversation was not altogether lost, though it was often replaced by insignificant gossip, in Paris at least. Morning visits still preserved the urbanity which had formerly characterized them, but even they were marred at last by the clash of political opinions. The number of unoccupied persons had also undergone considerable diminution, and it was only those who had carriages at their command who, by spending only five minutes at each house, could go the round of the salons on fixed days. Then was introduced the practice of replacing formal visits by merely inscribing one's name in the porter's visiting-book, and this we may call the final effort of French politeness in the 18th century.

Yet the broken remains of French society had an exaggerated idea of their importance and power. " Vain, inquisitive, capricious, and headstrong," to use the language of a contemporary who survived the final catastrophe, "this society had looked upon the words *reform* and *liberty* as it would a change in the shape of a dress or the tune of a couplet. It had so long possessed the right of citing everybody before its tribunal, that it could not abandon its habit of pronouncing judgment." It made light of the terrible events which were preparing after the triumph of popular revolt, crowned by the capture of the Bastille. But the last of the salons, which the tide of emigration had thinned, soon closed their doors. The course of political events led to the opening of clubs in every direction, and it may be said that the reign of ancient French society ended when that of the Jacobins began (1789).

CHAPTER XVIII.

TRAVEL

EVERYBODY travelled more or less in the interior of France during the eighteenth century, though the conveyances were heavy and unsafe, the roads bad and sometimes impassable, and the inns revolting; but Frenchmen were not readily tempted to make long journeys through Europe for the mere pleasure of travelling through new countries, and studying the manners and customs of the inhabitants. Those who had expatriated themselves for the purpose of making their fortune more rapidly than they could hope to do at home, returned to France as soon as they had saved up enough to ensure them a modest competence. This is how it was that throughout Europe, and we may say the world, certain trades were generally in the hands of Frenchmen, whose only thought was to grow rich and return home. The actors, barbers, milliners, musicians, and, we must also add, the adventurers, were generally of French and even Parisian origin. So at least the Flemish, Swiss, Piedmontese, and natives of Brabant dubbed themselves. Rousseau asserts in "Emile," that "only four classes of persons take long journeys,—sailors, merchants, soldiers, and missionaries. We cannot expect that either of the three former classes should supply acute observers."

J. J. Rousseau does not allude to many other categories of

ENTRY OF KING LOUIS XV. INTO STRASBURG IN 1744.

French travellers who visited, at least once in their lifetime, Italy, or Switzerland, or Holland, or Germany, or England. These consisted of young men belonging to rich families, whose parents sent them, accompanied by a tutor, to complete their education; of pious persons undertaking pilgrimages which were most frequent in jubilee years; of artists, and lovers of art, who also made a pilgrimage into Italy, but from different motives; of the admirers of nature, the veritable tourists, in search of picturesque and wild scenery, of mountains, glaciers, and torrents. But the number of travellers was nevertheless very far below what it now is. J. J. Rousseau, who was himself one of the most enthusiastic admirers of nature, thus alludes to the tastes of Englishmen and of Frenchmen for travel: "Of all the nations in the world, the Frenchman is the fondest of travelling. . . . There are Frenchmen to be met with in every corner of the globe. There is no country in which you will find so many people who have been abroad as you will in France. . . . The Englishman is also very fond of travelling, but in a different way. The English nobility travel, and the French nobility do not. The French people travel, and the English people do not. . . . The Frenchman has always some business in view when he travels, but the Englishman does not go to seek his fortune away from home, unless it is to make vast sums by commerce. When he travels it is to spend, not to make money. He is too proud to hold a subordinate position amongst strangers; this is why Englishmen gain more information when they are abroad than Frenchmen do."

Even in the time of Louis XIV. it was universally considered by all noble and wealthy families that no young man's education was complete, unless after leaving college he travelled through some part of Europe with a tutor. Thus Abbé Fléchier, after educating the son of M. de Caumartin, the Master of Requests, accompanied him through the South of France and Italy. As a general rule an ecclesiastic, or at all events a tutor wearing the ecclesiastical dress, was selected as companion for these travels, in the course of which information was conveyed in too pedagogic a form to do much towards developing the mind of the pupil. The Marquis de Pezay thus condemns what he calls the ridiculous mania of sending new-fledged collegians to travel: "Some schoolboy, who has never looked up at the statues in the Tuileries gardens, posts off to Utrecht to admire some very inferior ones in the gardens of Mme. Termer. Another, who has never seen the King's cabinet, gapes open-mouthed at Bâle before the shop-window of Bernouilli the apothecary, at six pairs of models, two agates, and a piece of coral. A Frenchman ought at least to be acquainted with the Louvre colonnade before he goes to kneel in the squares of St. Peter at Rome and St. Sophia at Constantinople."

These travels produced much better effects when the tutors took their pupils to the Alps or the Pyrenees, and made them familiar with those beauties of nature which cannot be seen in a large city or a provincial town. Many people travelled on foot amongst the mountains with a knapsack on their back and a stout stick in their hand, botanizing, or making collections of minerals, or studying natural history. J. J. Rousseau, with whom the love of nature was so overpowering a passion, often refers in the "Confessions" to the delight which he felt in travelling on foot through the mountainous districts of Switzerland. In one passage he says: "I like to walk at my own pace, and halt when I feel so inclined. A strolling life is what is best suited for me. To walk, during fine weather, through a picturesque country, without being hurried, and with a pleasant object at the end of one's journey, is, to my mind, the most delightful thing conceivable." But at the period when Rousseau was leaving his beloved Switzerland, then visited by few travellers, journeys on foot were not so frequent as they became after the publication of his dreamy writings, which gave birth to a new kind of traveller, who was in existence long before Sterne wrote his "Sentimental Journey." Rousseau, a few years before his death, regretted nothing so much as being unable to renew his mountain excursions, which he thus described: "It was only in my happy days that I journeyed on foot. Duty, business, and the increase of my luggage, soon compelled me to play the *gentleman* and hire carriages. Care, embarrassments, and constraint took their seats beside me, and from that time, instead of looking forward to my journey with pleasure, my only anxiety was to get to the end of it."

The mania of travelling, not only with a view of observing and taking notice of what one sees, but of making these observations, was not confined to France, but it extended to most European countries, Germany and England in particular. But the numerous books of travel written by Frenchmen, and even by Frenchwomen, generally testified to the levity of the national character, and it was of such writers that Voltaire said : " Some travellers think that the whole universe has its eyes upon the inns in which they have slept, and upon their wrangles with the customs' officers." He is also unkind enough to add that books of travel contain more falsehoods than any other kind, and this he instanced by an anecdote of what occurred at Blois. A German visitor, who had a quarrel with his red-haired hostess, wrote in his note-book : " All the women at Blois are red-haired and bad tempered." Montesquieu, meaning to signify that people travelled too rapidly to get any fair idea of the countries which they visited, says : " There are plenty of people who hire post-horses, but only a few travellers ; " and J. J. Rousseau thus defines the qualities required in a traveller : " There are many people who learn less from travelling than they do from reading. Others do not gain any knowledge because they travel with a very different object. Very often people happen to look at some object which does not strike them as beautiful, and then they cease their observations."

This will account for travelled and untravelled Frenchmen being so ignorant of geography, and of everything outside the narrow circle of their daily habits. Even those who had received a good education in many respects, knew as little of ethnography as persons utterly devoid of the most elementary instruction.

In the years preceding the Revolution, a great number of the inhabitants of Paris had never left the capital, or, at most, had gone but a few miles away from it. Néel, the author of a satirical pamphlet " From Paris to St. Cloud by Sea " (1760), says :—" There is no such greenhorn as your Parisian who has never been beyond the barriers, if he sees in the distance lands, woods, mountains, and meadows, he thinks they are uninhabitable ; he eats his bread, and drinks his wine in Paris, without having the least idea out of what they are made." These sarcasms fell harmless upon the imper-turbable Parisians, who would, perhaps, have derived scant benefit from travel. Mercier, writing in 1782, says :—" Though post-horses make travelling a very easy process, wealthy people move little from home, they will always prefer to reside in the centre of the capital, and the rest of France will be an unknown land to them. They will take up their quarters in Paris and Auteuil, or beside the banks of the Seine and the Marne." Thus the Parisians, as a rule, confined their excursions to the country near the capital.

Still a few daring spirits pushed their explorations farther afield, picnic parties being sometimes made up, which lasted three or four days, the company visiting different places within a radius of thirty or forty miles from Paris. Many people passed a day or two, during the summer or autumn, at Ermenonville, the splendid gardens at which place rivalled Chatsworth or Belvoir ; at Mortefontaine, where landscape gardening had enhanced the beauty of the scenery ; at Chantilly, famous for the château and palatial stables belonging to the Prince de Condé ; at Fontainebleau, where, in addition to the royal château of François I. and Henri II., the forest always attracted many visitors ; at Montmorency, where donkey-rides in the woods formed the chief attraction, and in the ancient towns of the Ile de France, in which there were always to be seen some local curiosities which formed a contrast with what Parisians were accustomed to witness at home. These excursions also formed a topic of pleasant conversa-tion afterwards, and the recollection of the various episodes connected with them broke the monotony of business.

The people of Paris also had their excursions during the summer and autumn months, frequenting the fêtes given in honour of the

Fig. 281.—Chantilly Park, the property of the Condés.

patron saints of the villages outside Paris, making pilgrimages to Argenteuil, St. Geneviève-aux-Bois, Larchan, &c., and visiting each Sunday the rural communes outside the walls, which have since become an integral part of the city.　Artizans, after completing their term of apprenticeship, generally made the tour of France, plying their trade in the different places they visited, and settling down as masters, after having travelled as journeymen.　These journeys were accomplished on foot, and the young workmen, who travelled sometimes alone, and sometimes in parties of three or four, always found at each stage a cordial welcome from the centre of journeymanship. Thus it was that most members of the trade corporations had, when young, visited various parts of the kingdom.

The King's journeys, which were very rare, excepting the ordinary visits to Marly, Fontainebleau, or Compiègne, and which only took place when an army was about to start on a campaign, or when a newly-conquered province had to be visited, were looked upon as important events by the population of the districts through which he passed, and gave rise to public rejoicings.　The journey of Louis XV. to Strasbourg was remarkable for the splendour and variety of the fêtes given on that occasion.

The nobility, rarely travelling out of France, generally passed a few months at their country houses, when these latter were not too far from Versailles, and when their position at Court enabled them to leave it without fear of being forgotten.　The nobles, moreover, possessing several properties very far apart from each other, could only visit them at rare intervals, sometimes but once in ten or fifteen years.　The Marquis de Mirabeau says :—" Let us suppose that a property in some distant province is left to some great family.　It was formerly in the hands of some worthy people who led a life of honest ease, bringing up their children, and spending their money in the district.　But, after passing into these new hands, the agent can scarcely scrape together enough to keep body and soul together, the timber is cut down, and the keep becomes a refuge for owls and bats, and with all this the new owner is none the better off."　The

FIREWORKS AT STRASBURG IN 1744.

Marquis de Mirabeau compares this deserted residence to that in which the owner spent a part of the year. The presence of the owner led to large outlays upon the property; the old castle was restored in modern style and newly furnished throughout; kitchen and flower gardens, terraces and hot-houses were added, and pieces of artificial water and fountains were formed at considerable expense. The household expenses swallowed up the rent, and the large hunting-parties, which often lasted the whole winter, further helped to encumber the fortune of the proprietor, who thus spent ten times more money in his country house than he would have done at Versailles. The magistracy did not spend so much when they paid their yearly visit to their country residences during the vacation. The members of the Parliaments also had vast hereditary possessions in the provinces, and their time, while visiting them, was taken up in inspecting the farms, receiving the rents, ascertaining the condition of their flocks and the result of the harvest, watching the grape-gathering, selecting the timber to be cut down, and in other matters connected with agriculture. The only festivities consisted of a few dinners with their neighbours, and a little fishing and shooting in a quiet way. The wealthiest of the magistrates posted to their country residences, but many others, less rich or more parsimonious, were content to take the diligence, then called the *carrosse*, which, though a less costly, was a much slower and more dangerous mode of transit.

Thus, the wealthy who did not travel or who did not care about travelling had every reason for avoiding the inconveniences and perils of a residence in the country, for by remaining at home they were not exposed to the annoyances of being upset in a dirty lane, of sleeping in some vile way-side inn, or of being rifled by highwaymen. They endeavoured to procure the pleasures of the country without moving far away from Paris. The anonymous author of "Les Numeros" says: "The great majority of wealthy and well-to-do people repair to the villages round Paris, such as Auteuil, Passy, St. Cloud, Sèvres, Nogent, Vincennes, St. Maur and Villejuif.

Those whose fortune allows it occupy magnificent residences surrounded by large and well-kept parks and gardens. Those who are less wealthy content themselves with small villas, the gardens of which are more like poultry-yards than anything else, and which remind one of the Rue St. Denis rather than of the country . . . . Both these classes lead the same life and see the same people as if they were in the heart of Paris . . . . They expect to find the country within a radius where art has altogether supplanted nature." At the same time the art of gardening had made wonderful progresses, and the Marquis de Girardin's ingenious theory "as to the composition of landscapes" could be put in practice within a very small extent of ground. Enormous sums of money had been spent on several estates near Paris, and even on residences within the walls, upon the creation of English gardens and fancy landscapes, whence the name of *follies*, as, for instance, the *folie-Beaujon*, belonging to Beaujon, the banker, the *folie-d'Orleans*, which was the Parc Monceau, and the *folie-Brunoy*, which was the ruin of the millionaire Marquis de Brunoy. Joseph de la Borde, farmer-general and banker to the Court, went even further, for he determined to prove that rocks and waterfalls and pine forests could exist within 10 leagues of Paris, as well as in the Alps, and, with this view, he spent more than a million sterling upon the construction, in the Beauce district, of the Folie-Méréville, and was in the habit of announcing to the guests whom he had driven down in his carriage and six : " Gentlemen, here we are in Switzerland, and we are now about to cross the devil's bridge, which, spanning a torrent and a precipice, will lead us to the marble temple which I have erected in honour of Friendship."

The bad state of the roads often rendered travelling very tedious. These roads had been made and were kept in repair by forced labour, but the work executed by the men pressed into service was nearly always scamped. Moreover, no change had been made in the laying of the roads, the causeway of which was always slightly convex, with avenues of trees on each side. But as the causeway was not wide

enough to admit of two vehicles passing each other, one or other of
them had to pull on one side, and this led to many accidents. Sometimes, the two vehicles came into collision, and in other cases the
one which was backing out of the way upset as it left the causeway.
The roads were much used by heavy waggons drawn by long teams

Fig. 282.—The death ; after Desportes.

of horses, and this, together with heavy thunderstorms, will account
for the deep ruts by which so many travelling carriages were upset
during dark nights. Louis XVI., who did away with the system of
forced labour (1776), decreed that the cost of making and repairs of
the main roads should be borne by the State, but the owners of the
property through which these roads ran asserted their feudal right,
and the system of forced labour was retained until the establishment
of the service of *ponts et chaussées* (bridges and roads). The *local
roads*, as they are now called, were, previous to the Revolution, so bad
that they can scarcely be classed as carriage-roads at all.

This was not the chief inconvenience in the way of travelling through France. People naturally dreaded having to sleep at the inns, though they were compelled to do so owing to the dangers of travelling after dark. In addition to the chances of accident, the highwaymen were very numerous, and certain places, such as the hills at Juvisy and Tarrare, were noted as being haunted by these malefactors, who generally selected for their attack rising grounds, so that the postilion might not have a chance of escaping by putting his horses into a gallop. The lonely inns had almost as bad a name as the highwaymen, and, though they were not always kept by cut-throats and thieves, they were invariably devoid of comfort. Most of them consisted only of three departments ; the stable, the kitchen, and a common sleeping-room, in which the traveller, whose evil fate compelled him to spend a night at the inn, had to share a bed with the innkeeper and his servants. Travelling by water was less dangerous, for the passengers slept in the *water-coaches*, as they were termed, but it was not more expeditious or comfortable. The water-coaches, which floated down stream and were pulled up stream by horses, were not built with a view to convenience, and the travellers, no matter to what rank they belonged, were crowded into a dark and close-smelling cabin, in which there were scarcely seats enough for all. So it was impossible to sleep, except in a sitting posture, for two or three nights, and those who had not taken the precaution to provide themselves with food often went fasting, for the provisions, always very bad, often ran short. All that the owner of the boats had a good supply of was wine and other intoxicating drinks, as he knew that these would be in great request with the country people, the workmen and the small tradespeople, who mostly travelled by them. They started every three days from the Quai des Célestins at Paris, and called at all the towns on the banks of the Seine as far as Montargis, all those on the banks of the Marne as far as Châlons, and all those upon the banks of the Yonne as far as Auxerre. They also went every other day to Rouen, where they formed a junction with the boats from Havre. Bertin in his

"Voyage de Bourgogne" thus describes his journey up the Seine from Paris to Montereau (September, 1774) : " The between-decks is occupied by monks, soldiers, nurses, and peasants, and it seems as if I was on board one of those vessels laden with animals which are being sent out to stock some newly discovered land. The *skipper*,

Fig. 283.—A wayside inn. (From the *Routes de France.*)

as they call him, has his berth near the helm. The den of the vivandière is not far off, and the place in which the provisions are kept is in unpleasant proximity to the bilge-pipe. The deck is covered with ropes and rigging, and moreover the weather does not admit of our remaining there. There are only six wretched berths, the possession of which is very highly prized." In reference to the way in which the boat is pulled up stream, the same writer adds : " I forgot to tell you that we have four strong horses to pull us along. They draw us by means of a rope attached to the mainmast, and these are our favourable winds. The Limousin quadrupeds are our zephyrs. This curious mode of locomotion sometimes gives rise to scenes worthy of Vernet's brush. Every now and then the horses stop, and the rope slackens and drops into the stream. With a crack of the whip, they start off again, and the rope, pulled taut, rises out of the water with snake-like contortions." Bertin terminates his description by a sketch of the horrible nights passed on the hard benches between decks.

Fig. 284.—The water-coach, on the Seine ; after Perronet.

A night in the diligence was almost as disagreeable, and a journey of four or five hundred miles was never got through without some accident, the least of which was an upset. The *carrosse de voiture*, as it was termed in the seventeenth century, was an enormous vehicle, of wood bolted with iron, with four wheels and shafts, seven feet long by five feet wide, and with room for eight or ten people on the front and back seats, and those placed against the doors. These doors could not open until the seats had been lifted up ; they had not any glass windows, as the berlins used in towns had, and their only protection from the wind, rain, or dust, were leather curtains. The top of the carriage was so loaded with luggage that it took eight horses to drag it over a bad piece of road. Subsequently, the travelling carriages were made still larger and heavier.

They were called *gondolas*, and room was made for twelve people by dividing the carriage into two compartments, to one of which access was gained from behind. The space was so limited that, to use Mercier's expression, " Everybody was asking his neighbour to give him back his leg or his arm when the time came to get out."

When it was proposed to entrust the repair of the roads to the State, upon the payment of a special tax, Turgot, the minister who had started the scheme, conceded the monopoly of the *messageries*

Fig. 285.—The Pannier, or land-coach ; fac simile, after Rigaud.

(stage coaches) to a company of speculators, who paid a large sum to the Crown for this privilege. It was the ruin of many small stage-coach proprietors, who were unable to compete against the new diligences, nicknamed *turgotines*, which were unshapely vehicles, drawn by gaunt animals that looked as if they had not a kick left in them.

The large four-wheeled travelling carriages used by families, with room for luggage before and behind, were very like the stage-coaches which had preceded the *turgotines*. The body of these carriages was also very heavy, and was very unsteady, owing to the bad quality of the springs, which were tied round with ropes to make them more powerful. There were three or four small windows, or casements, in the upper part of the carriage, access to the interior of which was through a narrow door on a level with the wheels, and with some steps leading up to it. These carriages, drawn by five or six horses, did about ten miles an hour when all went well. The

vehicles used for the post-office service, when it was in the hands of
the farmers-general, formed a singular contrast with the general
profusion of that body.   They were mere two-wheeled carts without
springs, with a tarpaulin stretched over some hoops for a hood.   The
wooden boxes and leather bags used for forwarding the letters and
parcels were packed into these carts under the supervision of the
courier, who distributed the mails in the towns and villages through
which he passed.   There were only twenty-seven couriers for the
whole of France, and in return for an annual allowance of 1000 livres

Fig. 286.—The "carabas" on the road to Versailles; fac-simile, after Rigaud.

(£40), they were required to provide the mail-carts, which were
horsed by the administration.   The couriers were allowed, by way of
compensation, to take one passenger and a small quantity of luggage.
These primitive arrangements were not altered until 1790, when the
farmers-general were deprived of the postal service.   It must be
said, however, that at this period it was safer and less expensive to
travel by the mail than in post-chaises.   The courier was excessively
attentive to his passenger, and this was also the case with the drivers
of the coaches previous to the establishment of the stage-coach
company alluded to in the preceding page.   The coachman, or
carrier, became as it were the host of the people who rode in his
carriage, and by exerting himself to make them comfortable, paved
the way for a *pourboire* at the end of the journey.

There was no end to the various kinds of vehicles, public conveyances with a fixed tariff, and carriages hired by private agree-

mer , which were running between Paris and the villages around it, throughout the whole of the eighteenth century, when the Court was in residence at Versailles, and the many ancient and modern châteaux within a radius of seventy miles from the capital, were inhabited by their owners. This was notably the case during the shooting and

Fig. 287.—Cart drawn by oxen.
(From the *Journal de mon retour de Saintonge*, by Robbé de Beauveset, 1760; drawings by Desfriches, engraved by C. Cochin.)

hunting seasons, but no heavy waggons, fourgons, cabriolets, or even empty fiacres, were allowed upon the Versailles road. In addition to these various conveyances, all more or less antiquated and cumbersome, the galiot and coach were much used for daily journeys to St. Cloud, and for going to Fontainebleau when the Court was in residence there. The price for going in the royal coach to Fontainebleau was two livres ten sols (about 2*s*. 3*d*.), and only five sols for a place in the galiot which went to St. Cloud. There were always an immense number of passengers for Versailles, where most of the public administrations had to maintain daily communications with the ministries and the King. Mercier, writing in the middle of the reign of Louis XVI., says : " Versailles is the land of horses, which are to be seen there by squadrons. The Princes have as many in their stables as the King ; and in spite of the weedings out, there are as many horses as there are human beings." At the same time the official residents at Versailles did not care to risk their valuable animals (for the English taste for good horses had become general amongst the French nobility) by using them to go to Paris, and they hired post-horses which, despite their half-starved looks, did the distance to and fro (not far short of twenty-four miles) in less than three hours, with a stoppage of an hour in Paris to allow the official time to transact his business at the ministry. The hire of these drudges (*enragés* was the term used) cost rather less than a sovereign.

But the conveyances which were most numerous on the road between Paris and Versailles were the *carabas* and the *coucou*. The former was a long wicker cage on mainbraces, with four or six wheels, capable of holding from twenty to four-and-twenty passengers, and drawn by six horses, which were six hours and a half in doing ten miles. The *coucou* was a more rapid mode of conveyance ; though constructed to hold five passengers, double that number were often huddled into it. This unsightly vehicle consisted of a body open in front, built upon two large wheels, and provided with two hard benches for the unhappy passengers whom the driver packed into it, without any regard to their comfort. The first-comers were nicknamed the *monkeys*, and those who arrived later had to sit beside the driver on a wooden plank, which was placed in front of the splashboard. These latter were called *rabbits*, and the whole number, after paying twelve sous (6*d.*) a-head for being half jolted to death for a couple of hours on the King's highway, emerged from their prison, either covered with dust, or perspiration, or mud, or numbed with the cold, according to the time of the year. Yet these disgraceful conveyances were allowed upon the road at all hours, and often met the court equipages, when the *rabbits* and *monkeys* were alike exposed to the jeers of the coachmen and footmen in their gorgeous liveries. The passengers adopted all kinds of stratagems to secure more than their share of room, and it is said that a *monkey*, with the cunning of the race after which he was nicknamed, obtained the seat belonging to a fat priest by telling him that he was not quite cured of an attack of hydrophobia. In fact, the Versailles *coucou* was about on a par, so far as comfort went, with the Chantilly *carriole*, which, according to the description of Jean-François Guichard (1760), was merely a covered cart with eight rickety stools, and a pair of steps to get into it.

CHAPTER XIX.

DRESS AND FASHIONS.

IN the sixth edition of "Les Caractères" (1691), La Bruyère pronounced what we may call a funeral oration upon the fashions of the 17th century: "A fashion has no sooner supplanted some other fashion than its place is taken by a new one, which in turn makes way for the next, and so on; such is the fickleness of our character. While these changes are taking place, a century has rolled away, relegating all this finery to the dominion of the past." La Bruyère might have added that fashion, like the phœnix, rises from her ashes, and that the supremacy of France, as the centre of fashions, was universally acknowledged—never more so than in the 18th century.

The moralists and philosophers, who set up to be the oracles of that age, never ventured to protest in very strong terms against the exaggerations and absurdities of dress, which they looked upon as a necessary, if not inevitable evil. The lawyer Alleaume, the imitator of La Bruyère, said in his "Suite des Caractères" that: "The foolish set the fashions; the wise do not make themselves conspicuous by dressing in opposition to them. Ridiculous as certain fashions may be, it is still more absurd to studiously avoid their adoption." Montesquieu ("Esprit des Lois"), while admitting that "fashions have their origin in vanity," did not go so far as to condemn them altogether, as he considered them conducive to the commercial prosperity of the country.   J.-J. Rousseau was even more severe on fashion, and on women who devoted most of their thoughts to it, for he declares that "an excessive love of dress is due rather to ennui than to vanity," though he allowed that "costly attire proves social rather than personal vanity, for its use is solely a matter of habit."   He also allowed that the personal appearance of many women was set off by good dress, though he dogmatically added, "but none can require expensive finery."   Buffon, on the other hand, openly declared that "dress is a part of ourselves."   Voltaire was equally lenient in regard to fashions, but as he saw them continually changing, he denied that they were governed by good taste.   In the "Questions sur l'Encyclopédie," he argues that "taste is arbitrary in many matters, as with dress, jewellery, equipages, and everything that does not come within the domain of the fine arts; and in these cases it may more appropriately be termed fancy.   It is fancy rather than taste which originates so many new fashions."   Whether fancy or taste, France had an almost complete monopoly of fashions during the 18th century, as was very cleverly shown by a celebrated caricature of the time of Louis XVI., in which the various peoples of Europe were represented with their national costumes.   The Frenchman alone was naked, holding under his arm a parcel upon which was written the following sentence:—"As the latter is continually changing his tastes and fashions, we have given him the material, so that he can have it made up in the way he likes best."

With all this, fashion had been almost banished from the Court during the last twenty years of the reign of Louis XIV., though it had found a refuge amongst the financial classes, and even with the wealthy representatives of the bourgeoisie, who were no longer under the subjection of sumptuary laws.   These laws, often renewed and put in force from 1660 to 1704, had only been intended by Colbert as an indirect means of protecting French industry from foreign competition, one of the most stringent clauses being that which prohibited the use of all articles of apparel, such as English and Dutch laces which were smuggled into the kingdom.   However,

whatever their object may have been, they were never strictly
observed, and they soon fell into disuse, except so far as they related
to the prohibition of stuffs into which gold or silver was worked.
The decree of 1704 was the last ever issued in France with regard

Fig. 288.—Dress; fac-simile, after a water-colour by Watteau.

to female attire, and those which were promulgated in other countries
were not any better observed than had been the case in France.

Male and female dress had undergone many characteristic modifications at Court since Madame de Maintenon's moral influence had
been so omnipotent with the King. The most marked change was
in respect to the colour of the apparel, showy and variegated colours
giving way to dresses of brown and sombre shades. Madame de

Maintenon dressed like a penitent, generally wearing a large black coif upon the head, but as Louis XIV. had a great dislike for mourning, she wore dresses of some dark colour other than black, though even so her attire had a monastic look about it which

Fig. 289.—Dress ; fac-simile, after a water-colour by Watteau.

harmonized with her general bearing and her manner. All ladies of her age copied her style, but the younger ones stood out as well as they could against these innovations. Thus they still wore as a head-dress the *fontange* (top-knot), which had been introduced in 1680, but they had effected several changes in its shape and style. St. Simon in his " Memoirs " satirically remarks : " The fontange was a structure of brass-wire, ribbons, hair and baubles of all sorts, about two feet high, which made a woman's face look as if it was in the middle of her body. At the slightest movement the edifice trembled and seemed ready to come down." The fontange had developed into this from a simple knot of ribbon tied in a knot across the forehead to keep up the hair which was brushed back to the crown of the head. In its perfected state, it was composed of pieces of gummed linen, rolled into circular bands, and used for keeping in place the bows, ribbons, feathers, and jewelled ornaments of this head-dress, which was also called *commode*, while the various articles which were attached with pins to form the fontange were known by such eccentric names as the *duchess*, the *solitaire*, the *cabbage*, the *collar*, the *musketeer*, the *palisade*, the *mouse*, &c. The *mouse*, as we learn from a comedy by Regnard called "Wait for me beneath the elm" (1694), was "a small bow of ribbon which is placed in the *wood*. I must tell you that a knot of frizzled hair which trims the lower part of the fontange is called the *little wood*."

The fashion of wearing fontanges had lasted nearly ten years (which for a fashion is equivalent to a century) when Louis XIV., who had long conceived a dislike to these voluminous head-dresses, formally condemned them, Sept. 23rd, 1699, as is recorded by the Marquis de Dangeau in his diary. The Princesses and the ladies of the court obeyed without murmur, and though some of the elder ladies stood out for a short time, the example of the exiled Queen of England (the wife of James II.) led to their submission. St. Simon says: "The pyramids fell with amazing rapidity, and in the twink-ling of an eye the ladies went from one extremity to the other." By which he intended to signify that the new mode was to wear head-dresses which laid quite flat upon the hair.

It was Mme. de Maintenon who introduced the use of *falbalas* (flounces), and even their abuse, for these flounces, plaited and slashed and puffed, which were so freely used for the petticoats and sleeves, made the dress look very heavy, concealing the good points as well as the defects of the wearer's figure. Regnard, in his comedy already referred to, is as severe upon the falbalas as upon

the fontanges, for he makes a valet in this piece say : " The Parisian
ladies only invent fashions with a view of concealing their defects.
The falbala corrects the imperfections of the waist and lower limbs,
while the *squinquerque* (cravat) has been invented for ladies who have
got a long neck and sunken throat." But the falbalas lasted longer
than the fontanges, which, left off at Versailles in 1699, did not
entirely disappear in Paris till after the Regency. The falbalas

Fig. 290.—A lady in the costume of Louis the Fourteenth's time, and wearing a "fontange," getting into her sedan-
chair; fac-simile, after a contemporary drawing.

were never given up, and the use of them was frequently carried to
such an excess that a caricaturist of the Regency drew a sketch of a
lady so enveloped in them that she looked like a turkey shaking its
feathers and spreading out its comb. This caricature gave rise to
a popular song called "La dinde aux falbalas," but, in despite of both
song and caricature, the falbala retained its popularity.

In many cases, the sudden discontinuance of a fashion was due
to the most trifling circumstances; sometimes the Court set the
example, and sometimes the town. Thus dresses looped up in front
with knots of ribbon like window curtains, so as to show a rich
petticoat made of some different material and trimmed with circular
bands laid one above the other, were still worn at Court, long after

the fashionable ladies of Paris had abandoned them for the *andrienne*, so called after Baron's comedy (Nov. 6, 1703), in which Marie Carton Dancourt appeared in a long dress with a low body. Such a dress was too "fast" for the Court of Louis XIV. and Mme. de Maintenon, and, moreover, the brocaded stuffs, with their flowers and arabesques, which were exclusively used for Court dresses, would have been too stiff and heavy for the *andriennes*, which required to be made of silk or light satin, so that they might undulate gracefully at the least motion. It is true that the young Princesses and the ladies of the Court who were of about the same age, encouraged by the example of the Duchesse de Bourgogne, revolted against the ancient modes, and occasionally dressed after the new ones originated in Paris, but not on state occasions, when the rules of etiquette could not be transgressed in the smallest particular.

The King himself, absolute as his authority was, was compelled to submit, in some things, to the exigencies of fashion. He continued to wear his enormous wigs when the dimension and the shape of wigs changed. This almost universal change was brought about by the perfumed starch powder which men used for their false hair. In this instance, it was the old who set the fashion instead of the young, and only powdered wigs were worn for the future, whether the hair of which they were made was dark or light. Louis XIV. at first denounced the use of powder very vigorously, but he was assured that it modified the effects of age and softened the expression of the face to which the black wig imparted a hard and forbidding air. He allowed himself to be persuaded into the use of powder, but he would not alter the shape of his wigs, though the gentlemen of the Court had brought into fashion several new kinds : the *cavalière* for the country, the *financière* for the town, the *square* wig, the *Spanish* wig, etc. People even wore horse-hair wigs, which did not uncurl when exposed to the air. But powder was the special attribute of the dandies, who never appeared in public without being powdered down even to their justaucorps.

Everybody rejoiced in a white head, and one courtier ventured to remark to Louis XIV. : " We all wish to appear old, so as to be taken for wise." Powder led the way to the reduction in the size of wigs, from beneath which gradually emerged the natural hair, powdered and pomaded, gathered up at the back of the neck with a piece of black ribbon, and enclosed in a net which fell upon the coat-collar.

Fig. 291.—Lady in a " chaise roulante " (reign of Louis XIV.) ; fac-simile, after Rigaud.

The fardingales of the 16th century reappeared at Court under the name of *panniers,* and they tended to increase the volume of petticoats and dresses which, narrowing from the waist downwards, took the shape of the round hoops, made either of whalebone, cane, or pliable wood, over which they were worn. The panniers, which were not preposterously large at first, imparted an air of dignity to Court dresses, and added grace to dresses with long trains ; but the wives of the financiers and of the bourgeois, as soon as they got hold of the new fashion, carried it to excess. The panniers assumed such monstrous proportions that, to borrow the expression of a satirist, they made short women look like balls, and tall ones like bells. The hoops, or *criardes* as they were also called, did not displace the falbalas and flounces which, on the contrary, were used for every part of the dress. It was in vain that the critics and caricaturists waged war upon a fashion which caused obstructions at the theatre, in the drawing-room, on the public promenades, and especially in a carriage. But the ladies did not give way before this coalition, and the panniers lasted, with certain modifications, until the reign of Louis XVI. Of all shapes and sizes, they were an indispensable part of the dress, even when the wearer was in the most negligée toilette. The ladies also increased the volume of their petticoats by the use of bustles, and it was about this time that Chevalier d'Hénissart published two or three very severe satires upon the women of the bourgeoisie who indulged in such extravagance of dress (1713). The fashion of wearing panniers was also held up to ridicule, though without effect, in a comedy played before the young King (Louis XV.) at Chantilly, on the 5th of Nov., 1722, and the size of the panniers continued to increase. The *Nouvelliste Universel* of August 21st, 1724, describes them as follows: "They are linen bells, kept in place by whalebone hoops;" and the same newspaper follows up the attack by enumerating the inconveniences which they caused in all places of public resort. The reign of Louis XIV. once at an end, and Mme. de Maintenon's black coif ceasing to cast its shadow over the Court, bright colours and stuffs of light material soon made their reappearance, and the dresses were made with a profusion of trimmings called *prétentailles*, numerous flounces, short open sleeves with *engageantes*, which had a treble row of embroidery, lace, guipure, ribbons and bows of all kinds. Amongst the curious names given to the various inventions of the fashionable dressmakers, we find *guenpes* (sic), *fard, postiches, boute-en-train, jardinières, coiffures à la culbute, galante* or *à la doguine, nonpareilles, abbatans, rayons, maris, colinettes, crémones, sourcils de hanneton, mousquetaires, souris, battans pouce, battans l'œil, assassins, suffoquans, favoris, bouquets, bagnolettes,* etc. (1724). This multiplicity of names for dress trimmings and head-dresses shows that the Regency, in encouraging everything in the way of pleasure and luxury, had inaugurated *the reign of the coquettes.* Dufresny declared in 1703 (as he might have done with still greater truth in 1715): "The contempt which women of high reputation profess for the coquettes does not prevent them from imitating these latter. They dress after them, and catch their way of talking. One must swim with the stream. The coquettes invent new fashions and new modes of speech, and they are all in all. He also compared women to "birds who change their plumage two or three times a day;" but this was moderation itself compared to the customs in 1746, when all fashionable ladies endeavoured to change their dresses four or five times at least. There was the morning toilette or *négligée*, the walking toilette, the theatre toilette, the supper toilette, and the night toilette, the last-mentioned not being the least sumptuous and complicated. The most singular vagary of fashion, the use of patches, was indulged in to such an extent that, as a contemporary critic declared, women's faces looked like the signs of the zodiac. The patches of black silk were, in fact, cut into the shape of a moon, sun, star, comet, and crescent. They had been used in the time of Louis XIV. to set off the whiteness of the skin, but only sparingly, and ladies of dark complexion took care not to put them on. They had almost died out of use when the Duchesse du Maine brought them into fashion again, and, thanks to her example, they came to be looked upon as the distinctive sign of a beautiful skin and an indispensable accessory to the play of feature, retaining their vogue until the middle of the reign of Louis XV. It required a special knack to place these patches where they would best set off the face—upon the temples, near the eyes, at the corners of the mouth, upon the forehead. A great lady always had seven or eight, and never went out without her patch-box, so that she might put on more if she felt so inclined, or replace those that might happen to come off. Each of these patches had a particular name. The one at the corner of the eye was the *passionate;* that on the middle of the cheek, the *gallant;* that on the nose, the *impudent;* that near the lips, the *coquette;* and one placed over a pimple, the *concealer* (*receleuse*), etc. The masks, which the ladies of the 17th century employed, less to hide their faces than to protect them from the sun and the wind, were no longer in use, except on certain delicate occasions when a lady did not wish to be recognised, either on horseback or in her carriage. But they were always taken off before going into a room where the

Fig. 292.—Male attire; fac-simile, after a water-colour by Watteau.

lady who had been wearing the mask would meet persons of a rank superior to her own.

Though men's dress had undergone fewer changes than that of women since the time of Louis XIV., it had lost a good deal of its heaviness and affectation; but fashion still delineated the characteristics of the time. The large coat embroidered with gold was still worn at Court ceremonies, sometimes open in front and sometimes buttoned up, with swordbelt or waistband; while the large wig, not yet powdered, flowed down over the back and shoulders. In private society, the coat was not so heavy and fitted closer to the figure; it was, moreover, shorter, and the sleeves were tighter. It

Fig. 293.—Male attire; fac-simile, after a water-colour by Watteau.

was extended in the back by the insertion of whalebone, and had a double row of silk or metal buttons, which varied in shape and size according to the fancy of the day. In 1719 these buttons were so small that, at a comedy called "La Mode" (Théâtre-Italien) they were represented as having been made so diminutive that it required a microscope to discover them. The waistcoat, cut low in front, displayed the frill of lace or embroidered muslin and the cravat made

of the same material. The breeches were no longer the plaited
trousses, or voluminous *canons*, which formerly fell in folds over the
white silk stockings. They were worn very narrow and led the way
to the use of the eighteenth-century breeches. The polished-leather
shoes had very high heels and covered the instep. The nobles, the
gentlemen and the Court people wore, as a distinctive mark, shoes
with red heels.

If men's fashions did not change very much, they were none the
less very expensive. The Duc de Villeroy, on paying a visit to the
Czar Peter I., in his capacity as governor of the young King (1717),
had a coat embroidered in fine gold, with designs of various kinds of
fruits and leaves. The Marquis de Nesle, who had sought the
honour of being sent to meet the Russian Monarch on his arrival in
France, started on his mission with an immense wardrobe of Court
dresses, wearing a fresh one every day. Peter I. did not appreciate
this delicate compliment, for he remarked to a courtier : " I am really
very sorry that M. de Nesle has got such a bad tailor that he cannot
find a single coat to his liking." Twenty-seven years after this, the
Court dresses were just as magnificent and even more expensive.
Upon the arrival of the Infanta of Spain, Maria-Theresa-Antoinette,
who had just been married to the Dauphin (1745), the costumes were
so costly that many people hired them instead of purchasing them.
Barbier states that the Marquis de Mirepoix paid his tailor £240
for the use of dresses which he only wore once. The Marquis de
Stainville, the Envoy of the Grand Duke of Tuscany, ordered for
the entertainments at Versailles a coat of silver cloth, embroidered
with gold and lined with sable, the lining alone costing £1000.
This excessive expenditure was often encouraged, where it was not
absolutely enjoined by the King himself, and Barbier, writing in
December, 1751, states that the courtiers launched into the most
reckless expenditure on the occasion of the fêtes given to celebrate
the birth of the Duc de Bourgogne : " The King has let all the
gentlemen and ladies of the Court understand that they must appear
in gorgeous dresses, and not in plain black velvet. This led to a

heavy expenditure. The Duc de Chartres and the Duc de Penthièvre were the most richly attired, the button-holes of their coats being sewn with diamonds ; the other guests were dressed in

Fig. 294.—The young sponsors ; after Moreau.

gold materials of great price, or coloured velvets embroidered with gold or trimmed with Spanish lace."

The magistracy and the higher bourgeoisie clung as long as possible to a simple and modest mode of dress, and Duclos records in his " Memoirs," written about 1740 : " Thirty years ago you would never have seen a pedestrian dressed in velvet, and M. de Caumartin, Councillor of State, who died in 1720, was the first gentleman of the long robe who adopted this custom . . . . While the highest branch of the magistracy displayed so much modesty, the financiers could not well be ostentatious, and even the wealthiest of them lived very quietly. I have seen some of them who were content with a plain carriage, lined with brown cloth, such as Serrefort recommends to Madame Patin in the comedy of 'Le Chevalier à la mode,' (played in 1687) . . . . In earlier times luxury of all kinds was not procured for money, for in some forms it was a mark of social superiority." Thus the bourgeois dressed in accordance with their rank, wearing stout cloth, rateen or barracan according to the season, though, however the material might vary, it was invariably of a dark colour. They wore small wigs, either round or square, which were not frizzled, and to which powder was applied but sparingly. Their shoes were plain and thick-soled, and they wore stockings of black or grey wool, with the garter buckled below the knee. The female members of the bourgeoisie wore, with few exceptions, plain woollen or cotton dresses of some neutral shade, without any ribbons, or embroidery, or lace. The only item of costume which they took from the Court fashions was the pannier, which was universally worn. But dress soon ceased to be a distinctive sign of the wearer's rank and profession, and Barbier complains in 1745 that money counts for everything in Paris, and that the middle-classes cannot keep their place.

The lower-classes, both in town and country, notwithstanding the daily changes of fashion which they saw going on around them, had not changed, in regard to dress, for the last century or two. They were poorly clad, in winter as in summer, but poorly provided with linen, and often going about with naked feet, but never without a covering to the head. Their garments often consisted of pieces of cloth of different colours sewn together, forming a coat which sometimes fell below the knee. They did not seem to feel this penury of raiment at all keenly, for the Marquis de Paulmy, in his "Précis de la Vie privée des Français" (1779), says: "Stout leather shoes are looked upon as a luxury by the poorer classes, who think themselves

fortunate when they have shoes with thick soles. In some parts of
the country, the peasants wear nothing but sandals, clogs, or pieces of

Fig. 295.—Morning undress ; after Chardin.

rope wound round the feet, and in others men and women alike wear
the sabot" (wooden shoe). Such contrasts, such striking anomalies
between the dress of the lower orders and the middle-classes, were
not to be seen in Paris and the large cities, where the poor dressed
in the left-off clothes of the rich. The result, of course, was that
the same clothes were worn in course of time, first when they were
new and afterwards as they were old, by the two extremities of the

social body. This was one of the most remarkable peculiarities in Parisian life : " Everybody is well clad there, and seems as if he could afford to change his linen and coat twice a day." Most of the artizans dressed in imitation of their betters when they were not at work, and it was no uncommon thing to meet in the streets a lot of

Fig. 296.—Girl wearing a straw hat.
Fig. 297.—Girl with a " bandeau d'amour " head-dress.

dandies, fashionably dressed and girt with a sword, who turned out to be barbers, printers, tailors, or shopmen. The females of the lower classes were always neatly dressed, sometimes with remarkably good taste, and the Paris grisette was renowned throughout the whole of the 18th century for her neatness of attire. Gorgy in his " Nouveau Voyage Sentimental " (1785), says : " The girls employed in shops of various kinds aspire to be classed above the lower ranks of the people ; their dress is plain and yet comely, and amongst them may be studied that sort of coquetry which Rousseau declares to be inherent in the female nature. It does not consist of a lot of gew-gaws which are but advertisements of the wealth of their wearers and the skill of their makers. These women wear only inexpensive dresses, with a little gauze and a few bits of ribbon, but they make the most of them, and produce considerable effect out of very little. Their coiffure is very simple, but it suits them so well

Fig. 293.—Costume à la Henri IV., worn at the court balls and fêtes given by the brothers of Louis XVI. in honour of the Archduke of Austria.

that it seems perfect." This corresponded very closely with J. J. Rousseau's opinions, for, in "Emile," he writes : "Give a young girl who has good taste and sets little store on the fashion of the hour, some ribbon, gauze, muslin, and flowers, and she will make, without the aid of diamonds, lace and trinkets, a head-dress which will suit her a hundred times better than all the jewellery of Duchapt could do." But a young girl who was capable of doing this would not have run counter to fashion.

The Marquis de Caraccioli in his "Voyage de la Raison" (1762), says : "To be in Paris without studying the fashions is to go about with one's eyes shut. The squares, streets, shops, carriages, people, the whole place is full of them. . . . . . When a fashion is first brought in, the capital goes mad over it, and nobody ventures to appear in public without it." One of the fashions most in vogue during the reign of Louis XV., was the *mode à la grecque*, which, in reality, was a single name given to many objects totally dissimilar. First of all there was the *coiffure à la grecque*, a way of dressing the hair that had nothing of the ancient or modern Greek about it, for the hair, crumpled and gathered into a knot, was covered with a lace cap bristling with feathers and flowers. The name was afterwards applied (in 1764) to all articles of attire, and even to shoes. This fashion probably originated in some theatre, where it was doubtless introduced by the reigning actress. The modes, previous to this designation, were *à la Ramponneau*, and this name was derived from the celebrated guinguette of La Courtille (see Chap. XIV.). As a general rule, a name had no connection with the fashion which it was made to designate. For instance, the following is the description of the costume à la Joan of Arc, which the ladies of the Dauphine (Marie-Antoinette) were unable to bring into fashion even at Court : "Dress *à l'austrasienne*, a sort of polonaise very open in front ; over this a vest *à la péruvienne*, surmounted by a *contentement* similar to the bows worn on *sabots ;* trimmings round the collar of a demi-Medicis shape ; Cretan cap, trimmed with flowers."

The male costume à la Henri IV. for men did not fare any better, though the leaders of fashion, at the request of the Comte d'Artois and Marie-Antoinette, endeavoured to introduce it, as a Court-dress, at the private entertainments given by the Princes of blood. The Comte de Ségur, who took part in them, says : " This costume was well enough for young men, but it did not at all suit middle-aged men, especially if they were short and inclined to corpulence. The silk mantles, the feathers, ribbons, and brilliant colours, made them look ridiculous."

The two sexes seemed to compete with one another in fashionable matters, and, as a general rule, a name given to some article of female dress eventually came to be used for male attire. After the marriage of Louis XV. with Marie Leczinska (1725) the fashions were all *à la polonaise*. The campaigns of Hungary and Germany led to the introduction of *hongrelines*, which had been in vogue a century before. The marriage of the Dauphin to the Infanta of

Fig. 299.—The ladies' tailor; after Watteau.

Spain (1745) led to a revival of Spanish fashions, which had never entirely died out at the French Court, where they had so often enjoyed high favour. Thus, in 1729, there was a revival of mantillas, not only in black and white lace or other light stuffs, but in velvet, satin, and even in fur. These mantillas were not worn upon the head, but the two ends were tied across the waist. The toilette of ladies who followed the fashions was completed by many accessory objects which were held to be indispensable to the dress of a lady of good condition or of *bon ton;* as for instance, trinkets, watches,

caskets, fans, and even canes.   Men had always carried canes, which
were made of bamboo, ebony wood, &c., with the head made of
metal or some other substance.   The long gold-headed cane, once
called cane à la Tronchin and afterwards à la Voltaire, was chiefly
used by elderly men, magistrates and dignified personages.   The

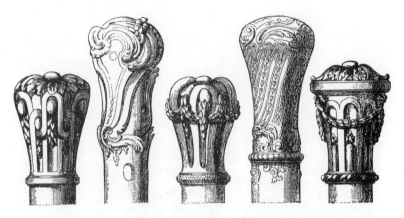

Fig. 300.—Gold and silver-headed canes.

pliant canes, varying in length, were only suitable for young men in
easy morning dress (*en chenille*).   The younger ladies eventually
took to using the long gold-headed cane, which they held in the
middle, like the *suisse* at the door of a nobleman's residence.   This
led to the introduction of very costly canes made of scented wood,
tortoise shell and ivory.   The fans, which were at first used for
fanning, eventually became more ornamental than useful, and the
commonest were made of scented wood, while the most expensive
were of tortoise shell and ivory, incrusted with ivory and precious
stones, and painted by artists of great talent.   The pocket handker-
chiefs, which were very small and were made of valuable lace embroidered with gold and coloured silks, also ceased to be more than
a mere set-off to the whole costume.

The reign of Louis XV. gave a wonderful impulse to two
branches of trade, which were looked upon as fine arts, viz., the
boot and shoe trade and that of the *coiffeur*.   The ladies' shoe-maker

was almost an artist, for he made such small shoes in every colour
of leather, set off with gold and silver embroidery, and with high

Fig. 301.—Shoe buckles.

narrow heels, that they were the most elegant part of the whole
dress.   The price of these luxurious shoes with their buckles in gold
or cut steel, was as great as that of many articles of jewellery.   The

prince of shoe-makers at that period was, thanks to the patronage of the Comtesse du Barry, a German called Efftein, who was succeeded by a Frenchman of the name of Bourdon. Men's shoes were also ornamented with buckles carved and chased (Fig. 301).

The fashions in head-dresses varied even oftener than those in shoes, and the number of ladies' hair-dressers increased so much, that there were no less than 1200 of them in Paris in 1769, when the corporation of wig-makers proceeded against them for exercising their trade without due authority. The advocate of the persecuted hair-dressers published the following laughable protest in defence of his clients :—" The art of dressing a lady's hair can only be attained by a man of genius, and is consequently a liberal and a free art. Moreover, the arrangement of the hair and the curls is not the whole of our work. We have the treasures of Golconda in our hands, for we arrange the diamonds, the crescents, the sultanas and the aigrettes." Having thus described his clients, he proceeded to demolish the master wig-makers, whom he thus caricatured : " The wig-maker works with the hair, the *coiffeur* on the hair. The wig-maker constructs artificial hair, such as wigs and curls ; the coiffeur merely arranges natural hair to the best advantage. The wig-maker is a tradesman who sells his materials and his work ; the coiffeur merely sells his services." The coiffeurs won the day, and one of them, Legros, founded an Academy of Hair-dressing, and published a large illustrated book called " The Art of Hair-dressing for French-women." Another hair-dresser and rival of Legros, one Léonard, conceived the idea of substituting for the cap generally worn pieces of gauze and other light material artistically folded in the hair, and he succeeded in placing fourteen ells of gauze in a single head-dress. He was the fashionable hair-dresser when the young Dauphiness set the seal to his reputation by patronizing him. Marie-Antoinette had a regular hair-dresser called Larseueur, who was the reverse of clever, and though so good-natured that, rather than dismiss him, she allowed him to do her hair regularly, he had no sooner completed his work, than Léonard came to undo all he had done, and build up a new edifice.

Léonard was the inventor of the wonderful modes of wearing the hair which were in vogue for more than ten years : the coiffure *à la dauphine*, in which the hair was gathered up and rolled into curls which fell on to the neck ; the coiffure *à la monte au ciel*, remarkable

Fig. 302.—Shop of a barber and wig-maker ; after Cochin.

for its extreme height ; the full-dress coiffure, called *loge d'opéra* (1772), which made a ladies' face seventy-two inches high from the chin to the top of the hair, which was divided into several zones, each one arranged in a different way, but invariably completed with three large feathers attached on the left temple, with a bow of rose coloured ribbon and a large ruby ; the coiffure *à la queasco* (1774), in which the three feathers referred to above were placed at the back of the head ; the *pouf* coiffure, which was a heterogeneous composition of feathers, jewellery, ribbons, and pins. Into this wonderful coiffure entered butterflies, birds, painted cupids, branches of trees, fruits, and even vegetables. In the month of April, the Duchesse de Chartres, daughter of the Duc de Penthièvre, appeared at the opera with her hair dressed in a *sentimental pouf*, upon which was represented her eldest son, the Duc de Beaujolais, in his nurse's arms, a parrot pecking at a cherry, a little negro boy, and the initials worked in hair from the heads of the Ducs d'Orleans, de Chartres, and de Penthièvre. It was popularly said that Marie-Antoinette was Queen of the coiffure before becoming Queen of France, and her husband's accession to the throne was hailed with delight by the hair-dressers and milliners. Soon afterwards appeared the head-dresses called *au temps présent*, which were caps trimmed with ears of corn, and crowned with two cornucopiæ. A colour called *cheveux de la Reine* was also invented, men and women's hats *aux délices du siècle d'Auguste,* and a fresh attempt was made to revive the costume à la Henri IV. After Louis XVI. had come to the throne, Marie-Antoinette exercised great influence, especially in everything connected with the fashions. Madame de Campan says in her " Memoirs " that the Queen had hitherto displayed great simplicity in her toilette, but her tastes became more expensive after her husband's accession, and as she was copied by the ladies of the Court many of them exceeded their means so much that their husbands began to complain. The King disapproved this excessive luxury of dress, but he did nothing to check it. It may be said that the most insignificant events during his reign were seized upon as pretexts for bringing in some new fashions which, whenever they were patronized by the Queen, obtained universal vogue. She was very fond of plumes, and the mania for them was carried to such a point that their price increased ten-fold, and the choicest had been known to fetch as much as fifty louis. Soularie in his " Historical Memoirs of the Reign of Louis XVI.," relates that " when the Queen passed along the gallery at Versailles, you could see nothing but a forest of feathers, rising a foot-and-a-half above the head, and nodding to and fro. The Princesses, aunts of Louis XVI., who could not make up their minds to adopt these new fashions and copy the Queen every day, called these feathers a *horse-trapping*." As the height of the

STATE CARRIAGES.

coiffures continued to increase, they at last reached such a pitch, says Madame de Campan, what with the strata of gauze, flowers, and feathers, that ladies found the roof of their carriage too low, and were either obliged to put their heads out of the window, or to ride in a kneeling posture. Nobody had so high a head-dress as the Queen.

It is impossible to describe in words these scaffoldings of hair, crimped, curled, frizzled, plaited, and surcharged with feathers, ribbons, gauze, wreaths, flowers, pearls, and diamonds. There were

Fig. 303.—Hats.—No. 1, à la Tarare.—No. 2, à l'Espagnole.—No. 3, Chapeau-bonnette.—No. 4, à l'Anglomane.

coiffures representing landscapes, English gardens, mountains, and forests. The fancy names given to them had rarely any analogy with their character or arrangement. The following are a few of the most eccentric of these names :—the *grecques à boucles badines*, the *oiseau royal*, the *chien couchant*, the *hérisson*, the hats *à l'enigme*, *à la mont-désir*, *à la économie du siècle*, *au désir de plaire*, the poufs *à la Pierrot*, the *parterres galants*, the *calèches retroussées*, the *thérèses à la Vénus pélerine*, the caps *au becquet*, *aux clochettes*, and *à la physionomie*, the bonnets *anonymes*, the cornet-caps *à la laitière*, the *baigneuses à la frivolité*, the coiffures *à la candeur*, *au berceau d'amour*, *au mirliton*, &c. When Marchand the lawyer, who was royal censor, published his book on head-dresses (1757), and, a few years afterwards his "Comédie des Panaches, as represented on the world's stage, and especially in Paris" (1769), the head-dresses which he satirized were only worn by coquettes and eccentric ladies, but in the reign of

Toque Alexandre

à la Modestie

Petite Palissade

Dormeuse

au Colisée

à la Silphide

à la Saporité

Toque à la Turque

le Chien couchant

Bonnet au Hérisson

en Ailes de Papillon panaché

à la Montgolfier

à la Noblesse

à la Persane

à la Recherche

à la Panurge

au Cerf-Volant

à la Cérès

Fig. 304.—Various head-dresses; from the books of fashion of the time.

en Fichu

à la Douce Raillerie

à la Grecque

à la Junon

en Echèlle

à la Distinction

à la Zéphire

Bonnet à l'Argus

en Rouleaux

Petite Palissade

à la Janot

Dormeuse

à la Harpie

à la Belle Poule

à la Reine

Baigneuse

Bonnet à la Candeur

le Parterre Galant

le Bandeau d'Amour

Baigneuse

Fig. 305.—Various head-dresses ; from the books of fashion of the time.

Louis XVI., the most staid persons were carried away by the Queen's example.

Satire, epigrams, and caricatures (see Figs. 306 to 308), secretly inspired by the King, were alike powerless against these extravagant head-dresses. For instance, there was a drawing which represented

Fig. 306.—The Baroness de Bel-Air, returning from the Palais-Royal; fac-simile of a caricature of the period.

an architect-coiffeur who had constructed some scaffolding so as to be able to reach the top-storey of a head-dress, and another caricature advertised a portable ladder for hair-dressers to move round a lady's head without disarranging the hair they were dressing. The police attempted to interfere in the matter, but all they could do was to prevent ladies from visiting a theatre if their head-dresses were large enough to obstruct the view. But, in spite of all this resistance, the principal feats of arms and politics were embodied in the head-dresses, and the successes of the French navy in 1778 gave rise to some twenty new modes of coiffure. One of them (see Fig. 305), invented after the naval combat, in which *La Belle-Poule* had figured to great advantage (June 17th, 1778), consisted in the imitation of the frigate itself, with its masts, rigging and guns. All this will explain the

Fig. 307.—Fac-simile of a caricature of the period.

Soutiens, Jasmin, je succombe,
Et prends bien garde, faquin,

Que si ma coiffure tombe,
Tu auras ton compte demain.

infatuation of one hair-dresser who, in a pamphlet eulogizing his profession, wrote : " The coiffeur's art is beyond question the most brilliant of all, inasmuch as it brings him in daily contact with the greatest, the most beautiful, and the most dignified people in the world."

The toilette of a pretty woman was a sort of intimate reception, held in the sanctuary where the coiffure was elaborated. The goddess of the sanctuary received her small circle of intimates, dressed in a plain peignoir of embroidered muslin, and the hair-dresser took an hour or more to complete his task. During that time, the conversation went on without interruption, dealing with all the novelties of the day, though in the time of Louis XVI. it was

Fig. 308.—Attempting to defraud the Paris custom-house ; fac-simile of a caricature of the period.

considered good taste to give it a literary, scientific, and philosophical turn. The toilet-table was covered with all the new books, and those on serious subjects were latterly predominant. The gentleman of the house invariably sent to say that breakfast was served, and Madame's reply generally was "not to wait for me." The night-toilet lasted almost as long as that in the morning, the only difference being that no company was admitted. Before retiring for the night, the lady's-maid was consulted as to what should be worn on the following day.

We will not attempt to enumerate the fashions which succeeded each other so rapidly from 1781 to 1788, though the Queen, seeing the evils of this reckless luxury of toilette for which she was mainly

Fig. 309.—The mysteries of the toilette ; fragment of a picture by Pater (in the Louvre).

responsible, endeavoured, but in vain, to moderate its excesses. The birth of the dauphin (October 22nd, 1781) was celebrated by the invention of head-dresses and costumes in commemoration of this auspicious event. The Queen had already diminished the height of her head-dresses, wearing caps *à la Henri IV., à la Gertrude, à la Colin-Maillard,* etc. But all these were discarded for the coiffure *à la Dauphin,* and the coiffure *aux relevailles de la Reine,* who no longer controlled the changes of fashion which were guided

by the caprices of the milliners and the hairdressers.   There was a
perpetual change in the materials used, but even these changes did
not keep pace with the change of names which were invented rather

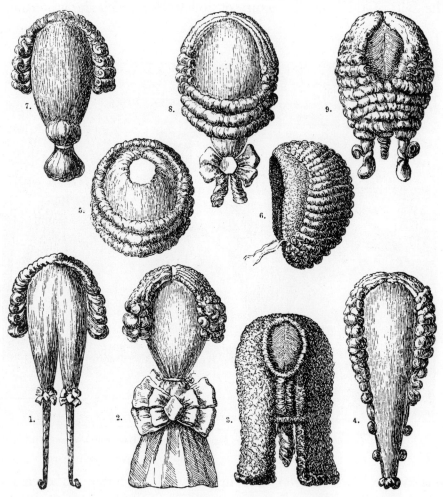

Figs. 310—318.—Wigs.—No. 1. Wig with two tails.—No. 2. Bag-wig.—No. 3. Square-wig.—No. 4. Newly-growing
wig.—No. 5. An abbé's wig.—No. 6. Woman's wig.—No. 7. Wig à catogan.—No. 8. Wig à la brigadière.—
No. 9.—Knotted wig.   (From Diderot's *Encyclopædia*.)

to designate the colours and shades of the materials than to attract
attention, such for instance as *fleas' bodies, fleas' stomachs, Paris Mud,
dandies' intestines, suppressed sighs, indiscreet tears,* etc.   Henceforward, the Queen was not so much the originator of the fashions as

she had been, though the famous *Chanson de Marlborough* was again brought into vogue because she had sung it (1782). The authors of the "Secret Memoirs" of Bachaumont say that "Since Marlborough's ditty, everything new is *à la Marlborough*. Ribbons, head-dresses, waistcoats and hats, the latter particularly, are *à la Marlborough*." When balloons were invented in 1783, everything was *au ballon, à la Montgolfier*, and so on. The success of "Le

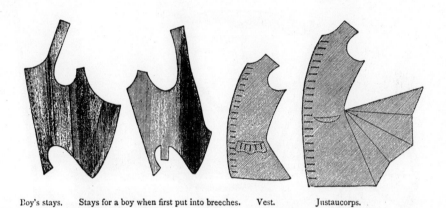

Boy's stays.　　Stays for a boy when first put into breeches.　　Vest.　　　Justaucorps.

Fig. 319.—Patterns of men's garments. (From Diderot's *Encyclopædia*.)

Mariage de Figaro" led to the invention of fashions named after personages in the piece : Chérubin, Suzanne, Basile, etc., and the popularity of the plays of Beaumarchais, Lemierre, Mercier and Monvel are attested by the fashions *aux Amours de Bayard, à la Veuve du Malabar, à la Brouette du vinaigrier, à la Tarare*, etc. The public newspapers published a description of some epicene animal said to have been found in Chili (1784), and all the previous fashions were eclipsed by the mode *à la harpie* (the name given to the animal in question). Men as well as women had been obliged to submit to the despotism of the tailor and the hairdressers. They wore their hair curled or plaited, in a pig-tail or rolled *à la Panurge*, and covered with pomade or powder. They still retained the small cocked-hat which they never wore but held under the arm or in the hand, and they adopted the use of hats *à la Hollandaise, à l'Anglo-*

Americaine, à la jockey, à l'Anglomane and *à l'independant.* Powder was used even by the cooks and footmen, and the republican, Sobry, in his treatise on "French Fashions," asserts that powder in the hair is becoming as well as agreeable, and has been regarded as a prime necessity by all civilized peoples. Men's costume was by no means in harmony with the gravity associated with a powdered head, for

Fig. 320.—Devil (shortened coach); after Lucotte.

they wore a coat with the skirts running to a point and with an up-right collar. This coat was either of wool or silk of some soft or showy colour, having, as a general rule, stripes of two colours, rose and blue, green and white, with a yellow or grey lining. Breeches made either of plush, rateen or rough cloth, a waistcoat of warped silk, and ribbed stockings completed the dress. A dandy looked more like a stage shepherd than anything else. Men were as fond of carrying gold-caskets, watches, rings, charms and buttons as the other sex were. The buttons used for the coat and waistcoat were of all shapes and of all materials: at one time in gold and silver with chased ornaments upon them; at another in mother of pearl and scented wood incrusted with precious stones; at another they consisted of gold and silver wrought into the shape of the wearer's initials, and they were also ornamented with paintings under glass, insects, minerals, objects of natural history, and so on. Some of these buttons were two inches in diameter, and on them were painted comic riddles, the portraits of the twelve Cæsars, the latest Kings of France, Ovid's Metamorphoses, etc. The waistcoats upon which

Fig. 321.—Gondola calash ; after Lucotte.

they were sewn were equally eccentric, hunting and military scenes, pastorals, and caricatures, being embroidered on them in silk of various colours. The dandies seemed to make themselves more conspicuous for their bad taste, in proportion as the ladies, under the influence of Marie-Antoinette, adopted simpler modes of dress. Mercier (1786) declared that "nothing can be more elegant and tasty than the present mode of female costume," but he could not have said this of male attire. Though Louis XVI. was very plain and even careless about dress, he was not copied even by the bourgeoisie, and when he visited the Hôtel Dieu in 1786 (February 27), people were astonished and even pained at his unkingly appearance. Restif de la Bretonne says : "This fat man, as they called him, had a badly combed round wig, and wore a seedy frock-coat."

The reform of the fashions, if not of all sumptuary profusion, began both at Court and amongst the public in 1783. Madame de Sartory wrote at that period (perhaps deceiving herself as to the progress of this reform which was very slow) : " Luxury is no longer displayed in buildings and external decorations. The carriages are plain (that this was a mistaken view may be gathered from Figs. 320 and 321), while the servants are less numerous, the fine clothes out of fashion, expensive horses are no longer kept, diamonds are at a discount, and jewellery has fallen into discredit." The time had arrived when the Queen, disgusted with politics, withdrew from the Court, and sought distraction in the rustic amusements of the Petit-Trianon, where she showed herself in the costume of an Alpine shepherdess to the ladies of her suite and the members of the royal family, though the dressmakers betrayed her secret to the whole world. Madame de Sartory, author of the " Petit Tableau de Paris," quoted above, says : " Women's dress was never so plain as it is now. You see no dresses surcharged with trimmings, or sleeves with three rows of lace. A straw-hat with a knot of ribbon, a plain neckerchief, and an apron for house wear have taken the place of curls, and frizzles, and falbalas. The men are dressed still more simply, and have discarded their embroidered coats, and scarves, and epaulettes."

The Court dress, with the panniers, the lappets, and the high head-dresses were still worn on state occasions, but outside the Court everything English and American was brought into vogue. Straw-hats attached with a piece of ribbon, short dresses of some light material, large aprons, enormous fichus, and shoes without high-heels were all the rage. Many women belonging to the upper bourgeoisie, and some of those appertaining to the highest classes of society, laid themselves out to be, or to appear to be very serious, and they assumed the air, and even, to a certain extent, the costume of the other sex. Mercier, writing in 1788, said : " Women actually go

LIGHT CARRIAGES.

about in male attire ; a frock-coat with three collars, the hair tied *à la catogan*, a switch-stick in their hands, shoes with low heels, two watches, and an open waistcoat." The men, as if to outdo these austere and incongruous fashions, had taken to the black frock, left off powder, and again wore the cocked-hat. They vied with one another in their imitations of the English and Americans, and the ladies went mad over hats *à l'Anglaise*, and *à la Jockey*, dresses made of English poplins, moiré, tulle, and lawn. Steel and glass-ware had taken the place of diamonds, and French fashion, so rich and so magnificent, so capricious and so varied, so elegant and so gracious, had almost disappeared at the dawn of the Revolution. It was a kingdom whose subjects had withdrawn from it their allegiance.

Fig. 322.—A restaurant-waiter (from a caricature).

THE END.

BRADBURY, AGNEW, & CO., PRINTERS, WHITEFRIARS, LONDON.